The Torchbearers

PHILANTHROPIC STUDIES

Robert L. Payton and Dwight F. Burlingame, general editors

The Torchbearers

WOMEN AND THEIR AMATEUR
ARTS ASSOCIATIONS IN
AMERICA, 1890–1930

Karen J. Blair

583597

Indiana University Press
Bloomington & Indianapolis

© 1994 by Karen J. Blair
All rights reserved

No part of this book may be reproduced or utilized in any form or by any means, electronic or mechanical, including photocopying and recording, or by any information storage and retrieval system, without permission in writing from the publisher. The Association of American University Presses' Resolution on Permissions constitutes the only exception to this prohibition.

The paper used in this publication meets the minimum requirements of American National Standard for Information Sciences—Permanence of Paper for Printed Library Materials, ANSI Z39.48-1984.

∞ ™

Manufactured in the United States of America

Library of Congress Cataloging-in-Publication Data
Blair, Karen J.
  The torchbearers : women and their amateur arts associations in America, 1890–1930 / Karen J. Blair.
    p.   cm. — (Philanthropic studies)
  Includes bibliographical references and index.
  ISBN 0-253-31192-6
  1. Feminism and the arts—United States—History—19th century.
  2. Feminism and the arts—United States—History—20th century.
  3. Women—United States—Societies and clubs.   I. Title.
  II. Series.
NX180.F4B63   1994
700'.1'03—dc20   93-485

1 2 3 4 5   99 98 97 96 95 94

To Cynthia Blair, my sister and friend

CONTENTS

Acknowledgments ix

Introduction 1

ONE
The Arts in Nineteenth-Century
American Women's Lives 12

TWO
Arts and Activism
An Overview of Women's Clubs, 1890–1930 29

THREE
"Hear America First"
Women's Amateur Musical Societies 44

FOUR
Women's Societies for the Visual Arts
The Struggle to Be Seen 76

FIVE
Pageantry and the Women's Rights Movement,
1905–1925 118

SIX
The Little Theater Movement 143

SEVEN
The Clubhouse as Arts Center 178

Notes 204
Selected Bibliography 239
Index 249

Illustrations follow page 106

ACKNOWLEDGMENTS

I wish to thank the Rockefeller Foundation for a Humanities Fellowship, the Smithsonian Institution for the Senior Post-Doctoral Fellowship, the Newberry Library for a summer grant and the Henry E. Huntington Library for two summertime Haynes Fellowships. My thanks to *Theatre Survey* for enabling me to use material from my article "Pageantry for Women's Rights: The Career of Hazel Mackaye, 1913–1923," from volume 31 (May 1990). The splendid librarians and library staff who have offered considerable assistance include: Leona Schoenfeld, Elsa Sink, Ginger Renner, and Doris Smedes at the Huntington Library; Pat Lynaugh, Cecilia Chinn, and Martin Kalfatovic at the National Museum of American Art; Tony Wren at the American Institute of Architects; Elizabeth Norris at the YWCA Headquarters in New York City; Cynthia Swanson at the General Federation of Women's Clubs; Glenda Pearson, Karyl Winn, and Richard Berner at the University of Washington; Eva Mosely and Katherine Draft at the Schlesinger Library; Marian Ritter of Western Washington University Music Library; Harriet Weston at the Massachusetts State Federation of Women's Clubs in Quincy; and Barbara Sellin at the National League of American Penwomen.

It was a privilege to work with Sue Davidson and Antoinette Wills, editors, and typists Kathy Sala and Linda Donnelly. I appreciate the student staff members of the Computer Center at Central Washington University, most especially Chris Prestin and Nancy Oakes-Width, who bailed me out of many a mechanical jam.

I wish also to thank several generous scholars for their help. Martin Ridge of the Henry E. Huntington Library and Helen Krich Chinoy and Helen L. Horowitz of Smith College discussed this material with me at length. Catherine Parsons Smith of the University of Nevada at Reno, Phyllis Peet of Monterey Community College, Susan Starbuck of North Seattle Community College, Cynthia Richardson of Western Washington University, and Anne Filiaci each read significant portions of the manuscript and offered excellent suggestions. Three supportive historians served as my sponsors during my year-long residence at the Smithsonian Institution. They are Lillian B. Miller, Deborah Warner, and Barbara Melosh. Barbara Melosh combed the entire manuscript and contributed insightful comments, most of which I was able, I hope, to incorporate into the work.

I have been terrifically fortunate to have the friendship of three individuals whose confidence in me and this project never wavered. My deepest appreciation goes to Jean Beck, Dan Ramsdell, and Marian Evans Kent.

My interest in this topic was initially sparked and then sustained by my instruction in piano playing and for that reason I wish to thank the teachers who introduced me to music-making—especially my mother, Josephine Blair, and Claude Gonvierre and Gary Towlen. I owe special thanks to Elma Schonbach, who opened the astonishing world of ensemble piano playing to me, and to the amateur pianists who have humored me in my quest to make eight hands into one voice—especially Jean Beck, Mark Walsen, Ruth Gerberding, Julann Chin, Way Hua, Gerte Shupe, and Shirley Crowley. Finally, I owe thanks to the patient scholars at the Huntington Library, who willingly trotted off to the Hollywood Bowl with me to relax after long days of research and writing, and to those at the National Museum of American Art of the Smithsonian Institution, who accompanied me to the Elizabeth Sprague Coolidge Chamber Music concerts to find the balance that scholarly endeavors tend to upset.

This book is dedicated to my sister, with whom I share the longest and steadiest history in the arts. Our collaborations, in storytelling, playmaking, singing, poetry writing, concert going, theater viewing and oboe/piano duets, go back almost as far as we do. In addition, she took precious time from her own writing to type some sections of this manuscript and to assist me in driving across this huge country twice, to facilitate my residency at the Smithsonian Institution. Because our familiarity and appreciation of the arts grew together, I am eager to share this work with her.

The Torchbearers

Introduction

Americans are a practical people and have never made peace with the arts. The mistrust of culture has been persistent throughout our past, beginning with the earliest settlements when there was no leisure time available for the fine arts. No one expected the colonists to compose a symphony or support a sculptor before their farmland was cleared and homes were built. But even with time, an anti-cultural bias persisted in the American populace.

Our forebears championed the citizen who tamed the land over the painter who preserved it in landscape; they celebrated the pioneer who settled the west over the novelist who mythologized the experience. By and large, U.S. history has revered as its most praiseworthy contributors those who invented machines, built factories, harnessed technology, carved a canal into the middle of the Western Hemisphere, and sent rockets to the moon. With few exceptions, Americans have met with suspicion any pursuit that did not appear to serve utilitarian purposes. Frontiersmen dismissed the lectures of Ralph Waldo Emerson, "who left his audience with only a meager fund of immediately useful knowledge."[1]

Fresh from victory in the Revolutionary War, most Americans felt a sense of superiority over "decadent" Europeans, and they worked hard at fostering a national image that rejected the European cultural environment. Although there were exceptional people who respected and fostered the Western cultural tradition on these shores, it was easy for most citizens to associate the Europe that produced great art with the Europe of rigid class distinctions, vice, and degeneracy. Both art and luxury, which required money and were consumed by an aristocracy of popes, cardinals, monarchs, and nobles, were dismissed by Americans as unnecessary.

Americans valued the self-made, practical, rugged individualist who conquered the "barbaric" Indian, not with the "artificial" knowledge of the European, but with clear, intuitive, simple common sense. Frederick Jackson Turner felt that the frontier that produced the American hero Andrew Jackson "was free from the influence of European ideas and institutions."[2] Actually, the frontier was not so devoid of European luxury that Jackson could not enjoy $1500 worth of cut glass and French hand-printed wallpaper in the hallway of his "Hermitage"; but this part of his background was obscured.[3] Instead, an image was built of the president that embodied America's image of itself. Mythmakers were totally successful in depicting Jackson as a natural, strong, rough-hewn frontiersman, the sensible balance between the savage Indian and the decadent European. Few suspected that "one of nature's noblemen"[4] had in fact never worked his own lands. The Jackson of "great urbanity and distinction of manner"[5] was obscured from those who knew him only by legend; the nickname "Old Hickory" was not accidental. The identification of the best American qualities in a virile president (1829–37) who publicly rejected the arts was damaging to American men who did choose to patronize or participate in them. If America's "real" men scorned culture, the manliness of those who did not was questionable. But while respectable men rejected the arts as unseemly for themselves, their abandonment of the field left it open to women.

Despite the identification of the American with open land, the Gilded Age saw the expansion of American cities, which challenged the ideal of smallness and individuality. The absurdity of placing state capitals in small towns like Albany and Montpelier "owed something to geography"[6] but also something to anti-urban prejudice. American distaste for the city was bolstered not only by the Jacksonian image but also by the association of cities with such European affectations as opera houses, conservatories, and art galleries. Glorification of nature at the expense of the city is evident in the philosophy of Thoreau, whose *Walden,* in its celebration of the isolated individual, may be considered a "bible of anti-urbanism." Similarly, Emerson found life in the city "artificial and curtailed."[7]

Public school education served to propagate these American values. According to Henry Steele Commager, the nineteenth-century attitude was that "Education was religion," but only if it "be practical and pay dividends."[8] In textbooks, scholarship and the fine arts were considered fields unfit for the American. The 1860 edition of the *New Juvenile Speaker* made it clear that Americans rejected the goals of their forebears across the sea:

> While many other nations are wasting the brilliant efforts of genius in moments of ingenious folly, to perpetuate their pride, the Americans, according to the true spirit of republicanism, are employed almost entirely in works of public and private utility.[9]

Despite America's reverence for practicality and scorn for European affectation, the burgeoning industrialization of the early nineteenth century softened the nation's suspicion of refinement a little. Newly prosperous middle-class men began to ape the aristocracy whom they had previously ridiculed. They expected their daughters and wives to assume a bit of polish, especially in the form of drawing and singing, and thereby planted the seeds of culture as woman's domain. A peculiarly American design for high culture was forged, however, one that took into account the national pride in practicality and industriousness. Thus, these pastimes were endorsed only with particular restrictions with which a female must comply. First, she must cultivate refinements in modest doses, never to the extent that they would divert her from her practical work of domestic responsibilities. Secondly, the accomplishments must be used in the service of her home and family. In this peculiar way, a new generation of girls was bred to acquire artistic interests. To them was assigned the duty of becoming repositories of the cultural frills that few men cared to cultivate, but now expected their households to offer.

A girl of the 1830s knew she should practice the piano an hour a day if she expected to become a proper lady—amusing, entertaining, the nourisher of culture and sensitivity in her husband's home. She also knew that if she practiced more than that, no one would marry her. The selfishness of self-cultivation was quite the opposite of the qualities embodied in a good wife, whose priority was to serve the members of her household. Such undesirable habits were therefore to be avoided. They would signal deviance and possibly foreshadow a path of strong-mindedness, leading to militant suffragism, a law career, or some other masculine posture unsuitable to women.

The mandate that a proper female be a dilettante, acquainted with the arts only enough to amuse and entertain, lingered well into the twentieth century despite the advent of painting academies, music conservatories, and colleges that provided talented women with the training to match that of men who became the respected artists in America. So firm was the opinion that women were designed to ornament rather than create and interpret that capable women were routinely denied opportunities in the professional art world.

This requirement, that the American non-wage-earning wife be familiar with art but not sufficiently accomplished to become a professional, resulted in the eruption of arts clubs for women amateurs that flourished from the 1880s to the late 1920s. These voluntary associations were popular in every geographical area of the country, especially among white, Protestant, Anglo-Saxon, urban, middle-class women. Throughout this work, when I use the words *woman* and *clubwoman,* I refer only to these particular women who constituted club membership. My generalizations are not constructed to apply to women of racial and ethnic minorities who were not admitted to the clubs.

Frank acknowledgment of clubwomen's exclusivity, especially in terms of race, religion, and class, must be made. Middle-class white Protestant women tended to prefer their own company and shape the constitution of their club's membership by limiting access to the circle. Club founders assessed the spaciousness of their meeting place and their ability to manage a large group, and then set a cap on the total membership. They collected like-minded women to fill vacancies by word of mouth. They reached women of similar background, who lived in the same neighborhoods, dressed and behaved in like manner. Once two members agreed to sponsor a new addition, the club's executive board considered her suitability. If two black balls were cast, the nominee would be rejected. Such screening ensured that many daughters-in-law, sisters, and neighbors would be included in clubs, and that most women of differing backgrounds would never gain access. Thus, the elite of American society—

the Rockefeller and Carnegie women, the Harrimans or Roosevelts, did not participate. Neither did clubs generally include women of color, immigrants, Catholics, Jewish women, or the working class.

Only occasionally was club homogeneity challenged, as when the Seattle Ladies Musical Club admitted a Jewish woman, Rose Morgenstern Gottstein, and honored her for her distinguished contributions in securing reknowned performers for their concert series. From Oklahoma, Roberta Campbell Lawson, whose mother was a Delaware Indian, enjoyed respect for her knowledge of Native American music. She was president of the entire General Federation of Women's Clubs from 1935 to 1938.

Of all the arenas for artistic expression considered in this study, the only one bringing more than casual multi-cultural cooperation was pageantry. In pageants, clubwomen often worked alongside members of all the ethnic and racial minority groups in the community. More typically, club consideration of cultural diversity was confined to programs on Negro spirituals and songs of the Sioux. The white, middle-class clubwomen left the many women in neighborhoods outside their own to form their own women's clubs. The rich story of minority arts clubs has not yet been fully researched, but several fine studies lay the foundation to address this question.[10]

Club recruitment styles also perpetuated homogeneity of marital status. Although many single career women participated, especially teachers, the societies tended to be dominated by women who had enjoyed some education in youth but who had married, run households, and raised children, with little time, space, money, or permission to pursue the arts. Once their children were grown, or at least in school, the mothers could devote their free afternoons to clubs. There they labored under the assumption that while they were somehow biologically attuned to beauty, their primary devotion to their families barred them from serious artistic careers. What resulted was a vast network of enthusiastic, organized women, who were less occupied with making art than with the advocacy of art for their loved ones—defined by them quite broadly, to include not only their families but their neighborhoods, social groups, communities, and municipalities as well. The story that follows is a tale of their success at perpetuating their own dilettantish status. At the same time, it records the clubwomen's energy and ingenuity in attempting to involve everyone in the arts. The women offered culture for all under the guise of maternal responsibility, and the outcome was an impressive array of permanent cultural programs and institutions.

How thoroughly did the women's art network impinge on the activities of the professional art world? Much of the time it was separate and self-defined, an invisible amateur arts subculture whose members were serious and knowledgeable but invisible and incapable of challenging the powerful mainstream. Clubwomen's steady deference to and cooperation with the "experts" enhanced the power of the museum directors, symphony conductors, and academy and conservatory instructors. Yet club influence developed from the sheer size, earnestness, and class privilege of the membership. Club preferences, from dislike of the avant-garde to curiosity about women's, minority, and

American-made arts, shaped the context in which professionals marketed their artistic wares. Certainly, the idea that clubwomen cultivated between the years 1890 and 1930, that every American, regardless of economic status or geographical circumstance, deserves access to the fine arts, is one the professionals accepted and one we have all come to take for granted. The programs clubwomen instituted to ensure that access include many that serve us still.

At first glance, Agnes De Mille's mother Anna, Mary McCarthy's great-aunt Rose, and Edward MacDowell's wife Marian may appear to have little in common beyond a family relationship with a noted American artist. Yet as volunteers in women's amateur arts clubs, these three women were key players in a creative enterprise during the Progressive Era, from 1890 to nearly 1930. The ingenuity, talent, and training in music, painting, and literature of America's great mass of volunteers in clubs were great, although the women's efforts did not make their names the household words that professional artists became. Nevertheless, despite previous neglect in cultural histories of this nation, their contributions are worth examining.

This study charts the evolution of clubs that women founded to study the arts and examines three themes dominant within those clubs. I intend to measure members' progress in educating themselves and their society in the pleasures of appreciating the American and European cultural traditions and encouraging all citizens to make art for themselves; to expose the cultural influence this activity had on their peers and the other beneficiaries of their efforts; and to weigh the relationship of their work to the political and social struggles of women of the era.

Why should we examine the work of amateur American women thespians, painters, or musicians, when only a handful of studies have addressed a more obvious area of interest, the accomplishments of the professional women in the arts? Why should we study the efforts of volunteer women's involvement in the turn of the century cultural arena when researchers are only beginning to create a literature on their activity in politics? The answer lies in the fact that for American women at that time, the distinctions between cultural and political change, and between professional and amateur achievement, are artificial. The relationships between these ideas illuminate the social and political structure in which women labored during this era. Generally, society has defined the professional artist as one who supports himself by his work. While a few of the women who became active in societies devoted to the arts were able to support themselves with their work—especially by teaching art in the schoolroom or giving piano lessons in the parlor—most were unable to do so. Their living expenses were met by working husbands or inheritances instead. However, since making a living in the arts is precarious whether the artist is male or female, society has sometimes defined the artist by intent; that is, the artist is one who is self-defined as a creator, whose daily endeavors focus on making art.

On this count as well, women pursuing the arts in clubs could not often measure up to generally accepted standards. Most were defined primarily as wives and mothers, with household responsibilities demanding most of their time and effort. They could not devote themselves single-mindedly to their art. Certainly there were some exceptional women who overcame the domestic obstacles to artistic creation, but they were few in number. No matter how ambitious women might be, to earn a living at their art or merely to work single-mindedly at it, let alone—if they dared express it—to become famous and respected as composers, playwrights, or painters, they faced tremendous barriers. They inevitably met a male-dominated world of orchestral conductors, newspaper critics, gallery owners, and art collectors who tended to dismiss their work, hamper their development, and exclude them from the customary channels for growth and exposure that male professionals enjoyed. Few women of this era were able to combat the perception that they were wives and mothers before they were anything else, in fact to the exclusion of anything else. Both they and those around them were generally unwilling and unable to view women as serious artists. The existence of a sexist society shaped the obstacles women faced and the development of a women's movement promised to remove them.

The membership of women's amateur arts clubs generally agreed that they constituted a large and significant portion of the Woman Movement of the day, a term which then was as problematical as "feminism" is today. The Woman Movement could be all things to all people, proving that the definition of women's rights was in the eye of the beholder. To some, the Woman Movement of the Progressive Era meant the controversial quest for woman suffrage, and full participation in public life, including such previously male-dominated careers as that of professional artist. For that reason, suffragists Charlotte Perkins Gilman, Susan B. Anthony, Olympia Brown, May Wright Sewall, and Abigail Scott Duniway courted women in arts clubs through speeches, lectures, and writings, expecting that the numbers there would bolster the bold political struggles that so shocked the age. To others, however, the Woman Movement stood for far less outrageous change, simply the permission for ladies to extend their age-old domestic responsibilities slightly beyond the home to the neighborhood, organized by like-minded women in societies and clubs.

How could the Woman Movement and the women's clubs that flourished in the era serve such varied needs? Yet they did. Women's clubs managed to appeal to so many on the grounds that women should seek influence outside the house through voluntary organizations, whether they sought to apply traditional nurturing qualities in the public arena or to master activities previously dominated by men. Clubs broadened their appeal by exercising extraordinary tolerance, flexibility, and politeness, banishing incendiary topics from the meetings, and stressing the commonalities among women rather than the differences. With their detachment from ideological commitment, women's clubs devoted to the subjects of literature and theater, painting, and music attracted millions of middle-class American women. For every dues-paying member who viewed her participation as another step toward women's equality and autonomy, there was another who joined for the club's virtue of enabling her to extend old-fashioned and supposedly biologically inherited traditional traits of patriotism, sensitivity, and maternal instincts to "mother" her extended family, her community. Yet undeniably, the conservative rationale for club membership also allowed women—even the timid ones—to be drawn into new and public realms of activity previously closed to them, providing unique vehicles for expressing their own vision of art and society.

Can we label club life as feminism? The very duality of conservatism and progressivism makes the term "Domestic Feminism," a term now used by many historians of women,[11] suitable to the brand of women's rights advocacy we will observe in women's clubs. Yes, their members were path-breaking in the founding of arts institutions and programs for culture, and in their support for professional arts institutions. They were visionary in creating new vehicles for community involvement in the arts. Their handling of finances, politics, and organization clearly places them in the arena of women who were breaking out of the domestic realm. Yet insofar as many members justified their behavior on the basis of old-fashioned goals like love of nation, family, beauty, home, and sharing, the work was acceptable and nonthreatening to upholders of the status quo.

The title of this work, *The Torchbearers,* is a term that was frequently used by clubwomen of the era about themselves and their work. It refers to the concept of leading others to the highest ideals, a concept which presupposes women's ability to march to a purer drummer than the men around them. Sculptor Anna Hyatt Huntington explained the term at the dedication of "Torchbearer," her bronze statue: "My Torch-Bearer does stand for the finer things of life that lead to Peace and I hope it can be placed to aid such ideals."[12] Likewise, Anna Blake Mezquida wrote a poem entitled "Torchbearer," which she dedicated to the California women memorialized in a 1922 *Who's Who among the Women of California*. In it she praised their various contributions to western society.[13] Alice Archer James wrote a light play entitled "Torchbearer" in the same year, referring also to the noble qualities women conveyed to society. Lotta Clark produced pageants by the same name in Minneapolis and Peterborough, New Hampshire. A history of the Women's Christian Temperance Union, published in the 1920s, used the title *Torchbearer* in reference to women's efforts to perfect society through the eradication of alcohol. Also in the 1920s, George Kelly named a comic play *The Torchbearers* in which he poked fun at the seriousness with which clubwomen attempted to reform society.

Like the phrase Woman Movement, "Torchbearers" is mercurial in that its definition and its meaning depend on the perspective of the user.[14] To some, the clubwoman who carried the light widened a path toward new roles for women. To others, the torchbearer's light represented the effort to protect an ancient path. Few enough are the moments in history when people with such variable points of view have cooperated, but women's amateur arts clubs nurtured a compatibility for forty years. If this is not a record, it is surely remarkable and deserving of our consideration. Ultimately, however, the conservative impulse limited the dimensions the club movement could take. This was defined by one club leader, Mary I. Wood, who observed in 1912:

> the inventive, aggressive, and creative functions of the twentieth century man is urging us on, but the price of such rapid advance must be paid, and that the cost may be less terrible, the conserving influence of organized womanhood is needed. Conservation, then, in its best and highest sense is the raison d'etre of the General Federation of Women's Clubs—conservation of life, of liberty and of happiness; conservation of child life, of womanhood, of civic and national integrity in matters of public and private import; conservation of the best and highest functions of womanhood which shall make her in very truth the conserver of all that is good in our advancing civilization, preserver of all that is good in the civilization of the past and helpmeet in the daily battle of life which is constantly going on about them.[15]

Readers will observe that I use the expressions *arts, fine arts,* and *culture* as synonyms. I have not used the word "culture" as an anthropologist would, to refer to broad social values. I am using all these terms to refer to literature, drama, dance, music, painting, and sculpture which have withstood the test of time and critics, to be accorded the status of classics by the learned and the affluent. Many early nineteenth century members of American women's clubs came to stretch this definition, however. Following their lead, I will include aspects of folk arts and crafts; popular expressions of inventiveness such as pageantry; and technological innovations such as photography under this rubric.

In an earlier work, *The Clubwoman as Feminist: True Womanhood Redefined, 1868–1914,*[16] I traced the origins and fruition of the civic reform aspect of the American woman's club movement and its relationship to, indeed its underpinning in, the budding Woman Movement of the day. So unyielding was turn-of-the-century woman's determination to forge a public voice that she created a massive yet viable vehicle to impress her will on a society which would have preferred to see her remain quietly at home. *The Clubwoman as Feminist,* while it overlaps in chronology with this volume, explored different themes than this monograph does. That is, *The Torchbearers* examines the strain of clubwomen who intended not to yield to civic reform impulses but to follow traditional paths of "beauty." Yet they found themselves persuaded by forces propelling them, too, to make their mark on a world wider than that of their own individual families.

The Torchbearers, then, doesn't elaborate on the political application of women's progressive work—support for civil service examinations, civics lessons, and the movements to institutionalize referendum, recall, and city managers. Instead the focus is on activity devoted to the nurturance of our culture. An impressive number of cultural institutions emerge from projects undertaken by clubwomen. The present study explores, as my previous study did not, the range of traditional impulses behind the self-improvement and community programs that clubwomen undertook. It has become clear to me that the caretaking impulse within the club population among the middle class is merely one aspect of women's constellation of reasons for support of cultural endeavors. Respected characteristics among clubwomen—patriotism, love of harmony, protection and conservation of western tradition in culture, cooperation with other women—accompanied them from domestic to public life. Thus, the alliance between modern activism and action motivated by traditional values built women's power that lasted for nearly four decades.

The modern reader, attuned to the mosaic of contributions from the rainbow of cultures that make up American life, may approach the history of white, Anglo-Saxon Protestant women's arts societies warily. Tea-sipping, turn-of-the-century leisured ladies with a reverence for high culture and old-fashioned values must have been complacent, snobbish, and intolerant, and as Lawrence Levine suggests in *Highbrow/Lowbrow*,[17] determined to foist their own definition of refinement on the unsuspecting masses to whom they have felt superior. Indeed, the women in these pages were reverential to the Western canon. Rembrandt, Beethoven, and Shakespeare were their gods. Yes, the members were repelled by the crass commercialized popular culture developing in their era. They rejected or at least underestimated the importance of the pastimes, parades and rituals of less privileged classes,[18] disdained the popularity of jazz and burlesque, and hoped to lure young people from entertainments they deemed shallow with more "uplifting" amusements. Clubwomen feared the boldness of abstract art and atonal music and shied from embracing new forms of expression in their programs. Unquestionably, they dedicated themselves wholeheartedly to proselytizing for programs they sanctioned, without considering how welcome their overtures might be.

Yet they broke with tradition in significant ways. They were not so enamored of the classical tradition that they accepted women's absence from it. They insisted that members of their sex were entitled to acquire top-notch training in the arts and exposure for the results of their effort. They identified and publicized the artistic contributions of women both in history and in their own day, and they funded the schooling of their girls with an optimistic view of the future. Arts club members rejected the notion that the work of European white males should monopolize the arts curriculum. Instead, they embraced the cultural contributions of American artists, including that of Native Americans, African-Americans, and regionalists. They refused to vacate the stage for professional artists, advocating the value of creative expression for amateurs, insisting that the spotlight be shared.

Moreover, members exuded humility as often as haughtiness—recognizing their privilege in possessing the resources to devote themselves to culture and determined to use the arts to solve social problems rather than to enhance their status. Thus, as philanthropists, they were reluctant to label the institutions they founded with plaques trumpeting their generosity, and they remained untroubled by the invisibility of their initiatives to their contemporaries. Admittedly, clubwomen were relentless in carrying their forms of the arts to the general public. But the forms they brought were broader than those sanctioned by professionals in the arts world. The clubwomen were respectful of the whole spectrum of the human creative spirit.

In all, many contradictory ideas coexisted within women's amateur arts associations of the Progressive Era—the value of the professional artist versus the value of amateur expression, the importance of the canon versus the importance of challenging it with women's work and contributions of minorities, an elitism coexisting with broadmindedness, an expectation of disseminating uplifting art in a world increasingly enveloped by popular culture. I have come to understand and hope to persuade in this work that the ability of women's clubs to tolerate, indeed absorb the contradictory ideals and methods held by women of the day not only was the source of club appeal from 1890 to 1930 but also explains its limited life thereafter.

Chapter 1, on women's arts experience in the nineteenth century, outlines the roots of the American lady's association with the arts for the sake of refinement and amusement, a mode she would attempt to outgrow with only limited success. Chapter 2 summarizes the changes in the women's club movement in the years 1890 to 1930, with emphasis on the pressure on members to move toward public activism, which arts lovers came to embrace. It identifies four stages in women's club behavior: self-instruction in the 1890s; delivering the arts to the community in the 1900s; facilitating community participation in making art cooperatively in the 1910s; and building grand clubhouses in the 1920s.

Chapter 3 describes women's ingenious efforts to bring professional musical talent to the general public and music training to school children. It also sets forth the patriotic justifications given for making music widely available, and shows women's success in associating music-making with love of country and with pride in America's new pre-eminence in world affairs.

Chapter 4 focuses on clubwomen's work in making America visually literate, especially via the traveling art shows which grew into museums and school education programs. It emphasizes the obstacles that diverted the women from their goals. Chapter 5, on pageantry, discusses three types of these gigantic shows: those that were community-wide; those confined to clubwomen; and the suffragist pageants created by Hazel MacKaye. All three types were supported by clubwomen, who aimed to instruct participants and observers in the values of collaboration and encourage the skills needed to produce pageants. In democratic fashion, the women attempted to weave the talents of many people into a harmonious enterprise richer than anything a few individuals could achieve alone. Chapter 6 focuses on the little theater movement, which grew out of clubwomen's determination to bring drama to every American community. These women were certain that opportunities for self-expression were as critical to a town's well-being as a settlement house was to the well-being of immigrants.

Chapter 7, on the architecture of clubhouses built to serve in part as arts centers in the 1920s, demonstrates the ambitions of clubwomen to use their money, power, skills, and intelligence to wed personal needs with community interests. The advent of these clubhouses caused terrific schisms in club ideology. Could clubhouses simultaneously serve as havens for members and as arts facilities for the town? Should clubhouses be run as businesses or homes? Should modern clubwomen emulate their businessmen husbands or their home-building grandmothers? The dilemma could not have been articulated before women had won the long-coveted political goal of suffrage, and before so many of them had left the home for war relief, education, or salaried work, as they had by the 1920s. Clubwoman leaders and followers who had managed to straddle the ideological fence for thirty years could do so no longer; they now polarized, weakening the movement they had so ably built.

Readers familiar with the recent wave of scholarly literature on the history of American women's organizational activity will recognize several themes in this study. I have emphasized, as have Estelle Freedman, Lynn Gordon, Ruth Bordin, and Leslie Epstein, the importance of women's untiring cooperation, in a sphere separate from men's, in launching their programs for social change.[19] I have observed women's willingness to justify their public activity on the basis of so-called female traits of gentleness, moral superiority, beauty, and sensitivity, a theme which has been examined by historians Robyn Muncy, Paula Baker, Anne Firor Scott, and Nancy Cott.[20] I have also embraced the suggestion of Cott, Scott, Muncy, and also of J. Stanley Lemons, that the continuities before and after the granting of woman suffrage in 1920 were more powerful than the discontinuities for women's public lives.[21] Just as Kathleen McCarthy found individual women in Chicago and New York City[22] to be key but undervalued players in effectively establishing arts institutions, I have discovered women in groups to be successful throughout the nation.

For all my indebtedness to the lively thinkers in my field, I hope I have filled a gap overlooked by others. The contribution I intend to make here is to emphasize the important relationship between women's arts interests and women's political interests during the Progressive Era. In this period women in their organizations used the arts, no less than they used political skills, to effect their vision for social change in America.

ONE

The Arts in Nineteenth-Century American Women's Lives

Historian Barbara Welter has deftly examined the "Cult of True Womanhood" which prescribed behavior for American women of the emerging middle class in the early nineteenth century. Piety, purity, domesticity and submissiveness were the basic virtues that defined the four corners of a woman's world, if she was to be perceived as a "lady." Beginning in girlhood, she was guided to develop self-sacrificing traits, which would assure her success in creating a harmonious, moral, and industrious household, and would inspire her husband, children, and neighbors to renounce temptation and become almost as good-hearted, hard-working, and God-fearing as she.[1] Scholars have persuasively documented the extensive propaganda to which antebellum women and girls were exposed in sermons, newspapers, magazines, etiquette books, fiction, instructional materials in the academies and seminaries, and in poetry and lyrics of popular songs.[2]

Little attention has been accorded, however, to society's emphasis on training young ladies in the arts, especially vocal and instrumental music, literary study, drawing, painting, and dance.[3] The ideal of ladydom not only shaped the arts instruction given to antebellum ladies, but tainted women's relationship with culture for generations to come. It is likely that the arts seemed so compatible with notions of proper activities for ladies because of society's assumption that both women and the arts were ruled by feeling rather than rationality. While it came to be widely held that woman was incapable of parsing passages of Latin and Greek or investigating the properties of elements on the periodic table, society agreed that her soft lullabies could calm a baby and her gentle drawings of wildflowers could warm the home's decor. An examination of the function of the arts in American ladies' lives reveals not only the tyranny of early nineteenth century roles for women, but the peculiar impression on both women and high culture that the early associations perpetuated well into our own century.

From all sides, the young woman in antebellum America was pressured to acquire facility in the arts.[4] The ladies' magazines regularly peddled poetry, reviews of concerts and theatrical performances, new fiction and nonfiction, anthologies of vocal music, articles on the lives of Beethoven, Correggio, and James Fenimore Cooper, and essays on the female characters in Shakespeare's plays. *The Ladies' Companion* serialized stories by Edgar Allan Poe and Charles Dickens. *The Ladies' Literary Cabinet* provided anecdotes about Milton, Hogarth, and Handel. Every month, *Godey's Lady's Book* printed an easy polka or song for the piano, with only a few sharps or flats. It also included at least one steel or copper engraving, a reproduction of a famous painting, or an original illustration for a piece of fiction, by such engravers as John Sartain, William Croome, W. E. Tucker, and others.[5]

Etiquette books of the day seconded the effort to identify the importance of the arts to ladies' good breeding. Florence Hartley's *Ladies' Book of Etiquette,* for example, advised the study of Italian for the purpose of singing lyrics in their original language and pronounced the piano the most fashionable musical instrument for ladies to study, well ahead of the harp and guitar. Hartley also explained that "no woman is fitted for society until she dances well."[6]

Educators championed the arts wholeheartedly. One survey of higher education of women in the antebellum South documents hundreds of parochial and secular seminaries and academies that included music and painting instruction as a regular part of the curriculum.[7] Judith Tick has described the strenuous musical training available to students at the Moravian Female Seminary in Bethlehem, Pennsylvania and the Cherry Valley Seminary in New York, where keyboard, guitar, and vocal instruction provided firsthand acquaintance with the works of Beethoven, Donizetti, and Herz, as well as American composers Gottschalk, Root, and Adele Hohnstock.[8] Thomas Woody, in his *History of Women's Education in the United States,* suggests that even the teachers most desirous of disseminating a solid curriculum of mathematics, science, and ancient languages, such as Mary Lyon and Zilpha Grant in their Ipswich, Massachusetts academy, "were unable to ignore the demand for vocal music, mezzotint, drawing and calisthenics."[9] When Lyon went on to found Mount Holyoke Seminary in South Hadley, Massachusetts, she provided drawing lessons from the start, and training for the school's choir. The piano was so much in demand that she added two additional pianos quickly.[10] Emma Willard, in describing her goals for the Troy, New York, Girls' Academy to the New York State legislators of 1819, rated literary and ornamental study alongside domestic, religious, and moral training for girls. She said she required a library, musical instruments, and some good paintings to do her work and she lauded the exercise and recreation that dance would provide to her students.[11] Almost twenty years later, she boasted about her success: "The education of a young lady now-a-days can hardly be considered provided for, unless she have the advantages of learning music. In the Troy Seminary this branch is taught extensively and scientifically. First-rate teachers of the piano, guitar and harp are employed; and some idea of the numbers which learn music may be inferred from the fact that fourteen pianos in the establishment are in almost constant requisition."[12]

Similarly, instructional materials of the period enjoyed enormous popularity among women. One hundred forty-five inexpensive drawing manuals published between 1820 and 1860[13] detailed the mysteries of perspective, geometry, and anatomy for all willing students. Only a few of these guides were pointedly prepared for ladies,[14] but this may be explained by their authors' desire to deliver the pastime from female hands to a broader public. After all, more than one worried observer proclaimed, "too many people view drawing only as suitable for young ladies to illustrate their album or some other genteel trifle, but not applicable to any other useful purpose."[15] Clearly, artists hoped to proselytize among a wider readership.

The arguments advanced by advocates of the arts for women were varied. Occasionally, culture study was justified for the aid it would provide its user along life's arduous paths. Educator Almira Phelps lauded music as a "resource against adversity." She promoted culture for other reasons as well, advising dance "to improve carriage of the body, provide pleasant form of exercise, and promote cheerfulness and good humor."[16] *Ladies' Wreath* asserted the usefulness of the arts as an alternative to wicked pastimes:

> A taste for reading fortifies the heart against the influence of vice and vicious habits, by occupying the leisure time which might otherwise be consumed in idleness, or wasted in fashionable dissipation, while it furnishes food for thought and rational entertainment, and thus creates an antagonist influence against the seductive brilliancy of worldly and sensual pleasures. It has also a direct tendency to elevate the soul above the low enjoyments of sense, and to give reason and conscience the ascendency over passions.[17]

Ladies' Garland, a Philadelphia magazine, stressed the vitality that the arts rekindled in humdrum lives, labeling music "the medicine of the mind—it rouses and revives the languishing soul; affects not only the ears, but the very arteries; awakens the dormant powers of life, raises the animal spirits, and renders the dull, severe, and sorrowful mind, erect and nimble."[18]

While artist Maria Turner contended that the study of painting instructed young women in botany (classification of flowers and fruits), natural philosophy (gravitation, refraction of colors, light and shadow, reflection on the water) and history (foreign scenes in history paintings), she also capitulated to the supremacy of domestic tasks by claiming "though I advocate the study of drawing and painting, I do not say that it is absolutely necessary to a young lady's education. There are many branches far more important."[19]

More regularly, however, arts education was portrayed as a handmaiden to the lady's duties in the service of her loved ones. Thus, her instruction in voice culture held entertainment value, for readings to her family. "Reading aloud, with propriety and grace, is an accomplishment, worthy of acquisition in females. It so often gives them an opportunity of imparting pleasure and improvement to an assembled family, during the winter evening, or the protracted storm."[20] Another essayist urged girls "to acquire an improved skill in any one branch of painting or drawing . . . ; to attain a moderate execution of music, with correct time and pure taste, so as to please others and amuse herself."[21] Even a mediocre result was entirely becoming if exhibited by a girl whose goal was to oblige her circle. Her singing supported her piety, when applied to sacred music. Lydia Sigourney wrote, "Young voices around the domestick altar, breathing sacred musick, at the hour of morning and evening devotion, are a sweet and touching accompaniment."[22] Similarly, Emma Willard wrote that "art enkindles the latent spark of taste, of sensibility for [Nature's] beauties, til it glows to adoration for their author, and a refined love of all His works."[23]

Her familiarity with the arts could help a lady bear up in the face of the dismal drudgery she would regularly face in the domestic sphere. Reading, declared one supporter of a rigorously literary curriculum—including English poetry, Blackstone's *Commentaries,* ancient history in the original languages, and novels by Sir Walter Scott—served to insulate women from the tedium of routine tasks, protecting them with high-minded thoughts. She argued for "the importance of the practical utility of a cultivated intellect, and the additional power and usefulness it confers,—raising its possessor above all the mean and petty cares of daily life, and enabling her to impart innobling influences to its most trifling details."[24]

The arts also armed a lady for her function as the inspirer of desirable behavior in those around her. Acres of verbiage were devoted, in nineteenth century publications, to the lady's noble role as a moral yardstick. An anonymous author in *Ladies' Garland* explained, "A female of cultivated taste, has an influence upon society wherever she moves. She carries with her that secret attractive charm which operates like magic upon the beholder, fixes the attention and softens the feelings of the heart like those benign influences over which we have no control."[25] In a like vein, Lydia Sigourney's publication, *Ladies' Companion,* proclaimed:

> The influence of women, in the endearing relations of sister, of wife, and of mother, exceeds all conception in its extent and its power. In this respect she is far superior to the sterner sex . . . How are the asperities of the husband softened, his evil habits corrected, and the nobler and better attributes of his nature developed in their lovely and exquisite proportions, by the captivating graces, the generous and self-sacrificing devotion of the wife of his bosom![26]

A girl quickly learned that she would grow to set behavioral and moral standards for her circle. One "Pupil of Troy Female Seminary" informed readers of *American Ladies' Magazine* that "this neglect of the female mind, will be regarded as a great political error when it is considered that women exert an important influence upon the moral, religious, manners and politics of a country." She went on to repeat the popular aphorism of Cato, "the Romans govern the world, but the women govern the Romans."[27] Clearly, the author intended to replicate this role in the United States of America.

Nineteenth-century publications for ladies bombarded their readership with arguments that their artistic accomplishments could sharpen the presumed natural character traits of their sex, which in turn would infuse their families with strengthened piety and purity. Quite baldly, middle-class society seemed to feel that specialization in character traits was as desirable as specialization in work. If it made sense to train technicians in a particular skill to share with the society at large, did it not also make sense to train women to be creatures of good character, to share with the larger society? Poetry by Homer, Shakespeare, Spenser, and Milton had the power to influence society for the better, and *Ladies' Keepsake and Home Library* expected women's familiarity with poetry to carry its beneficence to the family. "To gather the rays of divinity that are scattered amidst the clouds of this world into a pencil, to assist us to read the characters of wisdom that lie about us, is a most charitable and pious work. This is the highest promise of poetry, and those poets who have been faithful to their trust, have been both the patrons of sound philosophy, and the guardians of religion."[28] "Musick," argued Lydia Sigourney, "is a source of surpassing delight to many minds. From its power to sooth the feelings, and modify the passions, it seems desirable to understand it, if it does not involve too great expense of time."[29] Another writer drew on ancient literary works by Cassiodorus and Canus to argue that music could put unpleasant emotions in order. "We cannot deny that they . . . soothe disordered passions into peace . . . elevate the devotional feelings of the human heart."[30]

In her etiquette manual for ladies, Florence Hartley also expounded on the value of music instruction for putting passions in order. "It is not, as some will assert, a waste of time or money. Not only the fingers, voice, and figure are improved, but the heart and intellect will become refined, and the happiness greatly increased."[31] Another supporter of musical skill for girls linked its worth to religious piety as well as good character, praising "the concord of sweet sounds, which will enliven many a dull hour, and cheer many a desponding one, which will make them better worshippers in the sanctuary, and more cheerful members to their families."[32]

The mechanical aspects of home beautification, a duty of no small place among the lady's responsibilities, were said to be assisted by her familiarity with the arts. Modeling in clay, drawing portraits and miniatures in oils and watercolors, and painting on china plates, vases, velveteen, glass, or silk, were often given a place alongside crafts and home improvement techniques in the guidebooks. Quilting, embroidery, fashioning artificial fruits and flowers from wax, knitting, ceramics, macramé, papier-mâché, stencilling, woodcarving, basketmaking, rug making and crocheting dog muzzles were among the appropriate skills for household decoration, but they generally shared a place with instruction in arts for domestic training.[33] Thomas Woody's survey of women's education in the United States from 1749 to 1871 charts the numbers of art and music courses as equalling those in needlework in the early nineteenth century, with the arts gaining as the century progressed.[34]

For all the popularity of instructing young ladies in cultural accomplishments, not all Americans agreed that the arts afforded an appropriate vehicle for the concerns of girls and women. Both upholders of the ideal of ladydom and challengers of it put forward reasons why the arts should *not* be embraced by America's daughters of leisure. Many Americans suspected that the arts could corrupt their daughters, and steer them far from the prescribed paths of piety, domesticity, subservience, and purity. The dangers of dancing in crowded and overheated ballrooms, late into the night, appalled many social observers. They damned dancing, so troubled were they by the temptations flourishing at parties. They catalogued the reasons young ladies should confine their exercise to simple calisthenics, conducted modestly and in privacy at home. It was asserted that dancing parties might encourage vanity and competition in women, leading them to display themselves in elaborate, unhealthful, low-cut dresses. Some feared that licentiousness could arise, excited by the music, decor, costumes, and conversation at public dances.[35]

Ladies' attendance at theatrical entertainments and opera was also attacked for the corrupting influences of "indelicate" scenes and language, as well as the immodest costumes.[36] Girls' academies, seeking to protect their own reputations as well as those of their charges, promised to protect their inmates' virtue by denying them all public spectacles. "No pupil shall be allowed to attend balls, dancing parties, theatrical performances or festive entertainments," declared the bylaws of Elizabeth Academy in Old Washington, Mississippi in 1818.[37]

Reading was said to bear similar temptations for the female sex. Novels and romances, at least, "produce mischievous effects" and corrupt the mind.[38] Catharine Beecher claimed that "fictitious narrative" made "vice and crime alluring," transmitted a false view of life, and persuaded readers to abandon duty in search of unrealistic dreams.[39] A commentator writing in the *Young Lady's Guide* also promised nefarious results from familiarity with much fiction. "Bad novels enfeeble the intellect, impoverish the imagination, vulgarize taste and human nature, and waste precious time."[40] Likewise, the *Ladies' Garland* attacked "the pernicious influence novel reading exerts over the imagination." Mrs. H. O. Ward warned that "the flashy novels, the unclean novels, the novels that glow with fires of impure passions, are to be relentlessly proscribed."[41]

Such attacks on novel reading among women prompted lists of suitable titles to be publicized in periodicals and behavior guides for ladies. The favored works tended to be formidable in content, even leaden, especially heavy on history and biography, and cautious in their choice of fiction. Florence Hartley approved plays by Shakespeare, Sheridan, Knowles and Bulwer. *The Young Lady's Own Book*, published in 1836, recommended classics, travel, history, Fenelon, Sir Walter Scott, Washington Irving, Plutarch's *Lives*, Miss Sedgwick's *Redwood*, and the poems of Wordsworth and Coleridge.[42] Thirty-three years later in *Young Lady's Guide*, Henry Rogers recommended British essayists such as Macaulay, Milton, Gray, Cowper, Addison, Johnson, and Crabbe, and urged that light novels "be read now and then as a reward of strenuous exertion, or for having mastered some difficult book."[43] The *Handbook for Home Improvement* was quirky. It endorsed novels by Scott, Cooper, and Simms, which were "based on real historical events and can lead to more solid works," and recognized the universal popularity of Aesop's *Fables, The Arabian Nights, Robinson Crusoe, Pilgrim's Progress, Don Quixote, The Vicar of Wakefield, Paradise Lost,* and Shakespeare. It also sanctioned the study of phrenology and Mrs. Ellet's *History of American Women.*[44]

As for drawing, the exercise of sketching from nature was simply attacked as a waste of time, draining young women's energies from their real work of domestic tasks. The Rev. Charles Burroughs condemned the visual arts along with music as distractions from housework:

> Another common fault in the education of females is employing too much of their time merely in the acquisition of accomplishments. How many spend all their most important early years in unwearied attention to music, painting and dancing, under every variety of fashionable teachers, and neglect those studies, which are most essential to their usefulness and happiness. Accomplishments are generally of a temporary character. It often happens that females remarkable for their musical skill and attainments, leave their musical instruments almost entirely untouched, after they have once become occupied by the cares of domestic life.[45]

The notion of women sketching nude figures was simply not considered in antebellum America, so improper was the thought. The hazards of women's viewing unclad bodies would not even be addressed in print until post–Civil War arts institutions made life drawing available to its male students and excluded their female counterparts from classes.

The most consuming preoccupation of arts critics, however, involved neither the moral dangers of the arts nor their time-wasting elements. Rather, most faultfinders saw danger in the possibility that steady training in the arts, especially music, would produce preening performers, interested in self-display at the expense of womanly modesty. The girl who mastered a musical instrument would be inclined to promote herself and her skill at the expense of her family and home. No greater sin against the Cult of True Womanhood existed than the training of a woman in an activity that might lead her to be self-absorbed.

There were apprehensions that too steady a diet of culture might produce women artists with ambitions to show off their talents, to the detriment of woman's primary service to family. Such ambitions ran contrary to the calling approved for women—that of inspiring males to be breadwinners, risk takers, creators and interpreters, movers and shakers. Thus, women's cultural aspirations threatened to topple established social structures.

Charles Butler clarified the proper limits governing female attainments. "Their knowledge is not often like the learning of men, to be re-produced in some literary composition, nor even in any learned profession; but it is to come out in conduct."[46]

Another study of the day likewise disdained the tendency to train little girls to exhibit artistic ambitions, which nurtured display, competition, and vanity. "It is not to glitter in a sunbeam, and display a ceaseless variety of gay and gaudy colors, that woman should be educated, but to occupy her station with grace, and to fulfill its duties with humility." It was men who must study for careers. If "literary knowledge is indispensable to men," women did not need to master it as long as society agreed her duty was to serve as an auxiliary to him.[47]

Thus, the ideal woman was one who knew enough to admire her husband for knowing more. "My wife should have talent enough to be able to understand and value mine, but not sufficient to be able to shine herself," Ann Stephens asserted on behalf of the supposed typical husband. "I could never love a woman who was entirely occupied with literature. I want feeling, affection, devotion to myself—a domestic woman who would think my approbation sufficient for her happiness, and would have no desire for greater admiration. I could never be happy with an ambitious woman."[48] In 1836, Almira Phelps put it more plainly in her advice to the female student. Piano practice of one or two hours a day would sharpen her "taste, refinement and delicacy," but additional practice should be discouraged. Insofar as a young woman was permitted to achieve perfection at her art, she was simultaneously admitting that she had chosen to stint in the acquisition of "wifely qualifications."[49] In short, if a girl practiced long and hard, no man would marry her. Who would want a wife who put her own interests before her domestic cares? Many authors of the period cited actual case studies of girls who had practiced music twelve hours a day, or painted at the easel five hours a day, generally at a crazed father's insistence, only to achieve an unhappy result. Bachelors seeking a good marriage partner gave such women wide berth.[50]

Twenty years later, George Hogarth was repeating the same advice to the readers of the *Lady's Companion*. Music, he wrote, fulfills women's mission in that it sheds "a softening and refining influence over human society. It is not by brilliant displays of artistic acquirement and skill that music exerts its power in the circles of private life: it is in its simpler forms." He too attacked the woman who spent three to four hours a day indulging in musical practice for the purpose of preparing to display herself, and reminded her that such conduct served to distract her from her domestic labors.[51]

Popular literature in the early nineteenth century was littered with horror stories about the freakish women who ignored sound advice to renounce "brilliancy and fame" for usefulness, who embraced a "temporary power to dazzle and to charm" with the resulting "deadening within the heart of the feeling of love, which is the root of all influence."[52] A typical warning to women expounded on the futility of artistic training:

> She learns arts for strangers—to live for the applause of the foolish many.... To every thing gentle or refined, to everything lofty or dignified in the female character, this spirit is utterly opposed. Refinement would teach [her] to shun the vulgar applause which almost insults its object,—dignity would shrink from displaying before heartless crowds those emotions of the soul, without which all art is vulgar,—and how can women, who have neither refinement nor dignity, retail that influence which, rightly used, is to be so great an engine in the regeneration of society.[53]

Another writer warned succinctly that "vanity acts as a sort of refrigerator on all men."[54]

While adherents of the Cult of True Womanhood argued whether or not the arts played a constructive role in preparing young women to be self-sacrificing ladies, there were a few ideological combatants who rejected the self-sacrificing ideal altogether. These pariahs believed that women were capable of absorbing the same body of knowledge that men were learning in their colleges. Furthermore, they held that women need not confine the application of learning to domestic life, but could use it to enter the public arena, in such previously male-dominated careers as teaching, medicine, and missionary work. These path-breakers also dissected the role of the arts in women's lives. As antebellum champions of women's full participation in society, they tended to deplore arts education for girls. They suspected that culture was too trivial an activity for young minds, which needed to discard traditional ornamental work to construct a solid foundation of classical and scientific knowledge.

Writer and journalist Sarah Josepha Hale made a crusade of defending the ability of women to learn the most "masculine" subjects. In her 1843 essay arguing for the admission of her sex into the teaching profession she asked about women, "is it objected that they do not possess sufficient soundness of learning—that their acquirements are superficial, showy, frivolous? The fault is in their education, not in the female mind. Only afford them opportunities of improvement and motives for exertion."[55] In *American Ladies Magazine*, which Hale edited, she published an attack on tendencies in modern education for ladies, pitting the generally accepted arts curriculum against a call for instruction in government and politics. "We teach them accomplishments, they are ignorant of the laws of their country, but they can speak French, ... they have excellent notions of putting cows in watercolors."[56]

Hale did not stand alone in her campaign to entitle women to all the scholarly disciplines. *Young Lady's Own Book* decried the time wasted on the "inessential" arts by untalented girls, and insisted that girls needed more solid and less flashy educations, like those boys received.[57] *The Ladies' Literary Cabinet* also argued for solid subjects as opposed to the arts. "To be able to dance, sing, and play; to flirt at the theater, and faint in the ball room, is sufficient to obtain the highest admiration. A girl is sent to dancing schools, when she should be learning to spell ... I trust the day is not far distant, when female worth will be measured by solid acquirements, and the mere tinsel ornament of education will be properly estimated in society."[58]

In the early nineteenth century the newest academies for young women in America proposed to offer their students higher education, and to train women to be the nation's future teachers. The leading early schools with a rigorous curriculum included Catharine Beecher's Hartford Female Seminary, founded in 1828; Emma Willard's School in Troy, New York (1821); Zilpha Grant's school in Ipswich, Massachusetts (1828); and Mary Lyons's Mount Holyoke Female Seminary in South Hadley, Massachusetts (1837). The posture of these schools toward the arts was ambivalent. None could dispense with subjects that promised cultural attainments, for what parent would willingly expose a daughter to a course that rendered her a freak in society? All, however, were inclined to minimize their arts offerings and tout their instruction in math, science, philosophy and history, the subjects expected to train the mind as an instrument of reason.[59] In the latter half of the century, schools of higher learning for women would continue to need to make peace with the role of the arts in their students' educational lives.

There arose still other champions of women's abilities, who saw nothing unreasonable, second-rank or ridiculous about women's serious application to artistic endeavors. On the contrary, they argued that the women who received rigorous technical training in the arts could profit fully from the instruction. Furthermore, the students might achieve new power and respect, for themselves and for their art, by earning an honest living with their skill. These pioneers foreshadowed the post–Civil War explosion of arts institutes and conservatories that admitted women and provided them with as deep and sound an arts education as male students received.

In painting, several women distinguished themselves as founders of advanced art and design instruction for women. Ednah Dow Littlehale Cheney (1824–1904)—suffragist, civic reformer, clubwoman, biographer of Louisa May Alcott, Universalist, abolitionist, participant in Margaret Fuller's Conversations—was one of a handful of people of her day to suggest that formal art and design training for women could produce skilled workers who might become self-supporting while advancing the quality of American design available to consumers.[60] In a world in which husbands were not always willing or able to support wives to exercise their skills as helpmates and auxiliaries, women needed to obtain training to enhance their self-sufficiency. Ednah Littlehale helped found the New England School of Design for Women in Boston in October 1851. She served as its executive secretary until she married Boston etcher and portraitist Seth Cheney in 1853. The school appears to have continued throughout the decade, seeking and winning Massachusetts State support in 1853 and again in 1856.[61]

Ohio-born philanthropist Sarah Worthington King Peter (1800–1877) founded the Philadelphia School of Design for Women in her home in November 1848, and a few years later launched the Cincinnati society that would establish a co-educational art school and an art museum.[62] In New York, Mary A. Hamilton founded the Women's Art School in 1852, which merged with Cooper Union in 1859.[63]

Also during this era, women began to gain entry to previously male-only academies. The Pennsylvania Academy of Fine Arts in Philadelphia, founded in 1805, opened its doors to women in 1844. In 1856 the Academy allowed women to draw the nude figure—its genitals covered by fig leaves—alongside the men students. The National Academy of Design in New York admitted four women in 1846, twenty years after the school's founding, although it did not make women a permanent part of the school until 1865.

In music, antebellum women also began to gain access to formal institutions which provided advanced training for those aspiring to professional careers. Musicologist Judith Tick has identified Music Vale, or Salem Normal School, as the first music school for women in this country. Founded in 1835, and providing instruction until 1876, this Connecticut seminary for girls provided professional training in music theory, voice culture, notation, harmony, thorough bass, counterpoint, as well as lessons in organ, harp, guitar, and piano. As many as eighty girls, from locations throughout the Western hemisphere, were attracted by the advanced level of musical instruction offered there. In fact, female seminaries became a major employer of the best professional musicians in the country. Students at the Wesleyan Female Seminary in Wilmington, Delaware, could study music with Charles Grobe; with John Hill Hewitt at Chesapeake Female College in Hampton, Virginia; and with George Root at Abbot's Institute for Young Ladies.[64]

So began the formal training of women in the arts, permitting dilettantism to give way to professionalism while attempting to prevent indigency. Role models surfaced everywhere, further inspiring women to acquire the knowledge to pursue the arts vigorously. In music, the Swedish singer Jenny Lind became a household word as she toured the nation under P. T. Barnum's management in 1850. Adelina Patti followed in her footsteps a decade later, and American-born singer Clara Louise Kellogg enjoyed great acclaim in this era. Augusta Brown, Elizabeth and Anne Sloman, and Mrs. C. L. Hull were among the women composers whose songs were published in mid-century popular periodicals.[65]

In painting, Emma Stebbins exhibited portraits at the Pennsylvania Academy of Design in 1845 and 1847, and was elected an Associate at the National Academy of Design in New York. Elizabeth Ellet's history, *Women Artists in All Ages and Countries,* identifies several successful women artists in the period, including Ann Leslie Peale, Mrs. Wilson Peale, Mrs. Cornelius Dubois Peale, Anne Hall, Mary Swinton Legare, Hermionie Dassel, Lily M. Spencer, Louise Lander, Margaret Pillsbury Weston, and Anna Mary Freeman.[66] Several American women also distinguished themselves in sculpture. Harriet Hosmer journeyed to Rome in 1852, where she took on several private and public commissions, including a lifesized "Beatrice Cenci" for the St. Louis Mercantile Library and "Puck" for the Prince of Wales. Anne Whitney showed a marble bust of a child at the 1860 National Academy of Design. Edmonia Lewis, born of a black father and Chippewa Indian mother, sculpted several statues in the 1860s.

In theater, Fanny Kemble and Charlotte Cushman distinguished themselves as serious actors, a tall step above the burlesque queens who had heretofore been the only familiar female presence in professional theater. Writers were most successful of all. Fanny Fern (Sara Willis Parton), Elizabeth Stuart Phelps, Harriet Beecher Stowe, Catharine Maria Sedgwick, and Lydia Maria Child, were only a few of multitudes of women writers who earned a living and won wide fame and respect for their writing in antebellum America.[67] So popular became the occupation of writing for women that the *Behavior Book: A Manual for Ladies* devoted one chapter to "Suggestions to Inexperienced Authors, How Women Should Submit Manuscripts for Publication" and another to "Conduct to Literary Women," giving guidance on polite behavior with women authors one might meet.[68]

Despite these successes, women continued to feel they must defend their absorption in creating, as when Ann Stephens discussed the "Woman of Genius" in *Ladies' Companion*. "It is to be doubted," she said, "if the most industrious female writer among us spends more hours out of the twenty-four, at her desk, than the fashionable belle devotes to the adornment of her person."[69] Yet sufficient numbers of women in the arts gained a strong reputation that society began to reconcile the lady's traits with the woman's talent. "The works of the female authors of the present age are objects of no common interest—not only for their separate beauties, but for the new and lovely lights which they cast over the whole region of imagination and the nooks of the graceful loveliness which they have been first enabled to illume."[70] Not only might women have the ability and training to make art, they might even have something unique to contribute.

By midcentury, the nation was experiencing a tidal wave of women's rights activity. Women were visible in every phase of public life: in politics (through abolitionist activity and the drive for woman suffrage); in religion (becoming ministers and missionaries); in reform (in temperance and health); in salaried work (in teaching, the professions, business, and in factories and labor organizations); in volunteerism for the public good (via the Civil War Sanitary Commission and other types of social service activity); and in educational institutions (entering newly founded women's colleges and coeducational state universities). The shortage of eligible husbands, due to Civil War casualties, the gold rush, and the lure of the frontier, helped propel women's burgeoning determination to seek independence. In this environment, it should be no surprise that women found doors opening in the arts as well.

New avenues of instruction opened to them immediately after the Civil War. New educational institutions would launch armies of women students who thought it utterly suitable and possibly lucrative to acquire sound training in the arts. No longer entirely dominated by antebellum prescriptions that women should limit themselves to family life, America produced a new woman and sanctioned her association with serious cultural endeavors. At least twenty-eight societies for women can be identified as providing formal instruction in drawing between the years 1865 and 1882. The Pittsburgh School of Design for Women has the distinction of being the first, but groups in New York, Boston, Baltimore, New Orleans, Peoria, Cleveland, Salt Lake City, and San Francisco were not far behind.[71] New arts classes were also available to women at various branches of the Young Women's Christian Association and Women's Educational and Industrial Unions.

At the same time, coeducational institutions expanded their offerings to women. In 1868, the Pennsylvania Academy of Fine Arts initiated, on a trial basis, a life drawing class for women with a nude model. The following year it formalized the class. During the 1870s women entered the Art Students' League in New York, Boston Normal Art School, San Francisco School of

Design, and St. Louis School of Design. The National Academy of Design, where women came to occupy nearly one third of the student body, established a women's life drawing class in 1871. In the 1880s, women were admitted to Cleveland's Western Reserve School of Design for Women and to the Mississippi Industrial Institute and College for the Education of White Girls of the State of Mississippi in the Arts and Sciences.[72] By the early 1930s, it could be asserted that women comprised seventy percent of the students in art courses in colleges and universities.[73] A steady stream of young women also traveled to Europe to enroll in such institutions as Academie Julian and Academie Colorossi or to study independently with individual artists.

Meanwhile, American music conservatories were also opening their doors to women as students, scholarship recipients, student association officers, and teachers.[74] Women flooded the studios and classrooms, eager to gain professional training, not only in America but abroad, where the tradition of music conservatories had lasted since the eighteenth century.[75]

Probably the most prominent exemplar of Continental study was Amy Fay, who left the New England Conservatory in Boston at the age of twenty-five to study piano in Germany. From 1869 to 1875, she took private lessons with some of the most renowned pianists of her day—Carl Tausig, Franz Kullak, Franz Liszt, and Ludwig Deppe. Her letters home were first published in 1881, and must have been devoured by American music students, as evidenced by twenty-one printings of the memoir and the presence of nearly two thousand American students in Berlin alone in 1891.[76] Her account exuded enthusiasm. She exulted in the freedom women enjoyed in Europe. "Just think how convenient it is here with regard to public amusements, for ladies can go anywhere alone!" Fay used her new-found freedom to enrich her own musical education. She gushed over Clara Schumann's pianism: "It was worth a trip across the Atlantic just to hear those two performances. . . . She seemed full of fire, and when she played Bach, she ought to have been crowned with diamonds! Such noble playing I never heard." She noted that Deppe's top students, Steiniger and Warburg, were women; and she witnessed a concert by Alicia Hund, who composed and conducted a symphony. "That is quite a step for women in the musical line."[77]

Fay was only one of a long string of young American women who crossed the Atlantic for music study. Black students, facing discrimination at home, had better luck in Europe. Some, like the daughter of Booker T. Washington, Portia Washington Pittman, studied with Martin Krause in Berlin; and Hazel L. Harrison of La Porte, Indiana, toppled Ferruccio Busoni's resolve to take no more pupils.[78]

By the late nineteenth century, then, women who undertook the study of the arts could do so with serious purpose. Increasingly, musical and artistic training were no longer a prerequisite for girls; hence, most of the dilettantes dropped away, and those who chose to approach the arts did so with goals beyond social polish. "The new girl is too busy to play the piano unless she has the gift; then she plays it with consuming earnestness. We list to her, for we know that this is an age of specialization, an age when woman is coming into her own, be it nursing, electoral suffrage, or the writing of plays. . . . Never has the piano been so carefully studied as it is today."[79] Where antebellum musical instruction may have been limited to the goal of pleasing party guests with musical ditties, women now had access to all the mechanics of music. "Scarcely fifty years ago the subjects of harmony and counterpoint had been considered outside the province of women's education, and the acquirement of such knowledge, other than as a pastime, would have been regarded as a mental aberration. . . . It therefore must be considered a great point gained that it is no longer looked upon as an eccentricity for women to compose."[80] Musicologist Judith Tick has observed women's invasion of the music teaching profession. Between 1870 and 1910, the U.S. census records an eightfold increase from 36% to 60% of the profession.[81]

Professional training, in America and abroad, was not the only source of arts education for young women at the turn of the century. Colleges, too, were providing women with a more serious and formal foundation in music, art, and literature than schools had provided them before the Civil War. The new liberal arts colleges for women, founded in the second half of the nineteenth century, began to make peace, to varying degrees, with the serious education of their students and the incorporation of arts education into the curriculum. In general, these schools still shied from the association between cultural preoccupations and the female dabbler; but most of them began to move cautiously toward accepting the value of the arts in young women's lives.

The Mount Holyoke College solution was to teach the history and theory of art and music, rather than conferring academic credit on the practical application of arts skills. Vassar College took the plunge into initiating art instruction in the 1860s; Smith College created autonomous Schools of Music and Art in 1880, requiring only a high school qualification for entry. A generous gift from Northampton butcher Winthrop Hillyer enabled the school to build an American art gallery, which provided Smith students first-hand acquaintance with the development of art history. Wellesley College was perhaps bravest, opening a College of Music in 1881 for the plain purpose of providing instruction in singing and instrumental music, and also initiating a graduate program in art history and archaeology in 1897.[82] Not everyone was impressed with the quality of the instruction at the Seven Sisters colleges, however. James Huneker observed that the "great women's colleges" with "wonderful curriculums" nevertheless provided only a "comparatively humble position" for music."[83]

By and large, college students' actual participation in creative interpretation was confined to officially sanctioned extracurricular programs. For recreation, students wrote for their own literary magazines; they performed skits, tableaux, and plays for their peers; and they founded glee clubs, banjo societies, and Beethoven associations to entertain their campuses. In 1877, Wellesley students formed a Shakespeare Society, providing a vehicle of literary expression for the thespians and design experience for costume and scenery designers. The Vassar Glee Club raised scholarship money with a concert in New York City. At Bryn Mawr, nineteenth-century girls were steered away from the performance of French plays, but were encouraged in their production of Gilbert and Sullivan operettas. The Barnard College Greek Games and Bryn Mawr College May Day celebrations at the turn of the century, examined in my chapter on Pageantry, labeled theatrical expression an approved form of adolescent play. At coeducational colleges and universities, sororities and women's dormitories frequently sponsored similar artistic amusements.[84]

Not all colleges remained at arm's length from arts programs in the curriculum. H. Sophie Newcomb Memorial College, for example, opened a pottery decoration class in 1894. The instructor, Mary G. Sheerer, was so effective in launching a program for her New Orleans students that their work won an award at the Paris Exposition of 1900 and the college's strengths in art and craft became widely known and respected.[85] In 1873, the College of Fine Arts at Syracuse University became the first coeducational degree-granting college of fine arts in the United States.[86]

The college girl of the late nineteenth century, then, generally faced a notion of the arts' place quite different from that seen by her antebellum grandmother. The new woman was freed from expectations that she be acquainted with the arts for the delight of her family and social circle, while at the same time she enjoyed a rich association with the arts for relaxation, and sometimes even for college credit. Nevertheless, in higher education culture did not rank with the life of the mind, and so was still a step-child to studies that were considered serious intellectual fare.

Finally, private tutors at home and abroad met the artistic needs of some women. Wealthy families frequently provided intellectual and arts training through private instruction. Composer Amy Cheney Beach took piano lessons with Ernst Perabo, Junius W. Hill, and Carl Baermann in Boston. Hill provided the only formal instruction in harmony Beach ever received.[87] Cecilia Beaux took drawing lessons in the Philadelphia studios of Catharine Ann Drinker and Adolf Van der Whelen before she studied at the academy of Rodophe Julian in Paris.[88] Both diarist Alice James and novelist Edith Wharton were tutored by governesses in Europe and at home.[89]

By the late nineteenth century, however, the numbers of women with access to serious training in the arts were relatively great. The courses in art schools, music conservatories, colleges, and universities, in addition to the countless tutors who offered private instruction, produced a generation of women with greater knowledge of the arts than had ever existed before. Many fine talents emerged. Among them were pianist Julie Rive-King, pianist Miss Neally Stevens, and violinist Maud Powell.[90] In addition, foreign-born women artists won acclaim on American shores, teaching and inspiring American women to follow in their footsteps. Among these were pianist Theresa Careño from Venezuela and Austrian-born and American-raised Fannie Bloomfield Zeisler.[91]

However, not everyone had come to believe that women could excel in the arts. James Huneker observed inequities in ability between the sexes in music and attributed them to differences in physique. "The muscular conformation of a woman's arm militates against her throwing a stone as far as a man; it also operates adversely in modern piano-playing, where the triceps muscles are a necessity for a broad, sonorous tone."[92] An article printed in both *Living Age* and *Saturday Review* advised parents to discourage their daughters from drawing, because their docility caused them to copy the teacher and "merely reproduce the ideas of popular painters of the other sex, a little defaced, deformed, or emptied out" instead of inventing original interpretations.[93] Edith Brower told readers of the *Atlantic Monthly* that woman's aptitude for concrete thoughts made her a good housekeeper and manager of the family but a poor renderer of artistic ideas. She blasted the paintings of Rosa Bonheur and the fiction of George Eliot, drawing attention to the absence of a female Homer, Dante, Wagner, or Beethoven.[94] Similarly, George P. Upton saw woman as being incapable of using her emotional nature to its necessary fullness for art. "She lives in emotion and acts from emotion. She feels its influences, its control, and its power; but she does not see these results as man looks at them. He sees them in their full play, and can reproduce them in musical notation.... Man controls his emotions, and can give outward expression of them. In women they are the dominating element."[95] Even in fiction, such ideas persisted. Novelist Kate Chopin, writing *The Awakening* in 1899, suggested that the making of real art required a courage that protagonist Edna Ponteillier did not have. When Edna attempted to satisfy her emptiness by dabbling in art, another character, Mademoiselle Reisz, warned her against it because "to be an artist one must be courageous, to dare and defy."[96]

Mistrust about women's artistic capabilities persisted. Even the increased prominence of individual women performers could not mislead musical women into supposing that their sex had gained a firm footing in the male musical establishment. Male performers, orchestra conductors, critics, and teachers persisted in the view expressed by writer Anthony M. Ludovici that "women can at best make only an inferior display, even if she make any display at all."[97] In the orchestral world this attitude was rigid, causing social critic and feminist Suzanne La Follette to rail against "the prejudice of male musicians ... effective enough to exclude [women] from the personnel of our important orchestras."[98] London and Seattle Symphonies conductor Sir Thomas Beecham asserted the inability of male musicians to take female colleagues seriously:

> I do not like, and never will, the association of men and women in orchestras and other instrumental combinations.... My spirit is torn all the time between a natural inclination to let myself go and the depressing thought that I must behave like a gentleman. I have been unable to avoid noticing that the presence of a half-dozen good looking women in the orchestra is a distinctly distracting factor.[99]

Of similar mind, José Iturbi refused to accept female graduates from the Eastman School of Music in the Rochester Symphony he conducted. Only a handful of women, usually harpists, managed to win places in symphony orchestras, until the Cleveland Orchestra admitted a few female musicians in

1923, and San Francisco's ensemble admitted four violinists and a cellist in 1925. These steps, however, did not constitute a trend, and integration remained slight until the 1970s.

In addition, many people in American society still held the antebellum assumption that the ideal woman's primary role was service to her family. Once a girl grew up, she should follow society's dictates by marrying and beginning a family. Thus, most late nineteenth-century wives, like their early nineteenth-century counterparts, were expected to use their skills, no matter how finely honed, in only one way: in the service of others. Where, then, was such a woman to spend her hard-won arts training, once she had agreed to settle down and raise a family? Probably she was so busy running her household that she considered it an achievement to find the time to sing some lullabies to her babies, design costumes for their playtime, or compose snapshots of their outings. Until her children were grown, she most likely did not have permission, time, money, space, or peace to carry on any semblance of the artistic life she had once cultivated.

This book is a study of woman's quest, from 1890 to 1930, to use her literary, musical, and artistic knowledge and talent in a world that continued to legitimate only her role as a devoted mother. This is the story of the women who painted alongside Mary Cassatt, or took prizes with Cecilia Beaux at the Pennsylvania Academy of Art, or with Georgia O'Keeffe at the New York Art Student's League; who practiced scales with violinist Maud Powell at the Paris Conservatory; or turned in essays, like Emily Dickinson, for Mount Holyoke Seminary assignments—the women who did not build respected careers, the women who built families instead. As soon as their children were grown, these women created women's clubs as a vehicle to use their arts interests and talents more broadly than in their domiciles. This is the tale of their successes and failures in that effort.

It would be absurd, of course, to claim that all clubwomen had studied, as girls, in conservatories, design schools, or colleges with strong arts programs. It would also be faulty to assume that every woman with training in the arts turned to women's clubs to rekindle her youthful enthusiasms. Yet women's literary, painting, music, and theater clubs enjoyed a heyday between 1890 and 1930, and were frequently populated by women with some background in music, literature, or painting.[100] Clubs were by no means entirely successful at eradicating early images of women as dilettantes. Among professionals in the art world, among the women's rights activists of the period, and even among some of the women devotees themselves, earlier assumptions caused skepticism about the ability and sincerity women could bring to their creative enterprises. Yet women's amateur arts groups restored members' relationship to the arts, and they did so in ways that changed over the forty-year span of their heyday in history. An exploration of their history and the changes they underwent can create a context for their specific achievements and limitations in the fields of music, pageantry, drama, painting, and architecture. Whatever their limitations, the impact of the clubs on the women who participated in them and on the arts in America was extraordinary.

TWO

Arts and Activism

AN OVERVIEW OF WOMEN'S CLUBS,
1890–1930

Textbooks still teach us that the Progressive Era lasted about twenty years, from the turn of the century to World War I or 1920. Students of women's history, however, understand that women's organizations devoted to social change enjoyed a much longer life. Women's voluntary associations began to develop even before the 1890s and continued their reform efforts throughout much of the 1920s. This forty-year span of activity was naturally characterized by great changes in size of membership, goals of the leadership, and strategies for change. Scholars have heretofore neglected the shifts in the history of the woman's club movement, thereby missing much significant material. The clubs were unquestionably a major vehicle for the expression of women's public voices, in a time that was still trying to hold to the belief that woman's place was in the home. The identification of changing patterns in the clubs' history exposes changes in women's lives, changes in women's impact on society, and changes in the relationship of the women's clubs to the larger Woman Movement.

My observations are based largely on the records of women's literary and civic clubs and the General Federation of Women's Clubs with which they were affiliated. In addition, I have drawn on the local and national records of the National Federation of Music Clubs, the American Pageantry Association, the Drama League of America, and the American Federation of Arts. Patterns similar to those described here also emerge among the multitudes of cultural societies and civic organizations that never joined these national networks. Among them are alumnae associations, branches of the Association of Collegiate Alumnae (later the American Association of University Women), patriotic women's organizations, the Junior League of America, the National Association of Colored Women's Clubs, and countless other women's groups.

The historical records are to be found in public repositories and private hands throughout the country. Consisting largely of organizational minutes, correspondence, conference proceedings, newsletters, press releases, yearbooks, and annual reports that were generated by formal associations, the records yet manage to convey a sense of the individuals involved and their personal feelings about their volunteer efforts.

A clarification of the four stages, which did not unfold at identical times in every club, does much to explain the strengths and weaknesses of the woman's club movement of the Progressive period. The earliest stage in the evolution of women's clubs, blossoming by the 1890s, was one of self-development. Women assumed the right to engage in study for the joy of individual intellectual and cultural growth. It was an end that critics saw as far too selfish for so-called helpmates. In stage two, roughly during the first decade of the twentieth century, many women's clubs went on to offer community or social service programs to their neighbors. These activities were often labeled "Municipal Housekeeping," insofar as such volunteer efforts appeared to parallel—if widen, and remove from the private sphere—women's homemaking roles.

The third and most sophisticated stage of activity that women's clubs undertook consisted not of serving the community, as traditional women might have, but of engaging with it. In this stage, women fashioned such projects as pageants, Liberty Sings, and community art exhibitions in which no citizen was denied a role. Events of this kind were initiated to provide decision-making experience for the sponsoring club members and the rest of the participants. By inspiring observers to embrace their model, club members hoped to move all society closer to the democratic ideal they envisioned. Finally, in the 1920s, clubwomen entered an era of clubhouse building, which represented an ambitious effort to combine service to society with nurturance of their own membership. The new structures were designed to provide a lavish setting for the members' pleasure as they housed community projects for the general good.

It is possible to find precedents for women's club activities in mid-nineteenth-century America.[1] The idea of the woman's culture club did not bloom, however, until the 1890s, when the demands of earlier activists for women's political, social, educational, legal, and economic freedoms began to unlock the doors that had kept most middle-class women inside their homes. The woman drawn to a literary club in the final decade of the nineteenth century felt simultaneously relieved, delighted, excited, and afraid to embark on a course of study with six to thirty women neighbors in the parlors of their homes. It is likely that she had enjoyed reading, and perhaps even writing letters, poetry, or diaries as a schoolgirl, decades before. She may have studied voice, piano, or painting with some seriousness. Since marriage, however, her acquaintance with the arts had grown remote. The taxing and primary role of wife, mother, and housekeeper had not permitted her to pursue the arts even casually.

By 1895, over one hundred thousand women had formed women's societies, determined to encourage the discussion of literature, history, the arts, and current events for one afternoon a month.[2] In claiming her right to apply herself to the arts—not casually, as the antebellum girl had, but as deeply as circumstances would allow—the clubwoman was more like the woman engaged in professional training in the post–Civil War era. Whether her self-development demanded books, plays, a piano, or the sketch pad, she began to use the tools she needed to express the ideas she now believed she had a right to develop.

As might be expected, she was criticized, by family members and the press, for neglecting her home and family. Among those who disapproved was journalist E. Bok, publisher of the *Ladies' Home Journal*. In its May 1905 issue, Bok gave space to former President Grover Cleveland for an attack on clubwomen for neglecting their families.[3] Outraged clubs boycotted the magazine, which, in turn, sued one club under the Sherman anti-trust law.[4] Critics of the women's clubs might have tolerated selfless philanthropic endeavors on behalf of flood and famine victims; but new members regarded charitable work as an outdated occupation for modern women, and relegated it to a minor place in club life.

The late nineteenth-century clubwoman unashamedly proclaimed her goal as self-development. Such designations as the Women's Century Club and the Twentieth Century Club, in their anticipation of the new century, simultaneously anticipated a new use of women's developing talents. Although the idea of banding together was gaining acceptance in circles of forward-looking people, it required bravery for members to attempt to discuss new topics with one another, topics not previously addressed in a formal way, or to present a creative work for neighborly criticism. However rusty the club member's mind might feel, in middle age she certainly welcomed the chance to read again and discuss new ideas with her peers, to polish tired musical skills, to shed mundane and tedious responsibilities briefly, and enter the wider world of thought and beauty. She felt easier about presenting her original paper, on Shakespeare, Beethoven or Rembrandt, or about singing before the group, knowing she was surrounded by like-minded supporters. The intellectual stimulation stirred self-respect among the members again, and soon propelled women to initiate community programs such as the founding of town libraries, concert series, and art exhibitions.[5] Most importantly, clubs of the 1890s gave an opportunity for middle-class women to find a new confidence, a voice (both literally and figuratively), and a vehicle for both personal and social development.

The new women's groups of the 1890s, then, assisted members to rebuild their intellectual powers gone stale from the supremacy of domestic cares, and helped them feel entitled to self-expression. Clubs provided a reason and a forum for using reading, sketching, and practicing scales. They sharpened the researching and writing skills of members, as well as those in public speaking and Parliamentary procedure.

Clubwomen spoke in the strongest terms of the feelings of joy and comfort that their experience in the clubs brought them. Edna Dow Cheney wrote of her mid-nineteenth-century club experience in Boston, "I cannot express sufficient gratitude for the constant pleasure and comfort it has given me, the tie between the members was very strong, and we loved to be together, in the times of sadness as well as of joy and merriment."[6] Of the same era, Julia Ward Howe wrote, "I am anxious to get back to the Club.... To stay away from the Club seems like losing the comfort of one's family."[7] In New York, Cecilia Burleigh found at her club "atmosphere so genial, an appreciation so prompt, a faith so generous, that every possibility of my nature seemed intensified, and all its latent powers quickened into life."[8] Ellen M. Henrotin pinpointed the source of her joy as the dismissal of the social obligation by clubwomen to serve others relentlessly without thinking about themselves.

> Reciprocity is the foundation on which is built this great organization; the growing conviction that the giving and receiving are one, and that no one person should be placed in the position of always giving or always receiving, but that each one, according to her ability and opportunity, should be in a position to receive and to give.[9]

Cheney spoke publicly in 1890 of her feeling of "our club as a home, and of the tie that binds us together as a family tie. If it be possible to know a more sacred relation, I wish to say a word showing how we have known here a communion of souls, broader if not closer than the family tie, which we might not irreverently say has made this a true church to us, a company bound together by high thought and tender love."[10]

Contrary to scholars' assumptions that nineteenth-century patterns of women's culture, as a separate sphere from the men's world, toppled with the emergence of modern heterosocial structures, women's clubs would continue to attract women seeking to organize alongside other women. By the end of the first decade of the twentieth century, club life had flowered. The four hundred thousand women in the General Federation of Women's Clubs and ten thousand in the National Federation of Music Clubs represented only a portion of those interested.[11] The typical club had abandoned its limit of thirty members and its expectations that meetings could be held in members' homes. They succumbed to the pressure of friends and long waiting lists and admitted up to one hundred members, even if that meant renting public rooms in which to meet.

The great change that occurred in early twentieth-century club life was the pressure from the leadership to move away from the study of the arts, toward civic reform. "Dante is dead," cried General Federation of Women's Clubs president Sarah Platt Decker, throughout her administration from 1904 to 1908. In other words she was saying in effect, "don't waste your time on literature, music, and painting when municipal problems await your attention. Swell your ranks with new members! Use their signatures on petitions, their investigative talents on surveys, their connections with politicians, their energy on reform issues." Legions of clubwomen followed her advice, invigorating the civic reform movement we call Progressivism, giving women new clout in the public arena, but also, to a certain extent, putting arts adherents on the defensive. Today, club records dazzle researchers with their documentation of generally successful efforts to support, indeed to shape, the Progressive agenda: civil service, conservation, regulation of child labor and prostitution, inspection of factories, the creation of juvenile reformatories and mothers' pensions, enforcement of pure food and drug laws—to name only a handful of the measures that became the foundation of turn-of-the-century social, economic, and political reform. This strong civic reform strain in club activity has tended to obscure and diminish the contribution made by clubwomen who continued to concern themselves with the arts.

Decker's announcement seems to have commenced a war between the cultural advocates and the civic reformers that lasted a quarter century. However, the evidence suggests that the two camps were not really adversaries, and that the distinctions between them were insignificant. The social service forces felt that Municipal Housekeeping enabled women to charge into new territory, fitting themselves for work in public life and transforming the shape of social services in significant ways, and that the pursuit of beauty was a relic from a past that confined women. In fact, both schools of activity followed the age-old admonition that women should serve others. That was why the typical, non-militant, middle-class woman could easily embrace the Municipal Housekeeping of the clubs. The cultural advocates came to behave in ways identical to their civic-minded sisters, building the same impressive skills in lobbying, fundraising, and publicizing the creation of public institutions to reform the municipality for the common good. Not only did the two groups develop similar skills, but the goals of cultural and civic reform programs were the same: to improve the well-being of every American citizen. Most importantly, both sides shared the motivation to nurture the larger family, as all good women should. The establishment of a well-baby clinic and a Civil Service policy was no higher a manifestation of women's public activism than the founding of a city art museum or public concerts in the park. In sum, both factions labored to gain new skills in service of the same old service-oriented goals.

Not all political women of the day had Sarah Decker's difficulty in reconciling the idea that the arts and the civics branches of women's activism attained the same goals for individual women, for the women's rights movement, and for society's development. Feminist Charlotte Perkins Gilman, who had studied art at the Rhode Island School of Design as a young woman and supported herself as a writer and lecturer, saw no reason to pit women interested in art against women interested in reform. In her work, notably *The Man-Made World or, Our Androcentric Culture*,[12] she identified art as merely one of a wide variety of areas in western society where women's capabilities were overlooked or trivialized. Activists who dealt with the inequities in art, she believed, would assist in chipping away at the general sexism women faced. May Wright Sewall, suffragist, pacifist, and founder of the National and International Councils of Women, was another political dynamo who valued the arts. In 1883 she founded the Indianapolis Art Association and the affiliated art school which became the John Herron Art Institute in 1902. In Sewall's view, this work, to involve all interested citizens in creativity, in no way compromised women's goals for individual expression but fundamentally enhanced them. Melusina Fay Pierce, founder of the Boston cooperative household, had studied piano alongside her famous sister, Amy Fay, and expected that reduced household labor would yield women more time for cultural activities. Another woman activist who held the arts in high regard was trade union organizer Margaret Dreier Robins, who shared the same cultural upbringing that brought her sister Dorothea to paint and her sister Katherine to collect modern art. Her lifetime devoted to the rights of working women was fueled by the idea that no class of people should be denied the leisure to bring beauty into their lives.[13]

Women of the day, of course, enjoyed no monopoly on the understanding that art and politics could mix. The Greenwich Village radicals of the 1910s, including John Reed, Max Eastman, and Floyd Dell, embraced the compatibility of art and politics by acting on behalf of both. In *Women as World Builders,* Dell articulated his fear that a narrowness of vision would ultimately hamper the scope of the revolt women might bring about:

> It is the drawback of the woman's movement that in any one of its aspects . . . it may appear too fiercely narrow. That women should make so much fuss about getting the vote, or that they should so excite themselves over the prospect of working for wages, will appear incomprehensible to many people who have a proper regard for art, for literature. . . . It is only when the woman's movement is seen broadly, in a variety of its aspects, that there comes the realization that here is a cause in which every fine aspiration has a place, a cause from which sincere lovers of truth and beauty have nothing really to fear.[14]

Dell envisioned a woman's movement which incorporated the arts into the political struggle for a just society.

The reluctance of some to embrace women's involvement in the arts emanated, no doubt, from lingering associations of the Victorian lady's dilettantism. Professional musicians also abhorred the so-called "female sensitivity" that they believed produced the amateur's satisfaction with frothy, badly played or sourly sung romantic melodies. Although Woman Movement supporters generally lauded the supposed sensitivity attributed to the nineteenth-century woman, they sought to redirect this attribute toward her analysis of societal problems. Actually, the new rigor that arts clubs would impose upon their twentieth-century study of literature, music, and painting never buried the old assumption that it was woman's special sensitivity that provided her with a unique affinity for culture. This sentiment would continued to be voiced throughout the 1920s in such publications as *Etude,* a piano teacher's periodical:

> Music . . . is to myriads of women a solace and a joy, the means of preserving hallowed life ideas, spiritual values, without which humankind cannot survive. Oh, if men could only realize how much the very foundations of our civilization depended upon keeping these ideals, the shrines of womanhood, unsullied and undimmed.[15]

Increasingly, however, these romantic notions shared the stage with the admission of women's musical and artistic intelligence and of their ability to inject the arts with political significance by insisting on its accessibility to everyone.

Gradually, clubwomen would forge a constituency which endorsed the concept that serious music, theatre, and painting could serve as a legitimate tool for achieving Decker's dream of building a better nation. By the early 1920s, Massachusetts clubwomen had placed the arts alongside the necessities of life, declaring, "The four pillars that hold up the House of Life are food, shelter, love and beauty. Art is part of the joy and inspiration of living, whether we create or whether we appreciate."[16] On the other side of the continent, Washington state women told each other "to budget art at home and school, just like food, clothes, and recreation."[17]

Some clubwomen argued that music's soothing properties might ultimately energize the populace:

> Music is one of the most remarkable of constructive tonics for the tired brain and nerves. To many it revitalizes the beautiful in life and softens the brain-breaking, nerve-snapping strain of this high pressure era.[18]

Grace Poole, while president of the Massachusetts Federation of Women's Clubs, praised the arts as a tool for serving clubwomen and others better. In 1922, she urged that civic reform be accompanied by artistic endeavor. "While we are doing this work let us not forget to build for ourselves a little. Art, literature and music throw open wide their doors and ask us to enter. We must not pass them by. They will enrich us and, through us, all with whom we come in contact."[19]

Throughout the country, there were similar messages. The New York State Federation of Women's Clubs president, Katherine Hildreth, spoke of the refreshment that arts provided to active women. "I must pay tribute to our cultural clubs—literature, art and musical. These clubs meet our spiritual wants and teach us how to live." She went on to quote a phrase by Auerbach, often repeated in music club circles: "'Music washes away from the soul the dust of everyday life.'"[20] Even Alice Ames Winter, president of the General Federation of Women's Clubs in 1922, came around. A novelist, she was nevertheless devoted to civic reform, and apprehensive of clubwomen's deviation from overtly political action. Yet she felt obliged to follow the growing body of cultural converts, by asserting the importance of reflective pursuits: "If the club is to be the weapon we hope for the bettering of community and country it must know as well as act. The ideal club is the club that is neither all study club nor all working club, but a combination of the two."[21]

Modern historians have demonstrated the high regard for civic activism that the club leaders of the early twentieth century transmitted to their constituencies. Scholars have been so taken with clubs' energetic Municipal Housekeeping on behalf of civic reform that they have not documented the efforts of the club devotees of culture as carefully as those of club civic reformers during this decade.[22]

Did clubwomen follow President Decker's call to pack away their editions of Browning and close the lid on the piano keyboard to lobby City Hall for the appointment of police matrons or the registration of nurses? Certainly not. On the contrary, a few arts lovers were so disgruntled by the emphasis on civic reform that they split off from federated clubs to continue their original program, undisturbed, in small groups such as The Ten O'Clock (from the Woman's Department Club, Indianapolis) and the Art Study Club (from the Natchez Woman's Club, Mississippi).[23] New art, music, or theatre clubs were founded, whose members were adamant about remaining small in size and concentrating their attention on individual artistic endeavors. These clubs, including the Morning Musicale of Greencastle, Indiana; the Arts and Crafts Club of Hartford; and the Art Club of Fort Dodge, Iowa, have continued to be important in women's lives until the present time.

Most women, however, remained in their original clubs, which were devising a new format to accommodate the diverse interests of a growing membership. Within many clubs, women created "departments," or subsections that offered a concentration on a single interest topic for those members who had the enthusiasm to discuss it monthly or even weekly. Available to all, required of none, departments constantly shifted, developing or dying according to the enthusiasm of a supportive corps within the organization.

The newest generation of civic club leaders, then, did not drive the pro-arts dissidents out. They made room for the interests of all members, exhibiting an impressive degree of tolerance over a controversial question. For example, a society that grew to three hundred might create a department of literature, another for Civil Service reform, another for music, and still another for forestry. The Wednesday Club of St. Louis could boast, in 1898, that it had created six departments (literature and history, education, social economics, current topics, art, and science). Similarly, the Amherst Woman's Club in Massachusetts became a department club by devising seven sections, devoted to literature, social science, education, music, history, current events, and science.[24] A member could participate fully in one department and meet the other women only in monthly business meetings or social hours. Thus, social activists could meet regularly with like-minded reformers, while readers could assemble to share book reviews.

The larger clubs had more to gain by keeping the arts advocates allied in departments than by expelling them. Members paid dues to a common treasury that funded reform projects; they could be persuaded to sign petitions for street lights and write letters for clean waterways. A total membership of great size impressed the officials whom the reformers sought to challenge. In addition, club members provided musical entertainment at meetings and conventions, wrote club songs, and designed attractive party favors, club jewelry, yearbooks, and newsletters. Undoubtedly, some activists must have believed that cultural activity was less important than social reform work; but the artists continued to participate fully in club life.

It is of no small significance that as the department club grew in popularity, it attracted great numbers of arts supporters. Where a club may have boasted only a handful of trained musicians as members in 1895, by the early twentieth century many clubs held enough for a small choir or chamber group. While there may have been only a couple of painters in the club before, now there were enough to hire a teacher or model and arrange field trips to the studios of professional painters. Whereas early clubwomen had to be content to read a play together, now there was sufficient talent to stage a real production, with props, scenery, and costumes. In addition, the women in the arts departments enjoyed a large and appreciative audience from the larger membership for a gallery show or a performance of a string quartet. In short, clubs of increased size meant a higher quality of self-development was possible, thanks to the increased human and material resources.

Arts advocates in large department clubs paid a price for affiliation with the civic reformers. They felt and responded to the pressure to shape their interests along lines deemed practical, or relevant, by their civic-minded sisters. Many delighted, of course, in devising community sings, student art shows, immigrant festivals and other outreach programs to brighten the lives of all the municipality and satisfy the expectation that arts advocates frame their interests to meet social needs and solve urban problems. Not all women agreed that their work should be useful, however; and these were the women who split away from the department club, distracted by the focus of reform, and anxious to pursue their art single-mindedly in a separate arts society. However, even those who separated from large department clubs were not immune to the forces of reform. Painting or music societies, meeting for the object of cultural activity alone, were predictably generous in providing relief from a fire or storm, donating cash to a community fund, or adding signatures to a municipal streetlight campaign. When the Seattle Ladies Musical Club treasury paid for an ambulance during World War I or for beds for the children's hospital, or when Raleigh's Euterpe Club knit socks for the soldiers, the members were demonstrating their close connections to non-artistic community enterprises.

In their own way, then, the arts enthusiasts of the first decade of the twentieth century made contributions to the woman's movement in harmony with those that the civic activists defined as valuable. Having acquired the skills needed to initiate and sustain public projects, middle-class women embarked on programs designed to bring the arts they enjoyed to a wider citizenry. Civic-minded clubwomen brought their poor neighbors better health via well-baby clinics, visiting nurse programs, and clean milk campaigns; legal protection via free counseling bureaus and female jail matrons; joyful physical environments via public parks and sanitation regulation. Meanwhile, the arts lovers provided cultural services previously monopolized by affluent Americans, funding recitals by world renowned concert artists, sponsoring traveling art shows of portraits by leading painters, and presenting productions of Broadway theatrical sensations in isolated American towns. If club activists addressed the dearth of civic services in their communities, arts adherents could do no less. Although the war between reform and art or bread and roses seemed at first glance to signal victory for the advocates of reform, the roses hardly withered.

Whether women met in literature, art, music, or theatrical departments in large clubs, or created independent organizations for cultural study, they called attention to the previously undervalued contributions of professional women artists and supported their work. If their service-oriented projects tied them to old notions of women as domestic caretakers, their respect for talented women heralded a ground-breaking consciousness. While reform-minded clubwomen brought women's political values to the fore, the amateur artists brought women's artistic talents before a broader public. Certainly the clubwomen in arts societies deserve recognition for bringing professional women artists to their communities. Clubwomen enhanced the careers of internationally acclaimed women such as pianist Theresa Careño and soprano Madame Schumann-Heink, as well as American-born talents such as violinist Maud Powell, ethnomusicologist Alice Fletcher, sculptor Anna Hyatt Huntington, painter Elizabeth Nourse, and playwrights Alice Gerstenberg and Alice C. D. Riley. The Seattle Ladies Musical Club brought eighteen women to perform in their city between 1901 and 1930, a figure twice as large as the number of women performers that the male-dominated Seattle Symphony has featured in three quarters of a century. Not only did clubwomen champion their professional sisters on public occasions, but when the members played for each other, they were conscious of using the music of women composers, including works they had composed themselves. Clara Wieck Schumann, Fanny Mendelssohn, Cecile Chaminade, and Amy Beach were among their favorites.

Other ways in which the members encouraged women to expand their artistic expertise included providing scholarships to girls to study the arts. They responded to Marian MacDowell's plea for funds for the MacDowell Colony in Peterborough, New Hampshire, named for composer Edward MacDowell. Clubwomen applauded Marian MacDowell's performances of her husband's compositions and donated steady sums for the building of an artistic haven for the best talent in America. Cabins, library, swimming pool, amphitheatre, and other facilities were built through women's club contributions. In turn, Marian MacDowell saw that half the awards made in her lifetime went to women artists, writer Mary Wilkins Freeman and composer Amy Beach among them.

The artistic clubwoman of the first decade of the twentieth century, then, continued to develop her own appreciation and performance skills. In addition, she generally endorsed the reform component of the woman's club movement by tailoring her arts programs to meet social needs. She also encouraged professionalism among women in the arts by providing audiences for professional women's paintings, sculpture, books, plays, musical compositions, and their performances as actors and musicians. Perhaps most importantly, she observed the burgeoning political skills of her activist sisters and appropriated them for her own ends. In the following decade, she would apply these skills to a new slate of community arts projects which would meet both artistic and civic goals for American communities.

By the second decade of the twentieth century, the club movement was larger and stronger still, claiming over half a million members in thousands of clubs in the General Federation of Women's Clubs alone. The National Federation of Music Clubs had grown from 145 clubs in 1906, representing ten thousand members, to 440 clubs in 1917, probably including thirty thousand women. The new Drama League of America, founded in 1910, with sixty-three clubs (or ten thousand members), blossomed rapidly, to report one hundred thousand members by 1915. Although some clubs grew to thousands in membership, like the Wilshire Ebell in Los Angeles which had almost 1700 members in 1920, and the Friday Morning Club in Los Angeles, with over 1800 members, most art, music and literary clubs, and similar departments in large clubs, remained at a more manageable one hundred members or less.[25] American women were more welcome in colleges, professions, unions, businesses, and settlement work than they had ever been before, but this increase in alternative opportunities for women did not diminish their interest in the artistic and civic dimensions of club life.

In two ways, the artistic clubwomen moved into new realms of activity. First, taking a cue from the reformers, and echoing their stress on democratic accessibility to all social institutions, they continued to assert that the arts they loved should be made available to all Americans. They strengthened efforts to make available the finest professional work they could bring to their communities, inviting a broad audience to professional concerts, art shows, and theatrical performances. Perhaps the most outstanding example is that of Mrs. Artee Mason Carter's group, responsible for the establishment of the Hollywood Bowl in Los Angeles, an amphitheatre in the acoustically impressive Hollywood Hills. The Bowl seated eighteen thousand citizens at a time, who paid only twenty-five cents to hear the Los Angeles Philharmonic Orchestra under the stars.

Rather than remaining content to drink in the talents of the professionals, however, the clubwomen now eschewed class privilege to insist that all children, all immigrants, all poor, and all rural dwellers, have access to arts training so that they could involve themselves with the joy of making a play or performing a song, both for their own pleasure and to strengthen the nation with an active citizenry. Using the same organizational skills employed by the political activists, conducting surveys of community resources and needs, launching letter-writing campaigns, and establishing public relations committees that lobbied among the powerful of their communities, they introduced a variety of artistic institutions to society that invited wide community involvement. The clubwomen raised money to buy musical instruments for settlement houses. They sponsored art shows, pageants, and community sings, inviting everyone in town to participate. They lobbied state education systems to permit band, orchestra, chorus, and painting as extracurricular activities in the public schools. They pressed for elective credit for those subjects, and then for the licensing of trained teachers to instruct students. They initiated Municipal Art Commissions to encourage the purchase of public art for city streets.

As in the previous decade, when Municipal Housekeeping justified the public goals of both schools of clubwomen, arts clubs continued to operate in the 1910s from the same ideological motives as their colleagues devoted to civic reform. They continued to shape their newest outreach programs to attempt to solve the social problems of their day. When reformers addressed the Americanization of the foreign-born in the United States, the music clubs promised that piano lessons in the settlement houses would instill the best qualities of diligence and perseverance in immigrant children. Painting adherents claimed the same qualities would result from ethnic art festivals under the roofs of metropolitan museums. When war relief took center stage among the clubwomen devoted to social reform, music clubs donated Victrolas and records to the soldiers and the veterans. When food conservation came to the fore among the reform-minded, the theatrical supporters insisted that musical revues at the State Fairs, starring dancing potatoes, corn, and cabbage, would entertain and instruct more satisfactorily than pamphlets on vegetable canning ever could.

Alongside their efforts to support civic programs of the day, the lovers of literature, theatre, music, and the visual arts joined forces to produce the most ambitious forms of participatory arts exercises clubwomen had ever attempted. These new programs used the performing and creative arts to involve huge numbers of citizens in their communities in a common endeavor. Volunteers in every organization—scouts, immigrants, fire fighters, men, women, and children of every age, neighborhood, race, and ethnicity—were encouraged by clubwomen to cooperate in creating ambitious spectacles to entertain themselves and the rest of the local citizenry. Sizable projects of the era that clubwomen supported included theatrical pageants celebrating the anniversary of a town by reviewing its history; community sings in which citizens in record numbers formed massive choruses; "Safe and Sane" Fourth of July celebrations that moved the emphasis away from fireworks and toward parades; and neighborhood beautification campaigns in which townspeople labored to improve their own yards as well as public spaces. These projects are described more fully in the chapters to follow.

While these elaborate, demanding and cumbersome projects involved multitudes of amateurs in unfamiliar modes of artistic expression, they also served a larger purpose. From the clubwomen's point of view, the expansion of women's roles in the Progressive era opened the possibility of delivering new justice to American society. Women were determined to make a place for their sex and for neglected minorities of the population, in government and in every American institution. To achieve their goals they created projects over which the whole population united, each person bringing his or her individual talents and skills, all of which were essential to building an impressive result. The creators and observers of these productions learned the basic lesson of democracy, both literally and metaphorically; namely that their nation could be strengthened by utilizing the capabilities of everyone, for their own and for the common good.

The accomplishments of this stage are best reflected in the club members' support of pageants. In sponsoring pageants, clubwomen took a lesson from private women's colleges of the turn of the century. The Greek Games at Barnard College and the Elizabethan May Day celebrations of Bryn Mawr College demonstrated that it was possible to teach hundreds and even thousands of amateur performers to create and execute simple dances, lyrics, tunes, orchestrations, costumes, props, scenery, parades, and skits. Although the township often hired a professional pageant-maker to coordinate months of preparation, clubwomen played the critical role of locating, strong-arming, and organizing teachers, preachers, settlement workers, members of the chamber of commerce, government, and ethnic organizations to build a program to delight the townspeople. Few communities failed to produce pageants during this era. In Raleigh, North Carolina, the Daughters of the American Revolution coordinated the "History of Cape Fear." In 1914, on the 150th anniversary of St. Louis, seven thousand actors and seven thousand stagehands labored six months to produce a pageant and parade about the history of their city. On February 22, 1916, ninety-five pageants were staged simultaneously by the Young Women's Christian Association, in honor of its Jubilee. The California Federation of Women's Clubs staged the history of women's contribution to civilization at their Yosemite Convention, and the Texas Federation of Women's Clubs organized a pageant at the Texas State Fair. In 1916, the Shakespeare Tercentenary, and in 1921, the tricentennial of the Pilgrims' landing at Plymouth, clubwomen organized multitudes of other programs. Such labors laid the ideological and practical foundations for the federal and state legislation that would later ensure, through the New Deal and since 1965 the National Endowment for the Arts, the community arts projects that our contemporaries enjoy.

Among the admirers of pageantry were Alice Paul, the flamboyant suffragist who used elaborate parades effectively in her campaign to pressure for women's enfranchisement; the Patterson, New Jersey striking silk industry workers, who held a massive pageant in 1913 to raise funds for their cause; and Cecil B. De Mille, whose casts of thousands on the movie screen in small towns imitated real life for their viewers who had already produced such extravaganzas in their own backyards. But Hollywood only provided a secondhand view of the large scale interaction through its staged crowd scenes, a pale imitation of the actual empowerment real citizens experienced when they made their own dramas on the streets of their own cities through the agency of clubwomen.

World War I deflected this phase of club life with a heavy injection of traditional values. The impulse to serve—the country, our boys, the nation's new status as a world power—brought many women into clubs who had never sought a public life before. Women's clubs had previously paid but scant attention to charitable enterprises, such as sewing for the needy and feeding the poor, but now they dropped almost everything else to win the war, thereby inviting a new constituency to sign on. New members joined, those who had previously been unwilling to take on a public existence. The most important new groups to join were young mothers with toddlers and teenage girls in school, who found in the war a compelling reason to associate with other women in societies and clubs.

Never before had young mothers had the opportunity to leave their families for clubwork. The modern woman often had fewer children and a smaller home to care for, and more labor-saving devices to lighten her domestic responsibilities. It is likely that she would have begun to enter clubs even if no war emergency had invited her there, but the war argued compellingly for volunteer effort. Schoolgirls also came, glad to join in adult activities, emulating the mothers they had observed using clubs to participate in social change. They, too, found the time to swell the committees that rolled bandages, knit sweaters, collected items to amuse the soldiers, provided food at canteens and entertainment at boot camp, or raised and donated cash to purchase Liberty Bonds. Clubs, whether specifically devoted to music, theatre, or social welfare, revamped their agendas to recast their efforts toward winning the war.

Increased membership caused high hopes among the leadership that important new tasks could be accomplished by these greater numbers of women, once the emergency was over. But, fooled by wishful thinking, the leaders overestimated the interest of the new clubwomen, who remained in clubs only if they could serve there, in traditional ways, or if they could enjoy some relaxation from child raising. Such women did not view clubs as a means of entering into unprecedented social or cultural activism.

In the postwar era, the arts resurfaced, its advocates pursuing an impressive end, the unification of both major goals in the club tradition, namely the nurturance of women members and community service, in a single enterprise. To that end, the clubwoman created for herself the finest facilities to enjoy the arts that she had ever known, in the erection of clubhouses. The postwar decade, our fourth and last for consideration, saw women build over one thousand elaborate structures as meeting places, most of which contained state-of-the-art conference rooms, multiple auditoriums, reception areas, cooking and dining facilities, art galleries, libraries, and reading rooms. These new spaces enabled clubwomen to plan their cultural events and to stage plays and concerts by their own membership and by outsiders, fete the performers, present shows by visual artists, research cultural topics, and debate them in comfort. Insofar as members collectively purchased the best theatrical lighting, amplification systems, grand pianos, and luxurious furnishings that their treasuries could withstand, clubwomen established well-appointed arts centers for the use of their members and the general public.

Still, for all the pleasure and importance that the superlative arts facilities in clubhouses contributed, the maintenance of the structures demanded a great deal from the membership. The relentless repair of the buildings tested the decision-making mechanisms the members had devised, drained club treasuries, and, most especially, diverted energy from other projects the clubs might have undertaken. The inability of clubwomen to move beyond club housekeeping and find energy for more exciting work took its toll on the membership, which gradually fell away during the second half of the 1920s. Despite sincere efforts by club leadership, the decline could not be halted. The heyday of women's club life, in terms of numbers, enthusiasm, enterprise, and influence, was over.

By the end of the Progressive Era, clubwomen found themselves with expensive but gracious clubhouses in which to cultivate their love of the arts, and with declining resources to offer the community in which they functioned. Their nineteenth-century dreams of creating mechanisms by which they might improve themselves had now materialized, with justifiable satisfaction to the members. But the women achieved this goal at some social cost. Members' success at contributing to the artistic and social well-being of their neighbors, so strong in the early decades of the twentieth century and so utterly tied to traditional notions of women's nurturing responsibilities, had proved to be inextricably bound to women's own pleasure, power, and need to affiliate into women's clubs.

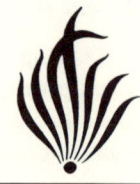

THREE

"Hear America First"

WOMEN'S AMATEUR MUSICAL SOCIETIES

"Everybody knows America wouldn't have any music if it weren't for women," observed the internationally renowned pianist Harold Bauer in 1924.[1] His remark saluted the phenomenon of women's musical clubs, which blossomed in the United States from 1890 to 1930, and it held a large measure of truth. There were, in thousands of communities, amateur women musicians who founded and sustained clubs that exhibited a wide range of musical strengths and achievements. An examination of their efforts yields an ingenious array of programs that shaped the musical taste of Americans. The collective accomplishments of women in music clubs demonstrate the degree to which concerned and united citizens, without the stature of professionals in the music world, could nevertheless make themselves heard. Through schools, arts colonies, wartime rituals, and other public forums, members injected their brand of good music firmly into American life.

Excluded from the male-dominated mainstream of musical performance and composition, increasing numbers of women in the late nineteenth century began to form separate musical associations. Initially, these groups maintained and expanded the musical knowledge and skills of women who, trained in music in their youth, devoted the bulk of their time to running households and rearing families; however, they soon came to embrace two additional important functions. The first of these was to assist the professional development of women performers and composers. To this end, the all-women's groups established musical scholarships for girls, created opportunities for performances of classic and contemporary works written by women, sponsored the MacDowell Colony for creative artists of both sexes, and supported women's orchestras. A second, civic-minded strain, always present, grew more prominent after World War I and pointed the way toward building a more democratic nation—an America, according to club ideology, in which no citizen would be denied the enjoyment of fine music. Working toward that goal, clubwomen brought artists of international reputation to perform in their towns, and successfully fostered music education for immigrants in the settlement houses and for youth in schools. Less obviously "feminist" in character, this second function nevertheless strengthened the new, growing public role of women; more subtly, its progressive thrust challenged the priorities of the male musical establishment.

Let us examine the origins and development of two key organizations which assisted in uniting musical women and bringing cohesion to the goals and projects of local clubs. The National Federation of Music Clubs (NFMC), with its emphasis on ensuring a musical future for the United States, put special effort into educating children. The General Federation of Women's Clubs (GFWC), with access to a wide range of interest groups, pressed for public access to classical and folk music in every social setting. The women's clubs that affiliated with these two associations won many victories in improving American training in musical performance and composition and delivering non-commercial music to the general public. A study of their efforts documents their tenacity and ingenuity in musicalizing Americans by reaching youth in schools, immigrants in settlement houses, patriots in wartime and post-war community gatherings, and in extending opportunities for women professionals in women's clubs, public forums, and arts colonies. Finally, we will examine the National Music Week, which annually invited amateurs and professionals alike to make music a priority for at least the beginning of May. That celebration, which thrived in the 1920s, was the culmination of decades of club work.

The National Federation of Music Clubs

The largest and most influential organization uniting women's musical societies originated in Chicago, at the World's Columbian Exposition of 1893. While the National Federation of Music Clubs did not actually form there, its antecedents arose when Rose Fay Thomas invited all forty-two known women's amateur music associations to convene at the exposition's Recital Hall to share music and prospects for their own and America's musical future.[2] The delegates represented thirty-four clubs, most of them less than a decade old.[3] The conference was chaired by Thomas, a pianist in her own right, who was president of Chicago's only women's amateur music club—appropriately called the Women's Amateur Musical Club. She was also the wife of Chicago Symphony Orchestra conductor Theodore Thomas.[4]

The delegates in the Windy City established their goals as three:

> To show the actual standard of musical culture among the best class of American women in all parts of the country, and the character and quality of the educational work in music being done by Woman's Amateur Musical Clubs; to stimulate the formation of clubs and improve the work of those already organized, by giving them an opportunity to measure themselves with each other; to give national

recognition to this department of women's educational work, hitherto overlooked.[5]

All of these goals would be met by century's end. Certainly participants would demonstrate a high level of performance and also composition, for their programs would include works written by the women themselves. As Thomas would later observe of club participants, "the standard of amateur music is astonishingly high in all parts of America."[6] The delegates would also keep their promise to share new ideas with sister clubs by reporting on their own club achievements and exchanging impressive accounts of club efforts to tutor their communities via musical programs.

In welcoming her sister musicians, Rose Fay Thomas articulated the enthusiasm of her peers. She attempted to express the attraction music held for amateurs, who might never achieve technical proficiency, but could become stronger human beings through their acquaintance with the arts:

> [In amateur clubs] musical art has its most powerful ally, and its most beneficent friend. The fundamental value of amateur music does not lie in the facility with which the fingers can manipulate the keys or the voice can trill a song, but in the deeper and broader culture it gives to the mind and heart—the power to think and feel with the mighty creators and their noble interpreters, and to follow them into those supernal realms of art whose portals only fully open to those who hold the mystic keys.[7]

Thomas also pointed out a reality that women's music clubs would strive to change: the general lack of interest in the arts, and its crippling of the development of a broad and rich American cultural strength. "It is a great pity," she said,

> that these clubs are nearly all confined to the female sex, and thus make the musical culture of America a one-sided affair. We ought to make it our next step in the march of progress to eradicate the word "woman's" from the title of the amateur musical club and bring into its pleasant circle the fathers, brothers and friends, whose love for and knowledge of music must be as carefully cultivated as that of the woman, if we are ever to be a musical nation or do anything genuinely great in this beautiful art.[8]

Thomas' attack on musical ignorance would serve as the war cry for four generations of clubwomen who were determined to match America's cultivation with that of any European power.

Interspersed among the recitals and performances by clubwomen at the Chicago fair were sessions critical to the growth of a national network, enabling club representatives to describe the organizational activities of their membership. In embryonic form, the representatives outlined the work that would be undertaken by growing numbers of women's music clubs for generations to come. The clubs emerged initially to satisfy the musical needs of the membership, a goal identified in Chapter 2 as the first stage of turn-of-the-century club life. A club could then stretch its musical horizons to bring professional solo artists to their town, to create a local orchestra, and finally to establish community festivals in which all segments of society could partake of music's pleasures. The women's reports indicated that the most common efforts at this time included the invention of club programs that encouraged members to research musical topics and perform for each other the compositions of the European masters or those they had written themselves. The women also offered musical services to individual members. For instance, when a member of the glee club within the Amateur Musical Club in Brooklyn married, her club sisters offered to sing her wedding hymns.[9] The level of performance was quite high, since club members were routinely required to audition for admission into the club, and they had to meet a standard that assured regular performances by each member. The Schubert Club of St. Paul went even further to maintain the high level of excellence that members possessed when they joined. "In order to maintain high standards," the Board decided "to have all active members examined once a year by a committee of accomplished musicians, outside the membership of the club. Anyone unable to pass such an examination became an associate member."[10] This clever technique removed judgment from the regular membership to disinterested musicians, enabling objective evaluations to be made, but channeling hurt and angry feelings away from the group. The Philharmonic Society in Topeka kept its membership in form by more tactful means, by requiring a monthly performance by every member. Anyone who allowed herself to get out of practice would be too embarrassed to remain a member.[11]

All musical activity in women's clubs was to be accomplished in a friendly setting. The Rubenstein Club, of Memphis, was careful to discourage all but amateur musicians from joining the organization. No self-supporting music teachers were welcome, for fear that this would set a competitive tone and an unrealistic standard for busy homemakers. "With other duties to interfere with our studies, we are not willing to place ourselves in a light to be criticized, or to compete with those whose life work alone consists of cultivating their talents," they explained.[12]

One realistic way for women to facilitate their musical development was to engage a director to lead a glee club of singers from the group.[13] Among the clubs who chose to initiate a choral program were the Zoch Club in Minneapolis, the Schubert Club in St. Paul, the Treble Clef Club in Los Angeles, the Matinee Musicale Club in Lafayette, Indiana, and the Amateur Musical Club in Brooklyn. These choruses, ranging in size from thirty-five to one hundred members, were all directed by men, presumably because women with comparable experience were unavailable. As time passed however, women tended to win these posts as club choral directors. In Los Angeles' Treble Clef Club, for example, when Mr. Henry Burton resigned, he was replaced by Mrs. Jirah D. Cole.[14]

In time, most clubs graduated to the more ambitious effort of bringing fine classical music to their neighbors. At a time when cultural opportunities were considerably more limited than they are today, these programs provided a genuine cultural service. Most members were too timid or modest to display their own talents before the general public on a regular basis; however, they did so for charitable events to raise funds for the social services that women routinely dispensed in their communities. The Ladies' Musical Club of Tacoma, Washington, for example, raised money for the Children's Home; the Abbey-Cheney Amateurs of San Francisco raised one thousand dollars for the San Francisco Children's Hospital; the Chicago Amateur Musical Club gave an annual charity concert at which one thousand to fifteen hundred dollars was raised; and six concerts by the Treble Clef Club of Philadelphia earned $1675 for good works.[15]

More often, clubwomen hired the most renowned concert artists they could afford to concertize in their town, no matter how small or remote from major centers of musical culture their community might be. This dimension of club life would reach impressive proportions, until most clubs brought major talents to communities throughout the nation. Thirty-five years after the original convocation of music clubs, the national association would report that "Through its individual clubs [our members handle] three-fourths of the concert engagements outside of the largest cities, spending annually nearly a million dollars for concert artists."[16] At the Chicago fair, three clubs reported on their success in broadening community access to high culture—the Morning Musical Club of Fort Wayne, Indiana, the Tuesday Musicale Club in Detroit, and the Ladies Musical Club of Cincinnati—but many of the others in attendance would follow suit quickly.

Early in their history women's clubs also took on the special responsibility of supporting the musical efforts of their sex. The Ladies' Musical Club in Tacoma, for example, reported at the 1893 fair that it had devoted one afternoon's meeting to the study of women composers.[17] In Brooklyn, the Amateur Musical Club informed other clubwomen that "we were able to advertise choir singers and music teachers, and gave several poor girls a helping hand toward independence."[18] Such activities by clubwomen presaged a future of attentive support to women performers and composers, both professional and amateur. By century's end it would be commonplace for women's musical clubs to invite leading women artists to perform in their communities, to present the compositions of women composers, to sponsor the concerts of all-women's orchestras and chamber ensembles, and to fund the education of budding young female musicians.

Finally, these early club reports exhibited the women's intention, which would later be successfully realized, to use music to build the nation culturally. With the expectation that the musical nurturance of a people could create a cultural force to be reckoned with, just as surely as military might and territorial conquests established a nation's political strength, clubwomen expressed the hope of raising American artistic standards and abilities to outdo those of European nations. The exposition delegates from Seattle, members of the Ladies Musical Club, reported that they had devoted themselves to the study of American music and inspired other clubs to do the same.[19] A representative from Duluth, Cecilian Society president Mrs. Stella Prince Stocker, herself a composer, predicted that women would transform a culturally backward society into a cultivated nation, as mighty musically as it was becoming politically:

> In order to be an artistic nation, with a national art, it must be here as it is in Germany, men and women, rich and poor, high and low, must require music, and all the time ... We live in a new country where all is turmoil and desire for conquest. Intense effort will win almost anything in lands, fortunes or political ascendency; hence our fevered, hurrying life. The men of our country have, as a rule, no time for the contemplation which is a necessity of art. Must it then be left to other nations to give us of their store? No, there is a vast population in this country not engaged in the frantic struggle for wealth and power. I refer to the women who live quietly at home, the sisters, wives and mothers of these busy men.[20]

As her remarks suggest, musical clubwomen would deluge the nation with fine music, in the hopes that American familiarity with the Western tradition of classics would breed a reverence for the European artistic foundations they hoped to build on and surpass.

While the women's Chicago conference emboldened existing musical clubs to attempt new projects, no national organization was immediately founded to facilitate musical club growth and development. Not until June 1897, at the New York City meeting of a National Music Teacher's Association, did a meeting of twenty women result in a call for the creation of a National Federation of Music Clubs.[21] It was apparent that the male-dominated Teacher's Association would provide no meaningful voice for amateur women musicians, nor for the many girls, widows, spinsters, and wives who provided musical instruction to supplement the family finances or support the family.[22] Likewise, other women's organizations, notably the General Federation of Women's Clubs, were providing little encouragement to the health of women's music clubs. Florence (Mrs. Theodore) Sutro, president of the temporary organizing committee, saw to it that a founding convention was held in Chicago on January 25 of the following year.[23]

Thus, the winter of 1898 saw the creation of The National Federation of Music Clubs (NFMC), committed "to bring into communication with one another the various musical clubs of the country, that they may compare methods of work and become mutually helpful." This simple statement of purpose soon expanded to include commitment not only to the musical growth of club members, but to the musical health of the entire nation. As the bylaws later articulated more clearly, the object of the Federation was "to bring into working relation with one another music clubs and other musical organizations and individuals directly, or indirectly, associated with musical activity, for the purpose of aiding and encouraging musical education and developing and maintaining high musical standards throughout America."[24] By the 1930s, the musical clubwomen's patriotic ambitions were even more baldly asserted. The NFMC desired "to make America the music center of the world."[25]

It is fitting that the National Federation of Music Clubs was founded in the year of the Spanish-American War, and would receive its greatest momentum during World War I, for its own growth and ideology were very much related to the United States' new self-consciousness about its potential power in the family of nations. As the country began to flex its military muscle power—through war, conquest, economic development, and nationalist pride—women patriots in music clubs wholeheartedly embraced the national agenda and attached their own musical dreams to this star. Increasingly, members became aware that their goals for their own and America's musical development might be linked to American dreams of surpassing Europe and assuming a primary role in world affairs. Clubwomen initiated an ingenious array of musical programs, all justified in terms of their contributions to fostering a more powerful America. Before we address the blatantly chauvinistic programs the clubs developed, let us examine the structure of the organization that generated the force to carry out these projects. Woven inextricably throughout are assumptions that the United States should and would assert musical dominance in the twentieth century.

The new officers of the National Federation of Music Clubs did not have to scramble for a structure. They simply duplicated that of other women's federations, notably the General Federation of Women's Clubs. Among the systems they employed to enhance cooperation and communication were the use of parliamentary procedure; regular elections of strong, competent, accessible officers; modest dues (ten cents per member per year); regular communication via an official publication (the *Musical Monitor,* from 1915 to 1922, and then the *Official Bulletin*); and the creation of a state federation in every state of the union, largely effected between the years 1915 and 1922. Like its forebears among American women's alliances, the NFMC created committees, of both clubwomen volunteers and professional experts, to tackle all the programs and issues the membership cared to address. By 1933, twenty-six priorities were addressed in committees devoted to various aspects of music.[26] In addition, the federation took on the responsibility of providing services that few clubs could provide for themselves. These came to include the compilation and circulation of a library of music; an Artist Bureau to encourage club bookings of young talents—American musicians whose modest fees would not strain the tiny club treasuries; and a Registry Bureau of club members who would perform at other women's clubs for mere reimbursement of travel expenses.

Biennial conventions in different American cities were also a staple of organizational life. The first of these was held in 1899, when the NFMC visited St. Louis, at the invitation of a healthy host club, to stimulate new membership and facilitate an exchange of ideas.[27] At the biennials, as at the initial meeting of 1893, delegates from member clubs could combine an honest evaluation of their own club efforts with a demonstration of their musical, intellectual, and organizational abilities, through performance, delivery of papers, and reports on committee accomplishments. In addition, national as well as state federation conventions showcased new and also mature talent in the form of performances and lectures by men and women professionals in the music world.²⁸ Among the lecturers on music education were leading experts in program areas that clubwomen chose to enter—pageants, community singing, the collection of the songs of minority populations in the United States, and instruction for children. Music history was little represented at conferences, and rarely did musicologists appear to discuss new academic arguments on the classical literature.

Like other women's club federations of the era, the NFMC had no trouble locating hard-working volunteer officers, with musical and organizational talent besides. Twelve presidents served between 1898 and 1930, having already proved themselves capable leaders in strong amateur women's music clubs in all areas of the country.²⁹

Other women who never reached the uppermost ranks of influence were also willing to devote their organizational talents to the NFMC. Bessie Bartlett (Mrs. Cecil) Frankel never rose above president of the California Federation of Music Clubs and first vice-president of the national organization, but her tenacity and drive delivered significant numbers to the NFMC. Her visit to Seattle, bringing representatives of thirty clubs together over lunch, launched the Washington State Federation of Music Clubs. Soon, as Extension Director for the NFMC, she traveled to Chicago, Detroit, New York, Boston, Washington D.C., and New Orleans, leaving a trail of music club federations in her wake and winning acclaim for multiplying the number of member clubs in the NFMC from 873 to 1,903.³⁰

Ella May Smith was another who made her mark on music clubs. A music teacher in Columbus, Ohio, and a well-known songwriter, she reorganized the Women's Music Club of Columbus in 1903, attracting three thousand dues-paying women. The club could then purchase musical materials for the Music Club Alcove in the Columbus Public Library from an endowment of two thousand dollars; buy an extravagant organ for the city's music hall; provide a one thousand dollar scholarship to train a girl in Europe for a year; bring renowned concert artists to perform in Columbus; and pay for music lessons for foreign children at several local settlement houses. No wonder the National Federation appointed Smith chairman of its education committee. Later, she became director of the federation's American Music Department, which she had developed in 1921; and chairman of the International Reciprocity for American Musicians Committee, to build friendliness abroad toward the work of American composers. She was a devoted volunteer who had innovative, viable ideas, and followed through on them with intelligence and zeal.³¹

Despite a talented leadership, the success in federation growth came slowly, the result of hard-won experience. At first, the officers of the NFMC were not aggressive in inviting amateur music clubs to join, or even to renew their memberships. Gradually, however, the numbers of women's music societies grew, sometimes as departments of larger literary or civic women's clubs; and they gravitated to the NFMC for programming ideas, organization advice, and the appealing agenda of making America the most musical nation in the world. Figures are sketchy for the formative years, but the states with the greatest numbers of clubs in the late 1920s were Texas, Missouri, Ohio, and Michigan.[32]

The NFMC came to attract an impressive collection of women's musical groups. In 1899, the federation roster listed seventy-six member clubs. By 1906, the count had doubled to 145, representing ten thousand women. By 1917, 440 clubs had joined; by 1925, the organization peaked at three thousand clubs with three hundred thousand members. This success was achieved in part by a continuing effort to create junior clubs for boys and girls, ages four to eighteen, and to count them as regular clubs. Therefore, in 1930, the NFMC could boast a membership of five thousand clubs and four hundred thousand members. Two thousand of those societies, however, were youth clubs which drained the federation organizationally, however profitable they might be ideologically. Insofar as junior clubs contributed lower dues, suffered high turnover, and required steady supervision by clubwomen and music teachers, they were a demanding dimension of musical club life.[33]

It was an inventive idea, to initiate young people into the joys of musical club life from the earliest possible age, and it was probably the major concern and achievement of the NFMC. Not only did the plan shape a music-loving public from its infancy, but it steered serious musicians into adult clubs, thus perpetuating the health of the national organization. No doubt the idea arose from observing the success of other teenage-oriented organizations such as the Scouts, the Camp Fire Girls, the 4-H Club, the YMCA and YWCA, the Young Men's and Young Women's Hebrew Associations, and the debutantes in the Junior League. Although every voluntary organization of women would enlist the support of younger people in the 1920s, none was as successful as the NFMC.

The heyday of junior music clubs spanned the 1920s. In 1920, 227 dues-paying junior clubs were reported in 26 states; by 1923, 732 clubs; and by 1929, 2,306. The clubs were numerically strongest in the southern states, perhaps in reaction to public school systems that were slow to offer music instruction.[34]

To be sure, women's music clubs did not hold a monopoly on the invention of children's societies. Many schools sponsored music clubs, and so did scout troops, industrial schools, settlement houses, and, of course, women's clubs. In essence, the junior clubs established a "second front" for meeting the same goals for music education that educators were developing in the classroom. The act of joining with peers, once a week or twice a month under the supervision of a trained volunteer, encouraged children to learn about musical instruments and the great works of classical music and to practice their own instruments in order to play together or for each other.

Acquaintance with quality music was believed to build good character by distracting young people from the pernicious influences of popular music. "The tune we know best is the best tune we know," recited members of Illinois junior music clubs,[35] reassuring clubwomen who hoped that familiarity with the classics could pull the United States through its "grave musical crisis," checking the "degeneracy in our modern public music into rag time," and luring potential "delinquents" from the "suggestive words of popular songs" and the unacceptable behavior they believed was sure to follow. Instead of succumbing to a commercial and popular musical path strewn with dangerous allure, students with classical musical training were provided with "the training to keep still, listen, and concentrate on learning." *Etude Magazine* advised that music practice would teach youth to: "(1) think more clearly, quickly, and with more appreciation of beauty, (2) remember better, (3) coordinate the body, (4) develop more personality." Furthermore, it was claimed that music could enliven the small and sleepy communities from which youth, increasingly, were fleeing. "Make it a lovely place to live in so that nobody cares to leave it," suggested one clubwoman to rural villages afraid of losing their population to the "wicked" cities.[36] Additional attacks on "evil songs and jazz music" are also put forward in General Federation of Women's Clubs literature.[37]

Clubs attracted young members by sponsoring a wide variety of participatory activities. The children, divided by age group, were enticed into junior club participation, with such inducements as musical memory contests. Patterned after spelling bees, these contests tested familiarity with staples from the classical, and also American, musical tradition. Melodies were excerpted on Victrolas and listeners were invited to compete in identifying the composers, their countries of origin, and the types and names of the pieces of music played. Based on a hearing of a few phrases of Beethoven's *Moonlight Sonata*, Verdi's *Anvil Chorus* from *Il Trovatore*, Brahms' *Hungarian Dances*, or the "Negro" spiritual "Swing Low Sweet Chariot," many children could demonstrate their familiarity with a broad range of works.[38]

If informed listening was encouraged in children, actual performance was even more valued. One junior club held a contest of eighty-five days to reward the member who could practice the most.[39] The National Association of Colored Women publicized the music contests of the junior membership of its affiliated group, in Oakland, and gave prizes for Regional Chorus, Glee Club, Quartette, Trio, Duet, Solo Voice, and Solo Instrument.[40] Several clubs performed operettas created especially for boys and girls, such as *Candy Land* by Manna Zucca, *Magic Rose* by Grace Porterfield Polk (the first junior club director), *Cinderella* by Frederick Jacobi, and *Princess of the Fountain*. All four of these works were performed by the Junior Musical Club of Miami, thanks to the stamina of volunteer supervisors.[41]

Other groups carolled at Christmas, made floats for local parades, performed for orphans, and donated the proceeds of their concerts to children's homes or impoverished rural schools for the purchase of musical materials. Such activities were said to serve students well, even to work miracles. "I have seen little incorrigibles in our neighborhood come, in just a short time, to be staunch upholders of right principles, through the influence of the club. Movies have lost their dangerous hold on the minds of the club members and music now holds their place," boasted Miss Jean Duthy, leader of the Junior Fortnightly Music Club in Indianapolis, and proud general in the war against popular culture.[42]

The rewards of junior music clubs were felt by clubwomen to be even greater for more devoted students than for the casual participant. The cream of the crop could be channeled through local, state, and finally national performance competitions, with monetary awards, scholarships, and, not insignificantly, valuable exposure through performance opportunities. NFMC publications touted compositions by eleven-year-old Marguerite Maitland, a member of the Song Birds in Philadelphia, and adult clubs enjoyed concerts by children's ensembles like the "Toy Symphony." This institution, sometimes tapping the energy of fifty children under the age of ten, initiated them in the playing of bells, triangles, tambourines, cymbals, xylophones, rhythm sticks, gongs, drums, bugles, cuckoo whistles, and sand blocks.[43] The Norfleet Trio, a touring band of youthful musicians who played regularly for club functions, attracted much attention.

The object of the musical programs for young people was to provide basic instruction for musically deprived children, rather than to create a club monopoly on training. Thus, clubwomen were delighted to persuade or cooperate with school systems to integrate the aforementioned programs into the regular curriculum. Increasingly, members succeeded in ensuring that after-school clubs or even credit-bearing courses taught by accredited music teachers were available to pupils from kindergarten through college. Even so, they continued to maintain healthy club programs for young people.

The General Federation of Music Clubs

Despite its premier role in defining worthwhile musical activity for daily American life, the NFMC did not remain the sole women's voluntary association dedicated to this proposition. The literary- and civic-oriented General Federation of Women's Clubs (GFWC) included member clubs, such as the New Century Club of Wilmington, Delaware, that maintained departments devoted to the study of music.[44] The leadership of the GFWC was preoccupied with other concerns for two decades, but in 1910 they decided to create a Music Committee, in response to club demands for services to the music departments emerging within its large and diverse membership.[45] Because the General Federation of Women's Clubs included many members uninterested in music, however, the organization is more noteworthy for its efforts to deliver a musical education to the majority than for its assistance to the converted. Like the National Federation of Music Clubs, the GFWC leadership promised to inaugurate an outreach program to the general public. The GFWC Department for Music chairman, Mrs. Lawrence Maxwell, praised the NFMC for having "led the way," but stressed that her organization would develop "lines of progress heretofore untouched, more philanthropic and fruitful in unselfish accomplishments."[46] Her underlying assumption was that the NFMC was preoccupied with the concerns of its musical constituency to the exclusion of public programming; however this belief exaggerates the differences between the programs of the two federations.

The GFWC was no less successful than the NFMC in its campaign to musicalize America. The organization provided leadership positions to clubwomen with a love for, training in, and commitment to music, and these women applied considerable inventiveness to the goal of involving more citizens in artistic avenues of expression. Eva Perry (Mrs. Philip North) Moore, president of the entire GFWC from 1908 to 1912, had come up the ranks of club life in part through her musical interests. She had served as president of the St. Louis Musical Club from 1892 to 1903, was vice-president of the St. Louis Symphony Society until 1918, and served as vice-president in the NFMC from 1901 to 1903. In 1906, it was she who whetted GFWC interest in establishing a committee for music by arranging a session on women composers at the St. Paul convention, at which delegates were treated to an evening of compositions by women.[47]

Once the Department of Music (later called a Division of Music) was created within the GFWC, energetic leaders continued to populate the decision-making positions. Probably the most successful music educator among them was Anne Shaw Faulkner (Mrs. Marx E.) Oberndorfer, who published several works that assisted clubwomen in doing their musical work.[48]

Roberta Campbell (Mrs. Eugene B.) Lawson was another musical clubwoman of distinction. A Native American raised in Nowata, Oklahoma, she championed the collection of Native American songs and rose through the ranks of the GFWC Music Division to preside over the entire organization. Lawson was elected GFWC president in 1935, and served in that capacity until 1938. She was the first and only woman of color to preside over the largest, and largely white, woman's voluntary organization in America. Her book, *Indian Music Programs for Clubs and Special Music Days* (1926) is an impressive compendium designed to popularize the Native American musical heritage. From her research, she produced study guidelines for women's clubs, such as "Indian Music Programs for Clubs and Special Music Days," which provided suggestions for performance and papers to deliver at meetings.[49]

To meet its responsibility to bring music to all clubwomen, the GFWC Music Committee adopted a variety of approaches for broadening public programming. Leaders encouraged performances at club meetings everywhere, by club choruses, talented children, or professionals. The professionals, they chided their volunteer constituency, deserved to be paid for their efforts. The committee tapped into new technology, circulating recordings of Hopi songs, Beethoven symphonies, and American classics. They distributed program ideas on a range of American and European musical topics that held appeal for the general membership.

Programming assistance began in 1917 with a handful of free pamphlets, and grew to include an endorsement of an official four-year program of four textbooks. In 1917, the Department of Music's chairman, Mrs. Steele, wrote a pamphlet entitled *Patriotic Songs of America*. She also secured authors for club guides on "Opera Study," "American Musical Tendencies," "Music's

Place in Education," and "The Importance of School Music."[50] In 1923, the NFMC recommended a four-year course of study, identifying *Fundamentals of Music* by Karl W. Gehrkens, *From Song to Symphony* by Daniel Gregory Mason, *Musical Instruments* by Edgar Stillman Kelley, and *Epochs in Musical Progress* by Clarence G. Hamilton as worthy of careful examination.[51] At conventions, organizers initiated group sings on the excursion boats, to involve members in the joys of music making. In 1910 they supplied the finest music available, by inviting the Cincinnati Orchestra, conducted by Leopold Stokowski, to perform works by Gluck, Wagner, and Tchaikovsky for the delegates' pleasure and edification.

The Music Committee did not neglect the organization's mandate to serve the community. When Sarah Platt Decker, author of the "Dante is Dead" statement, heard that a woman's music club was declining for lack of enthusiasm, she suggested a predictable cure for its malady: "Sing for someone else," she advised.[52] To that end, the organization supported a wide range of initiatives to enrich the musical life of their neighborhoods. Club leaders pressured the radio broadcasting companies and the motion picture industry to improve the quality of music disseminated through the media.[53] The leadership built alliances with any likely groups that might support their goals: they cooperated with the Mutual Welfare League to bring good music to prisoners; they joined with Kiwanis and Rotary, and Quota Clubs of businesswomen, to encourage community support for quality music. By the 1920s, they were willing to engage in negative campaigning, allying with the National Dancing Masters Association to eliminate jazz from dance halls, and supporting legislation against the "evil songs and jazz music of the day."[54] This latter tactic, which amounted to outright censorship, was not a technique characteristically embraced by women's club members, but it was a logical result of their fervent adherence to canonical definitions of musical excellence.

Music in the Service of Nationalism

Numerous women's musical clubs in American cities and towns did not make a distinction between the ideals and services of the two national women's amateur music federations. Clubs joined both federations if their treasuries permitted the expenditures of two sets of dues. Regardless of whether a music club belonged to one, both, or neither of the national federations, it was likely to embrace a program that emphasized the advancement of American music. This program meant three things: (1) the nurturance of American composers and performers, and the schools, conservatories, teachers, scholarships, and artists' colonies that would train talent on United States soil, rather than in Europe; (2) the collection and appreciation of America's traditional music, including Native American, "Negro," lumberjack, cowboy, mining, and Appalachian songs; and (3) the education of the general public in "good" music of the Western classical tradition, rather than the popular contemporary tunes peddled by the commercial music industry. This three-pronged attack was intended to eradicate America's musical deficiencies.

American clubwomen rarely extolled American music making by deprecating the achievements of the Europeans. They respected the European tradition, including the contributions of the great composers, patrons, performers, and conservatories. They did, however, hold every expectation that the United States could surpass the Old World in music making, just as it would in political, military, technological, and economic arenas.

Members' solid respect for their European musical forebears broke down once, during World War I. They were generally reconciled to President Wilson's decision to enter the war, and wholeheartedly enthusiastic about contributing to victory once the United States entered the conflict; accordingly, they damned "the Huns" in this period, often turning their backs on all German music, both contemporary and historical. Apart from this interlude, however, music clubs generally worked to meet and then surpass foreign creativity in a less confrontational mode. By and large, the clubwomen's brand of Americanism was founded on three principles. First, confidence in their nation's bounty, natural beauty, and material resources, which could provide inspiration and cultivation to anyone who chose to use them. Second, a trust in the creative capacities of various groups in the population—in the privileged classes, to which clubwomen generally belonged; in the foreign-born immigrants who would contribute to the nation's development; and in the Native Americans and African-Americans, whose musical traditions clubwomen resurrected and publicized. Finally, they took pride in their country's democratic political structure, which they believed protected political liberty as well as creative development. On these principles, clubwomen established an ideology which deemed reprehensible the denial of access to political and artistic participation for all. The suffrage that was about to be granted to all women and to all Native Americans was seen as not only the tangible evidence of the United States' evolution toward full political participation, but a metaphor for the artistic participation a free nation could and would offer.

To cultivate the three areas they had identified as necessary to build musical power, clubwomen launched an effort they termed "Hear America First." It consisted of a wide range of projects, seven of which deserve consideration here: (1) women's pressure for a national and official sanctioning of American musical life; (2) club competitions and creative colonies to encourage the productivity of American composers; (3) the preservation and dissemination of American folk music; (4) support for opera in English; (5) the pressure to hire American musicians rather than their more glamorous European counterparts; (6) the support of music for newcomers to America at settlement houses in immigrant neighborhoods; and (7) community sings for the American public, a forum that blossomed out of World War I service programs. Clubwomen sought support for their agenda by asserting that this patriotic path was a logical contribution to the nation building of a nascent world power. The encouragement of our best music, they argued, would bolster the strength of the nation.

A national sanction for musical development could come in two ways, clubwomen asserted. First, the federal government could establish a Cabinet position, the Department of Fine Arts, to ensure artistic support from the highest levels of government. Secondly, the United States could establish a National Conservatory of Music, where raw American talent might be honed. Achieving success with neither of these ideas, clubwomen settled instead for supporting the establishment, immediately after the Allied victory over Germany in World War I, of several private American conservatories of music—the Juilliard School of Music in New York City, the Curtis School of Music in Philadelphia, and the Eastman School of Music in Rochester, New York.[55]

The notion of nurturing native creativity was exceedingly attractive to American women, so much so that the NFMC credited the sudden growth of the organization to its 1907 decision to hold competitions for music composed by American-born artists.[56] One convention speaker insisted that "the first step toward freeing the musical life of the nation from foreign domination was made by the National Federation of Music Clubs in its biennial competition for works by native composers."[57] Within the space of ten years, the organization held four competitions, with fifty-three judges, and awarded prizes totalling $5,650 for five symphonic works, one choral piece, two chamber works, one piano sonata, five songs, one operetta for schoolchildren, and one part song.[58]

Many of these works, as well as others by composer clubwomen, enjoyed premieres at club conventions and meetings. Frequently clubwomen composers, like Mary Carr Moore, who sought participation in the mostly male and mostly European professional musical world, enjoyed their largest audiences and steadiest acclaim in local club meetings and national club competitions.[59] New York State clubwomen became acquainted with the work of Mabel Wood Hill and Fannie Dillon from programs featuring American composers.[60] Other American women composers who enjoyed club attention in the 1920s included Mrs. H. H. A. Beach and Gena Branscombe.[61] Black composers, including Rosamund Johnson, enjoyed a hearing at a concert of American music sponsored by a branch of the MacDowell Club in New York City.[62] Both the NFMC and the GFWC tried to promote the composition by a woman of an official federation anthem and hymn; but awards committees were too unimpressed with the entries to confer any prizes. Finally, the leadership of both groups settled on the use of Katharine Lee Bates's widely sung anthem, "America, the Beautiful," while the GFWC also adopted Harriet Ware's *Woman's Triumphal March,* in 1927.[63]

The clubwomen saw still another opportunity to develop American composition in the establishment of the MacDowell Colony in Peterborough, New Hampshire. It was to be a haven for composers, but also for writers, painters, and sculptors in need of solitude, workspace, inexpensive room and board, and prepared meals, so that they would not need to devote an ounce of energy to nonartistic endeavors. Not surprisingly, clubwomen became important financial backers of this still lively and prestigious summer hideaway for American creative artists.

The colony was a project undertaken by Marian Nevins MacDowell, an American-born pianist, who "showed evidence of her rare musical gifts at a very early age."⁶⁴ Nevertheless, she had abandoned her European musical training to marry and serve her creative husband. Even before Edward MacDowell's untimely death in 1908, and certainly afterward, he was widely saluted in American musical circles as "our first great American composer" and "America's greatest composer."⁶⁵ After his death, Marian made plans for their summer cottage to become a workspace for American artists. To that end, she embarked upon a forty-nine year career of regular concert tours to women's clubs and conventions, publicizing her dream of establishing a retreat "where working conditions most favorable to the production of enduring works of imagination shall be provided for creative artists."⁶⁶ Her tireless efforts to publicize and finance this dream in four hundred cities earned the colony one hundred thousand dollars, much of it donated by members of women's clubs.

Marion MacDowell sought and won respect, enthusiasm, and money for her colony from the women's clubs in the GFWC and the NFMC. The membership responded generously. Even before the composer's death, seventy-five women's organizations had already pledged contributions.⁶⁷ This degree of enthusiasm was sustained for decades. In 1919 the NFMC raised two thousand dollars to purchase stone seats for an outdoor amphitheatre at the colony. The women of the NFMC raised over ten thousand dollars in the 1920s, and the Junior Division collected a matching sum.⁶⁸ By 1925, the MacDowell Colony was a thriving institution. Its original eighty acres had grown to five hundred, its three original buildings were in the company of thirty more. Fifty artists each summer engaged in the work of producing an American culture on par with that of Europe. Clubwomen had helped to make another of their musical dreams come true.

In return for the patronage of club members, Marian MacDowell's colony was unusually hospitable to creative women. While she maintained control over the fellowship procedure, the bulk of awards were given to women.⁶⁹ Oddly enough, working women in arts other than music received the lion's share of awards, and later, of fame. Clubwomen showed their appreciation for this support of the creativity of their sex. In 1923, women's club leaders, who dominated a committee selected by the publication *Pictorial Review* to award five thousand dollars to a worthy project, deemed Marian MacDowell most deserving.⁷⁰ In a flattering portrait of her in the League of Women Voters publication, *Woman Citizen,* she was commended for being "responsible— who knows?—for developing some unknown woman's genius that would otherwise be smothered under the pressure of ordinary life.... It is quite possible that one of the reasons why women have not equalled men in creative achievement is that they have not had any one to give them the freedom of mind and body which most men have had."⁷¹

Just as women had hoped, this sort of encouragement did indeed yield noteworthy creations. If Pulitzer Prizes were awarded to MacDowell projects by Edwin Arlington Robinson, Thornton Wilder, Stephen Vincent Benét, Aaron Copland, and Norman Dello Joio, so did they also go to Margaret Widemer (in 1919, for *Old Road to Paradise*); Willa Cather (in 1923, for

One of Ours); Leonora Speyer (in 1927, for *Fiddler's Farewell*); and Julia Peterkin (in 1929, for *Scarlet Sister Mary*). The MacDowell Colony was doing its part to put creative Americans, female as well as male, on the artistic map.

Toward the achievement of similarly pro-American ends, the music clubs took steps to demystify the allure of European performers by calling for the employment of American musicians for club meetings and for other concerts in their communities. This was an uphill battle, and only somewhat successful among listeners entranced by the allure of foreign-born musicians. GFWC Music Chair Anne Oberndorfer warned NFMC convention delegates, "We women . . . do not realize our own personal, individual responsibility to the art that surrounds us . . . we feel that great singers with foreign names are better than our own."[72] Women in Chicago's Amateur Musical Club went so far as to refuse its scholarship to students embarking on European study, insisting that its award money be spent at home-grown institutions.[73]

As early as 1901, Adella Prentiss (later Hughes), manager of the Cleveland Symphony Orchestra, was hired by the NFMC to administer an Artists' Committee that would secure affordable local talent to perform at club functions. This scheme was intended not only to ensure exposure for new American talent, but to provide employment for beginning musicians. The idea failed miserably, being impractical in the light of club realities. The meager treasuries of most clubs put members in the position of performing gratis for each other at their own meetings, while occasionally employing European celebrities capable of luring the general public to community concerts. The committee was dismantled quickly. It was replaced by a Bureau of Registry, which facilitated club exchanges of their own talent, a less ambitious outcome of a noble goal.[74]

Although the clubs were most successful at providing a hearing for their own membership, they also created performance opportunities for notably talented students in their communities, and for regional artists, especially women, who would otherwise have had little access to the professional concert stage. Musicians of color could take advantage of this relatively open forum. Pianist Maud Cuney Hare and baritone William H. Richardson toured the state of Massachusetts, singing for such groups as the Stoneham Woman's Club, "one of the largest white women's clubs in Massachusetts."[75] Azalia Hackley, a black musician with a wide following among black women's clubs, performed extensively on the church, community, and club circuits "to instill in the hearts of Negro youth and the masses the urge to grasp the higher and finer things in life; the love of Negro folk songs—the only true American music."[76] Similarly, the black women of St. Paul who formed the Folk Song Coterie studied Negro folksongs, spirituals, and art music by contemporary black composers, and presented them to wide audiences.[77]

In nurturing women-made music, the clubs naturally gravitated toward the turn-of-the-century phenomenon of the all-women's orchestra. When women performers, barred from established professional symphonies, formed their own separate orchestras, women's music clubs took steps to ensure the health of these alternative institutions. They did so by contributing money, publicizing their engagements, selling tickets, filling concert halls with their own members, inviting the orchestras to play at their conventions, and reporting, in their own publications, on the tours, reviews, and successes of these ensembles.[78] Naturally, they also invited the women's orchestras to play at their meetings. At the Friday Morning Club of Los Angeles, one clubwoman said of the Women's Symphony Orchestra of Los Angeles, "We were glad to present an aggregation of women players, whose ensemble work compares favorably with many of the better known orchestras."[79] The same group performed at the California convention of the NFMC and at the California convention of the GFWC.[80] Likewise, the Chicago Woman's Symphony Orchestra, conducted by Elena Moneak, performed at the formal opening of the NFMC convention in 1927.[81]

The oldest women's symphony orchestra in this country, The Fadettes, was founded in Boston in 1888 by Caroline Nicholas. The group was named for a protagonist in George Sand's novel *La Petite Fadette*. By 1920, it had performed six thousand concerts to critical acclaim all over North America. The *Boston Transcript* observed: "The time for qualifying every remark about the playing of this orchestra with a hasty, 'for an organization composed entirely of women,' has gone by. In solidity of tone, vigor and self-confidence, in elasticity and precision, this orchestra ranks high among orchestras everywhere."[82] The Fadettes was quickly adopted by the Massachusetts State Federation of Women's Clubs, which permitted the orchestra to join as if it were a women's club. In annual reports, the federation documented the acclaim enjoyed by the orchestra and provided it with important exposure.

Dozens of other orchestras of women playing classical repertoire—in Salt Lake City, Chicago, Philadelphia, Los Angeles, New York, and Minneapolis—were founded in the first third of the century, and adopted by women's music clubs.[83] In philosophy, the two groups were likely allies, for music clubs and women's orchestras shared basic premises on the important contribution women could make to American music, particularly if they cooperated to win a hearing for each other.

Women's amateur music clubs also raised interest in the production of opera in the English language. In 1922, the GFWC passed a resolution in support of opera in English.[84] During the 1920s, the NFMC disseminated a list of sixty-six composers of American opera, including four women, to educate its membership about the talent at home.[85] The organization allied with the Opera in Our Language Federation, chaired by Edith Rockefeller McCormick, and attempted to raise ten thousand dollars for the American Opera Association in Los Angeles.[86] It publicized the national tours of the latter company, such as when it brought 126 performances of *Madame Butterfly*, in English, to Washington D.C., New York, Boston and Chicago.[87] Clubs publicized the work of the three-thousand member National Opera Club of America, in New York City, which sought to create a string of state-supported opera companies in this country that performed in the English language.[88]

The encouragement of American music was not confined to elite forms, but also extended to the American folk music tradition. Members sought the advice of ethnomusicologists, including Alice Fletcher, Natalie Curtis, Frances

Densmore, Nedda Hewitt Stevens, Arthur Farwell, and Charles Wakefield Cadman, to prepare materials and programs on Native American and "Negro" folk music for their regular meetings and conventions. This enthusiasm served to popularize America's earliest musical traditions. At the 1921 convention of the NFMC some of Fletcher's discoveries were performed, a fitting tribute to her knowledge and her audience, since her career as a lecturer had begun in a music club twenty-six years before.[89] The program included performances of seven Native American melodies that she had collected as well as six "Old Negro Melodies and Plantation Songs" collected by Stevens.[90] Arthur Farwell spoke at conventions of both major women's music organizations, and wrote for their periodicals.[91]

While clubwomen celebrated minority folk traditions, they condemned the contemporary contributions of African-Americans, who were making an indelible mark on popular song. Musical clubwomen were careful to clarify the difference between "good Negro ragtime," and the distressing "jazz" they sought to eradicate. The former, explained Anne Faulkner, "is one of the most important and distinctively American expressions to be found in our folk music," whereas jazz, or "the putting rhythm, melody, harmony out of joint," was "bolshevism in its disregard for the elements of music."[92] Despite professions of respect for traditional black music, however, the racism of the era was apparent; for example, African-Americans were not always called upon to perform their own music, by clubwomen or by other groups. Consider for example the Society for the Preservation of Spirituals, one hundred twenty Charleston men and women, who described themselves as "prompted by their love for their old servants, their interest in negro folk lore and their appreciation of the beautiful religious songs or spirituals sung by the negroes,"—but it was whites who comprised the choirs and promised authentic interpretations "with clapping hands, patting feet and a rhythmic sway."[93] Black performers did not join them. Likewise, Katharine Tift Jones of Georgia performed a "delightful impersonation of the Negro of the south," in costume, for the NFMC 1923 convention.[94]

Early twentieth-century clubwomen did not altogether neglect to invite representatives of minority groups themselves to share their expertise. Native American Roberta Campbell Lawson, referred to earlier as an officer of the GFWC, was a collector of Native American songs, and a consultant to federal government efforts to preserve Native American music. She lectured to clubwomen on "Music and the Mysticism of the American Indians," singing excerpts by way of illustration.[95] Indian princess Tsianina was a popular performer at meetings and conferences. She presented Native American songs, in costume, for attentive clubwomen.

Although minority musical heritage entered club life in this era, there is no doubt that folk music rooted in white America's experience received greater attention from members. Clubwomen argued that native-born whites in this country were as ignorant of their own musical tradition as the immigrants they expected to "Americanize." One clubwoman asserted, "Americanization means Education—not only of the foreigner, but also of the American."[96]

Therefore, clubwomen intended that no one should go without exposure to the music created by the wide variety of people who had settled the nation—cowboys, French Creoles, Kentucky mountaineers, miners, sailors, lumberjacks, Southwestern Hispanics, and others. The songbooks and bibliographies circulated by clubwomen contained music from the foregoing categories, as well as Native American, African-American, and patriotic songs, favorite hymns of America, and the songs of Stephen Foster.[97] In keeping with their respect for the European tradition, these compilations also included examples of songs inherited from all over Europe. Clubwomen used these songbooks themselves at their meetings, and they pressed their community's schools, churches, scouts, and—most fervently—settlement houses to adopt them. As a result, it was nearly impossible for an American to advance to adulthood in the 1910s without learning *Yankee Doodle, Swing Low, Sweet Chariot, Home on the Range,* the *Marseillaise,* and *Silent Night.*

Clubwomen made special efforts, generally through the settlement houses, to acquaint immigrant communities with America's new enthusiasm for music. Like their civic-minded sisters, musical members endorsed the importance of "Americanizing" immigrants, by which they meant assisting them in acquiring the skills they would need to contribute to American life. The degree to which this process challenged the culture of the immigrant's native country varied, depending on the sensitivity of the Americanizers. By and large, clubwomen—musical and otherwise—agreed that foreigners needed to learn to speak the language of their new country to understand its ideals, political principles, and governmental structure, to learn American history and customs, and become citizens. Adherents of music agreed that song was an ideal way to introduce foreigners to the English language. They also believed that beyond any other means, teaching immigrants patriotic songs for participation in holiday rituals and ceremonies would instill in them a sense of Americanism.

For the newcomers to American shores, clubwomen also hoped that music would provide nourishment and solace in lives sapped by struggle. "If it means a great deal for the rich, who are surrounded by beautiful things, to have music in their homes, those who have only poverty have even greater need of it," remarked one settlement music supporter.[98] By offsetting the immigrants' struggles, clubwomen expected that music would cultivate the qualities contributing to good citizenship. Susan Hart Dyer, director of the New Haven Settlement Music School, director of the Music Department of the Florida Federation of Women's Clubs, and leader of the Liberty Chorus for the Florida Council of Defense during the war, stressed that music, like other intellectual pursuits, was essential for health and happiness:

> It is, of course, a truism that a healthy happy human being makes a better citizen than a morbid unhealthy one; and also that the more normal mental and emotional outlets the individual has, the most chance there is of his remaining healthy and happy and a good citizen. Everyone remembers having watched the 'intellectual breadline' which forms in the evening at the desk of the public library. Settlement music school offers emotional and intellectual outlets which are so

necessary to normal existence anywhere, but especially important to the youth reared in the artificial and overstimulating atmosphere of our congested cities.[99]

Similarly Frances McElwee McFarland, who surveyed music in New York settlements for the city's Welfare Council, observed that "the intimate connection between a genuine appreciation of good music and the cultivation of fine character has become the wisdom of the ages."[100]

Some idealists among the clubwomen looked upon music shared by native-born Americans and immigrants as a true international language, a vehicle for communication among the diverse groups settled in America, or even, perhaps, around the world, contributing to international peace—"Art unifying mankind in the common cult of beauty."[101]

In many American cities, clubwomen saw to it that settlement houses sponsored music schools that provided foreigners from Europe and Asia, or African-Americans, with free or inexpensive lessons in piano, violin, and voice, and an opportunity to participate in a chorus or orchestra. In the largest programs, training was also available in other instruments of the orchestra and in theory, harmony, ear training, sight reading, orchestration, music appreciation, and instrument making. Music libraries of sheet music, scores, Victrolas, recordings, and written material on music were also provided. Instruments on which to practice, including pianos, were donated. A few settlements even managed to provide summer music camps for their most talented urban musicians.[102]

The music was not limited to immigrant children in the settlements. For the general foreign population there were harmonica bands, community sings, choruses for every age group, and celebratory pageants full of music, not solely American in origin or even classical, but including folk songs from every land. Thus, it was possible to hear mothers sing their folk tunes while kindergartners marched in rhythm bands, groups of boys harmonized sailor songs, young girls performed *Madame Butterfly,* and orchestras and choruses of all ages prepared a varied repertoire for neighborhood audiences on settlement anniversaries and national and religious holidays.

How significant was the contribution clubwomen made to the immigrant's musical world? Despite the rise of professional social workers in settlement houses, volunteer clubwomen were still welcome in the area of music as fundraisers as well as instructors. Few schools could rely on a generous angel to pay the bills, as Philadelphia's Settlement Music School relied on Mary Louise Curtis Bok Zimbalist.[103] Rarely did a school enjoy the teaching services of professional instructors, as the Neighborhood Music School in New Haven did when the Yale University Music Department donated lessons.[104] Thus, most settlements drew on women's clubs for a great variety of assistance—not only for money for instruction and supplies, but also to teach and coordinate lessons, to supplement local audiences of settlement house performances, and to invite immigrant musicians to play at their club meetings.

It was the Schubert Club in St. Paul, for instance, that actually initiated music classes at the West Side Neighborhood House in 1911. Beginning with fourteen "worthy" students who could only afford to pay twenty-five cents for a half-hour lesson from a Schubert Club member, the program grew steadily. Eventually, the St. Paul clubwomen served twelve settlement houses and provided full scholarships for a series of twenty-four lessons in piano, voice, or violin.[105] In Columbus, Ohio, the story of the Women's Music Club was similar. In 1914, club president Ella May (Dunning) Smith placed volunteer teachers in eight settlement houses; by 1928, the program had grown to supply thirty-five teachers, who gave 1,353 lessons that year. In addition, donations enabled awards of scholarship.[106] In Kansas City, the Musical Club raised money to support a school of almost eighty pupils. The members who taught were paid from this fund and through modest payments by the children.[107] The Thursday Musical Club of Minneapolis could boast an ambitious program as well. In the space of eight years, from 1914 to 1922, its members gave 11,670 free lessons in piano, violin, and voice.[108] In New York, Junior League members gave the lessons at the Union Music School, although the settlement director was nervous about ensuring quality control over her young, affluent volunteers. Therefore, "each week I met with the delightful and gifted young 'faculty' so that its members might keep at least one lesson ahead of the pupils."[109] The Junior League's musical members in New Haven did not teach, but supported programs by ushering at the concerts of the settlement music school.

For music clubs without the personnel to provide lessons to the immigrants, fund-raising was a tremendously welcome contribution to the health of music. One thousand dollars was raised by the Fortnightly Club in Cleveland for the Cleveland Music School Settlement.[110] The Buffalo Chromatic Club raised five hundred dollars annually for the music settlement with a benefit concert. In Kansas City, the Music Club raised five to six hundred dollars each year for the Swope Music Settlement it had founded. The Morning Musical Club of New York sent five hundred to nine hundred dollars each year to settlement music programs.[111] In Los Angeles, the Wilshire Ebell's Music Department contributed one member to the vice-presidency of the Music Settlement School Association board of directors, whose responsibilities included the financing of programs.[112] Beginning in 1914, Seattle's Ladies Musical Club funded instruction for children at the Settlement Music School, serving a Russian-Jewish neighborhood.[113] Both the facilities of the settlements and their links to the broader community would have been significantly diminished without the involvement of the musical clubwomen.

America's entrance into World War I interrupted club work and forced a major recasting of club activity. Efforts to ameliorate conditions for women and to improve American life took a back seat, as patriotic service and benevolent work dominated club life so substantially that it would never be the same. "While we may again take time for the cultural development of life as interpreted through music, art, and literature, it is to the practical things that we must direct our best thought and energy," advised the President of the

Massachusetts State Federation of Women's Clubs.[114] The call to service would outlive the national emergency, and would slow future initiatives by members to devise new vehicles for their own growth.

The GFWC and its seven thousand member clubs and the 2.5 million women it claimed to represent had taken a pacifist stance before the United States went to war. At the 1916 biennial convention in New York City, twenty thousand women applauded speeches on the importance of peace. However, when Wilson declared war, the federation supported him thoroughly, raising $4.8 million in Liberty Bonds, $55,128 in thrift stamps, $90,000 for the Red Cross, $55,106 for military camp library funds, and $89,788 for the YMCA's war-support work.[115] Clubwomen from organizations of every stripe united on 21 April 1917 to create the Council of National Defense Committee on Woman's Defense Work. Chaired by suffragist Rev. Anna Howard Shaw, it included the leaders of the major women's federations of the era. Among them was Ione (Mrs. Josiah E.) Cowles, who represented the GFWC, and Eva Perry (Mrs. Philip North) Moore, representing the National Council of Women.

For all the emphasis on service, however, music clubs and music departments in civic and literary clubs used the topical theme of patriotism to their advantage while the war was in progress. Suddenly, members' earlier efforts to Americanize the new foreign community and strengthen patriotism among American citizens was widely perceived as filling a wartime need. It satisfied a general awareness of the desirability of nurturing American self-consciousness and pride. Musical clubwomen, in addition to participating in fund-raising, gardening, and bandage rolling, also applied music to the national emergency. No NFMC convention was held during the war,[116] but members were made aware, by means of club publications and word of mouth, of the importance of pitching in with musical relief. Salt Lake City clubwomen were typical in sending 3,500 recordings to soldiers at American hospitals and European battlefields.

Many clubs used their musical talents to raise money for the war. In October of 1918, for example, the Schubert Club in St. Paul sponsored a recital of the Metropolitan Opera soprano Mabel Garrison as a benefit for the American Friends of Musicians in France.[117] Clubs sent musical instruments and Victrolas to camps, YMCA buildings, and ships, so that soldiers could amuse and educate themselves,[118] and the women made music for soldiers in training. Joining the call for respect for the flag, music club members urged Americans to stand for the national anthem.[119] They devoured copies of "National Songs of America" to use at their own meetings and to circulate to other groups. They cheered at the promises of the Cleveland and Buffalo Philharmonic Orchestras to play the work of an American composer at each of its twenty-two concerts of the season.[120] Even when they indulged in their favorite pastime of attending concerts, they did not fail to bring their knitting. In fact, the professional musicians of New York, Boston, and Cleveland objected to the distracting click of needles, and tried to say so patriotically:

[The New York] Philharmonic Society fully appreciates the spirit that prompts charitable assistance in the great world's calamity caused by the European war, but many complaints have been received from patrons of the concerts who are annoyed by knitting during performances, and the directors respectfully request that this practice, which interferes with the artistic enjoyment of the music, be omitted.[121]

The war prompted clubwomen to re-evaluate earlier assumptions that the German listening public must be inherently more receptive than the American, and that German music conservatories must necessarily remain superior to American ones. A Washington State clubwoman wrote in 1917:

Hundreds of thousands of this country's money have been spent yearly by students of music in European cities.... We have not the musical atmosphere of older civilizations. It is our privilege to see to it that this atmosphere is created and maintained, in order that American women may be trained under the protection of our own wholesome institutions.

There are indications that we are about ready to replace our old-world culture with something radically our own. Let us make it unnecessary that any of our good American dollars shall be changed into marks in Leipsic or Berlin.[122]

Similarly, Artee Mason Carter, who organized the building of the Hollywood Bowl after the war, remained resentful of German supremacy in music: "No nation is great so long as it borrows or buys its culture. Imagine an orchestra in Berlin made up of more than half Americans, with American conductors playing American music! You couldn't imagine it—it couldn't exist."[123]

Sometimes clubwomen's musical prejudices reached proportions unthinkable in peacetime. The New England Conservatory Club, formed by Conservatory alumnae in Portland, Oregon, exhibited its hatred of the Germans in deciding not to devote its October 1918 meeting to the music of Robert Schumann. Although one clubmember objected, pleading that "our country was not making war upon art," the club voted to present a program of French music instead.[124] Similarly, the Rhode Island Federation of Women's Clubs grew incensed when the German-born conductor of the visiting Boston Symphony Orchestra, Dr. Karl Muck, failed to begin a wartime concert with the national anthem. The Providence clubs participated in lodging a complaint about his loyalty, and helped ensure the cancellation of the remaining concerts in the series, the barring of the orchestra from many other cities, and Muck's internment for the duration of the war in an American prison in Oglethorpe, Georgia. The clubs also went on record as supporting an effort "by the Police Commissioners of Providence to refuse permission to appear before or entertain any audience in Providence to any and all musicians who decline to stand, sing, or play in the presence of the American flag."[125]

In general, German musicians discovered that American audiences, clubwomen among them, were unwilling to patronize their talents in wartime, and these performers found it wisest to lie low. The cause of the German-born musician was further damaged in America when childhood loyalties steered some of them home to fight for the Kaiser, as was true of several performers in the Cincinnati orchestra. It was said at the time that the musical life of the city was so dominated by German trained artists that the city's cultural life was brought to a standstill. The same issue split the clubwomen of Florida, where members objected to any German music being played at federation functions. "At the 1917 convention so many protested over the music committee's plans to play selections from Beethoven, Mendelssohn, and Wagner that President Wilson himself was wired and asked for an opinion. He replied that he did not regard the use of good music as unpatriotic."[126]

Even after the war, there were clubwomen who remained suspicious of German music, and urged that its role become subservient to home-grown culture. The postwar era brought musical refugees from Europe to America, in search of employment and in search of American respect for their musical tradition and excellent training. They discovered American musicians and their champions rising to defend their newly won turf, insisting that Americans could make their own music. The delegates to the 1922 conference of the New York State Federation of Music Clubs heard that many foreign artists were leaving war-devastated Europe for America, and were crowding out some fine American artists. The speaker, Eleanor De Ciseros, "urged music clubs, music committees to do all in their power to aid our own artists, to have at least fifty per cent of the program artists American."[127]

After the war, music clubs also attempted to define the proper way to memorialize the catastrophe, deciding finally on the commission of a carillon. Club leaders, among them Anne Oberndorfer, made an unsuccessful attempt to raise two million dollars for a bell tower "to commemorate at the nation's capitol the victory over imperialism."[128] Musical clubwomen also called for the establishment of a convalescent home for wounded musicians at the MacDowell Colony, another plan that never materialized.[129]

One of the war's great legacies to musical clubwomen was a heightened understanding of the value of community singing. To a certain extent, they had already become aware of the importance of community singing to their goal of mass participation in creative endeavors. Group choruses of untrained immigrants had become a staple of settlement festival life even before the war. Fifteen hundred singers welcomed Admiral Dewey home on his return from Manila after the Spanish-American War of 1898. Two thousand New Yorkers sang in the new century on 31 December 1899, and three thousand voices joined to sing at the dedication of Grant's tomb.[130]

During World War I, however, the general perception of the usefulness of community singing was much expanded. Clubwomen increasingly tapped the ritual of community sings, now termed Liberty Sings, in club meetings and, more importantly, in any public demonstrations they could influence. These activities became popular throughout the nation.[131] In San Francisco, ten thousand people united for the purpose of singing.[132] Bessie Bartlett Frankel presided over the Hollywood Community Chorus to generate community singing to raise spirit and money for a Liberty Loan Drive at the Women's Club of

Hollywood on the Fourth of July 1917. Her effort seeded the movement that founded the Hollywood Bowl.[133] Supporters of the phenomenon observed, "Community music is a fact in all sorts of places from New York down to the smallest rural hamlet. The people have at last found their voices. Our emotions have been bottled up for generations. We have had no real vent for them since the Civil War."[134] Soon American music—a mixture of popular tunes, patriotic anthems, and Christian hymns—was being sung at patriotic festivals, holiday gatherings, and mass meetings called simply for the purpose of singing. *Keep the Home Fires Burning, Dixie, America, Onward Christian Soldiers,* and *Swanee River* could be heard in town halls, churches, canvas tents, and, when these proved too small to meet community needs, in country fields and city parks.[135]

The reasons given for encouraging community sings were many. There was general accord that music could be a patriotic stimulant, and would loosen "the people's purse strings" at events designed to sell Liberty Bonds. Music would "comfort citizens whose relatives were fighting on the front lines, and inspire soldiers to greater vitality."[136] Clubwomen felt confident that music "is universally recognized as a conspicuous factor in the transformation of raw recruits into a fighting army which won the admiration of Europe."[137] Furthermore, singing was said to heal class divisiveness at a time when the nation needed to move in solidarity to win the war. Never was it more important to "assimilate and Americanize our alien population," and song could do this, as foreigners were taught to salute the flag and sing their respects to the nation. "Music acts as a social solvent, bringing all classes together," J. Lawrence Erb told women delegates to their federation convention of 1918.[138]

Clubwomen quickly gravitated toward the community sing for its expression of an ideal that they came to embrace wholeheartedly during the second decade of the twentieth century. Like the women in theatre clubs who would popularize the community pageantry movement and amateur drama efforts, or those in painting clubs who championed public art shows displaying the work of schoolchildren, the musical clubwomen invented opportunities for all Americans to express their creativity. In the belief that individual participation in artistic enterprises shaped a population of better character, greater happiness, and a deeper understanding of the desirability of shared talent in a democracy, they used community music to build a stronger America, in peacetime as well as wartime.

After the war, well into the 1920s, Americans continued to come together to sing American songs or foreign hymns that held relevance for this nation. At Christmastime, many communities recaptured the wartime spirit of unity, revitalizing the public enthusiasm through song. In 1923, the Philadelphia Music League secured two hundred and fifty choirs and choruses for its Christmas carolling program. Its effort climaxed at City Hall Plaza, when ten thousand Philadelphians attended a massive concert directed by Leopold Stokowski.[139]

Philadelphia prided itself on being "The Singing City," and boasted that its record of community singing at mass meetings, conventions, Navy Yard Sings, and church and fraternal meetings was unbeatable. Philadelphia clubwomen distributed song sheets to multitudes of citizens, schools, manufacturing plans, mills, factories, and stores. On Thanksgiving Day in 1920, one hundred thousand people attended exercises in forty-four city parks. At the Christmas season, forty groups of church choirs sang carols in the streets; and on New Year's Eve, Philadelphians "sang the old year out and the new one in" at Broad and Chestnut Streets. In summer, community sings were held in cooperation with the Police Band.[140] Clubwomen, in fact, lent their support to countless such programs, to celebrate Armistice Day, the Fourth of July, or any song-worthy occasion. Their enthusiasm grew to include a more ambitious effort in the 1920s, the plan to combine community singing with several other aspects of music making in every American town.

One musical project promoted by clubwomen stands out as most effectively embracing their ideals and achieving their goals. The celebration of National Music Week during the 1920s, undertaken by clubwomen in collaboration with other civic-minded members of their communities, invited all citizens to inject some music into their lives in settings throughout the community. During the first week of May, from 1924 into the mid-1930s, musical club members allied with many community institutions to generate occasions for music making. Eight major women's organizations lent support: the GFWC, the NFMC, the Camp Fire Girls, the Council of Jewish Women, the Girl Scouts, the YWCA, the National Congress of Mothers and Parent-Teachers' Association, and the National Council of Women. Additional organizations signed on as well—the Grange, men's service organizations, chambers of commerce, churches, schools, conservatories of music, libraries, colleges, government, professional organizations, unions, motion picture houses, theatres, settlements, charitable institutions, hotels, concert halls, workplaces, radio broadcasting stations, and commercial enterprises, especially those in the music trades, like the Victor Talking Machine Company, Steinway and Sons, and the National Association of Music Merchandisers—to facilitate the success of city-wide music festivals.[141]

Clubwomen did not invent the idea of a sustained period of citizen participation in musical events. The orchestra conductor Theodore Thomas, as director of Cincinnati's biennial music festivals from 1872 to 1902, probably deserves the distinction of uncovering the excitement and pride a town could experience through exposure to a serious dose of musical events. Other antecedents for National Music Week have been noted,[142] but it appears that the New York City festival, 1–7 February, 1920, fired the enthusiasm of the women's clubs.

Once clubwomen decided that the concept embodied their musical and social goals, they were tenacious in their efforts to engage their towns in a special week of music making. If clubwomen's efforts in major cities were obscured by the participation of famous musical celebrities, they were indisputably the mainstays of the celebrations in smaller towns. In Arkansas, where the school system did not offer the massive assistance that they did elsewhere, women's clubs carried off Music Week almost single-handedly.[143] In fact, most states contained a splendid array of women workers provided through music clubs.[144] Their role did not go unrecognized by government officials who were invited to sanction the local celebrations. In his proclamation for National Music Week, the Governor of Ohio specifically named women's clubs as generators of the state's music. In Tucson, Mayor Rasmessen described the Saturday Morning Musical Club as "deserving the support of every other organization of a civic or semi-civic nature in the effort to make this week a success."[145] The major historian of the Music Week movement conceded the women's importance: "Possibly no local contacts were responsible for more Music Weeks than those of the National Federation of Music Clubs."[146]

With finances from a patchwork of sources—from government, from private donations, and even from corporate foundations—[147] and with armies of volunteers to implement it, early May became the season for music making in America of the 1920s and 1930s. A Rip Van Winkle who awakened to National Music Week, having slept through all the advance preparations, would have been staggered by the level of participation. In 1923, 116 cities observed Music Week, while other communities initiated more modest activities. 572 cities reported holding Musical Memory Competitions, and 1,441 cities held Christmas carolling events.[148] By May 1924, National Music Week had snowballed—452 cities and towns celebrated with a wide spectrum of musical events. Another 328 cities and towns participated to a lesser extent, and sixty-eight communities held Music Weeks at a different time of year.[149] By 1935, two thousand cities and towns held observances; twenty-five states appointed state music week chairmen; and forty-seven governors and President Franklin Roosevelt accepted Honorary Committee member status.[150]

The celebrations made an effort to involve as many citizens as possible at least as spectators, and stressed the performance of American rather than foreign music. Church choirs competed against one another. School children performed for their peers, their parents, and their neighbors. Glee clubs and choruses assembled to regenerate the large-scale community sings that had been such a comfort during World War I. The public library displayed books about music. Schools held Musical Memory Contests. Colleges and Normal Schools presented operettas or pageants. Volunteers sang in prisons, hospitals, soldiers' homes, and orphanages. In Harrisburg, Pennsylvania, noontime organ recitals were held in the churches. In New York City, industrial plants and department stores hosted concerts, noonday sings, and tableaux.[151] Renowned musicians were invited to hold concerts, Vladimir de Pachmann appearing in Lancaster, Pennsylvania, and Ossip Gabrilowitsch in Spokane, Washington. The principal hotels offered Saturday evening concerts in Roseburg, Oregon. Municipal bands played at many a courthouse square. Churches in Altoona, Pennsylvania rang their chimes. In Boston and in Lebanon, Pennsylvania, parades were held, with bands representing many corners of the city. In New York City, the St. Cecilia Club presented a Toy Symphony at the Presbyterian Church. The Benedictine Sisters in Oil City, Pennsylvania, performed music by composers of their state. The Monticello, Arkansas Music Club furnished prizes for the best high school essays on "How to Cultivate a Love for Good Music in Preference to Jazz."[152] And, naturally, clubwomen gave recitals, in their clubs and for the public, and used the occasion to focus publicity on their ongoing junior club recruitment efforts.

African-American musicians shared their talents throughout the South. The Jubilee Club of the "Negro" schools sang in Dothan, Alabama; and Gadsden, Alabama's church programs included twilight musicales by black singers.[153] The Colored Jubilee Singers sang at Orlando, Florida's 1927 celebration.[154]

The rationales that adherents articulated to justify and champion National Music Week can be categorized into several themes, three of them familiar by now to students of the period. As might be predicted, many argued that the enterprise was worthwhile because the arts served the goals of democracy, sharing a valuable exercise widely, and diminishing differences.[155] Others emphasized the hope that morality would be strengthened by exposure to music. Finally, the use of music to harmonize discord was touted.[156]

New reasons for wide musical participation emerged in the mid-1920s. Some asserted the value of music to mental health. One report described the salutary effects of music on mental patients: "Of a band composed entirely of patients ninety percent were released from the institution the first year."[157] For the less extremely afflicted, mental benefits were also in the offing. Oliver Wendell Holmes was quoted: "Take a music bath once or twice a week for a few seasons. You will find it is to the soul what a water bath is to the body. This elevates and tends to maintain tone to one's mind."[158]

Another cause that won advocacy was music for relaxation. "The world is now waking up to a retarded realization of the relaxation music brings to the nerve-tired business man and the body-tired factory worker when there is opportunity for relaxation."[159] Music for the economy's sake was another reason asserted in the 1920s. "Music is an economic asset to the world and should be more widely used as such. It increases the earning power of the worker and at the same time makes his work easier. It aids the employer to the exact degree that it benefits the worker in his work. It makes life more enjoyable at the same time that it makes man more productive."[160]

National Music Week launched significant permanent musical institutions in some communities. In the wake of the celebration, the Arcata Woman's Club in California formed a women's chorus, while the town's business and professional men formed a civic quartet. The community of Beverly Hills began its plans for a civic music and art association. In California, the Inglewood Music Club formed to sponsor National Music Week and immediately took steps to create a junior club. Sandy Lake, Pennsylvania, started a music library; the state college bought new equipment for its music department through the proceeds of its performance of the *H.M.S. Pinafore;* and the people of Sunbury, Pennsylvania, created a permanent Oratorio Society as an outgrowth of their performance of *Elijah.*

The level of activity generated by National Music Week, along with the many other programs musical women had supported, demonstrate their success in rallying the citizenry to their call for a musical nation. Clubwomen justifiably praised themselves for the transformation:

> Before the world war, the majority of Americans believed that our country had no folk music of its own, that our artists were only fitted to appear if they had any foreign training, that we were absolutely devoid of American composers, that our operas and vocal numbers must all be presented in a foreign language, because English could not be sung; and that America would probably always be subservient to foreign powers in music.[161]

The implication was that thanks to the efforts of clubwomen, these mistaken beliefs had been largely eradicated.

How significant was the impact of clubwomen on the American musical world? Their efforts scarcely constituted a frontal assault on the male-dominated musical establishment of the early part of this century, yet many male critics expressed their discomfort at the increased feminization of the musical public. Failing to appreciate that club members had subordinated their own musical development in order to champion established musical values among women, children, and immigrants, these men felt threatened by women's presence in the musical world. Walter Damrosch, conductor of the New York Philharmonic Orchestra, complained in his autobiography:

> Women's musical clubs began to form in many a village, town, and city, and these clubs became the active and efficient nucleus of the entire musical life of the community, but alas, again principally the feminine community. It is to these women's clubs that the managers turned for fat guarantees for appearances of their artists, it is before audiences of whom 75% are women that these artists disport themselves.[162]

Joseph Hergeshever, a contributor to the *Yale Review*, positively despaired of women's success. "The leaving of all aesthetic questions to women has serious consequences," he said.

> One result of this is that music, except as the lyrical accomplishments to semicircles of legs, has almost ceased to exist as a masculine pleasure. In Philadelphia, for example, it is impossible to have a concert in the evenings for the reason that many women cannot very well go alone ... an amazing number of men ... think that music is effeminate ... because music has been so wholly delegated to women.[163]

Earl Barnes, in *Women in Modern Society* (1912), recognized the same phenomenon:

> Who, fifty years ago, could have imagined that to-day women would be steadily monopolizing learning, teaching, literature, and the fine arts, music, the church and the theatre? ... We may scoff at the way women are doing the work and

reject the product, but that does not alter the fact that step by step women are taking over the field of liberal culture.[164]

Others expressed resignation at the trend, following the suit of George Reynolds, who simply assigned cultural concerns to the twentieth-century woman as he assigned sports to men:

> Most of our Chambers of Commerce, men's organizations, you notice, are strong for good roads and golf links and Sunday baseball, to provide the amenities of life and opportunities for the enjoyment of the leisure with which our society seems almost to be threatened, but it is the women's clubs which mainly advocate those diversions of life which, from the days of primitive man, have enlivened his soul and ennobled his days, the great arts.[165]

Such acceptance of women's growing role in shaping musical taste was the exception. When the Curtis School of Music opened in 1919, it was realized that two-thirds of its students were women, so the admissions staff cut back on acceptances until, by the decade's end, women represented only a third of the student body.[166] At Ginn and Company, publishers of music, Edbridge W. Newton attempted to bolster men's acceptance of music by hawking its virtues to them: "We too look upon music as effeminate, and think only girls should study it. This is not true. To be a good musician requires brains of the highest order. Boys, be not afraid to study music, there is nothing more worthy of the masculine mind."[167] Women's support of music persisted nevertheless, despite the massive gulf that still existed between their musical accomplishments as amateurs and their acceptance as respected professionals.

Indeed, like a mutual protection association for women in music, the range of opportunities that music associations provided for its members and their families was impressive. For the beginner, the loans and scholarships, instruction and contests, the exposure and support, even the safe dormitories for music students in strange cities, identified and then developed budding performers and composers. For the mature woman artist, who might have been a full-time, widely recognized professional in a world without sexism, the clubs reaffirmed the importance of her ability and nurtured its growth. They constituted a crucial network for the professional women who did surface—with alliances among the teachers who shared educational techniques and news of openings in schools, with exposure at regional meetings, prize money, and acclaim for the ambitious concertizers and composers.

The federation's focus, away from the training of individual women in favor of acquainting all segments of society with the classics and indigenous American songs, lent such efforts a seriousness unmatched anywhere else in society. Sheer tenacity pushed clubwomen beyond mere lobbying for accessibility to music to include the institution of contests, concerts, prizes, and classes in schools or settlements. While members seldom received praise from the male musical establishment, their efforts made an enormous impact on American musical life. This relentless cultivation of musical taste built the respect that Americans developed for music and the enthusiasm that they applied to the federal music programs of the Depression years. The clubs' public programs also shaped the future supporters of the town symphony, the subscribers to the chamber music festivals, and the donors to music schools throughout the nation.

Without a doubt, club members' motives were many. Apart from blind patriotism, they were motivated by the desire to repress popular music and homogenize the taste of youth and immigrants until they conformed with traditional standards of good taste. These nationalistic motives coexisted with other, more progressive and liberated aims. These aims included the effort to develop an arena for women's influence in society; to retrieve the folk music of Native Americans, African-Americans, and all traditions in the United States; and to share the musical beauty that had heretofore been monopolized by elites. On all counts, the clubs' organization was impressive, the variety and ingeniousness of their projects dazzling, and their success broad. Women's societies, however detached from the musical mainstream, effectively shaped musical taste in the early twentieth century, and served as a major force in American music.

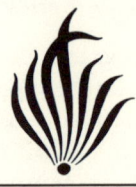

FOUR

Women's Societies for the Visual Arts

THE STRUGGLE TO BE SEEN

No group of arts lovers met more resistance in proving the worth of their work and justifying their cause than the advocates of the visual arts. Smaller in number and less tightly organized than the women supporting music, pageantry, little theatre, or literature, they struggled to proselytize among the wary. Rose Berry, speaking before the General Federation of Women's Clubs convention about the art committee she chaired, observed that art supporters were trying to "serve the people who do not know how badly they need service."[1] Despite this stubborn difficulty, Berry and other clubwomen devoted to fine art broadened access to art for the masses. When Berry declared, "In the United States today, there is no longer any doubt as to there being a renaissance, it is more than that: it is literally a new spirit, a new desire reaching out for the beautiful,"[2] she did not speak altogether in hyperbole. Yet the success of the women who preached the power of painting and sculpture was hard won, for these missionaries resigned themselves to subordinating their own love of art in order to carry its message to the untutored.

Early on, in the last decades of the nineteenth century, women's clubs formed for the specific purpose of instructing members in the Western art tradition. In time, they expanded their interests beyond the Old Masters whom the experts had taught them to revere, and gave equally serious attention to two other interests: woman-made art, both historical and contemporary, and regionally produced works, especially landscapes of local scenes. The clubwomen were influenced by respect for the acknowledged greatness of the Western tradition; by delight in the efforts of their own sex; and by loyalty to their own regions of the country. These factors, plus an aversion to controversy and modernity in artistic techniques, shaped their decisions about the work they studied, purchased, and made available to America's citizenry.

For all the diversity of approaches to art that this chapter surveys, certain truths remain constant. All the American women's visual arts clubs of the late nineteenth and early twentieth centuries were characterized by love of visual arts, willingness to meet regularly with other women to learn more in a formal setting, insistence on using refreshments and conversation to foster sociability among members, respect for peers from whom they felt they could learn, ingenuity about locating and using arts resources in their communities, and an understanding that they could have wide impact by cooperating with other women's arts clubs to accomplish grand goals. It is significant that women decided to associate with other women, for they might have joined coeducational organizations devoted to the arts, which were plentiful by the turn of the century. However, in mixed-sex groups women did not generally enjoy the decision-making power they did in all-women's organizations. Women frequently served as secretary in these organizations, for example, but rarely as presiding officer.

Like their sisters in other types of arts clubs, women in visual arts societies moved through four stages: (1) providing art and art history instruction for themselves; (2) providing access to art and art training for their neighbors; (3) undertaking art projects with other members of their communities; (4) embracing clubhouse decoration in the 1920s.

The earliest women's art clubs devoted their efforts to develop painting and design skills among their membership. Soon, they moved on to the second stage, providing generous access to traditional forms of fine art to a large public by founding or helping to found schools, museums, and traveling exhibitions, and providing lodgings for professional art students. Most impressively, in the third stage of their development clubwomen invented situations in which many citizens could pool their artistic contributions. We shall see examples of this effort in community art shows and state fairs, where school children's sketches were displayed alongside the work of renowned painters, and in the city museums that invited immigrants to bring their crafts, costumes, and music to special ethnic festivals. The most sophisticated of these efforts to bring people together to combine their artistic vision was achieved in the community pageants that clubwomen organized, inviting non-members with artistic ability to contribute ideas, materials, and hard labor to make a colorful, beautiful spectacle for all the townspeople to enjoy. These pageants are treated in Chapter 5. Finally, in stage four, during the period immediately after World War I, clubwomen applied their talents to adorning the private clubhouses they built. This subject is explored in the final chapter, on arts center architecture and decor in women's clubhouses.

While there were many similarities among women's art clubs, their approaches to art varied, reflecting the diversity of public activity clubwomen of the era were willing to undertake. Six major types of women's art organizations existed at the turn of the century. The first was to be of service to students of art history. These groups emphasized self-instruction through the study of the history of the Western art tradition, one of the most basic and early forms of club activity. For those ambitious to become professional artists, a second type of group was founded to enhance art technique among the members. A third type, museum founders, brought traveling exhibitions to town as a route to the establishment of a permanent museum. The next type, art school founders, addressing women's early enthusiasm for educating their children, founded a mechanism for practical art instruction. The fifth and most numerous and probably most influential type of woman's art club, created the art department, an oasis for arts lovers in the middle of the giant woman's civic association. Here, devotees of fine art diluted their own agenda to win wider support for their cause from more reform-minded sisters in the larger organization. Finally, a few women's art groups supported careers for women artists by funding lodgings or lounges for women art students far from home attending art schools in major cities. Such clubwomen provided financial support for a safe home for women, to foster a new generation of independent women, the professional artists.[3]

No specific organization comparable to the National Federation of Music Clubs developed to unite all types of amateur women's associations devoted to the visual arts. Instead, the groups tended to ally with two major networks, which offered different but compatible services: the General Federation of Women's Clubs (GFWC) and the American Federation of Arts (AFA). It is important to remember, however, that many other national organizations also served the needs of women's associations that expressed some interest in the arts. The American Association of University Women, the National Council of Catholic Women, and the National Association of Colored Women's Clubs were among the many nationwide networks that provided art study outlines and bibliographies to women's groups.[4] But the AFA and the GFWC were the most useful to women's art clubs—the AFA through its connections with the established art world of museums, galleries, and dealers, and the GFWC through its ability to promote the consideration of art to huge numbers of clubwomen. An understanding of the importance of both national networks is critical to a study of the dynamics of women's visual arts societies, for the affiliation with both defined the limits and expanded the horizons of the women in the member clubs. As we shall see, the two giant federations provided not only information and resources to clubs, but also priorities, leadership, and role models. They enlisted enthusiasm for art projects undertaken, generated positive publicity, conferred status by allying with renowned experts in the field, and generated growth and development through the conferences they sponsored. Responding to the needs and preferences of the membership, the federations provided a genuine exchange that made clubwomen participants rather than observers. The two federations served very practically to unify the work of clubs. They did this so effectively that even non-member clubs devoted to the arts came to know that they were a small but critical part of one of the largest, most far-reaching, and certainly most ambitious art movements in the United States.

American Federation of Arts

The AFA was the smaller of the two networks, but it enjoyed more prestige and firmer connections in the professional art world. Dominated by men who steered the elite arts institutions in America, and by the industrialists who funded the growth of those facilities, it united some of the most influential arts figures in the nation. Women's efforts were peripheral to the vision of the AFA, but their clubs were welcome to join, and members took away much information and direction from AFA's service bureaus.

The American art world had exploded in size at the turn of the century. The AFA formed in 1909 to bring some cohesiveness to the massive growth. Nineteenth-century museums, like the Metropolitan Museum of Art in New York and the Museum of Fine Arts in Boston, received huge donations of art and cash, enabling them to house new collections in new and grand wings. In addition, many new museums were founded during this era, including the Fogg in Boston, the Huntington in Southern California, the Heckscher Museum in Huntington, Long Island, the Henry Gallery in Seattle, and the Isabella Stewart Gardiner House in Boston, to name just a few. Colleges followed suit, scrambling to establish advanced art training and study collections, on a par with the art academies. A 1910 survey reported that there were 102 art schools in America, serving 13,710 students, and 170 colleges with art programs, enrolling 111,401 students.[5]

It was Glenn Brown, an architect and the secretary of the American Institute of Architects, who after discussion with influential art supporters sent out a call inviting representatives of art societies to form a national art federation to serve as a clearing house or general bureau of information to a broad constituency of arts enthusiasts. The proposed federation would also "stimulate appreciation of art all over the United States among all classes of citizens," and educate them by circulating paintings, lectures with slides, and publications.[6]

That the founders hoped to tap the goodwill and expertise of museum professionals was clear in their choice of president. Charles L. Hutchinson was already president of the illustrious Art Institute of Chicago. He served for three years and was succeeded by Robert W. DeForest, president of the Metropolitan Museum of Art in New York City, who presided over the AFA well into the end of the 1920s. The selection of early officers, regents, and board members reads like a *Who's Who* not only of museum directors, but also of generous fine art philanthropists (Archer Huntington, Andrew Mellon) and leading artists of the day (Augustus Saint-Gaudens, Cecilia Beaux). Soon the organization attracted a diverse membership of individual painters, sculptors, and architects. It also invited sympathetic legislators like New York Senator Elihu Root; major museums; chapters of the American Institute of Architects; and respected schools of art. Organizations of arts-related professions were also welcome—such as the American Society of Landscape Architects, the American Water Color Society, the National Sculpture Society, the National Society of Mural Painters, the National Society of Mural Craftsmen, and the Archaeological Institute of America. The National League of Handicraft Societies even joined for a time, although craft, with its association with utility, has had uneven reception by fine artists historically.

Not insignificantly for our story, the AFA was quickly populated by the city and state arts societies, many of them dominated, if not monopolized, by women, and by the women's art clubs. Individual women's clubs, including those in Farmville, Virginia and Pendleton, Oregon, also joined. Sometimes only the pertinent departments of large clubs signed on, like the Literature and Art Department of the North Carolina Woman's Club. The GFWC itself, and several state federations such as the California, Kentucky, and Connecticut Federations of Women's Clubs, also acquired AFA memberships.

A loyal following of arts adherents united at the founding meeting in Washington D.C., with eighty delegates from various of America's art institutions. The AFA grew steadily, to include 120 chapters by 1911, 200 by 1914, 313 by 1921, 411 by 1926, and 438 by 1929. The leadership reflected only minor awareness of clubwomen's enthusiasm for art. Four of the 32 original regents were women, among them Mrs. Phoebe Hearst, a California clubwoman of prominence—but also a monied benefactor of arts causes. Three of the twelve vice-presidents of 1910 were women, including Alice M. Gould (Mrs. Everett W.) Pattison, Art Chairman of the GFWC Art Department. However, women were featured but rarely on the dais of the AFA's annual conventions.[7] Most of the multitudes of speeches that filled three days of sessions each year were given by male leaders of museums and other art institutions. At the 1914 meeting, the listeners heard from the president of the American Institute of Architects, the director of the Minnesota State Art Society, the founder of the Art in Trades Club of New York, a member of the National Commission on Fine Arts, the president of the Chicago Art Institute, and the director of Fine Arts at the Panama-Pacific Exposition in San Francisco. There is special irony in this inequity, in light of the women's dominance in the audience. Their presence so surprised one convention speaker, Congressman John Slayden, that he observed: "I knew the ladies very soon expected to assume the entire political control of the country, but I did not know before that they were such an overwhelming percentage of the art movement. This audience indicates that in a very short time our architects, painters and sculptors will all be of the class that Miss Rankin represents politically.[8]

An important contributor to the alliance clubwomen built with the male-dominated AFA was the cordiality of two key female AFA staff members, Florence Levy and Leila Mechlin. New York City-born Florence Nightingale Levy (1870–1947) had studied art and art history at the National Academy of Design and in Europe. In 1898 she began to edit the *American Art Annual,* a publication the AFA started to sponsor in 1913. As the compiler of a comprehensive directory on art exhibits, art schools, museums, galleries, sales, art societies, and clubs, Levy was in a position to dignify the efforts of women's art organizations, applauding them for their "massive interest." Levy stepped down to become associate editor in 1918, and went on to work for the art world in additional capacities, implementing many of clubwomen's outreach projects through the Baltimore museum.[9]

Leila Mechlin (1874–1949) spent her entire life in Washington D.C. She studied at the Corcoran School of Art in the 1890s and served as art critic for the *Washington Evening and Sunday Star* from 1900 to 1945. One of the founders of the AFA, she immediately came on board as an assistant secretary and was elected secretary from 1912 to 1930. Quite importantly, she edited the official magazine of the organization (entitled *Art and Progress* from 1909 to 1915, *American Magazine of Art* from 1915 to 1919, and *Magazine of Art* after 1919). At first her support of clubwomen, like Levy's, tended toward the steady and subtle inclusion of notes on their successful projects rather than the use of bold feature stories. Occasional exceptions to Mechlin's low-key publicity for women's art club activity are in evidence, such as a reprint of the full text of a speech by S. Henrietta Housch, past president of the Ruskin Art Club and the Fine Arts League in Los Angeles.[10] She grew bolder in the 1920s, publishing a faithful round of feature articles in her monthly magazine that championed the work of women artists.[11] The clubwomen among her readership praised the change, applauding the new celebrity and prestige for women's accomplishments, which were long overdue.

Probably the greatest service that the AFA offered to clubwomen was its collection of traveling exhibitions. Professional arts groups, like the American Water Color Society, the Brooklyn Society of Etchers, or the National Association of Women Painters and Sculptors, were eager to give their artists exposure and sales.[12] The member groups in the AFA could become sponsors, bringing to their towns such portable works as oils, watercolors, student art, etchings, small sculptures and, after World War I, photographs of war memorials. The steady growth of the program attests to its popularity.[13] Some of the sponsoring groups sought to create a festival around the visiting art works, requesting special lectures, with slides, to attract the general public.[14] Here was an inexpensive way for a women's club with a low budget and high enthusiasm to produce an art fair worthy of note in the community.

For the clubwoman with an arts inclination, the AFA opened doors to professional circles of art expertise. As a vehicle for getting in touch with the best art advice available in America, the organization's effort was timely, responsive, and generous. It saw in clubs, quite rightly, a route to achieve its own goal of broadening intelligent understanding of fine art in the nation. Clubwomen had no role in shaping the association. Rather, women molded many of their attitudes to conform to those the AFA leadership espoused. The GFWC, the second great organizational influence on women's art clubs, gave clubwomen a freer hand in shaping art policy at the top; but it also exacted a price from its membership, that of diverting club attentions to peripheral programs nurtured by civic-minded constituencies within the woman's club federation.

General Federation of Women's Clubs

The General Federation of Women's Clubs (GFWC) formed in 1890, a union of women's literary clubs throughout the nation. Its national leadership, biennial conventions, and publications served to standardize efforts of women's literary and civic societies and prioritize projects undertaken by its membership.

The GFWC formally recognized the value of art to its organization in 1896, in response to the art clubs that had joined the federation in its infancy.[15] Music and theatre pursuits would have to wait years for similar recognition inside the federation. At its fourth biennial conference, members observed that twenty-four of the 595 women's clubs already federated had established distinct art departments. It became clear that women in other clubs sought instruction and involvement in art as well, and so the convention delegates resolved to create an Art Section, "the object being to advance the study of art, history, theory and criticism, and the employment of practical methods whereby art interest shall be promoted and supported in America, such as exhibitions of sculpture and painting, and the bringing together of the artists and the people."[16]

The representatives at the 1895 meeting enthusiastically received reports from club members describing their accomplishments. The Minnesota Federation of Women's Clubs had purchased its own stereopticon for surveying the history of art, with slides available to its member clubs. The Arundell Club of Baltimore held a regular sketch class; the Arlington, Massachusetts women's club had paid for the service of an art instructor; and the Heptorean Club in Somerville, Massachusetts, sent its art lovers on trips to local galleries, to private exhibitions, and to the magnificently decorated library in Boston.[17] The list of possible activities sounded tantalizing to other clubwomen, who voted to create a federation committee to assist all federated clubs in initiating art activity. The membership responded warmly, with two thousand clubs reporting art lectures during 1912, and three hundred clubs sponsoring art exhibitions. By 1922, 350 arts clubs belonged to the GFWC, and considerable numbers of department clubs included art departments for their memberships.

The GFWC, unlike the AFA, was eager to feature talented women in the arts in leadership positions. Among the most impressive of the GFWC's art committee chairpersons was Ella Bond Johnston. An officer from 1912 to 1916, she had trained for her post with remarkable service for art in Indiana. There she had brought together a variety of community-minded citizens who established the Richmond Art Association in 1897. She presided over the organization from 1899 until 1913, and served as director of its museum from 1914 until her death in 1951. Under her leadership, the group had acquired by donation or purchase a permanent collection of art, with emphasis on the work of Indiana artists like painter William Merritt Chase and sculptor Janet Scudder. The group exhibited this work, as well as traveling exhibitions, at the public school, drawing on the help of teachers, florists, musicians, and the press. When a new high school building was needed, the city of Richmond included a state-of-the-art gallery on the top floor, with skylights and special artificial lighting. So attractive were the group's shows to schoolchildren that it was rumored that art appreciation had stamped out bad habits: "There was less loitering on the streets and less common gossip among the pupils."[18] Johnston's philosophy and achievements, in bringing art to a wide public, made her ideal for meeting democratic federation goals.

Other effective promoters of art for the GFWC included Virginia Stewart

Berry of Berkeley, California, who served as art chairman in the early 1920s. She had studied music and art appreciation in leading art schools and museums of Europe for seven years, and had become a senior docent at the 1915 Panama-Pacific International Exposition art exhibition. She published a survey of American sculpture at the Palace of the Legion of Honor and a study of John Singer Sargent; and she also collected into a book a series of columns she had written to assist clubwomen in attempting group study of art history. [19]

The federated clubs enjoyed the services of many other capable women, trained in the arts. Florence Levy, staff member at the AFA and long-time editor of the *Annual of American Art,* served the Art Division of the Maryland Federation of Women's Clubs in the 1920s while she directed the Baltimore Museum of Art. Mrs. Randall Hutchinson, artist and former pupil of William Merritt Chase, served as the Art Chairman for the Friday Morning Club in Los Angeles.[20] L. Pearl Sanders, who studied at the Chicago Art Institute and the New York Art Students' League, won the William Merritt Chase prize in France, directed the School of Art and Applied Design in Nashville, and served as chairman of the Tennessee Federation of Women's Clubs Art Department.

The federation also sought the advice and expertise of women celebrities in the field of art. Among its honorary advisors were Violet Oakley, the Philadelphia muralist (consulting on fine arts and painting), Anne Coleman Ladd (sculpture), Jessie Wilcox Smith (graphic art), Mrs. James Earle Fraser (civic art and war memorials), Helen Cleavis (school and industrial art), Mrs. Douglas Donaldson (arts and crafts), Mrs. John W. Alexander (art in the home), and Mrs. Herman Rossi (art and the garden).[21] In addition, the federation's program committees invited women in art to speak to the delegates at their biennial conventions. Maud Mason, painter and also president of the Association of Women Painters and Sculptors, joined sculptor Lorado Taft and painters William Merritt Chase and Edward Robinson in making brief presentations at the New York Biennial. At the 1926 conference, the federation displayed fifty sculptures by twenty American women.[22]

Publications of the GFWC likewise emphasized women's contributions to the arts. Rose Berry distributed bibliographies on fourteen American women sculptors and twenty-four American women painters to guide club members through extended studies of these topics.[23]

While the study of paintings and sculpture by the great masters of Western civilization was effectively initiated by arts supporters in clubs, many other clubwomen in the GFWC, drawn to membership for the sake of public issues, found this approach, if not dull, at least irrelevant to a practical society that rejected the affectations of European aristocracy and sought immediate solutions to the pressing problems of the day. The GFWC Art Department chairman, Mrs. Cyrus Perkins, baldly asserted, "There is no disguising the fact— the majority of people do not care for the Fine Arts."[24]

Accordingly, the art programs and projects wandered away from a study of the Old Masters to include a wide range of civic-related art topics. Art was packaged to appeal to any and all other interest groups in the club world. Its new goals could assist the conservationists in the beautification of the environment. Art could serve the home economics devotees, who sought beauty in the home. In the hopes of appealing to pro-education forces, arts advocates claimed art could build the character of school children. Aiming at those concerned about the quality of life of rural Americans, arts lovers insisted that access to beauty could relieve the grimness of the farm and countryside. Art would educate, welcome, and impress the foreign-born, Americanization advocates were told. Arts-related industries were said to provide new jobs for women, an argument generated to build alliances with women's rights advocates.

The arts adherents themselves, never single-minded purists in their attentiveness to the Western canon of Great Masters, readily embraced more accessible types of art and art forms. If this stretched the narrowest definition of art, it also widened the appeal of and sympathy for a great variety of arts projects among clubwomen.

In the celebration of American-made crafts, the arts advocates in clubs could coexist with a great variety of other constituencies populating the GFWC. Crafts, it seemed, could satisfy the broader membership as the Western tradition of painting, however tempered with women's contributions, could not. In fact, crafts won wide approval among women's clubs because they could be all things to all people. On at least four counts, the study and exhibition of art pottery, basketry, metalwork, embroidery, wood carving, hammered brass, leatherwork, weaving, rug making, and, to a lesser extent, candle making, quilting, and furniture making, catalyzed the enthusiasm of clubwomen.

First, American craft appealed to the clubwomen whose object was to improve the American home. As soon as they became convinced that household decoration with well-designed crafted objects could achieve their ends, they championed lectures, exhibitions, and classes devoted to crafts. "Art for Home's Sake" was a topic that was considered widely among clubwomen in 1919, when the GFWC created a special subcommittee to publicize the importance of art in the home.[25]

Second, American crafts won the hearts of clubwomen who sought economic relief for impoverished women. Disturbed by the low wages and limited work opportunities that faced their working-class sisters, they hoped craftswomen could sell their work in Women's Exchanges, or non-profit shops offering goods produced by housebound women. Clubwomen also sponsored "Home Industries" production among rural people—the Woman's Club of Central Kentucky opened a market for the sale of work by mountain people; the Vermont Federation of Women's Clubs sponsored classes in tapestry weaving and rug hooking; and the New York City Federation of Women's Clubs commissioned lace and weaving by girls trained at the Greenwich Handicraft School in upstate New York.[26] Club women of Santa Fe called for Native Americans to produce traditional pottery and silver jewelry rather than capitulating to tourists with cheaper, more commercial souvenirs.[27]

A third group of clubwomen that embraced the growing enthusiasm for crafts were members who sought new career opportunities for the modern, path-breaking woman. In particular, they lauded the vogue for art pottery, which was increasingly produced by women in women-managed potteries. The trend had begun in Cincinnati in the 1870s, when Maria Longworth, Mary Louise McLaughlin, and others formed the Women's Pottery Club and won international distinction with their Rookwood Pottery. By the early twentieth century, women's contributions were central to a significant number of American potteries.[28] Thus it was American art pottery, perhaps more than any other of the crafts, that charmed clubwomen and prompted popular tours of home-produced pottery throughout women's clubs in the early decades of the twentieth century. When the GFWC wanted to present a gift to President Anna Pennybacker, nothing would do but a piece of Overbeck pottery.[29]

Finally, crafts appealed to the patriots in women's clubs. Their nostalgia for America's proud colonial heritage moved them to join their peers in addressing craft with new seriousness of purpose. They praised the revival of colonial linen production by the Deerfield (Massachusetts) Society of Arts and Crafts,[30] and publicized the achievements of Candace Wheeler's New York Society of Decorative Art and of the Philadelphia School of Design and other craft ateliers of the period. Their praise also went out to contemporary crafts, made from local clays and other materials, an expression of the proud regionalism that accompanied this era's strident Americanism.

Among twentieth century clubwomen, then, craft generated more excitement than did painting and sculpture. Members studied the finest examples of ceramics at their meetings, and sometimes attempted their own designs. The GFWC circulated fifty pieces of art pottery, representing the Grueby, Marblehead, Frackelton, McLaughlin, Newcomb, Niloak, Overbeck, Revere, Van Briggle, and Webb potteries.[31] At the biennial convention of 1900, the Milwaukee hosts prided themselves on providing exposure to "practical" artwork for the delegates, assembling carvings in wood, leatherwork, bookbinding, metalworking, enameling, gem setting, basketmaking, pottery, porcelain, painting, furniture designs, and textiles, including rugs, spreads, hangings, dress materials, lace, embroidery, dyes, designs, and craft tools.[32]

However valuable their association with the large and influential GFWC, arts advocates who functioned there quickly realized that they would need to adjust their goals to a public more attracted by issues other than "art for arts sake" if they cared to broaden support for the visual arts. If they cared to be heard at all, they had to compromise with the other interests within the club movement. This they did, centering their efforts on the art education of Americans, creating Municipal Arts Commissions, supporting an unspoiled environment, and lobbying for tasteful war memorials.

Art Education

Despite the limits of the AFA and GFWC, the two organizations had a hand in educating arts advocates in women's clubs, who then launched ambitious campaigns in their communities to bring art to everyone. Public schools and libraries, their own clubhouses, department stores, and state fairs were among members' favorite places for acquainting their neighbors with the visual arts.

Considering the scarcity of Great Masters and the expense involved in circulating original works of the European classical canon clubwomen settled on a more realistic scope for their shows. Their exhibits tended to feature work that was more readily available; notably, inexpensive regional paintings of non-controversial subject matter, particularly landscapes. Work by local artists was likely to attract many buyers. It was regional pride, as much as admiration for objects of beauty in the environment, that ignited many a community to view a touring exhibition and perhaps to build an art collection for itself. The Arche Club in Chicago primarily sponsored Chicago artists, as did at least twenty-five other Chicago clubs, making a priority of purchasing work by local artists. The Hoosier Salon was an annual exhibition in Chicago of work by Indiana artists, sponsored by fifty clubs, many of them women's clubs, in the Indiana Federation of Arts.[33]

Women's art was well represented in these exhibitions, in affirmation of clubwomen's steadfast belief that women were able to do anything well, even in arenas where they had been excluded previously. For example, the One Hundred Friends in Pittsburgh, organized in 1916 to purchase local works of art for the public schools, had acquired by the 1980s 416 works of art by 283 local painters, print makers, and photographers. In the first two decades, it acquired 47 works by women, out of 134 collected.[34]

Usually, women with aspirations to spread knowledge and appreciation of the visual arts found easy entry into the public schools. While women in organizations successfully pressed for school libraries and playgrounds, for vocational training and sanitary drinking fountains, women's call for attractive schoolrooms decorated with fine art was just another aspect of maternal concern for the welfare of America's youth. On the grounds that art education for children created an everlasting market for beauty, Mary Gibson, officer in the California Federation of Women's Clubs, supported the suggestion that each of the two hundred clubs in the sunshine state decorate at least one schoolroom: "No higher service can be rendered the art of the future than in cultivating a sense of color and proportion in the minds of the children of today."[35]

Art in the Schools

Art enthusiasts of the period seemed to agree that the youth were the most expedient target for producing new art lovers in a society largely scornful of art. As Lorado Taft, famed Chicago sculptor and endorser of progressive arts outreach, suggested, "We cannot do much for grown people; our work must be largely with children."[36] Tennessee clubwomen hoped that by putting art within reach of schoolchildren, youth "would acquire the language by which were expressed emotion, a tool to face the problems of life, and a key to unlock the store-house of happiness."[37] It was widely believed that the rising generation would use art as a vehicle to acquire countless desirable characteristics. "As industry takes the raw material of wood, and coal, and iron, and shapes them into the necessities and comforts of life, so Art takes the raw material of leisure, ambition, and desire, and creates with them forces for the refinement of living."[38]

Meeting this challenge, women began routinely to pressure public school officials to paint classrooms in attractive colors and to permit clubs to fund the purchase of framed art works for the classrooms, hallways, or auditoriums. The AFA polled experts in 1925 and produced a list of the specific masterpieces appropriate to the classroom.[39] This list bears witness to the kind of art that fit the clubs' agenda. It was not modern, abstract, or controversial. It included lush American landscapes, portraits of leaders in history, and works by the Old Masters. The emphasis on children as subject matter was no doubt intended to resonate with the schoolroom viewers; at the same time, the choices tended to project an old-fashioned naiveté.[40] The Chicago Public School Art Society had already placed works of this kind, including two Donatello casts of a *Mother and Child,* for the Polk Street School, and Della Robbia casts of *Singing Boys* and *Baby* for the Andrew Jackson School, and the Goodrich and Jones schools, respectively.[41] Likewise, when communities assembled temporary shows in schools for public exhibition, the subject matter gravitated toward gentle and laudatory images, especially of American scenery. For example, in McPherson, Kansas, the seventh annual high school art exhibition included B. Sandzen's *Rocky Mountain National Park,* Oscar Jacobson desert scenes, Anna Keener's *Mountain Ranch,* C. Raymond Johnson's *Colorado Landscape,* and Henry V. Poor's Santa Clara Valley portrayals.[42]

Clubs were quick to obtain permission to provide art works for local pupils. In Massachusetts in 1909, eighteen women's clubs reported buying original contemporary paintings, reproductions of Old Masters, or plaster casts of sculptural treasures of antiquity for school decoration. In Tacoma, Washington, the Aloha Club gave 175 framed photographs of masterpieces to the high school. In St. Louis, Missouri, the clubs gave fifty dollars' worth of casts to the State School for the Blind. Taking to heart the admonition of GFWC Art Committee chairman Adelaide S. Hall that communities needn't be afraid to place noble statues of nude Greeks before the eyes of children, the Alabama Federation of Women's Clubs Art Committee in 1910 gave plaster casts of the Winged Victory of Samothrace to the Girls' High School in Montgomery and to the Tuscaloosa High School.[43]

Not content to decorate the schools with paintings, prints, and statuary, clubs sought to make more permanent their artistic impact on institutions of learning. Foreshadowing the rage for murals during the WPA Art Project of the 1930s, clubwomen supported efforts to commission such works as *George Washington at the Battle of Monmouth* at Shorewood Grade School in Milwaukee and Olive Rush's *House that Jack Built* at Nathaniel Hawthorne School in Indianapolis.[44]

Clubs could not always afford to make such generous gifts as entire art collections or murals to schools, however, and had to devise cheaper ways to encourage the love of art in children. In North Dakota, clubwomen sent one picture a month to one rural school at a time. Schools had the option to buy the picture if they wanted to, members thereby moving the responsibility to educators to supply the students with permanent prints.[45] In Kansas, children were encouraged to purchase art on exhibition at McPherson High School. When they bought inexpensive prints, delighted art advocates dubbed them as "the de medici of the Smoky Hill Valley."[46]

Clubwomen found other ways to assist the art education of youth. They pressured for art history and practical art training in the schools, trips to museums, poster contests, and bookplate competitions, for which they awarded not the traditional ugly trophy but a handsome print or a bronze statuette, consistent with their program to disseminate quality art whenever possible. Some clubs raised scholarship money to provide talented young people with professional training. The Tourist Club of Minneapolis gave $150 for a three-year scholarship to the Minneapolis School of Art, for example.[47] The Tuesday Art and Travel Club in Chicago awarded five $100 scholarships to students at the Chicago Art Institute in 1907.

In conjunction with clubwomen's enthusiasm for art study, teachers also pressed for art resources from inside the school systems. In many cities, public school art associations formed to pool the determination of teachers, clubwomen, and other interested parties. The Public School Art Society formed in Chicago in 1894, uniting teachers and clubwomen and supplying one hundred schools with art reproductions, mural decorations, and art libraries, and spending $18,000 by 1910.[48] Six years later, Chicago club officer Mrs. Jean Sherwood lectured in Houston, Texas, and inspired the founding of the Public School Art League for the same purpose. The Public Education Association of New York City made a special effort to elicit gifts for particular schools from specific individuals of means.[49] Much to clubwomen's delight, city or state public school art directors were appointed in New York City, New York State, Massachusetts, and Pennsylvania.

Once art classes were available to students, the most successful could display their own work alongside that of the Old Masters hanging in the hallways.[50] Student art was exhibited, for example, in the Cloonan School Library in Stamford, Connecticut. In a poll of school systems in 1925, surveyors found that some school systems were providing specific space for art exhibitions in the new school buildings of Chicago; the state of Maine; Indianapolis; Pueblo, Colorado; Beatrice, Nebraska; and Portland, Oregon.[51] In Chicago, seventy-five new junior high schools were designed to include 53' × 30' art galleries on the top floor, with skylights to illuminate plaster casts in the collections.[52]

For all their support for placing fine art in the public schools, women's art clubs did not view the school system as the only logical recipient of their patronage. They sought a wider constituency, and used other public buildings to display art as well. Arguments circulated that the public library was the best place to exhibit art, because it served a wide segment of the population, and because the library held books, pamphlets, and clippings about the subject of the painting or the artist, thus enabling interested people to learn more about the work immediately.[53] The Melrose, Massachusetts, Woman's Club spent one thousand dollars on art books and photographs of fine paintings for the public library. Illinois clubs sent art work to the juvenile court of Chicago, presumably to brighten a somber setting and perhaps even uplift those headed on the wrong path.[54] In 1915, the Kentucky Federation of Women's Clubs circulated 240 pictures by forty Kentucky artists in Lexington's Carnegie Library. The Art Association of Charleston, Illinois, made up entirely of women's clubs, purchased a picture by C. E. Dana for their library. In 1912, the Women's Art Club of Cincinnati presented a painting by Mary Spencer to the Cincinnati Art Museum. The Nashville Art Association, a group substantially composed of women, won an appropriation of one thousand dollars from the city to purchase work for the municipal gallery.[55]

Women's purchase of art work for the enjoyment of the community, whether placed in a school, library, or some other public building, was made in the hopes that the objects would serve as the seed of a collection that would become a museum. In Duluth, Minnesota, for example, the Twentieth Century Club purchased pictures to found an art museum. The Wednesday Club of Fort Worth was successful in helping to start a public gallery.[56] The Richmond Art Association in Indiana, which initially used the high school to display art, built an Art Museum attached to the new high school.

Art for Clubwomen

Despite their predilection for community art programs, clubwomen lived by the motto that charity begins at home—right in their own clubrooms. Women's art clubs turned inward in the 1920s, despite their fine track record at creating art programs for the general public. The wave of clubhouse building after World War I provided luxurious art gallery space, never before available to clubwomen. The new spaces provided institutional sanction for a steady number and wide range of art shows. Clubs could enjoy the luxury of providing displays such as the traveling exhibitions of the AFA for the pleasure and edification of their membership. Or they could present the results of a class the members had taken, much as a school might hang art by prize pupils. Sometimes clubs exhibited art by artists of the community, and opened up their private gallery for community attendance. Clubs could offer space to show collections loaned by an affluent member. And increasingly, as generous clubwomen donated more works of art to the clubhouse than could be used to decorate the reception rooms, clubs built permanent collections of their own, supplemented by bequests from deceased clubwomen. All of these occasions necessitated receptions at which the artists or the works could be launched in style. Art gallery space in clubhouses helped mark the club and its members as knowledgeable, refined, and cultured. It also removed them further from the artistic life of their communities than clubwomen had been for two decades.

In Illinois alone, thirty clubs built their own collections of art for members' viewing. The Moultrie, Georgia, women's clubs did likewise. The Des Moines

Women's Club added a gallery to its clubhouse, to show off its collection of thirty-two paintings. Massachusetts clubs bought a New England rural scene for the headquarters of the Massachusetts Federation of Women's Clubs in Quincy. The swank Cosmopolitan Club in New York supplemented the art work on its walls with a steady round of small exhibitions, a different one each month, simply for the pleasure of members. The New Jersey Federation of Women's Clubs supported the work of Helen Maria Turner, when Mrs. Alvoni Rallen in Jersey City spent two thousand dollars on Turner's *Golden Hours,* a painting of a woman sewing, to award to a federated club showing the greatest interest in art. The presentation was made to the Contemporary Club in Newark at the Atlantic City convention in 1928, where the painting was displayed. Turner enjoyed the respect of other clubs as well, winning the Mary B. Elling Prize Award in 1910 from the Women's Art Club of New York and another prize at the Cosmopolitan Club in New York City in 1914–15. The Paducah Woman's Club, proud of the Kentucky artist, also bought a Helen Maria Turner.[57]

Several clubs that had their own clubhouses lent their art collections to less affluent clubs, seeing temporary exhibits as a way to enrich the artistic lives of sister club members. The St. Louis women's clubs sent an art show to the Canal Zone in 1910, for the pleasure of American wives of engineers in Panama, who had recently formed a club of their own. Chicago women lent their collections of art work to Nebraska clubs for the examination of entire Nebraska communities, if the local clubwomen chose to invite the public.

Some women's organizations that existed for purposes far distant from the cause of fine art nevertheless became patrons of the arts to accomplish their work. The Women's Christian Temperance Union, in its war against alcohol, invited sculptors to create drinking fountains it donated to towns around the nation. Patriotic societies of women needed designers for tablets, historical plaques, memorials, markers, and statues of heroes. The Women's Roosevelt Society, for example, sought a bronze medal with the image of Theodore Roosevelt in 1919, and they commissioned Anna Hyatt (Huntington) to design it. She would also create a bronze statue of Sybil Luddington, Revolutionary War heroine, for the Daughters of the American Revolution.

Much of the work that women's clubs commissioned for the decoration of their clubhouses was created by women artists. The Daughters of the American Revolution purchased work by L. Pearl Sanders for Continental Hall in Washington D.C., and by Gertrude Vanderbilt Whitney, whose statue was unveiled in 1929 for the courtyard at DAR headquarters. Violet Oakley, renowned for her mural paintings at the Pennsylvania State Capitol Building at Harrisburg, was revered by the Philadelphia Republican Women's Club, which bought the home of Charlton Yarnall to save Oakley's mural decorations inside it. A bronze fountain by Janet Scudder was commissioned as a memorial shrine to Mrs. E. J. Robison, president and founder of the Woman's Department Club in Indianapolis, and was placed at the entrance to the main hall of the clubhouse. The Junior Lounge of the American Women's Association clubhouse in Manhattan contained a series of murals by Lucile Howard and

M. Elizabeth Price. The Wednesday Club in San Diego hired Anna Valentien to produce all of the door plates, hardware, and copper and glass lanterns for their clubhouse. The Daughters of the Republic of Texas commissioned statues of Stephen Austin and Sam Houston by Elisabet Ney, which never adorned their clubrooms, but went to the United States Capitol Building.[58]

Even the more single-mindedly political organizations of women came to use fine art in their campaigns to win funding, publicity, and support for woman suffrage. The New York City–based Women's Political Union, bankrolled by wives of some of the most affluent industrialists in America, provides a stunning example. Suffragist Louisine Havemeyer, in possession of the American Sugar Refining Company fortune, possessed an extraordinary collection of Old Masters that had been obtained on the advice of the Philadelphia-born Impressionist painter Mary Cassatt. Although the works were enjoyed solely by wealthy friends of the Havemeyers, it appears that Louisine was persuaded by suffragist Harriot Stanton Blatch to loan anonymously her El Grecos and Goyas for exhibition at the Knoedler Gallery in New York, in April 1912, as a fund-raiser for the suffragist cause. Again, in April 1915, Havemeyer placed in exhibition her masterpieces by Degas, Cassatt, Bronzino, Van Dyck, Holbein, de Hooch, Rembrandt, Rubens, and Vermeer. She also persuaded other collectors to lend some of their works by Degas and Cassatt. The exhibition was controversial, since many art collectors were disdainful of its association with woman suffrage. Some feminists questioned the propriety of flaunting aristocratic playthings while many women starved. Still, the suffrage movement benefitted from the admission fees and many suffragists were untroubled, indeed delighted, by the suggestion that beauty was part of women's agenda for a brighter future.[59]

The most militant feminists of the period, in the National Woman's Party, who were also financed by wealthy women with political commitments, understood the significance of ennobling their heroines in statuary. The party's fairy godmother, Alva Belmont, commissioned marble busts of its leadership. Most importantly, Adelaide Johnson's seven-ton monument to the woman's rights triumvirate of Lucretia Mott, Susan B. Anthony, and Elizabeth Cady Stanton was dedicated at the United States Capitol Building, where it continues to be displayed, on the 15 February 1921 anniversary of Anthony's birth.[60] Replicas of the three busts also adorn the Washington D.C. headquarters of the National Woman's Party, alongside a gallery of portraits of suffrage leaders painted by women artists.

Outreach

Often the acquisition of permanent art works was not a realistic way for women's clubs to introduce art to a community. Touring exhibits were sometimes a more feasible way for women's clubs to acquaint the local citizenry with fine art. As always, clubwomen utilized avenues readily available to them—schools, libraries, and their own clubhouses—for the shows they assembled or borrowed on a temporary basis. Members also used additional public spaces to win wide exposure for their shows. The town hall, settlement houses, shop windows, community rooms in department stores, and state fairs all provided traffic for the collections clubs wished to display.

The GFWC and the AFA assisted their member clubs by assembling and serving as brokers for shows that were thought to appeal to clubwomen and the communities they served. At first, the GFWC created circulating exhibits intended to illustrate straightforward lessons in art history, painting, and sculpture. Quickly, however, the art committee decided to add flamboyant programs. Admitting that "this study does not appeal to a large proportion of our people," federation art leaders advised dealing with more accessible exhibitions, "with beauty in dress, home, garden, school . . . pioneer work in taste."[61] The federation enjoyed marked success circulating exhibitions of art by schoolchildren, graphic arts, or crafts. Fifty donated pieces of American art pottery, including clay pots from representative American potteries such as Rookwood and Grueby, toured to enthusiastic audiences, until the fragile pieces were retired in 1927 to national headquarters for safekeeping.[62] Another popular exhibit among women's clubs, "Made in the USA," illustrated concepts of sophisticated designs for the home. This show included samples of upholstery, silks, plushes, velours, velvets, laces, rugs, and wallpapers, as well as thirty photographs of furniture, fixtures, fireplace fittings, mantels, and silverware.[63] Fifty paintings by women artists, under the auspices of the Association of Women Painters and Sculptors, also traveled widely. By 1930, the GFWC launched its Penny Art Fund, which urged each member of a club to donate a penny to build a fund for the purchase of art by local talent, to be sent on tour.[64]

Department stores became willing allies of women who hoped to introduce art to constituencies beyond club membership. Robert Grier Cooke, president of the Fifth Avenue Association, promised the AFA's members that the New York displays would serve as leaders in encouraging art in commerce. In 1929 the Retail Trade Board of Boston agreed to support Art Week, a festival to create art awareness in the community.[65] Clubwomen in Boston decorated Filene's windows with merchandise selected by a jury of well-known artists for its artistic merit. In Dayton, Ohio, women's clubs united with the chamber of commerce, the retail merchants association, and the Display Men's Association to create "art windows" and merchandise artistically displayed during Art Week in February 1927. They thereby succeeded in bringing thousands of visitors to town in the dead shopping period between January sales and the arrival of the spring merchandise. Clearly, the goals of clubwomen in visual arts could unite with those of commerce.[66]

Clubwomen perceived that one of the most promising avenues for bringing visual art to the people was at the state or county fair. Members had been providing hospitality, tea, lounge areas, and sometimes even daycare facilities for women at fairs as a matter of course. It seemed logical that they should expand their services to include art exhibitions. Clubwomen were aware that forty million people attended state and county fairs each year, including rural people eager to see a wide variety of exhibits. For both the Spokane Art

League and the Michigan State Federation of Women's Clubs, the Women's Building at their states' fairs served as home for their arts and crafts exhibitions. Not everyone agreed that a fairground woman's building was the appropriate place for art to be shown, however. Jeannette Scott, an art instructor at Syracuse University, scorned the offer to exhibit industrial art by her students and by local Onondaga Reservation Indians in the Woman's Building at the New York State Fair. After two seasons in that female environment, she refused to be "relegated" there. More often, however, the coexistence of art with women's concerns won out. In Massachusetts, arts clubs linked their efforts with home economics clubs to put on a Better Homes Conference at the Eastern State Fairgrounds.[67]

By the early 1920s, clubwomen enjoyed success at persuading respected art institutions to loan fine art for the duration of the fair. In 1922, New York's Metropolitan Museum of Art displayed thirty oil paintings at the Oregon State Fair in Salem. Water colors graced the Tri-State Fair in Memphis; the National Academy of Design sent oils to the Tennessee State Fair in Nashville; and the American Society of Landscape Architecture sent garden photography to the Michigan State Fair in Detroit.[68]

Another route that art clubs used to make the arts more accessible was to bridge the distance between the general population and the art museum. Clubwomen became staunch advocates of museum outreach programs. This was a golden age for American art museums, insofar as numbers of donations and facilities multiplied rapidly, and this increase was due in part to the assistance of women's clubs. Now the women sought to deliver new audiences to tour the museum collections.

Clubwomen particularly applauded efforts to invite schoolchildren to exhibits, and to provide either knowledgeable docents or training for classroom teachers so that the young visitors would be guided to learn from the art treasures they viewed in municipal galleries. With luck, they would return with their parents, instructing them about the beauty in their city. In the hope of drawing new immigrants to the museum, art club members championed special festivals in which museums invited ethnic minorities to lend the handicrafts of their native lands for public examination. Clubwomen also endorsed the free admission policy that brought low-income citizens to the museums.[69] Museum administrators who told tales of the Polish worker who spent his Sundays enthralled at the Chicago Art Institute, or the black preacher who brought his Sunday school charges to take strength from the works of black painters, nurtured clubwomen's expectations that art could mend society's schisms.[70]

Members devised additional efforts to develop new friendships between paintings and people. This work to create an arts-loving America included the formation of Municipal Art Commissions, the erection of war memorials after World War I, and efforts to heighten the attractiveness of the cityscape and countryside. But as their history of frustration with a generally unresponsive wider club world and a skeptical public might have forewarned, they frequently found their own aspirations tamed, diluted, and even abandoned to meet the needs and fuel the dreams of other reformers. Repeatedly, the arts advocates accommodated conservationists, city planners, chambers of commerce, and boards of tourism in their communities.

Arts Outreach

One of clubwomen's least-known achievements is their collaboration with government to enhance public awareness of the importance of the arts. Like most reformers of the Progressive era, clubwomen trusted government. They had faith that their political leaders would respond to their calls for beauty in America. Clubwomen supportive of the arts began to urge Congress at the dawn of the twentieth century to fund a National Gallery for the Arts in Washington D.C.—an institution that would not be authorized until 1937. One element of their campaign to influence legislators and the executive branch consisted of inspiring schoolchildren to lobby their representatives. In the mid-1920s, clubwomen prepared to offer Anna Hyatt Huntington's bronze statue *Diana* as a prize to the high school that produced the most persuasive teenage lobbyist.[71]

In 1909, clubwomen also supported the Payne Tariff Bill, which admitted into the United States, free of duty, works of art over twenty years old. In 1913, they applauded Congressional removal of tariffs on new art as well. In 1921 and 1929, they opposed efforts to reinstate the tariff, on the grounds that obstacles to imported works of art reduced the strength of private collections that would eventually be donated to museums, ultimately educating the public. Clubwomen also supported the creation of the U.S. Commission of Fine Arts, created by Executive Order under Theodore Roosevelt in 1909, and established more firmly by legislative mandate in 1910. This permitted the President to appoint seven well-qualified judges of fine art to advise upon the location of statues, fountains, and monuments in the public squares, streets, and parks of the nation's capital city, and to review the artists and the work to be placed.

Municipal Art Commissions

One of the most important public arts issues clubwomen faced was the creation of Municipal Art Commissions (MACs). As early as 1906, clubwomen took on the mission of creating MACs in towns of every size "so adornment may be in the hands of experts, not politicians." The commissions were structured much like the U.S. Commission of Fine Arts. They consisted of boards of seven to ten artists and influential citizens, appointed by the mayor, to serve as a bridge between art experts, "whose interest lies entirely with the aesthetic side" of municipal life, and the large and practical general public, which was largely ignorant of the value of art.[72]

Clubwomen embraced the notion that these new governmental agencies could improve the taste of the general public by appointing professional artists to review proposals for future statues and monuments to be erected under the aegis of the government. While commissions never won the authority to destroy poor designs already executed, clubwomen hoped the supervision of new plans would serve to surround Americans with beauty and teach them to know and demand the best. They believed that the country's artistic strength would soon equal its political and economic power, and further define the United States as a world leader. A University of Chicago social scientist articulated these hopes, asking, "Shall she [the United States of America] not by being true to her traditions and her destiny, her manifest destiny, a democracy grand and great, develop an art such as the world has not yet seen?"[73] No more would schoolchildren pass through streets "embellished with grotesque monuments and inartistic drinking fountains."[74] Instead, works of beauty would become commonplace, "genuine works of art, works that will live through the decades, works that will speak of civic pride, patriotism and consideration of the future."[75] Even GFWC President Sarah Platt Decker, who had so succinctly dismissed the importance of Dante and, by implication, all the arts and their relevance to contemporary life, praised the founding of Municipal Art Commissions at the Boston Biennial of 1908. Instead of selecting the lowest bidder to create public monuments and memorials, she suggested, let our government officials defer to the expertise of professional artists to select the artists who would create civic art "to cultivate the eye and soul."[76]

It is generally conceded that New York City's Municipal Art Commission, founded as a private institution in the late nineteenth century, inspired those that followed it. It was formed out of the commitment of private individuals "to provide adequate sculptural and pictorial decorations for the public buildings and parks of the city of New York."[77] Its affluent male members raised money to place a mural in a courtroom, erect a memorial on Fifth Avenue to Richard Morris Hunt, and hold a competition and offer a prize for a well-designed City Hall flagstaff and drinking fountain. It was eventually chartered by the City of New York, in 1897. This status it would lose in 1927, to be regained later. In 1913 it held a convention, hosting representatives from twelve of the seventeen Municipal Art Commissions that had formed all around the nation. The cities of Baltimore (whose commission was founded in 1895), Los Angeles (1903), New Haven (1913), Philadelphia (1907), Milwaukee, Mount Vernon, New York, and the District of Columbia sent participants. So did the states of Connecticut and Massachusetts and the National Commission of Fine Arts. Not insignificantly, GFWC Art chairman, the tireless Mrs. Pattison of St. Louis, attended this Manhattan meeting, determined to suggest to both the existing commissions and the cities that still contemplated the formation of commissions, that clubwomen could be useful, indeed instrumental, in the success of these bodies.[78]

Clubwomen worked behind the scenes to create the commissions. In 1909 the AFA had announced that "the Federation of Women's Clubs, in membership eight hundred thousand strong, is found to be making a concerted and in some cases effectual, effort to secure the establishment of expert art commissions in every state."[79] The GFWC *Federation Bulletin* reproduced a draft of sample legislation that members could employ in their lobbying. Essentially providing a blueprint for the establishment of a Municipal Arts Commission in every town, the article advised that support for the commission be drawn from stronger bodies, like the local Civic League, Art Society, Business Men's League, Chamber of Commerce, mayor's "kitchen cabinet" of advisors, or federated women's club.[80]

Support for the formation of the commissions did not come only from arts advocates. MACs also won support from men and women who objected to traditional political patronage in government—a system under which not much respect had been shown for arts expertise as a qualification for an arts position. Support even came from those who were impatient with art, but eager to sensitize the public to other types of urban unsightliness:

> Civic art, the expression of civic life, is too often understood to consist in filling our streets with marble fountains, dotting our squares with groups of statuary, twining our lampposts with wriggling acanthus leaves or dolphins' tails, and our buildings with meaningless bunches of fruit and flowers tied up with impossible stone ribbons.[81]

Another supporter, secretary of the American Civic Association, sought to link the goals of the Civic Betterment Movement with MACs. He wanted the commissions to inspire tidiness, better sanitation, window boxes, tablets on surviving landmarks, and tree planting as their mission.[82] His notions prevailed. The MACs did indeed drift into civic beautification issues, and ultimately spent far greater efforts on landscaping than on sponsorship of public art.

It is not widely realized that clubwomen were a pivotal force in the creation and maintenance of the arts commissions—the forerunners of today's local arts councils—in hundreds of communities. For example, the Minnesota Commission was formed in 1903, thanks in large part to pressure from Minnesota's State Federation of Women's Clubs. Members of St. Cloud's Art and History Club, while studying the subject of France, observed the phenomenon of support for arts by the French government. Determined to replicate this arrangement, the group's officers introduced the concept at their district convention in 1898, and won the support of the president of Minnesota's State Federation of Women's Clubs, Mrs. Margaret J. Evans. With the entire federation behind the proposal, Governor Van Sant and the 1903 legislature agreed to establish a state art commission (also known as the State Art Society). They appropriated two thousand dollars per year to the endeavor. The commission's objects were ambitious: "to advance the interest of the fine arts, to develop the influence of art in education and foster the introduction of art in manufactures." The modest budget of the Minnesota art commission, even supplemented by memberships and donations, would not have permitted appreciable activity had not women's volunteer power fueled the agency. Clubwomen on the State Art Society Board delivered the unpaid labor that established a lecture service, a traveling exhibition program, the loan of photographs of masterpieces of Western art, and the beginnings of an original art collection. Through the cooperation of the St. Cloud Reading Room Society, the society initiated an annual exhibition. In 1911, with an increased appropriation of $7,500, the society was able to hire Maurice Irwin Flagg as part-time director to expand the services. This advance did not mean that clubwomen dropped out, however. The financial support of the Farm Woman's Congress, for instance, erected a prize-winning farmhouse at the 1915 State Fair. In wartime, state funding for such projects collapsed, but clubwomen revived the Minnesota State Art Society in 1921. It foundered in 1927, and was again revived in the mid-1940s.[83]

Certainly the record documents the appointment of club members to serve on municipal or state commissions. Among these were the two members of the Ruskin Art Club in Los Angeles who served on the 1907 Los Angeles Art Commission. In 1930, the Ebell Club of Los Angeles was proud to announce the appointment of one of its members as president of the Los Angeles City Art Commission.[84] In Utah, Miss Mabel Frazer of Salt Lake City served in the early 1920s on the Utah State Art Commission, in addition to her service as president of the Utah Educational Association's Art Section, and as president of Associated Craftsmen, a club that included members of both sexes. In 1930, Miss Rena Olsen of Salt Lake City served on the Utah Art Commission; she was also elected vice-president of the Utah Art Institute, an AFA affiliate. In Alabama, Mrs. Frank Elmore of Montgomery was appointed to the state art commission in 1921, while she served as vice-president of the Alabama Art League. Mrs. J. Howard Palmer of Minneapolis served as vice-president of the Minnesota State Art Commission in 1921, while she also served as the Minnesota Art chairman for the GFWC.[85]

More often than they themselves served on the commissions, however, clubwomen simply took a stand in favor of the appointment of art experts to the commissions, and opposed decision making by politicians and their associates. At the 1910 Biennial Conference of the GFWC, Art chairman Alice Pattison addressed this patient willingness of clubwomen to remain invisible:

> Many of the best organized and most successful Civic Art movements have originated in Women's Clubs. I have in mind a very large civic body which owes its inception and many of its working methods to one club woman. This woman, by her courageous persistence, enlisted a large membership, raised a fund, very cleverly put the right men into office, and persuaded the right women to serve upon the committees. The dear men were so pleased with the success of her efforts, that they gradually came to consider the whole movement their own. The women have gracefully withdrawn from prominence, while keeping a watchful eye upon plan and performance, and they rejoice in the new parks and city lighting, in the new statues and fountains, in the boulevard system and in the proposed Art Commission ... the women have suggested and initiated, the men adopted and completed. If the desired results are obtained, we women are more than half content; yet the Commission of both men and women is a higher ideal.[86]

In this respect, club members' support of a concept, rather than the lobbying for clubwomen to populate the commission, resembled their efforts in civil service reform and sanitation inspection.

Who served on the commissions, if clubwomen generally did not? The Municipal Art Commission members usually consisted of two different types of individuals. First were the art professionals. Three professional artists, painters, architects, and landscape architects generally advised on the proposed statues, fountains, and war memorials in the town. The other group that served on the Commissions were prominent individuals in the town: philanthropic industrialists, directors of arts institutions, respected businessmen—said "to keep the artists down to earth,"[87]—and increasingly, representatives of civic associations in the community such as arts associations. The boards were purposely devised to include participation from several constituencies. While the MACs fell far short of representing universal participation in public artistic questions, they managed to act as brokers for the knowledgeable public. In so doing, the commission furthered the clubwomen's aim of widening citizen participation or community self-determination.

Clubwomen's anonymity in establishing these cultural advisory bodies and their infrequent direct participation is puzzling until we remember that most women at the turn of the century were not motivated by the desire to bask in the spotlight or to assume power for the glory of it. Rather, they were content to defer to arts experts and the monied, powerful men in their towns who enjoyed wide respect and influence, in order to see that their aim of placing the finest art before the public was realized. Clubwomen remained behind the scenes, agitating to make sure the commissions were established to supervise quality art. Hence, their central role has been overlooked, although their success was formidable.

The alliance of various community groups supporting MACs did not protect them from controversy. Particularly when they were perceived to attack the methods whereby businesspeople attracted customers—as when they withheld approval of billboards—the art faction ran afoul of more powerful forces. In a small village in metropolitan New York, an all-woman board, carrying out "an essentially feminine beautification mission,"[88] asked a butcher to remove unsightly gizzards from his display window. The mayor disbanded the commission in the face of outrage at the women's obstruction of commerce. Similarly, the members of the board in Cincinnati[89] felt they had to back off from their attack on billboards, so deeply did it anger local influential businessmen.

Adherents of MACs soon learned that their survival depended on diminishing their antagonism toward commerce and emphasizing the assistance the commissions could lend. Boards bent over backwards to claim that the beautiful city they advocated was less a burden to taxpayers than a boon to commercial development. One sociologist promised that "beautiful and picturesque features of a city will raise the value of real estate, make higher rents, and increase business prosperity in general, attracting desirable visitors, and drawing to it and keeping residents who have the means to go where they will."[90] Others echoed the sentiment that "beauty is an excellent investment, a wise commercial policy."[91] Many MACs persuaded the railroads to landscape the approach to their yards, on the grounds that rail travelers' first impression of the town would be a more positive one, which would boost general confidence in the community.[92]

Thus, public support for MACs came to depend upon the commission's promotion of city beautification—however distant this might carry arts advocates from their desire for quality statuary. The success the MACs enjoyed was due less to the conversion of the general public to appreciation of fine art than to other interests. The ability of arts advocates to piggyback on the wider enthusiasm for humanizing urban life assured their inclusion in the municipal improvement momentum that institutionalized better sewage disposal, street lights, and sanitation inspections, and generated pocket parks out of unsightly vacant lots, street trees to unify neighborhood landscapes, and playgrounds to keep children safely out of traffic. Not surprisingly, the same clubwomen who awarded prizes for school gardens, planted trees in the parks on Arbor Day, and advocated the use of "smokeless" coal, joined their art-loving sisters to rally behind the call for MACs, if only to ensure the attractiveness of public spaces. The existence of the MAC, in the eyes of clubwomen, did more than wrest artistic control from political incompetents and place it in the hands of experts. The commission also spread responsibility and decentralized authority, by engaging representatives of artistically knowledgeable citizen groups to assist in decision making about the design of their town.

Women in art clubs planted the notion of establishing MACs in cities of every size. In the long run, their effort flowered into the elaborate network of government-funded arts councils, populated by arts experts who today review public arts proposals for federal, state, or local grants. Since 1965, the federal government has assisted state governments to follow the model of the New York state plan, implemented by Governor Nelson Rockefeller in 1960, a scheme, in turn, closely modeled on early twentieth century MACs.

Insofar as MACs acted as censors, rejecting art that was too flagrantly modern for the taste of the members (as when the National Commission of Fine Arts rejected Gertrude Whitney's Red Cross nurse in modern dress for one in classical attire), or at least remained stubbornly mindful of the neoclassical preferences of the public, they passed on, unsolved, the tangles of fashion and social pressure in determining the so-called quality of art. With all their limitations and their achievements of democratizing public access to the arts, MACs can be said to have framed the issues of content and form in government support for art with which the modern United States has continued to struggle.

Two other successful programs on which women's visual arts clubs embarked during the Progressive Era can only broadly be defined as art-related. These two campaigns—one opposing billboards on the highways, and the other supporting the creation of war monuments after World War I—require considerable latitude to be connected with the concerns of the world of visual arts. The application of art club energies toward such widely divergent issues testifies to the meager support for art appreciation accorded by either the parent club movement or the broader public. The only way to comprehend such diverse interests among so-called art lovers is to view their entire activity as a campaign for an attractive environment. While arts clubs made paintings available in museums, schools, and temporary exhibitions, they also put considerable effort into achieving an uncluttered landscape, clear of billboards, and into the placement of statuary commemorating the war dead. The aim of these undertakings was to establish surroundings more beautiful and uplifting than had been available previously. In so defining their work, art lovers could lure the clubwomen who were unresponsive to the charms of the Old Masters, to work for a more wholesome American environment. If their goals were diluted, their program was far-reaching; and their forces were staggering, in numbers, talent, and energy.

Arts Clubs Work for Natural Beauty

One of the issues most vehemently supported by women in art clubs was not an art issue at all. The eradication of billboards from highways became a major plank in the club platforms. At the expense of projects more closely allied with fine arts, art club members devoted countless local meetings, general conferences, publications, newsletters, and influence to seeking the demise of roadside advertising. A rural counterpart of the City Beautiful Movement tapped by the MAC campaign, billboard opposition enjoyed the support of a whole range of women environmentalists, among them members of the Forestry or Conservation Departments of federated clubs; the Women's Outdoor Art League; and the Garden Club of America. All advocated the removal of new, unsightly advertising along the roadways.

Arts club women understood the fragility of the landscape in their era. The preservation of the American wilderness was a patriotic notion in the 1920s, a notion women's clubs had played no small part in nurturing. Women devoted to fine art were invited to broaden their work to promote beauty outdoors, and they rode the coattails of the more popular issue, no doubt sympathetic with its goals and with the patriotic impulses underneath it, and perhaps hopeful that if they supported the lovers of natural beauty, their projects would be supported in turn. The two movements did reciprocate, insofar as the leadership of the GFWC permitted the public to perceive all its million members as endorsing art education in the schools.

Members of the art clubs, then, stepped into the world of nature lovers and worked alongside their civic-minded sisters to protect the natural environment. In Miami, Florida, for example, clubwomen in 1916 purchased and then maintained for thirty-one years the four-thousand acre Royal Palm Park. Afterwards, it became Everglades National Park. In 1929, Maryland women collected $325 to buy a 160-acre Maryland Federation Forest in the western part of their state and aspired to acquire similar groves in Southern Maryland and on the Eastern Shore. In 1926, Washington State women began collecting the $25,000 needed to purchase its Federation Forest from the Snoqualamie Falls Lumber Company. The forest was dedicated to Washington State Federation of Women's Clubs' environmentalist president Esther Maltby. Likewise, in 1925, the Shakespeare Club of Pasadena, California, held a "Save the Redwoods" benefit, with films and a performance of bird calls, to raise money toward the purchase of Redwood Grove in Jordan Creek, Humboldt County. A marker recognizes a grove that was preserved thanks to the $45,000 raised for this purpose by the California Federation of Women's Clubs; and a Federation Hearthstone, conceived by architect Julia Morgan, encourages picnickers to linger there.[93]

Women's clubs' interest in nature was not confined to rural America. The urban scene was also scrutinized for elements of ugliness. Officers of the GFWC and AFA were present at the American Civic Association Conference at which City Beautiful was proposed as the theme for year-long efforts. In downtown Baltimore, the Women's Civil League cooperated with the Home Garden Committee and the Municipal Art Society to sponsor a plant fair, at which cuttings were sold at the foot of the Washington Monument to yard-starved city dwellers. They spent the proceeds to establish gardens in vacant lots in the city. Members of Sorosis, in Wilmington, North Carolina, initially met with little success in urging the neighbors of each residential street to select their own flower for planting, for the purpose of creating distinctive neighborhoods. However interest skyrocketed once the clubwomen had persuaded a local corporation to offer a prize of $250 for the most beautiful yard, plaza, and hedge. The club used this momentum to initiate a clean-up day, and to assist school children in planting a school garden.[94] At this time Shakespeare Gardens enjoyed a vogue among clubwomen, who planted each of the specimens mentioned in Shakespeare's plays in the gardens of their clubhouses, their public libraries, women's colleges, and public parks. Here was an ingenious way to wed the interests of readers with outdoorspeople.

Billboards

To clubwomen no problem bespoke the modern threat to natural beauty more clearly than the popularity of the roadside billboard. At first, the strategies employed by clubwomen to oppose billboards were utterly predictable. These included publicizing the unattractiveness of roadside advertising at conventions, and inviting the companies that advertised on billboards to refrain from further use of them. These methods enjoyed only limited success. In 1910, however, GFWC delegates to the national convention discussed a resolution to boycott offending companies. Characteristically, they defeated the measure, which they perceived as a negative attack on U.S. corporations. The censorship of advertising simply would not wash with the ladies. Throughout their history, clubs preferred to bring about change by creating new institutions or reforming old ones, rather than challenging existing structures. Their rejection of the boycott reaffirms their positive approach to politics. The Women's Christian Temperance Union's effort to legalize the prohibition of alcohol, for example, was one from which the GFWC kept its distance. Instead, their style was to embrace the funding of public drinking fountains for the abstinent.

However positive they attempted to be in their approaches, clubwomen came to feel stymied by the absence of voluntary cooperation by advertisers. Attempting a fresh start after wartime and post-war distractions, the GFWC united with forty other organizations in December 1923, over the issue of roadside billboard removal.[95] They formed the National Committee for Restriction of Outdoor Advertising. Among the members of the Executive Committee were art committee leaders Rose Berry and Anna Maxwell Jones. The object of this alliance was to pressure advertisers whose billboards were seen as defacing the countryside.[96] The women were careful to draw a distinction between the restriction, as opposed to the abolition, of signboard advertising in order to save scenic beauty.

The anti-billboard alliance enjoyed a victory in 1925, when an impressive list of national advertisers agreed to confine their billboards to commercial locations.[97] Thereafter club successes multiplied. Local groups were effective in winning support close to home. Southern clubs persuaded the Daytona Beach Chamber of Commerce not to erect one thousand billboards planned for highways of Florida, Georgia, and the Carolinas. Standard Oil Company of California removed twelve hundred signs from five states, while the Benoit Company of Portland, Maine, removed four hundred billboards.[98]

Not all effort was rewarded with success, however. As we have already observed, the Cincinnati companies that advertised with billboards were incensed at this perceived interference, and forced the local Municipal Art Commission to back off from its criticism. The commission withdrew its request for abolition of roadside advertising to preserve itself. In three states, clubwomen could not agitate against the advertisers of billboards, for they had accepted free advertising for their own projects from the offenders.[99]

Clearly, seeking capitulation from individual companies was a Sisyphean labor. Recognizing this fact, clubwomen moved to legislation to deal with the billboard problem. "Do not for a moment think that Self-Regulation by the Billboard Industry will do it," warned Mrs. W. L. Lawton at the 1927 Biennial, despite her report that more and more individual companies had agreed to restrict their advertising.[100] Furthermore, where legislation had been enacted, clubwomen realized that they needed to demand enforcement of the unenforced state laws. One clubwoman claimed that the 1925 Massachusetts billboard law had been ignored for six years.[101]

Only in the late 1920s did clubwomen move to launch an aggressive plan against companies' use of billboards. Mindful of the collective refusal to endorse a boycott in 1910, they decided to stop short of a boycott, and instead reward companies that conceded to anti-billboard demands, much as the National Women's Trade Union League had used White Lists to reward companies that provided fair conditions for women workers. Regional associations of clubs, in the eastern part of the United States, the Midwest, the West, and finally the Southeast, publicized the companies that withdrew their billboard advertising, and resolved to use their products over those of companies still defacing the landscape.[102] The fight continued into the 1930s, when gains continued to be made through the constant vigilance of clubwomen.

Art and War

World War I provided another vital issue around which art clubs rallied. Since American involvement in the war became almost universally supported, members could once again attach their dreams for a more artistic America to a popular issue. Like members of music clubs, art clubwomen first used the war to demonstrate the relevance of art to support for the emergency effort. They praised the painters of camouflage that masked defenses on U.S. soil. They attested to the importance of stirring patriotism, inspiring loyalty, and selling Liberty Bonds through eye-catching posters designed by artists. When museums created war-related exhibitions—photographs of the Italian front, water color sketches for YMCA huts in France, and cartoons by Raemaekers, to name a few—clubwomen were quick to recommend the shows to their memberships and their neighbors.[103] Art clubs themselves also circulated war picture exhibits that had been assembled by the AFA, including lithographs of munitions plants, photographs of French cathedrals and churches in the war zone, and Lucien Jonas's scenes of France, illustrating the valor of the French people.[104] The members of the Art Association of Newport, Rhode Island opened clubhouse doors on Sunday afternoons to provide special classes in drawing for the navy men stationed in their city.[105]

In order that no one might dismiss art advocacy as trivial during the emergency, art clubs aggressively appealed to the wartime patriotic impulse. Art lovers used the war effectively to make the point that art was essential to refresh the spirit, and to keep basic values in perspective—in times of catastrophe, no less than in peacetime. Massachusetts clubwomen emphasized the importance of boosting morale for those at home. "We entreat you not to drop your art activity because we are a nation at war. If we anticipate times of stress and gloom, let us not prepare by abandoning all that is cheerful. Rather let us get ready by keeping alive every interest which brightens and gives color to existence," one clubwoman admonished her sisters.[106] Charles Dudley Watson, in a speech to clubwomen, insisted that art could teach responsible leadership skills to a nation emerging as a world power. "With the establishment of world democracy and lasting peace in the hands of America," he asked, "is it not up to us as individuals to learn all we can of the laws of order, harmony and beauty? Is it not a natural obligation, an essential part of true patriotism!"[107] However the pages of the *American Art Annual* spoke more succinctly, admonishing its subscribers to cultivate painting now more than ever, with the biblical injunction "without vision the people perish."[108]

War Memorials

Once the Armistice was signed, art supporters assumed an authoritative role, warning Americans to erect war memorials of taste, by knowledgeable American sculptors, rather than succumbing to flashy, impressive, empty, and inexpensive markers peddled by cemetery salesmen. "Hundreds of war memorials will within the next few years be erected in all parts of our country and pity indeed will it be if instead of worthily commemorating the noble spirit of the youth of our land they merely testify to the ignorance and misguided zeal of those by whom they are erected," admonished one advocate of tasteful statuary.[109] Clubwomen called on every community to commemorate the valor of American soldiers by erecting a special war monument, shaped to the needs of the particular town. They scorned the Civil War memorials that dotted the American landscape, uninspired statues of a single soldier, each one just like all the others. Art Chairman Mrs. Cyrus Perkins warned, "What is feared is a repetition of the artistic crimes committed after the Civil War as typified by the commercial stone soldier standing around in most of our towns.[110] A speaker at the Pennsylvania Convention of clubwomen went so far as to joke about the abominations: "After the Civil War, someone in surveying a soldiers' monument sadly remarked, 'now I understand the horrors of war.'"[111]

The women joined in a call for individually designed bronze or marble statuary (or flagpoles, benches, or tablets for less affluent communities) that specifically reflected the expression, and perhaps the building materials, native to the individual locale. The arts organizations self-consciously advised any and all listeners to consider seriously the elements—site, form, simplicity, and lettering—that would contribute to an artistic rendering of the town's patriotism.[112] They assured impoverished city councils that a wide variety of memorials were appropriate to the community unable to afford a commission of several thousand dollars by a renowned sculptor. They suggested commissioning a flagstaff with memorial base, or a fountain, bridge, building, tablets, gateways, symbolic groups of statuary, portrait statues of individuals, medals, stained glass windows, the creation of a village green, a bell tower, even a memorial doorway or room.[113] They published the likely costs of such memorials, to encourage even small communities to erect something tasteful. A stone seat could be had for five hundred dollars, a fifty-five foot flagstaff on a stone platform for four thousand dollars; a bandstand for twenty thousand, and an elaborate fountain in a serene green space, for fifty thousand dollars.[114]

Clubwomen hoped that wide discussion of the elements in war memorial design would tutor Americans in stylistic lessons they had never learned before. The search for an appropriate and attractive plan, before the monument even stood in the town square, presented to any community a lesson in the importance of knowledge and appreciation of art and in giving the people's abstract vision a visual form. This movement, wedding the goals of fine arts advocates with the public outpouring of grief for the war dead and, more particularly, with the pain of club members who had lost sons to the cause, seemed to win universal approval within women's clubs.

Far from delivering the decision making to the mayor and his friends, the women wanted to see their neighbors come together to define the type of statement they wished to make about their nation. This process of ordinary Americans shaping the symbols of themselves perpetuated the commitment to democracy for which the soldiers had died. It also echoed the clubwomen's steadfast advocacy of drawing the people together to exercise their prerogatives. As was true for the Liberty Sings, town history pageants, and community theatres, the public debate over the choice of a war memorial would school Americans afresh in the mechanisms of democratic behavior.

Fast on the heels of post-war enthusiasm for well-designed monuments came, predictably, dissent. Women skilled in attacking social problems directly by funding post-war orphanages, veterans' hospitals, and relief for war-torn Europe, called for more practical types of war memorials. Echoing the lack of enthusiasm for fine art that had beset art lovers and caused them to join the attack on billboards, a call arose, within clubs and without, for "living" memorials; that is, for more useful statements of commemoration. This call spelled disaster for the members of art clubs. Suddenly, support for fine statuary waned, as mourners realized they could honor the dead by planting rows of trees along the highway, or by erecting municipal recreation centers, auditoriums, or swimming pools, thereby creating pleasant gathering places in which the living might enjoy life fully, as the nation's war casualties could not.

Arts advocates protested vehemently. They perceived an insincere linkage between the building of a long-needed playground that had never previously enjoyed sufficient financial support, and the patriotic impulse to memorialize the war dead. Club members asserted that this was a despicable way to pretend to celebrate wartime valor.[115] One disappointed supporter of statues wrote:

> Let us not dishonor the noble spirit we would commemorate by using the sentiment of the hour merely to attain a desired material end. . . . A name on a building or a park ceases with the passing of years to convey special meaning other than designation. Our war memorials . . . must speak the language understood by all people—the universal language of art—must be beautiful, as beautiful as it is possible for genius to conceive and man to create.[116]

Nevertheless, the examples of memorials that were tied to the interests of conservationists and urban reformers were many. Among the living memorials with which nature-loving clubwomen became involved most earnestly were programs to plant trees on the community landscape. Minneapolis clubwomen planted five thousand trees along Victory Drive in memory of their dead soldiers after the war, while Seattle and Tacoma women planted elms along Hiline Highway for the veterans. Trees hugging George Washington Parkway, along the Potomac River, also represented clubwomen's memorialization of the war dead.[117]

Undoubtedly, part of the reason for the popularity of planting trees to memorialize war dead was its relatively low cost compared to the expense of sculpture. The arts advocates who had hoped to sprinkle the nation with fine statuary by respected American artists shared the wealth, once again, with adherents of natural beauty and urban reform.

Unlike the performing arts of music, pageantry, and theatre, visual arts did not enjoy wide appeal in the Progressive Era. Clubwomen could not make artists out of every American citizen and newcomer to our shores. The clubs' efforts to teach art history to children and other citizens in schools, libraries, museums, state fairs, and department stores, brought only limited success, insofar as most Americans remained skeptical about the utility of absorbing the accomplishments of the Old Masters, or even of local painters and sculptors. Instead, clubwomen discovered a compromise position in arguing that their communities required more beautiful environments; that their cities, the surrounding countryside, and even their homes could make them better people, if only attention were paid to beauty. This compromise brought them into increasing contact with the movements for city planning, conservation, patriotism, and home economics. Arts adherents lent enormous support to these movements, and enabled them to make great strides in social reform.

Thus, arts clubwomen often found themselves far from their love of art. Diluting their passion for visual arts more than any of their counterparts in theatre and music clubs, they were least successful in justifying their goals in a social context. Instead, they brought their energy to the creation and functioning of the Municipal Art Commissions, especially in their role of watchdogs for war memorials and supporters of American-made crafts. When they had the opportunity to bring visual arts to public attention, they favored conventional styles. Their respect for the Old Masters, in deference to the professional experts, was strong. Their distaste for the avant-garde and controversial was genuine, while their attention to the work of local artists arose from an unquestioning patriotism. Only their regard for professional women's art broke rank with conservative traditionalism. In this area they achieved the goals of many feminists of the day, in seeking new opportunities for the modern woman.

The clubwomen's call for the availability of art to all people was legitimated by their role as mothers to the community. Importantly, that call shaped the ideals that helped move the federal government to fund the Works Progress Administration in the 1930s, and laid the groundwork for the National Endowment for the Arts in the 1960s. The controversies that have since beset both federal programs also reflect the issues debated years earlier by arts advocates in women's clubs.

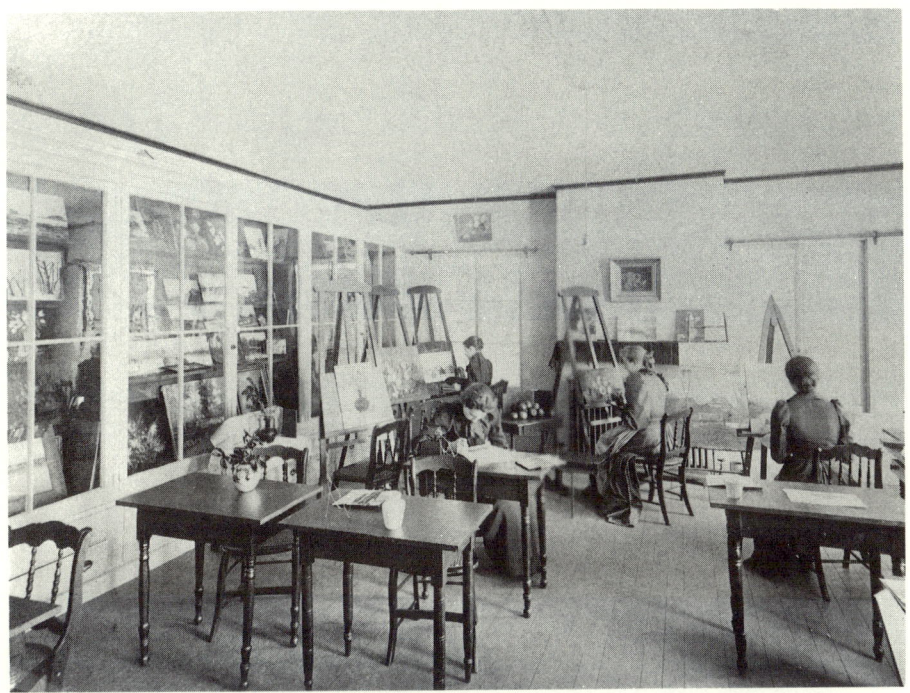

Women students in art studio, Mount Holyoke College, South Hadley, Massachusetts (Mount Holyoke College Library/Archives)

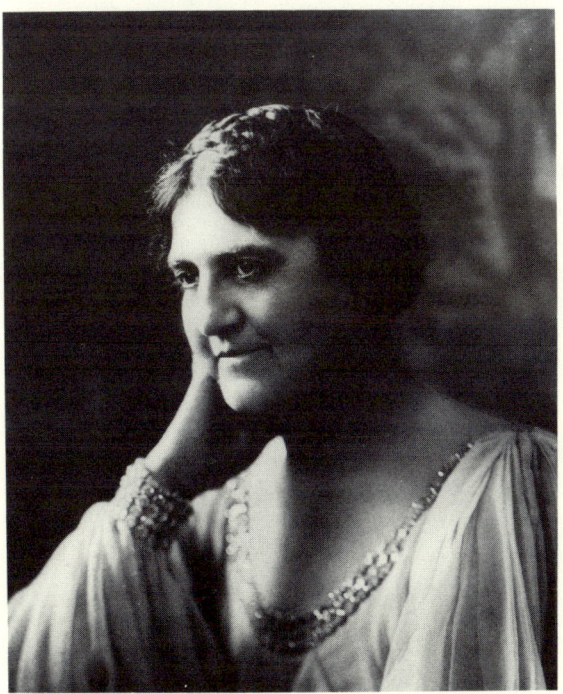

Roberta Campbell Lawson, expert on Native American music and president of the General Federation of Women's Clubs, 1935 to 1938 (Photo courtesy of the General Federation of Women's Clubs Archives)

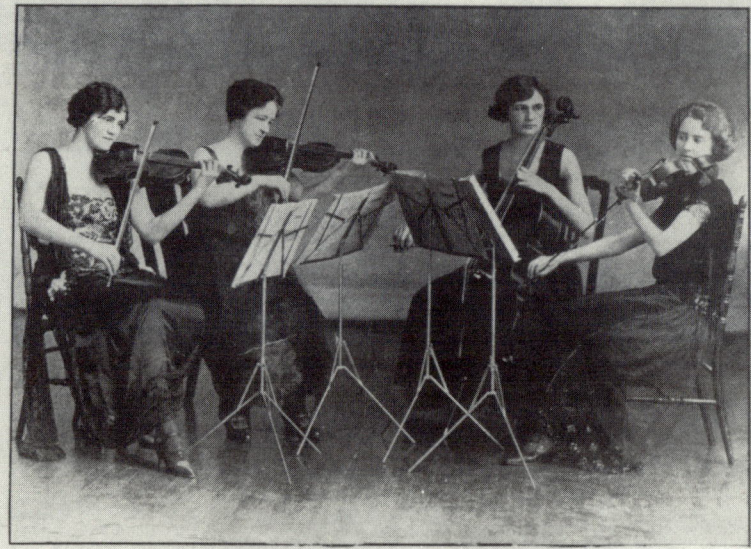

Four members of the Seattle Ladies Musical Club formed a string quartet, which performed during the 1920s. From left to right: Margaret McCullough, first violin; Alice Williams Sherman, second violin; Iris Canfield, cello; Louise Benton, viola (Museum of History and Industry, Seattle, Washington)

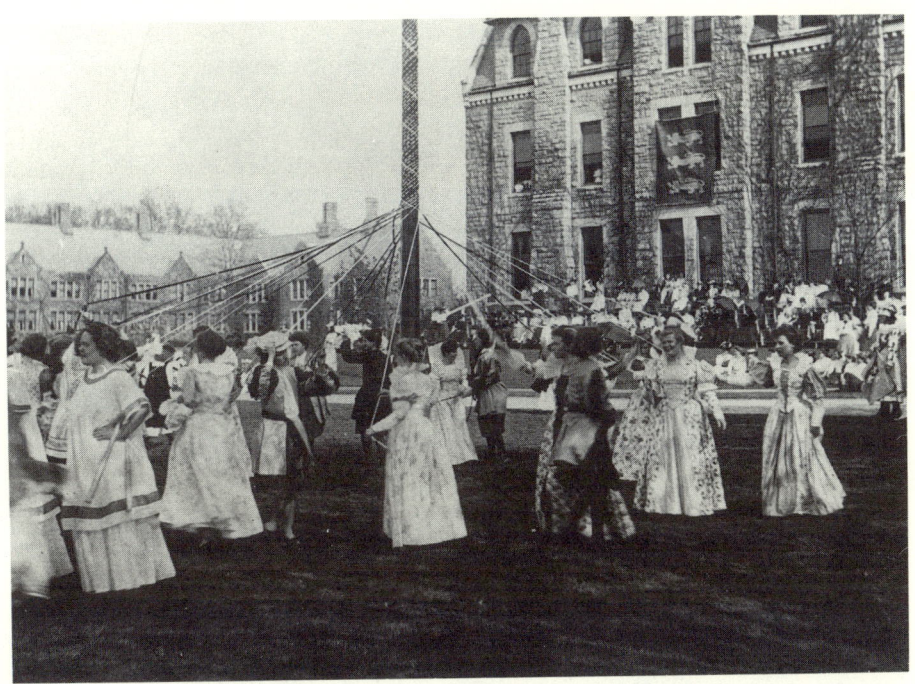

The first May Day celebration, Bryn Mawr College, Bryn Mawr, Pennsylvania (Bryn Mawr College Archives)

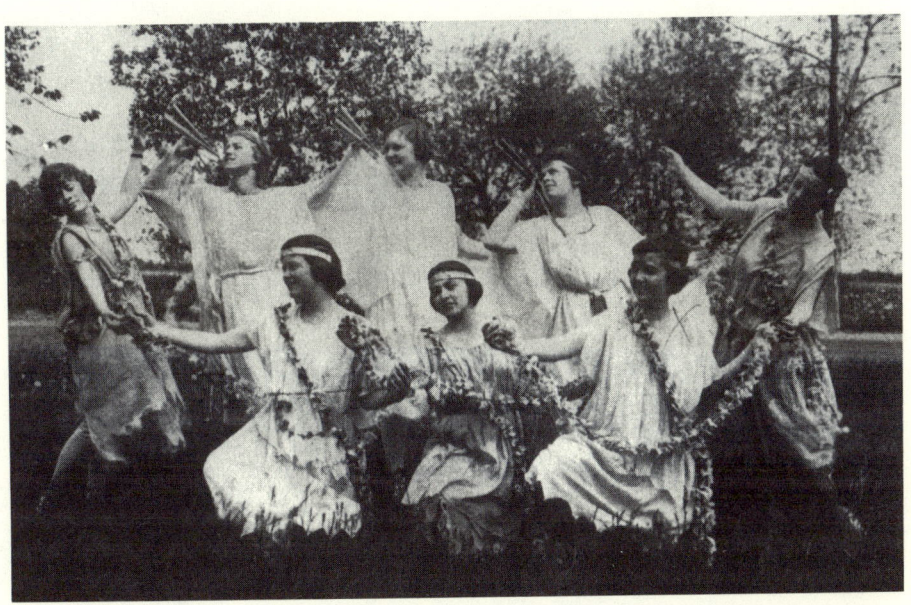

"Art and Poetry," a scene from Nina B. Lamkin's pageant, *The Passing of the Kings*, performed at Northwestern University in June 1919 (From Nina B. Lamkin, *The Passing of the Kings*. Chicago: T. S. Denison and Co., 1920)

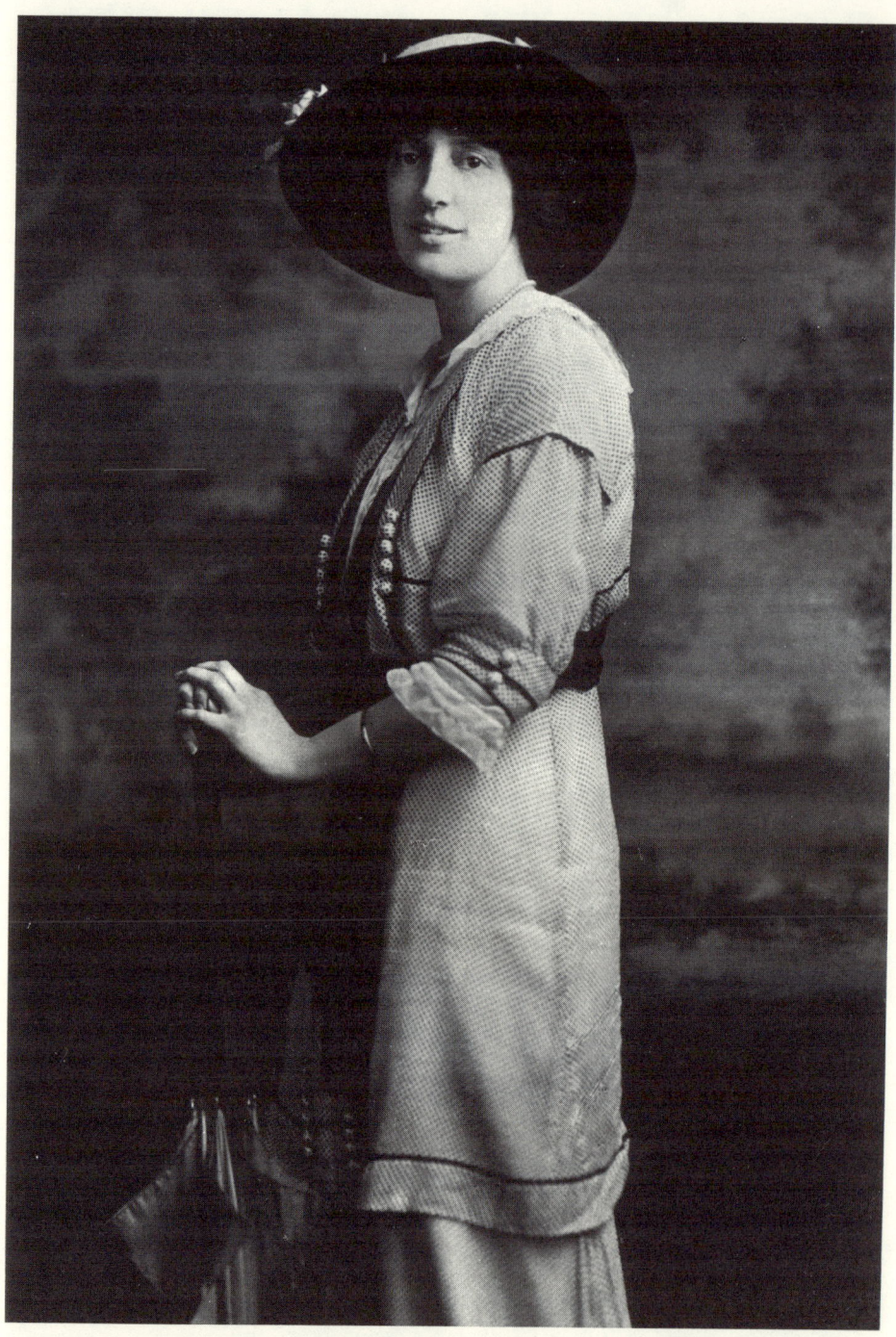

Hazel MacKaye, Pageant-Maker (Library of Congress)

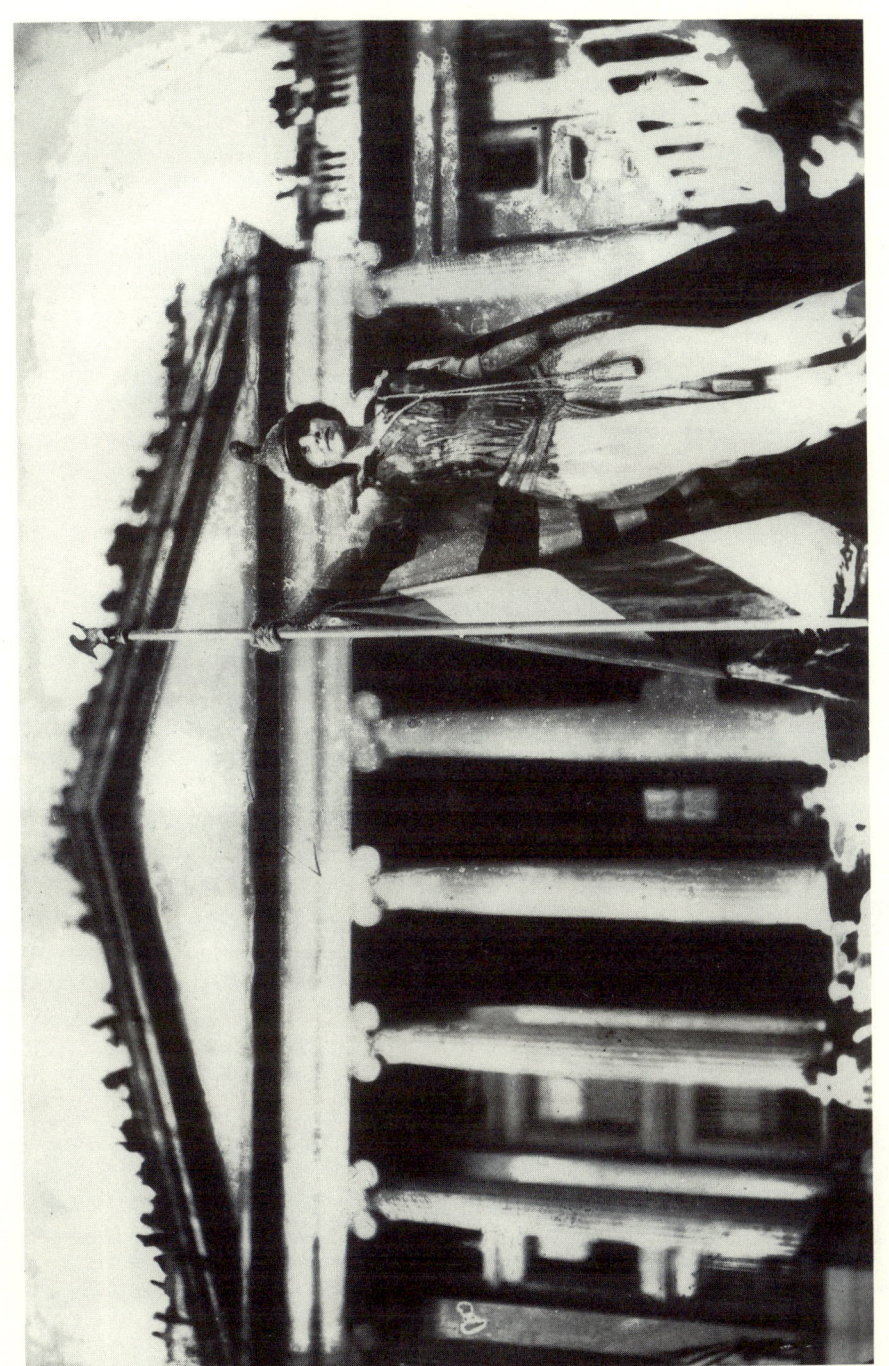

Scene from *Allegory*, Hazel MacKaye's pageant for the National American Woman's Suffrage Party, performed in Washington, D.C., in March 1913 (Library of Congress)

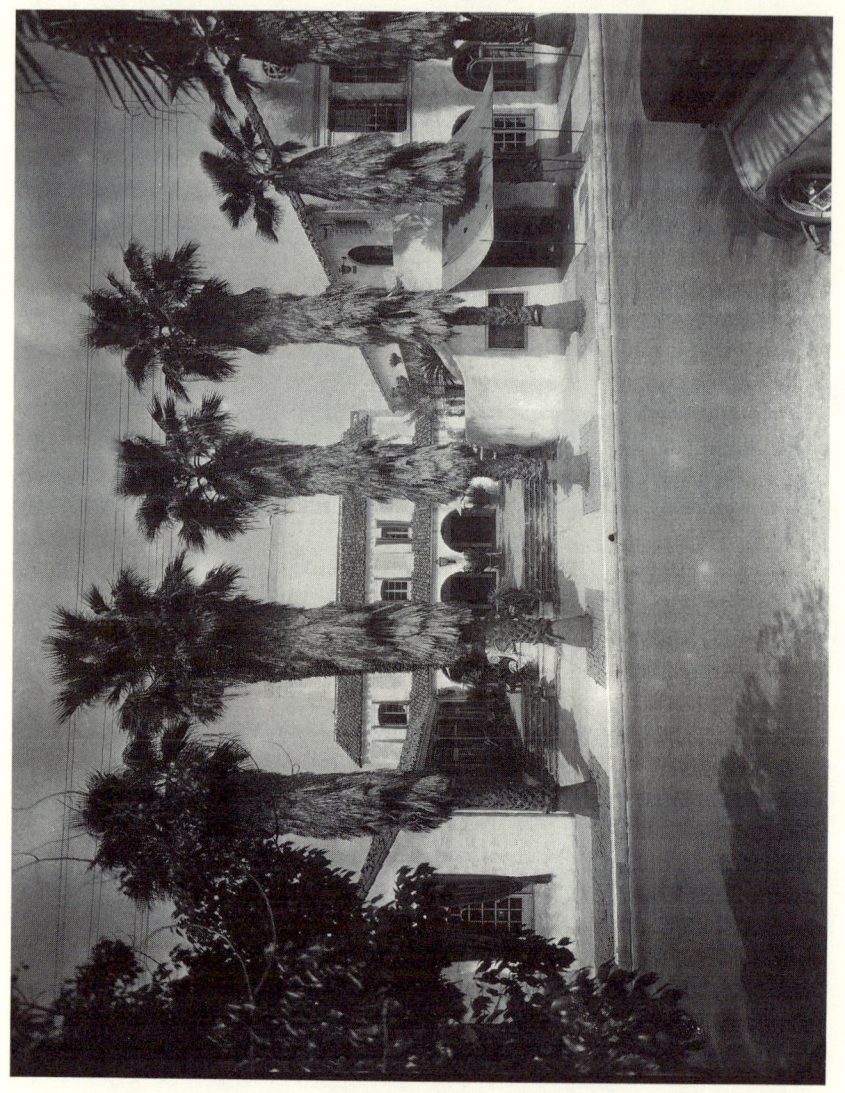

Exterior of the Pasadena Community Playhouse in 1928 (Huntington Library, San Marino, California)

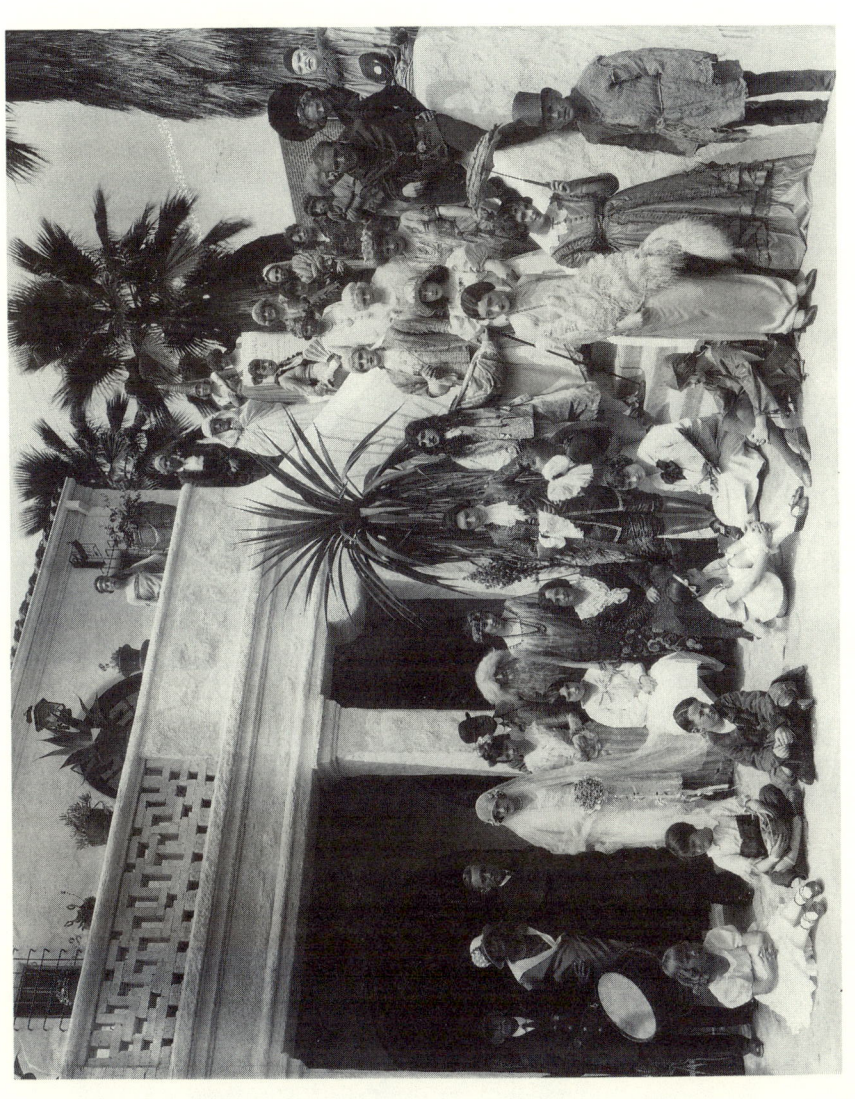

The cast of *The Amethyst*, at the Pasadena Community Playhouse, 1925 (Huntington Library, San Marino, California)

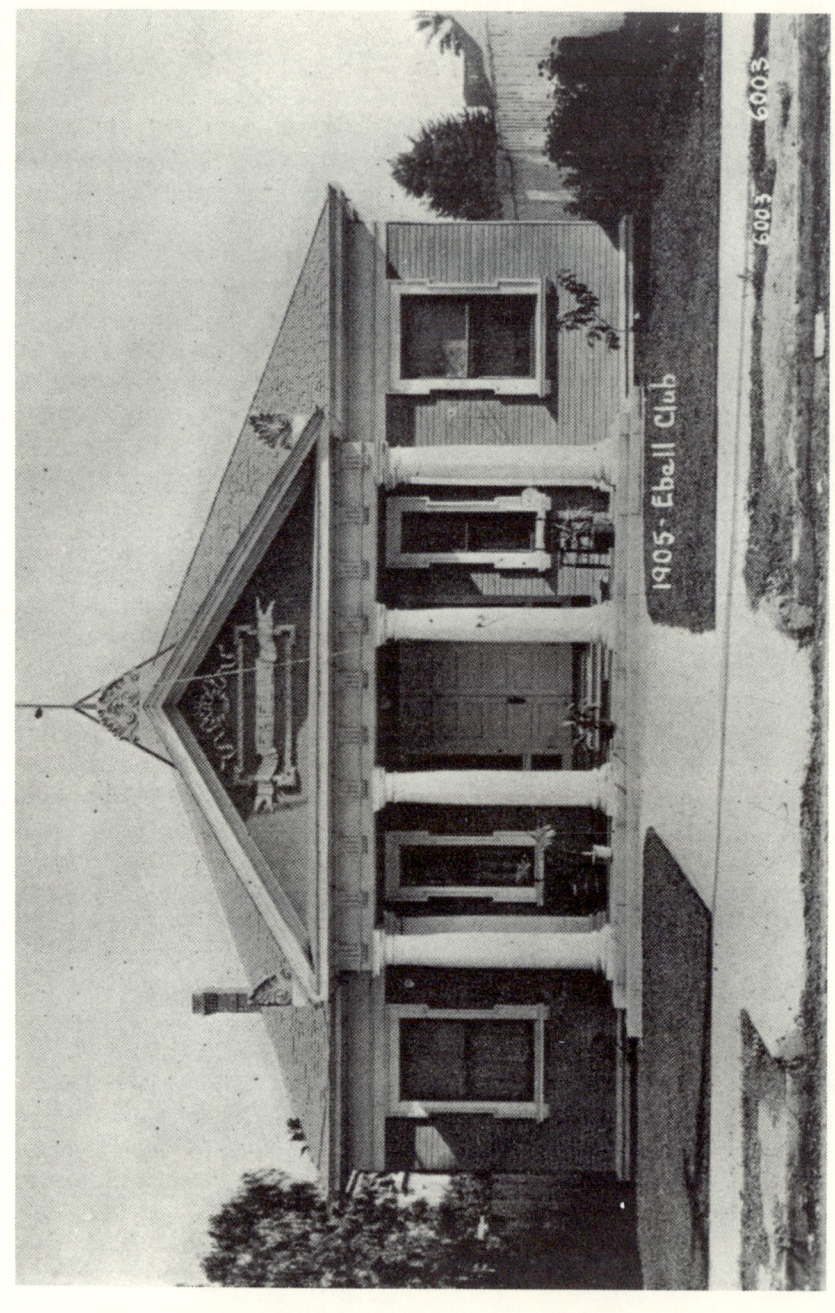

Exterior of the Ebell Club's fourth clubhouse (1897–1902) at 724 South Broadway, Los Angeles, California (Huntington Library, San Marino, California)

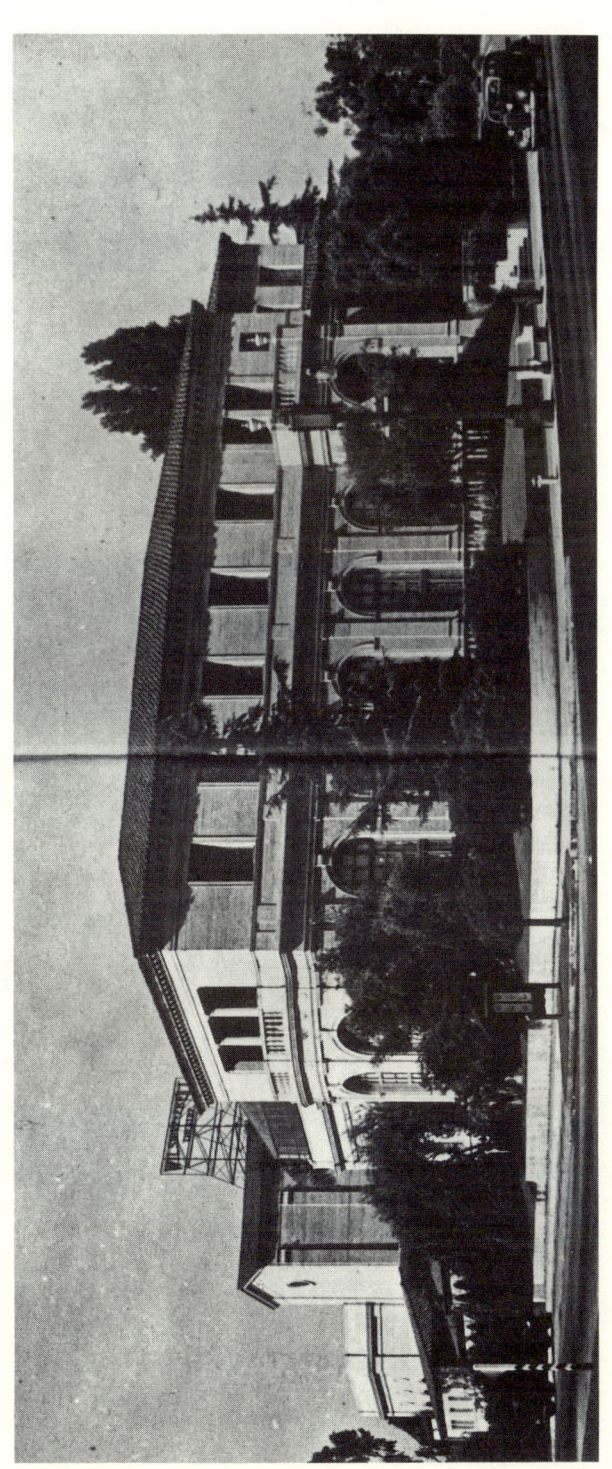

Exterior of the Ebell Club's seventh clubhouse (1927–present) on Wilshire Boulevard, Los Angeles, California (Ebell Club)

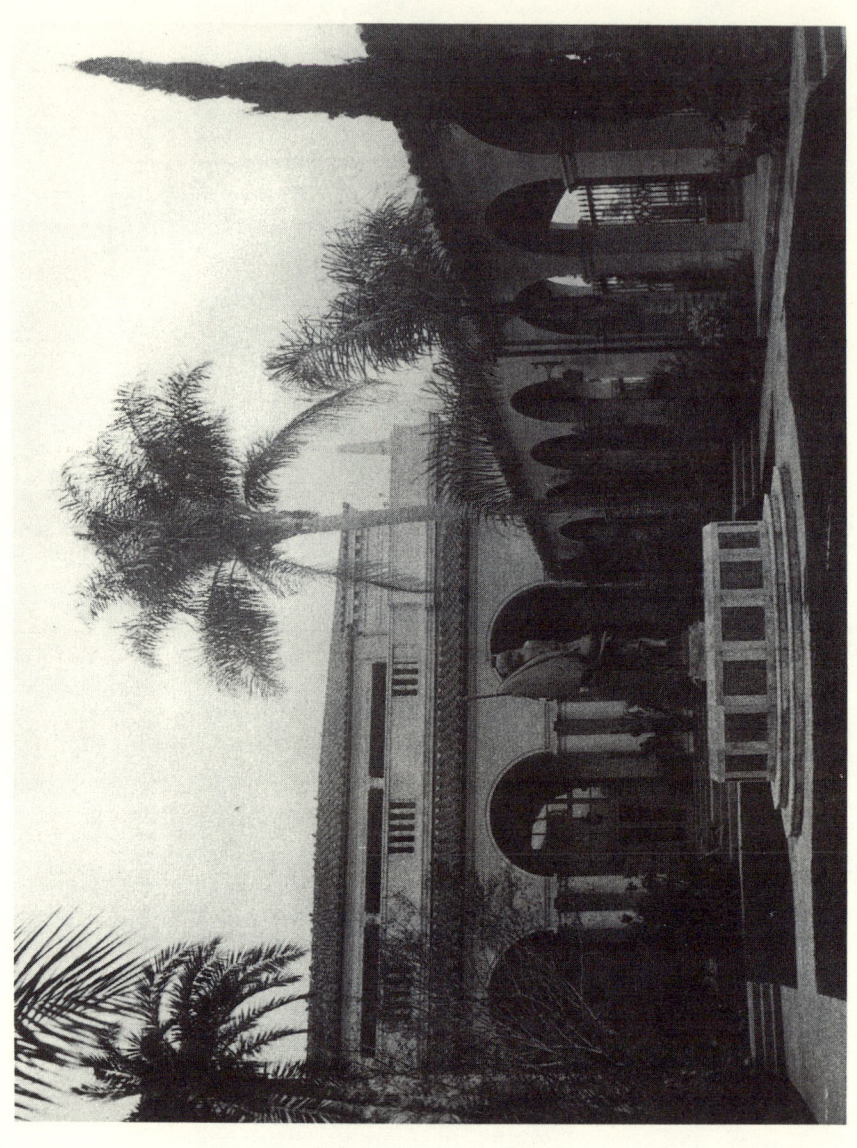

The Fountain of Honor in the courtyard of Ebell's luxurious 1927 clubhouse (Ebell Club)

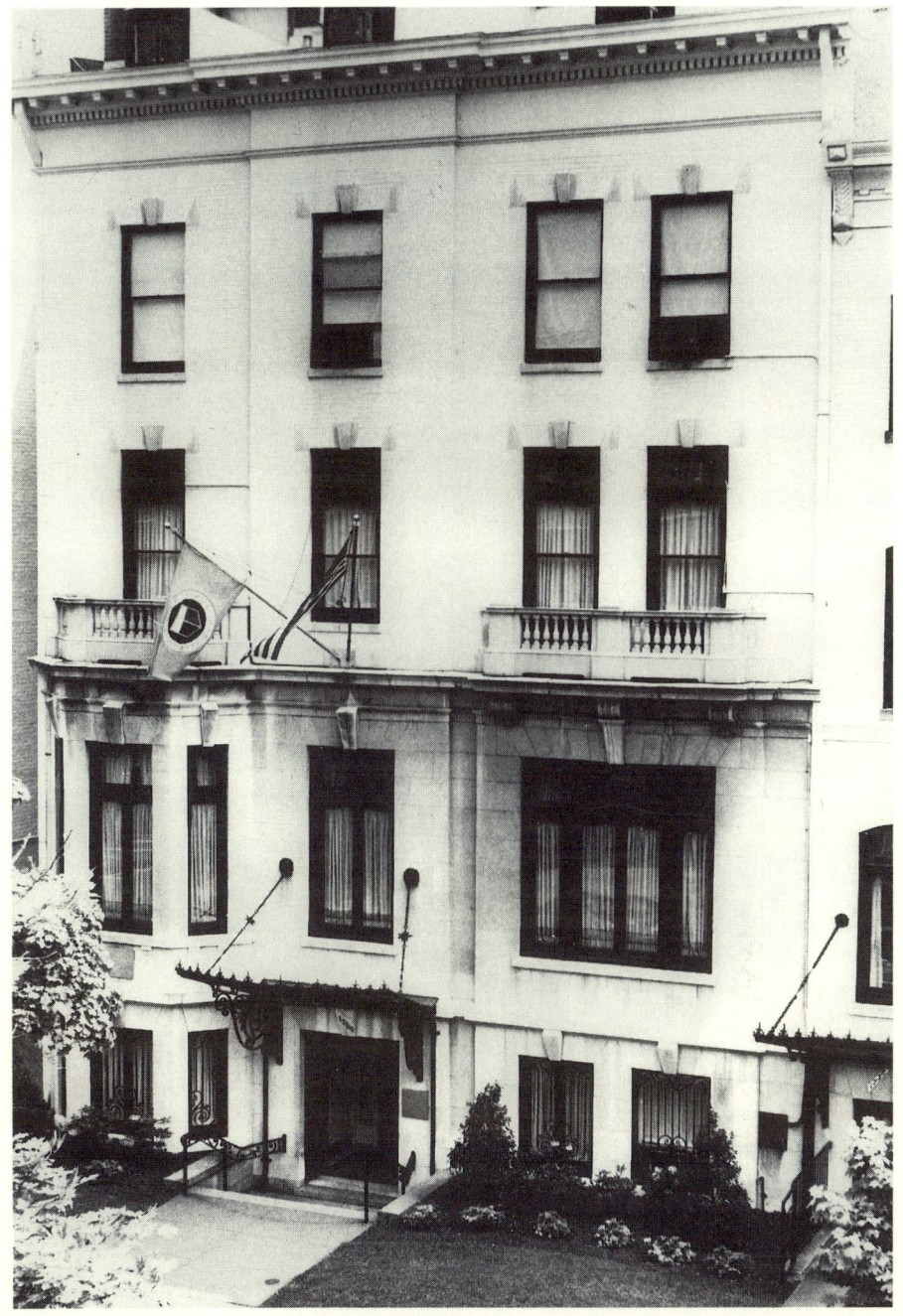

The General Federation of Women's Clubs established a national headquarters in Washington, D.C., in 1922, by purchasing this 1873 mansion at 1734 N Street Northwest (Photo courtesy of the General Federation of Women's Clubs)

FIVE

Pageantry and the Women's Rights Movement, 1905–1925

The pageant was a large and spectacular outdoor civic rite that enjoyed enormous popularity from 1905 to 1925. While this art form has recently begun to enjoy a long-deserved scrutiny by historians, the still sparse scholarship too heavily emphasizes the male contribution and obscures the key role women played in its development.[1] Pageantry served clubwomen's artistic and political needs admirably and deserves careful examination for its effective expression of their social aspirations for their era.

The pageant, ordinarily a two-and-a-half-hour program, was devised and enacted by huge numbers of amateur performers. Utilizing acting, singing, orchestral accompaniment, dancing, costumes, and props, it generally consisted of six twenty-minute episodes, placed in chronological sequence to illuminate a common theme such as the history of a town or, with some frequency, the history of women's contributions to civilization. The scenes were typically interspersed with brief interludes in which young girls dancing in Greek tunics represented abstract values and ancient ideals. The program finale consisted of a giant parade that included all the actors, plus clusters of community club members who represented associations that had supported the pageant with money, personnel, or enthusiasm.

Pageants were created by citizens in every corner of the country. They were staged by children in Sunday schools, summer camps, kindergartens, playgrounds, and Scout meetings; by foreigners in settlements and churches; by Black students in colleges and Native Americans on reservations; by women in the YWCA, clubs, state fairs, and World War I canteens; by strikers on picket lines and peace advocates in the classroom; and by whole communities celebrating the Fourth of July or the anniversary of their town.

Pageants were wholeheartedly supported by a wide range of progressive reformers who wished to deliver wholesome and uplifting entertainment to the general public. The middle-class clubwoman also embraced this goal, but there were additional considerations that led her to a special interest in pageantry. From the point of view of the member who championed the arts, the pageant was an ideal mechanism to weave together all the arts she revered. The format required the use of music, movement, poetry, drama, and the visual arts. In addition, it engaged the community with the arts in a more ambitious way than prior club arts projects had; instead of clubwomen inviting passive observers to attend a concert or an exhibition, pageants demanded the participation of large numbers of citizens who created the program alongside, not under the largesse of, the clubwomen who sponsored the effort. Pageants further served clubwomen's goals for community partnership because they prevented no one from making some essential contribution to the program; that is, pageants did not require of participants an advanced level of artistic training.

Insofar as the form welcomed the gifts of every one of its many contributors, it satisfied several important ends of the sponsoring women's organizations. On the most basic level, pageants served to stretch the artistic capacities of the general population by creating a grandiose excuse for using the talents of each citizen. Beyond the individual growth they invited, pageants also brought people together to appreciate the skills of their neighbors, finally bringing about the union of the members of the ensemble. A production by large numbers was inevitably more impressive in scope than any that a lone individual performer could enact. Beyond the artistic merits of the exercise, therefore, clubwomen hoped the cooperative experience would instill important lessons in its participants and audiences. Metaphorically as well as literally, members sought to convey a wide understanding that communal endeavors nurtured a democratic society, and that the nation and its citizens would be stronger for the people's willingness to act together, toward common goals. Pageants, then, taught clubwomen and their neighbors good civic habits more surely than any of their other art forms had. Insofar as pageants called for wide involvement, close cooperation, community strength, and respect for the diversity of talents available, they represented one of the most sophisticated forms for instilling republican precepts that clubwomen would endorse.

Since the pageant celebrated everyone, even the underdog, it comes as no surprise that it was a vehicle for touting women's own contributions to society. Women who were organized in clubs, as well as in schools and other social institutions, created all-women's pageants that propagandized for non-controversial ends endorsed by women's groups, such as the study of Shakespeare or love of country. Others campaigned for more controversial causes, such as world peace. Many pageants proclaimed women's contributions to history and the present. Finally, some boldly advocated women's rights in general and woman suffrage in particular. In this last category, the work of a single individual, Hazel MacKaye, was the primary influence. I will therefore deal with MacKaye's career in special detail.

Clubwomen devoted to the arts were not the only women to champion pageantry. They shared their support for the movement with women in other walks of life—settlement workers, school teachers, playground supervisors, college students, voice teachers, dance instructors, Sunday school leaders and others. As one contemporary of the period accurately observed:

> From the movement's birth, women took the lead in the creation, direction and dissemination of a new theatrical and recreational form. The first American pageants resulted largely from the vision and work of a handful of daring and spirited women, who, year after year, traversed the country, engineering and executing mass dramatic celebrations.[2]

In this chapter, we will observe the contributions of women from a wide variety of organizations, including educational institutions. Still, clubwomen's contributions will receive special attention, because of their previously unnoticed but substantial contributions in initiating plans to create town pageants with other segments of their communities, in serving on ad hoc committees of clubwomen only or of community-wide representatives to carry the plan to completion, or in devoting considerable resources, money, connections, education, training, and experience to the pageants of the era.

Women's Contributions to Historical Pageantry

Pageantry enjoys a long tradition in Western civilization. Elements of pageantry existed in ancient Greek celebrations, medieval morality plays, and ceremonies performed in Elizabethan England. In the United States, historians of working-class culture have noted pageantry's success in creating class awareness, republican ideology, and community cohesiveness.[3] Historians of leisure and recreation have made brief note of its presence.[4] While American theater histories tend to concentrate on the professional stage, a few have noted the popularity of pageantry during the Progressive Era.[5] Theater historians tend to credit the spark for the early twentieth-century American phenomenon to Louis N. Parker's pageant, *The Sherbourne Pageant,* held in England in 1905. Sources assert that Parker was immediately emulated by Percy MacKaye, who won instant acclaim in Cornish, New Hampshire, for his ambitious staging of *Masque of the Golden Bowl* in honor of the sculptor Augustus Saint-Gaudens. These two events are often said to have inspired the rage for pageantry that swept America for the next twenty years.[6]

As is so often the case, these accounts of the origin of pageantry in America overlook the contribution of women's groups. In 1888, the Marietta Woman's Association called for a pageant to celebrate the hundredth anniversary of its Ohio community.[7] In 1900 and 1903, respectively, Bryn Mawr College and Barnard College initiated springtime festivals, which incorporated many elements of pageantry.

Whether men or women should be credited with originating the popular enthusiasm for pageantry from 1905 to 1925, the fact remains that its support came largely from middle-class female and some male progressive reformers. Clubwomen were dominant among them because pageantry spoke so well to their social concerns. To the extent that progressives sought to ensure a decent, happy, and healthy nation of citizens who would contribute to the betterment of the whole, the theatrical format and the content of pageants assisted them in pursuit of their civic goals.

The grounds on which clubwomen could endorse pageantry were many. Like most progressive reformers of their day, they identified the availability of wholesome recreation as a desirable aspect of a democratic society, and pageantry satisfied this requirement. Not only could pageants alleviate the "humdrum of daily lives" of rural women,[8] but they could lure away idle youths from the morally degrading temptations of "languor, social decay, alcoholism, morbidity."[9] One pageant supporter praised pageantry for its educational value, calling it "a hundred-headed teacher, converting the pasture into a schoolroom."[10] Still another pageant enthusiast claimed that its historical plots could enliven history: "It covers the dry bones of fact with a mantle of glamour."[11]

Progressives also praised pageantry for its efforts to provide an important aesthetic experience. The spectacles could serve as a vehicle for citizens to both express and enjoy artistic creativity; their color, splendor, ambition, and themes fed a human spiritual need for ennoblement. Even a highly critical observer was moved to admit: "No matter how half-baked the pageant artistry may be, it slakes, in some measure, the gnawing hunger for artistic nourishment. The spectator returns home with elated spirit."[12] Even Hazel MacKaye, who politicized women's rights issues in pageantry, did not overlook its aesthetic elements:

> I stress the beauty of the ceremony because I have an intense belief in the importance of beauty to the health of the world.... In modern society where the creation of beauty is considered the specialized foundation of a class apart (the artist), this lack of aesthetic expression has stifled the sensuous life of the average man.[13]

Some reformers favored the pageants because they demonstrated America's special democratic effort to involve all its citizens in all its work. Percy MacKaye, Hazel's brother and a renowned pageant director, urged that "Every property, costume, symbol, insignium, banner and humblest buckel designed for their festivals should ultimately become the product of the people themselves, under leadership of their fellows—the artists of the civic theatre."[14] Other progressives, frightened of the heterogeneity of America's population and eager to tame it, argued that pageantry could assist in unifying the population. For example, Constance D'Arcy MacKay (no relation to the MacKayes) insisted:

> The historical pageant quickens the sense of nationalism as well as the art sense of the community. It possesses a power for unification and coordination of large groups of people that a play does not possess. It is a civilizer.... It is an arouser of patriotism, and through arousing patriotism, makes for Americanism.[15]

With claims such as these for pageantry, it is no wonder that progressive institutions like the Russell Sage Foundation and the National Recreation and Playground Association supported pageantry with funding and personnel.[16]

To be sure, all elements of pageantry did not conspire to provide every citizen with the quality recreation, beauty, and moral uplift that the most comfortable citizens enjoyed. In fact, certain of its aspects reinforced patriarchal, elitist, and exclusionary middle-class beliefs. To these functions of pageantry its middle-class supporters were blind. Thus stereotypes reflecting sexism, racism, ageism, and classism were not banished from the stage. A reverence for law and order, blue-blooded ancestors taming the land without regard for the environment, and praise for established institutions were the themes regularly articulated in pageants. It would be a misstatement to claim that pageants promoted or reflected a classless American utopia. Still, they attempted on an unprecedented scale to bring about a more inclusive vision of society than was usual in the popular culture of the time.

As we examine the town histories and all-women's pageants, the tension between the middle-class clubwoman's avowed democratic ideals and the limits of that vision is nowhere more plain than in the constant presence of ancient Greek imagery. This was especially evident in the allegorical interludes between scenes of historical events. Here, young barefoot girls dressed in sheer white Grecian gowns, performed dances with highly stylized motions to symbolize basic human emotions. Today only Isadora Duncan is remembered as an exponent of François Delsarte's system of gymnastic harmony of expression. At the time, however, Delsartian dance movements were enormously popular for their allusion to the Greek democracy of antiquity. Proponents of the Delsarte system were able to overlook, forgive, or remain unconscious of ancient Greek imperialism, wars, slavery, and deprecation of women. They habitually invoked a golden age that celebrated the Spartans' physical prowess and Athenian mental development, both qualities that American women were now attempting to acquire. This idealized image of ancient civilization had no consideration for the vast population excluded from beneficence. Pageantry's references to Greece, through classical architecture, costumes, and the open-air theatre, evoked for the clubwoman a reverence for a respected culture's philosophy, poetry, and mathematics and also for the democratic tradition she hoped to expand still further in the United States.

Town history pageants preceded women's pageants in popularity. Before 1910, the majority of town history pageants were held in New England and these most frequently represented the history of a particular town on the occasion of an anniversary.[17] As New England towns continued to celebrate town history with pageants after 1910,[18] the rest of the country quickly came to embrace the concept.[19] Indiana and Illinois celebrated state centennials in 1916 and 1918, respectively; Madison, Wisconsin, marked the hundredth anniversary of the writing of *The Star Spangled Banner;* while Cleveland, Detroit, and Washington, D.C., celebrated the Fourth of July with pageants in 1910.

At a typical pageant, upon arrival at a clear slope of grass in a park the spectators might purchase a souvenir program explaining the story to come and listing the hundreds of amateur performers and the volunteers behind the scenes, whose numbers frequently matched or exceeded the large numbers in the cast. Viewers would then take seats with thousands of other eager neighbors and friends, often townspeople related to cast members or citizens who had painted swords, helped children memorize the lyrics to the *Battle Hymn of the Republic,* or offered rehearsal space in spare barns. Trumpets announced the beginning of the program and the arrival of the narrator, who briefly delivered a verse prologue for the scenes to follow.

Pageants typically consisted of six scenes. The first scene was likely to portray a local Indian tribe, played by actual tribe members, oftentimes descendants of the chiefs.[20] The men polished weapons while the women prepared food at a campfire, wove baskets or beaded moccasins. The dramatic action flared when the white settlers arrived. A noisy battle might ensue or perhaps the signing of a treaty and the smoking of a peace pipe.

Between the first and second scene there might be a brief interlude of interpretive dance performed by young girls dressed in flowing white Grecian tunics and carrying decorative garlands to identify themselves as daisies, bluebells, dragonflies, wood nymphs, or water sprites. Their postures and movements were designed to signify the virgin forests in the early days of settlement.

The second scene might recreate a colonial event—a royal Governor's wedding, the rebellion against the Stamp Act, or a call to arms for the American Revolution. The last-mentioned used the descendants of the town's forefathers whenever possible, who sometimes even carried the actual swords handed down in their families. Each script closely reflected the particular features of the specific community. In Elizabeth, New Jersey, a slave market was depicted, played sometimes by African-Americans but sometimes by whites in blackface.[21] In Ohio towns the underground railroad was portrayed. In the St. Louis pageant, the Lewis and Clark Expedition departed for the western exploration. "The Coming of the Immigrant" was an occasion for colorful ethnic costumes and a rich assortment of dances and songs from the Scottish fling to the Polish polka. Western towns featured the coming of the railroad, the westward wagon trains, or barn raisings followed by hoedowns and Virginia reels. In the Southwest, Spanish mission scenes were depicted.

At the end of the program all the actors in their costumes re-emerged in a grand procession of history. Last in the line of march, and identified by banners, were large contingents of contemporary history builders—members of the Boy Scouts, the Girl Scouts, YWCA, YMCA, Women's Christian Temperance Union, Rotary Club, war veterans, fire department, and whole parishes of ethnic churches, the last dressed in brilliant costumes reflecting their national origin. These contingents offered the audience the assurance that contemporary citizens, no less varied and energetic than their forebears, were continuing to build upon their illustrious foundations.

At first glance, the casual observer might see nothing in such productions to complement the clubwoman's aspirations. In fact, the shows might well appear to have done little except perpetuate traditional patriarchal perspectives on history. Far from inviting criticism, they exuded the same reverence for war heroes and government leaders, for the cavalry and the law, as did the textbooks. They were euphorically self-congratulatory in their presentation of a triumphant record purged of scandal, controversy, mistakes, and injustices.

The inclination to dismiss these town history pageants as silly, time consuming diversions that lured the club member from important public work should be tempered with the realization that they offered important routes for her social advancement. Under the respectable cover of civic pride and community boosterism, pageants enabled her to smash a variety of traditional assumptions that set limits on her development. Certainly pageants satisfied her impulse to bury restrictive notions about the impropriety of women performing on the stage. They provided a new channel for her artistic expression, inviting her to abandon the embroidery she had created in domestic seclusion in favor of designing scenery, painting flats, conducting choruses, choreographing dances, researching history, or writing scripts for the entire population of her city. Pageantry's popularity indicated women's success at fashioning an engrossing recreational alternative to the hollow, commercial theatrical entertainments, like burlesque and sometimes vaudeville, that demeaned her. In addition, pageantry gave the women's club members new opportunities to learn a variety of organizational skills or to apply skills they had recently learned in other settings.

Not unimportantly, these dramatic extravaganzas gave club supporters a public forum and a wide audience for their message. That is, the sheer size and complexity of the pageant expressed metaphorically clubwomen's vision of a more perfect democracy, one in which every citizen, even women, would contribute to and receive from the collective wisdom. As pageant director Mary Porter Beegle explained, "Pageantry's whole point lies in the fact that it is not, and cannot be, the work of a single individual. It is a cooperative art in which there is opportunity for all to share according to the measure of their time and skill."[22] Or, as another enthusiastic supporter put it, "No one says *my* pageant [emphasis original]."[23]

With that democratic vision in mind, the women's club sponsor invited people of all ages, races, and economic and ethnic backgrounds to participate in the pageants she created. She attempted to exhibit sensitivity to the integrity of unfamiliar songs, dances, costumes, and music. She ensured that handicapped veterans would be transported to front row seats, that amateur artistic effort would be valued above that of professionals. She saw to it that whenever possible groups rather than individuals would collect material, write it down, and perform it. In short, every step taught the same lesson, that the community was stronger using the talents of all than those of the few.

The non-exclusionary aspects of pageantry were especially attractive to women on the verge of full citizenship. For participants and viewers, access to pageants was the keynote, breaking the barriers of professional theater's emphasis on stardom and individuality. Invitations to participate were nearly universal. With few exceptions, amateurs, huge numbers of them, dominated every aspect of the production. In fact, professional actors, writers, singers, and carpenters need not apply. Budding designers, seamstresses, ticket sellers, printers, painters, ushers, and publicists were the rule.

The form prevented celebrities from emerging in the production. Starring roles were non-existent, for the town's story became the star of the production. Whenever possible, the parts were distributed broadly. Scripts called for a troop of soldiers rather than a general, a band of hunters rather than a single Indian, a cluster of wood sprites when one might do. This device bestowed popular acclaim over all players rather than a few. Dialogue was generally sparse as well, eliminating the assignment of a few key parts to a handful of influential or experienced individuals. An emphasis on the visual rather than the aural also ensured that non-English-speaking listeners, small children incapable of concentration, or those who had to sit great distances from the stage would be able to understand the story.

The public did not expect a professional level of acting, artistic design, or musicianship. Easy-to-sew costumes and minimal props and scenery became the norm. Simple new lyrics set to familiar classics and popular tunes made the music easy to learn and listen to. Patriotic songs were a staple. Uncomplicated dances with repetitious patterns made it possible for large numbers to participate.

Simplicity served to counteract the commercial theater's artificiality. A natural setting in a familiar park, unspoiled by buildings and urban noise, was the favored location for pageants. Local audiences associated the green vistas of the public park with a respite from life's commitments and troubles. The absence of a formal stage reduced the traditional distance between actors and audience.

An examination of the varied pageant duties that the women's club organizer took on reveals that she mastered every skill necessary to production. It also yields evidence that the women's roles ranged from the very traditional work of sewing costumes to the ambitious and progressive goal of interjecting women's and children's contributions to history onto the stage. In between fell a wide category of talents many women had already begun to acquire in civic and social organizations—sponsoring public events, attracting influential supporters, allying with other community associations, raising money, donating time, acquiring and distributing information, and collaborating on presentations. Women with experience in club activity now applied these skills to pageantry, while newcomers to public life acquired them on the spot.

Frequently, it was a women's association which initiated the pageant by calling for the community's celebration of a holiday or anniversary. In Georgia, it was the Daughters of the American Revolution who called for a "History of Georgia Pageant" in 1914. In 1924, the Wa-Pe-la-Way chapter of the DAR in Hendricks County called for a pageant in Danville, Illinois. The Drama League in Pasadena, California, sponsored the annual Easter Pageant on the lawn of the Huntington Hotel. The Hollywood Woman's Club urged that a Thanksgiving Pageant take place in the new Hollywood Bowl in 1920. The Arlington, Massachusetts, Woman's Club raised a seed-fund of a thousand dollars to launch the town's pageant; the Sioux City Woman's Club in Iowa sponsored the community Peace Pageant; in Chicago, Savannah, and Nashville, it was the women's organizations that developed the community historical pageant. In 1910, the million-member General Federation of Women's Clubs, impressed with Fourth of July pageants in Detroit and Cleveland that lured children away from dangerous fireworks, called on its thousands of affiliated clubs to initiate "Safe and Sane" patriotic celebrations in their towns throughout the nation.[24]

So common was clubwomen's initiation of pageants that one pageant director, Margaret MacLaren Eager, advised readers of the American Pageant Association *Bulletin* to "approach the local Woman's Club, the Societies of the DAR and American Revolution, Colonial Dames."[25] A women's club could then create a board of distinguished townspeople, inviting individuals with strong links to the businessmen, Rotarians, educators, clergymen, social workers, and clubwomen who could provide the cash, enthusiasm, audiences, respectability, and volunteer actors and workers needed for the spectacle. There are numerous examples of cooperative efforts, as in North Dakota, where the Drama League, an association mostly of women devoted to the theatre, joined with the University of North Dakota to present a pageant. Similarly, the Illinois Federation of Women's Clubs allied with the Audubon Society and Chicago Art Institute to sponsor the Dunes Pageant Association in 1917 to save the Illinois beach from commercial development.[26]

Once representatives of all the supporting groups met, they would hire the single paid employee of the entire enterprise. This person was the "pageantmaster," as they termed the post, who coordinated or directed the complex event. While a handful of men, notably Thomas Wood Stevens, William Chauncy Langdon, and Percy MacKaye, have enjoyed considerable acclaim for the numerous pageants they directed, women actually dominated the field. Among them were Margaret Eager, Constance D'Arcy MacKay, Esther Bates, Mary Porter Beegle, Nina Lamkin, Ethel Rockwell, Virginia Tanner, Virginia Dallin, Lotta Clark, and Hazel MacKaye (sister of Percy MacKaye). Collectively, these women were responsible for well over one hundred pageants. In hundreds of other instances, women, often fresh out of college, were invited by the citizens of their hometowns to create a single pageant.[27] Occasionally, pairs of women shared the work and the credit for the key role they assumed together.[28]

The pageant-maker began her job three to six months before the date of the actual performance. First, she secured the assistance of several volunteers—a business manager; directors of music, dance, lighting, and episodes; scenic technicians; a costumer; and an advertising manager. If she was inexperienced in pageant making, she could secure technical advice from a variety of printed sources, often written by other women who published the results of their newly acquired expertise.

A great number of women wrote books with extensive bibliographies, musical suggestions, and costume patterns, which enabled novices to direct a first-rate pageant. These reference works attempted to provide historically authentic songs, dances, facts, costumes, and props. The guidelines were often sufficiently detailed to warn readers of potential pitfalls. They enumerated such hazards of staging as the incongruity of standing tropical plants next to pine trees, of standing tall performers next to short ones, and of standing at a spinning wheel without pretending to use it.[29] Experienced pageant-makers also published their pageants, with texts, stage directions, music, and photographs, for others to borrow. Sometimes, in a spirit of generosity toward communitarianism, no royalty was required.[30]

Women's agencies frequently distributed pageantry information for members. The General Federation of Women's Clubs, for example, circulated to its huge membership the Drama League's bibliographies, such as the *Material for Festival Pageantry and Dramatic Presentation for the Celebration of the Tercentenary of the Landing of the Pilgrims*. Magazines such as the *Woman's Home Companion* printed pageants and enthusiastic stories about pageants.[31] University extension programs, too, responded to interests of their constituencies by publishing guides and texts pertinent to pageantry.[32] Finally, subscribers to the *Bulletin* of the American Pageant Association, a small society that acted as a clearinghouse for information, could study technical articles by some of the leading pageant makers of the day.[33] The publication also announced ambitious undertakings by dozens of women pageant-masters, and readers saw that women served as officers and directors in the association itself.[34]

The acquisition of a script was a crucial step, requiring not only a mastery of the town's history, but also a generous attitude that welcomed researchers, writers, and eventually players of every stripe. Not content to draw on standard textbooks of the region, the pageant-master often engaged a broad segment of the population in the investigation of the past. Clubwomen and school children began a new and deep examination of local history. Teachers instructed teenagers to interview the elderly for personal reminiscences of the town's early development; this activity yielded previously unrecorded details and built respect between the generations. Other townspeople ransacked the attics of descendants of early settlers in search of original garments, swords, bonnets, and uniforms to use as authentic costumes and props, or tracked down photographs to verify the scenery's accuracy. These efforts encouraged the interest of townfolk in the contributions of their ancestors. They also led to pageant texts that did not limit praise to the work of presidents and generals, but lauded all citizens' efforts.

In Great Barrington, Vermont, a one-hundred-fifty-year-old play was discovered during such a search and was modified for use in abridged form.[35] Most towns, however, created new productions by drawing together committees to write down the research material that others had collected. In the Wilmington, North Carolina, Sorosis club, five members synthesized the research of fifteen amateur historians. The *Pageant of the Lower Cape Fear Valley*, was composed by Delaware DAR members, and at the State University of Montana, eighteen students wrote *Selish*, about Missoula's indigenous people.

Once a script was produced, parts could be assigned with the help of the clubs, schools, social agencies, and church groups that came forward with players. The numbers they secured were impressive. In Peterborough, New Hampshire, for example, two hundred played in the program. Old Deerfield, Massachusetts, used three hundred citizens; Westchester, New York, four hundred; Brattleboro, Vermont, seven hundred; Machias, Maine, one thousand; Salem, Massachusetts, twelve hundred; Hadley, Massachusetts, eighteen hundred; Gloucester and Brooklyn two thousand each; Philadelphia, five thousand; and St. Louis, the grandest of them all, utilized seventy-five hundred people in the cast.

The composition of the casts, in particular, reflected the enthusiasm of women for pageantry. Children came from the classrooms of women elementary school teachers, Sunday school volunteers, and dancing instructors; immigrants from the settlement houses staffed by women social workers; clubwomen from women's own social networks; and youth from the Scout troops, YWCAs, and playgrounds supervised by women. It frequently fell to the women teachers, settlement house volunteers, and municipal playground supervisors to teach the boy scout "Red Coats" or sailors the lyrics to their songs, or to rehearse the YWCA Indian princesses or sunflowers in the appropriate dances, using Delsartian movements. High school girls provided wholesale child care, finding ways to occupy and quiet the legions of restless sunbeams awaiting their entrances at rehearsals and performances.

Since women recruited players mainly from their own circles of activity, women and children dominated the casts. This circumstance served to modify the official histories as presented in standard texts to include considerable female and juvenile participation in great events. It recast the public's view of history to include everyday unspectacular occurrences in which goodwives and their children took part. To be sure, Paul Revere, George Washington, and John Paul Jones were still prominent in the stage histories, but the mob scenes of rebels or celebrants contained large percentages of women and children. A balance was thus achieved between the supremacy of government or the glory of battle, and the weight of domestic routines.

In addition, women's participation tempered the impulse to dwell entirely on political events. Audiences saw episodes documenting Yankee farm girls who became the earliest textile factory operatives. They watched the schoolteacher supervise her charges at recess. Female Indians cooked at the campfire; nurses worked at the battle lines. When slaves escaped, they were likely to be mothers, and Quaker women assisted them; when wedding vows were exchanged, women and children figured prominently in the church scenes. In Maine, *Dame Creel of Portland* starred the colonial rebel who melted her pewter down for bullets.[36] In all, the heretofore invisible players of history saw new recognition in the pageants. Women and children demonstrated that they had had an important role in shaping the past.

Behind the scenes as well, women with the leisure to do so labored at the supporting tasks with enthusiasm. One of the major jobs was the creation of costumes, hundreds of them, for all the players. In Newark, New Jersey, 403 women volunteered to sew feathered headdresses for tribesmen, waistcoats for colonials, antebellum hoop skirts, Blue and Grey Civil War uniforms, and filmy robes for youthful butterflies, raindrops, and zephyrs. Portsmouth, New Hampshire, called on ninety-two seamstresses, while Westchester women made 645 costumes for the roles of the English, Dutch, French, Indians, and colonials. In St. Louis, 583 women were enlisted as costume or property-makers.[37]

Women were prominent in other vital capacities as well, from selling tickets to ushering, to seeking donations. Women extracted money, favors, and services from businesses and from their neighbors and friends. Would the high school, the YWCA, and Farmer's Hall permit rehearsals on their premises? Would the lumber company send supplies, the stable lend some horses, the National Guard put in phones so that the conductor, directors, and stage hands could communicate? Could the public works department donate a clean-up committee, the utility company send lighting experts? Would the newspaper sponsor a contest for the poster design, the local button company contribute its wares for costumes? In Newark, women approached the stores and manufacturing establishments for dress forms, hats, fur pieces, spectacles, hat and shoe buckles, and other trimmings. Women also secured vehicles to transport the handicapped viewers, determined that no interested citizen should miss the event.[38]

Women negotiated for especially appropriate pageant settings. Would the city council permit the use of space where a significant historical event took place? *St. Mary's Pageant* was performed on a stage erected twenty feet from Maryland's first council chamber, using the structure as a backdrop. In Plymouth, the landing of the Pilgrims was reenacted at Plymouth Rock. In Gloucester, the seashore set the stage for the growth of a seaport. The *Hudson-Fulton Pageant* used the Hudson River for a spectacular naval display. In each of these cases, pageant enthusiasts had to win permission from male politicians for use of the site.

Women made generous contributions to complement those they solicited from others. The Raleigh Woman's Club gave five thousand dollars towards pageant expenses in its town. Woman's clubhouses, classrooms, and homes served as rehearsal halls. They lent plants, furniture, and vintage clothing to the cause.

The many women who participated in all these activities came away with more than sharpened organizing skills and an acceptable vehicle for theatrical self-expression. Their pageants yielded many tangible benefits for their towns, in the form of profits for civic causes, for instance. In St. Louis, the pageant's $139,000 earnings netted a profit of $17,000, enough to construct a Little Theatre Playhouse and support a twenty-nationality choral society. In Baltimore, pageant profits established the Vagabond Players, a community drama association. The Boston Teachers' Mutual Benefit Association earned money for its work, and the Red Cross pageants made substantial surpluses for Liberty Bonds in wartime. The Minneapolis pageant raised ten thousand dollars for the Jewish War Relief Fund, and Plymouth, Massachusetts, was able to restore a church.

To create the town history pageants, each member of an organized sisterhood took on a wide range of public activities that had not necessarily been prescribed for her. Yet her efforts were tolerated, indeed welcomed, by her community, for she appeared to be engaged in woman's traditional role, that of serving others, guiding and assisting her larger family to enjoy a wholesome type of amusement. In this contentional guise, however, she acted as a leader and an innovator. She reached beyond her immediate circle to include in her town histories an unusually broad swath of the society. Also, by bringing women and children onstage in generous numbers, she gave visibility to their role in history. These experiments also laid the foundation for a more ambitious expansion of the pageant format beyond serving the community's needs for definition, history, ritual, self-expression, and celebration. The modern generation of clubwomen began to use pageantry for themselves.

All-Women's Pageants

The New Woman of the early twentieth century had begun to dwell in a more public world than her mother and grandmother had. Both the broader career options now open to her and the general acceptance of her efforts to create civic improvements are illustrations of this trend. Even so, the New Woman, a beneficiary of her forebear's activism, did not abandon the separate women's societies and institutions built on the foundation of the nineteenth-century "woman's sphere." Not surprisingly, then, women's academies and colleges, as well as societies and clubs, provided the setting for great numbers of pageants, this time created and executed solely by women. Like town history pageants, the all-women's spectacles gave the members of women's organizations an opportunity to develop and use artistic and organizational skills. They provided a vehicle for creative expression and demonstrated women's continuing commitment to communicating their moral and social values to a broad audience. They widened women's choices for leisure time activity, and offered them a way of engaging in cooperative effort.

Beyond such benefits for the individual, all-women's pageants served some larger social and political purposes embraced by women. First, pageants were used to publicize and argue various causes that women supported. We will examine here the pageants that promoted the aims of women's Shakespeare clubs and patriotic associations, as well as the more controversial aims of women's peace societies. Next, all-women's pageants in federated clubs and colleges celebrated women's contributions to society. Finally, women's groups began using pageantry to advocate equal rights for women. The pageants by Hazel MacKaye, especially those commissioned by women's suffrage associations, will be examined as examples of the modern woman's use of pageantry for her own political advocacy.

The earliest of the women's pageants predated the town history pageants.

They originated at eastern women's colleges as part of elaborate springtime rituals deriving their inspiration from the classical traditions prominent in the college curricula. Both the Bryn Mawr College May Day Festival, begun in 1900, and the Barnard College Greek Games, begun in 1903, exerted important influences on the pageants that followed.

Bryn Mawr's May Day ritual—which the college continues to the present time—was first organized with an Elizabethan theme by alumna Evangeline W. Andrews (class of '93) in 1900. Thousands of spectators gathered to attend seven period plays, including *Robin Hood* and *Midsummer Night's Dream*, to watch the elaborate ribbon dance around the maypole, and to feast on English delicacies. The day's revels began with a huge procession, which would become a staple in pageants. Five hundred students marched alongside alumnae, musicians, heralds on horseback, marshals, milkmaids in hay wagons, shepherdesses in ox-carts, white oxen hauling a fresh maypole cut in the woods, chimney sweeps, Morris dancers, actors, and Maid Marian, the Queen of the May.[39]

Bryn Mawr's colorful program was perceived by some viewers as defying propriety and decorum. There were complaints that it was not appropriate for young ladies to wear men's fashions, short garments, or diaphanous costumes. Such complaints threatened to halt the New Woman's attempts to bury sanctions against her participation in public rituals. This dilemma was solved by forbidding reporters to take photographs or to disclose the names of the participants.[40] Taste and modesty were thereby protected, enabling the pageant tradition to flourish among women.

Barnard College followed Bryn Mawr with its Greek Games, in which sophomores and freshmen first competed in April 1903. Each year thereafter, a goddess from antiquity such as Athena, Demeter, Persephone, or Aphrodite, or sometimes a classical male god, was selected to be honored at the games. Student poets wrote odes, and the physical education department supervised the preparation for athletic competitions in relay races of hoop rolling, torch racing and chariot riding. By 1908, choral and dance programs, based on gymnastic instruction bearing credit, expanded the celebration. Once again, an elaborate procession opened the event and a series of episodes followed, using half the student body to tell the myth of the deity. At the conclusion of the games there was a wreath-granting ceremony for the winners.[41]

As at Bryn Mawr, the issue of immodest costumes was raised. The college solved the problem with the following admonitions: "To avoid embarrassment large people should be in long costumes, women should wear long slips or nightgowns under diaphanous cheesecloth, and everyone should wear a brassiere."[42] The event continued annually into the 1930s. Its use of classical Greek themes had considerable impact on the development of pageants. The costumes, dances, and symbols of the Greek Games came to embellish town histories set in America, and they also enjoyed special prominence in many of the women's rights pageants.

The use of Elizabethan imagery at Bryn Mawr and Grecian imagery at Barnard, besides reflecting the colleges' classical curriculum, reveal the caution with which women approached these early theatrical experiments. How safe these nostalgic frolics were! No harsh naturalistic descriptions of history were attempted in 1900, although they were attempted by 1915. These college revels gently bridged the distance between earlier types of women's dramatic expression and the bolder forms to come. The theatrical endeavors of proper women of the late nineteenth century had consisted of either charades in the parlor or tableaux (stationary and therefore modest representations of one or more persons costumed and posed to replicate a picture, statue, or scene). The college festivals moved one step further, to set the stage for the all-women's pageants designed to gain support for causes championed by women.

Among the causes promoted by women of the early twentieth century was the appreciation of the classics of English literature. These devotees worked through associations for the regular study of William Shakespeare's plays, which leisured middle-class women of the late nineteenth century had founded.[43] Readings and discussions of the Bard's great works satisfied the enthusiasts initially, but in the early twentieth century his April birthday occasioned a spring celebration of bolder consequence. By the turn of the century, clubwomen in the Pomona, California, Shakespeare Club appeared in the costumes of favorite characters from the plays and performed brief excerpts on the lawn of a member's home.[44] In Evanston, Illinois, the Drama Circle, another women's literary society, toured schools and YWCA's presenting excerpts from the plays.[45] In these ways, women devotees of Shakespeare's work grew accustomed to sharing their delight in Elizabethan drama with friends, neighbors, and young people in their communities. How eagerly, then, they awaited the tercentenary in 1916 of Shakespeare's death to attempt more ambitious celebrations. Thousands of women, reluctant to execute full-length productions of Shakespeare's plays, instead launched pageants that consisted of brief excerpts from the canon. They hoped both to deepen their own familiarity with the Bard's work and to introduce their audiences to its richness. They succeeded on both counts.[46]

Women's patriotic associations also used pageantry in an effort to build a love of America. Every Fourth of July and George Washington's birthday provided opportunities for the Daughters of the American Revolution and other patriotic groups to initiate a historical rendering of the American past. "Uncle Sam's 137th Birthday Party" at the Washington Monument on 4 July 1913 brought out miniature costumed George and Martha Washingtons from the Thomas Welles Society of Children of the American Revolution.[47] The 1920 Tercentenary of the Pilgrims' Landing at Plymouth Rock presented another opportunity to revere the American past, especially in Massachusetts. In 1925, the anniversary of the selling of Manhattan Island to the Dutch was the cause for celebration in New York State. During World War I, the YWCA participated widely in patriotic pageants. Y members performed wholesome entertainment for soldiers at camps and canteens, raised money for Liberty Bonds among citizens, and taught the public the importance of food conservation during the emergency.[48]

Peace pageants were created by pacifist women before and after World War

I, although none appears to have been tolerated during American involvement in the fighting. Many peace plays were presented for and with children, in the hopes of raising a new generation of pacifists. The productions attempted to lift children out of American provincialism by emphasizing the colorful games, habits, and costumes of their peers in other countries. In 1921, the National Council for the Prevention of War sponsored *Good Will, the Magician,* in which the players concentrated on the joys of cooperation rather than the ravages of war. Will, the balloon man, gave American youth a bouquet of magic balloons, each one of which yielded a child in the native costume of another land who recited a rhyme—about the politeness of Spanish children, the obedience of Chinese children, and the skating ability of Dutch children. Then each visitor called up a band of compatriots who taught a dance, game, or song from their nation to American children in the school pageant. The program emphasized the joy of sharing and closed with a Red Cross song:

> In hearts too young for enmity
> There lies the way to make men free;
> While children's friendships are world-wide,
> New ages will be glorified.
> Let child love child and strife will cease.
> Disarm the hearts, for that is peace.[49]

For adults, pacifist women used sterner stuff. A 1915 production of the Woman's Peace Party, *War and Women's Awakening,* employed a brutal realism. A narrator read a text embellished with grim action on the stage. A little boy, at play with his sword, pretended to decapitate the head of a girl's doll. The plot implied that belligerent habits developed in grown men who then groveled at the feet of "Commerce," for whom government rulers were mere puppets. Young men, entranced by the glamour of the nation's wars for profit, broke from their mothers and sisters to enlist. The gory result was a battle attended by darkness, thunder, lightning, cannon fire, smoke, and screams, accompanied by rapists and threats against women. Finally, women demanded cessation of hostilities, and Justice deemed their claims sound. She freed the Herald of Civilization to escort Art, Science, and Plenty onto center stage at last. Pageant author, Hazel MacKaye, expressed her hope of gripping the audience with the possibilities for peace. "It is necessary," she said, "to color peace pursuits with the same thrill and imagination as war," carrying out her intent of using theatre to dramatize the "moral equivalent of war."[50]

Women's use of pageantry was not limited to issues of literature, patriotism, and peace. On the contrary, women concerned about child labor, Americanization, and education all embraced the pageant format to publicize their concerns.[51] In addition, women's associations used pageantry to celebrate their histories and achievements and those of women generally.[52] They developed dramatic renderings of domestic and public scenes that conveyed women's contributions to civilization. These productions included not only the women who had found a place in history, but also the invisible and unacknowledged. Thus, the YWCA production of *The Torchbearers* at the 1919 Texas State Fair, which predictably portrayed Joan of Arc, also represented the bravery of cave women protecting their children. When the YWCA celebrated its Jubilee on 22 February 1916 with ninety-five simultaneous pageants in clubs throughout the nation, anonymous nurses, college students, and women from all nations received attention. So, too, the Detroit working women who produced *Through the Centuries: Women in Industry* paid homage to nameless colonial seamstresses and to militant trade union women on the picket lines.

The California Federation of Women's Clubs prepared an impressive presentation in May 1921 at their twentieth annual convention.[53] *California, a Land of Dreams,* written by the renowned California novelist Gertrude Atherton, was performed with a breathtaking natural backdrop at Yosemite National Park. Six episodes, performed by different women's clubs in the federation, addressed historical situations in which women's contributions, heretofore ignored or trivialized, were elevated for consideration and praise. Not surprisingly, the perspective on history remained limited to that of the dominant white groups represented in the clubs. Thus the episode that dealt with the incursion of the Spanish, although it focused on women, celebrated "The Emancipation of Squaws through Christian Marriage," and emphasized the successful proselytizing of Native American women by Spanish women settlers. The pageant nonetheless exposed the audience to a broader view than was available in most accounts of the state and its history, dramatizing such subjects as "Women's Work During the Gold Rush." This pageant also highlighted the numerous women who had made and were continuing to make a significant contribution to public life. An episode entitled "Contemporary Dreams of Service" included tableaux of Art, Music, Literature, Conservation, and Education, and demonstrated the powerful range of talents women were exercising. The spectacle closed, of course, with a massive parade of all the actors and of women representing each club in the federation.

Some pageants enumerated, chronologically, the great women in history. Vassar College, for example, observed its fiftieth anniversary in 1915 with a *Pageant of Athena*.[54] This resurrected from obscurity such learned women as Sappho, Hortensia of Rome, the Abbess Hilda of Whitby, Marie de France, Isabella d'Este, Lady Jane Grey, and Elena Lucrezia Cornaro—the first woman to earn a doctorate, at the University of Padua in the seventeenth century. The intent was to inspire students to expand the "Web of Knowledge" these forebears had begun to weave. The undergraduate "priestesses," among them Edna St. Vincent Millay, heard Athena recite in a Poughkeepsie glade a lyric invoking the age-old variety and power of women's contributions, which would, if permitted to flourish, make incalculable contributions to civilization. The use of needlework imagery in the text reflects a typical respect in pageantry for women's work and women's culture:

> Bright in the skein of time gleam many strands,
> Endlessly varied. I have chosen those

Of flame, of fire, or rich, luxuriant gold,
And those whose beauty lies in their clear strength.
My will it is to weave them, strand on strand,
Tracing the course of learning through the years
In one close-wrought design. And those who come
Shall pause before this fabric, ages old,
Shaped by past lives in symmetry and truth,
And glorying in design so well begun
Themselves shall add thereto. And this my web
Shall weaving be forever, never done.[55]

The Vassar program, like the California production, gave its participants a sense of their growing strengths. That the complex job of presenting it was successfully accomplished by women alone spoke as clearly of the abilities of cooperative womanhood as the affirming messages in the storyline. If the town history pageants had served as a tribute to the community, then the all-women's pageants announced that women shared a proud history, which had never received proper recognition, and the talent to shape a more just future for themselves.

The exhilaration they experienced at creating a grand and stirring spectacle inspired many women to use pageantry as a political tool to call for woman suffrage and women's rights. Several unusually political women's pageants were created by Hazel MacKaye. They were sponsored by the Congressional Union (later called the National Woman's Party), seen by most observers as one of the most daring and militant suffrage organizations of its time. Yet its pageants had an impact well beyond its roster of membership. Its performances would touch the lives of multitudes of Americans, including great numbers of women who were about to win the vote.

Hazel MacKaye, Pageant-Maker

One outstanding individual took women's pageantry well beyond the popular forms described so far, to propagandize vigorously for the women's rights movement of the day. Hazel MacKaye (1888–1944) brought a unique background of political activism and theatrical experience to the distinctive women's pageants she created. Although her work, from 1913 to 1923, was embraced by the most active feminists of the radical Congressional Union and the National Woman's Party, it was attacked by more traditional pageant-makers for selling out their art form to special interests—and to a controversial interest at that. Pageant enthusiast Ralph Davol, for example, accused the women's rights pageants of "erroneous methods and false ideals, . . . commercialism, sensationalism and feminism."[56] Nevertheless, MacKaye continued to experiment ingeniously with pageantry's form and content in order to unite the women participating and elicit sympathy for the cause from indifferent or hostile audiences.

Hazel MacKaye's biography explains her ease and familiarity with the theatrical world.[57] She was born in 1888, the daughter of (Harold) Steele MacKaye and Mary Keith Medbery MacKaye. Hazel's father was a popular nineteenth-century playwright, and she was named for his play, *Hazel Kirke,* which claimed to enjoy more performances than any other in America but *Uncle Tom's Cabin.* Steele MacKaye had studied movement with Delsarte in Europe, years before Hazel was born. He lectured throughout America on the Delsarte system and is credited with being its primary exponent in the United States. Thus, Hazel was initiated early into this system of harmonic gymnastics. She would eventually use and champion the system in her pageants, especially in her interludes, which employed formal physical gestures meant to indicate harmony between life, mind, and soul.[58]

Hazel's mother published a dramatization of Jane Austen's *Pride and Prejudice* in 1906 and 1928, and acted in it at many universities.[59] Not insignificantly, Hazel's oldest sibling, Percy (1875–1956), enjoyed respect and fame as one of the founders of the American pageantry movement, creator of the prologue to the influential Cornish, New Hampshire, pageant in honor of Augustus Saint-Gaudens. He is best known for masterminding the 1914 St. Louis Centenary pageant with 7,500 people in the cast and for creating *Caliban,* the Shakespeare sampler of 1916.[60] These works represent only a small portion of his original and ingenious output.

With such a background, it is hardly surprising that Hazel MacKaye found her career in the theater. Forsaking her earliest dreams of becoming a concert pianist, she enrolled in 1907 in George Pierce Baker's pioneering theater classes at Radcliffe College. However, she never became more than an "honorary member" of her college class, withdrawing from Radcliffe the better to pursue her theatrical interests.

MacKaye spent the next fifteen years learning everything she could about the theater, and then working for women's groups that commissioned her to dramatize their messages.[61] From the start, MacKaye successfully challenged the limitations placed upon women, off stage or on. Her first job application was for the position of assistant to the director of the *Pageant of Darkness and Light,* a history of the missionary movement. Although the Englishman who interviewed her was unaccustomed to hiring women, she got the job, and then went so far as to hire the Boston Ladies' Orchestra to supply the music. She went on to assist Thomas Wood Stevens in the *Pageant of Illinois* and her brother in his *Canterbury Pilgrims' Pageant* and later in *Caliban.* Through her work in these productions, she gained firsthand experience in tapping the resources of individual women and women's groups enthusiastic about pageantry. An early devotee of the form, Hazel became a charter member of the American Pageant Association in 1913 and wrote a "Who's Who in Pageantry" for the membership.

MacKaye also stepped outside of pageantry to work in more traditional forms of drama. She toured the country in a variety of roles with Winthrop Ames's respected Castle Square Stock Company of Boston, and she grappled with impressive female roles in two of her brother's plays, *Sappho and Phaon* and *Jeanne D'Arc.* In New York City, she became an instructor in the pioneering Children's Educational Theatre, thus becoming keenly aware of techniques in theater for young people. None of these experiences would remain untapped in her development of women's rights pageants.

MacKaye developed multiple ties with the questioning New Woman of her day. She was a charter member of the Women's City Club in Manhattan and lived in Greenwich Settlement House. She worked in voluntary associations dominated by women with progressive interests, including the Drama League of America, the Community Drama Association in New York City, and the Meriden Bird Club in New Hampshire. She was present at the first meeting of Alice Paul's spirited Congressional Committee, when it was still allied with the National American Woman Suffrage Association; thus, she participated in the beginnings of the National Woman's Party. To the end of her life she saved the ribbons from suffrage parades in which she had marched. She wrote in favor of the Equal Rights Amendment when few others supported it,[62] and she devoted herself to assisting outsiders, especially women, children, and working people, to make themselves heard through the medium of pageantry.

The first milestone in MacKaye's development of political pageantry was achieved on 3 March 1913. A stunning theatrical spectacle on the marble steps of the Treasury Building in Washington D.C., it entertained three thousand seated dignitaries and countless more observers on Pennsylvania Avenue. Maidens blowing trumpets, dressed in flowing white Grecian robes, heralded the hour-long *Allegory*. The National American Women's Suffrage Party commissioned the pageant, and it was a coup for its most radical leader, Alice Paul, who admired the English militant suffragists' use of spectacle.[63] Here a government building, no less, with majestic marble columns and grand staircase, gave the pageant its splendid backdrop.

The action began when the massive doors swung open before the crowds to feature the figure of Columbia, who descended a flight of stairs as a gigantic American flag was unfurled. She summoned a series of symbolic figures: first Justice, in purple robes, accompanied by female attendants in violet, all making their obeisance to the majestic strains of the *Pilgrims' Chorus;* then Charity, preceded by little girls strewing her path with roses; next a statuesque Liberty, who raced down the stairs followed by "brave" girls decked with red and gold scarves. Next Peace entered, dressed in silver and white, sending a dove to the White House nearby. She was followed by Plenty, surrounded by maidens carrying cornucopias of fruit. Finally came Hope, shyly venturing forth, with girls dressed in rainbow colors, dancing and releasing bouquets of balloons.[64]

This part of the show was merely a preliminary to the great procession of suffragists who marched past the cast, now frozen in salute to the paraders. First came the floats representing Norway, Finland, New Zealand, and Australia, the countries where women held full suffrage. These were followed by floats representing nations in which women had won partial suffrage. The last floats represented countries in which women were still working for political freedom. Several floats, portraying seventy-five years of suffrage struggle in America, held tableaux of 1840, 1870, 1890, and 1913. The 5,000 to 10,000 marchers trooped by the 250,000 spectators, many in town for President

Wilson's inauguration. The women marched with banners identifying suffragist farmers, homemakers, patriots, educators, lawyers, physicians, pharmacists, wage earners, government employees, businesswomen, teachers, social workers, librarians, writers, artists, actresses, and musicians, as well as male politicians supporting women's suffrage. Then came delegations of women from the nine suffrage states. In all, the parade provided dazzling testimony to women's contributions to society and to the importance of including them in the nation's governance.[65]

This parade of women representing various groups had quickly become a staple following New York City's 1910 suffrage parade. Hazel MacKaye did not invent the use of parades to argue the strength of prosuffrage forces. Still the diversity of women in her parade, of all ages, occupations, incomes, nationalities, and religions, anonymous shop girls alongside society matrons, Senators, and celebrated feminists, spoke effectively again to the breadth of support behind the cause. MacKaye's genius was to wed the parade to her *Allegory,* to show that the power of contemporary women to win rights and exert influence rested on the foundations of the abstract virtues. The enormous parade of living women inspired confidence that they would carry out the noble aspirations of the ancients.

At the time, the reviewers were ecstatic about MacKaye's production and their commendations established her on the theatrical map. The *Washington Herald* proclaimed the *Allegory* "one of the most beautiful dramatic pictures ever seen on the stage or in the open in Washington." *The New York Times* was more extravagant, labeling it "one of the most impressively beautiful spectacles ever staged in this country."[66] The *Woman's Journal* addressed considerations worrisome to feminists of every period:

> To those who feared that equal suffrage would make women less womanly, to those who feared that in becoming politically free woman will become coarse and mannish looking, to those who fear the loss of beauty and grace, art and poetry, with the advent of universal suffrage, the pageant offered the final word, the most convincing argument that human ingenuity can devise.[67]

The spectacle heralded a future of responsible, non-threatening woman citizens, not harpies who threatened to dislodge civilization as it was known.

Had violence not erupted, the day might have been remembered only for its crowds of supporters and for Hazel MacKaye's clever use of color, music, dance, costume, flowers, birds, flags, balloons, banners, scarves, and imagery. Instead, both contemporary and historical accounts concentrate on the hecklers who disrupted the parade with hoots, jeers, and obscenities, even loosening rats to cause havoc.[68] Because the antisuffragist Chief of Police Sylvester looked the other way, three hundred marching women were hospitalized before Secretary of War William Simpson called in the National Guard from Fort Meyers to restore order. Thus, despite all but universal praise, the inspiring pageant has been overshadowed by the focus on its detractors.

For all her aesthetic sense, Hazel MacKaye was a realist who had a shrewd appreciation of theater as a practical political tool. She clearly articulated her practical purposes in creating *Allegory* when she lectured at the School for Suffrage in Washington, D.C., several months after it was staged. There she stressed the political and propagandistic value of theater. A showy demonstration on stage of women's ideals and their service to contemporary activism fired audiences to respect both. An appeal to the audience's emotions, to their senses of sight and sound, won support as no written argument or debate ever could. The effort additionally touched the actors who played the roles: "These women today were going on with the noble traditions of the past . . . not one of those women or girls who participated in the pageant could ever feel indifference toward the cause of Equal Rights."[69] Playacting built commitment to the movement.

MacKaye also cogently pointed out that suffrage theatre raised immediately tangible support in the form of money. Three thousand spectators had paid five dollars a head for the privilege of viewing her pageant and the procession which followed. MacKaye noted that if celebrities like young activists from wealthy families were in the cast, these "drawing cards" could arouse the public's curiosity; a previously indifferent populace might attend for amusement, but leave instructed.[70]

The success of the *Allegory* opened many opportunities for MacKaye to create pageants in the decade that followed. Not content to reproduce her first victorious effort, she continued to experiment, testing the form to develop variations that would delight and startle her sponsors, workers, and viewers.

In 1914, she staged her most controversial pageant when the New York City Men's League for Woman Suffrage engaged her to direct *The American Woman: Six Periods of American Life*. The pageant took place in the seventy-first Regimental Armory.[71] Emboldened by her brother's recent use of a cast of thousands to enact the history of St. Louis, MacKaye enlisted 500 players— five times the number she had marshalled in the District of Columbia. Repeating a tactic that had proved alluring to Washington press and public, she included in the cast some prominent society leaders.

In a parody of the town histories that sanctified the American past, MacKaye's new production used historical scenes to expose the specific economic, political, and social oppressions of American women. Throughout the production, she paired men's freedoms with women's limitations, and pointedly placed the blame for the inequities on the men. The script was biting, not subtle, and bared centuries of sexism endured by American women. Its baldness was unusual for its time and medium; certainly no pageant before this one had taken so firm a position on so controversial a topic.

In the first scene, Native American men relaxed after the hunt while women worked at preparing food, grinding corn, weaving mats, and beading moccasins. When white traders came offering bows and arrows for their wars, the men merrily exchanged the items the women made, without the women's assent, and eventually even traded away their daughters. In the next scene, the Puritan men exhibited similar brutality, hanging a woman healer for witchcraft. The male and female colonists were later portrayed working side by side, until it was time for the town meeting. Then the women were invited to leave. The scene on Reconstruction featured Susan B. Anthony calling for the woman's vote to accompany that of the Black man; she was denied. The contemporary episode dramatized the continuing denial of woman's equality before the law, and showed turn-of-the-century women as disorganized and discouraged. Then the suffragists marched onstage to unite women and channel their disquiet into useful paths. Finally, "the future," borrowed from the *Allegory,* alleviated the relentless darkness with a flash of optimism. A parade of all the actors marched before Justice to witness a dance by the Spirit of Freedom and her supporters in golden costumes, celebrating to triumphant music the day when equality would reign in America.

If the twenty-five hundred viewers who contributed to the coffers of the Men's League for Woman Suffrage expected another production as uplifting as the *Allegory,* they must have been disappointed. In tone and content, the pageant was grim; its message was depressing, if not paralyzing. To many feminists, the pageant simply relayed the truth, but to the skeptics whom it sought to convert, it rang of bitter feelings and unreasonable expectations. In seeming to pervert the town histories, to ridicule their exuberance and reinterpret the past in so disrespectful a manner, MacKaye set no precedents with *Six Periods in American Life.* So unpopular was it that neither she nor anyone else ever touched its angry realism again in women's rights pageantry.

MacKaye restored her good name the following year, when Alice Paul's militant political faction, which had broken away from the moderate National American Woman Suffrage Association, requested a pageant that could be used in lobbying for suffrage. MacKaye bent over backwards to create an unambiguously inspirational pageant, and she succeeded brilliantly. For this occasion she chose to feature the biography of a single individual. This was an unusual, indeed daring, innovation. The American pageant was intended to convey universal national themes, which no one person's story seemed able to provide. Nevertheless, MacKaye's pageant deifying Susan B. Anthony achieved all its aims. It enraptured the audience of three thousand legislators, society people of influence, and suffragists at Convention Hall, while arguing cogently for a suffrage amendment to the United States Constitution. It also netted four thousand dollars for the Congressional Union.

Susan B. Anthony assembled a company of four hundred women actors, sixty choristers, and twenty-five musicians. It consisted of ten biographical scenes interspersed with five symbolic tableaux. The latter showed Anthony's family sheltering a freed woman in the 1920s—a reference to her Quaker heritage; Anthony's meeting with Elizabeth Cady Stanton; her trial for voting illegally; her lobbying at legislative hearings; and her eightieth birthday in 1900, when she saw four states embracing enfranchisement of women.[72]

Every scene plainly argued the immediate issues of the suffrage question. Through various historical episodes, actors articulated the justice of the woman suffrage cause and the ways in which the world would benefit from women's political participation. The pageant reminded listeners that the vote was already a fact of life in some states. Huge investments of time and effort had already been expended by suffragists; the time had come for contemporary women to realize the dreams of many generations of women. Those powerful lawmakers in the audience could assist a great deal. The pageant served as a practical tool for addressing the major questions and synthesizing the major arguments of the militants.

The production proved to be so clear, appealing, and useful that other cities clamored to reproduce it. MacKaye outlined a plan for distant suffragists to follow. She insisted that six hundred dollars (for seventy costumes, stage props, and her royalty) would meet the costs of a performance if local communities donated publicity, lighting, cast, transportation, performance space, and live music. The program was seen in Cleveland where it was titled *A Dream of Freedom,* and the New York State Woman Suffrage Association sponsored it in Syracuse, Albany, Rochester, Buffalo, and smaller communities within the state. The wide exposure gave MacKaye confidence that her message would have great effect. "It seems to me," she wrote, "that a pageant is the most potent means of welding the women themselves together as well as poignantly to set the question of suffrage before the voters."[73] Thus, for its durability and adaptability, MacKaye considered *Susan B. Anthony* to be her most significant contribution to the Woman Movement.[74]

While productions for schools, colleges, laborers, feminists, and pacifists kept MacKaye busy for many years, the climax of her career occurred in 1923, on the occasion of the seventy-fifth anniversary of the Seneca Falls Women's Rights Convention. The National Woman's Party, the direct descendant of the Congressional Union, planned a major celebration. It would take place at the Seneca Falls, New York, birthplace of the woman's movement, where a weekend conference would launch a new campaign for an Equal Rights Amendment to the United States Constitution.[75] An Equal Rights Pageant, its purpose to inspire pride in women's past, would kick off the conference.

The pageant created by MacKaye was an extravaganza combining the grandest elements of a generation of her previous pageants. No women's pageant had ever used so many actors; one thousand women portrayed the historical evolution of the women's rights movement. They began with a gigantic parade, the blockbusting element which, in the past, had generally signaled the grand finale. Now trumpeters and a chorus of two hundred women welcomed five hundred banner bearers and garland carriers, dressed in white and carrying flags of purple, gold, and white, the colors of the National Woman's Party. Illuminated barges floating in the darkness on Seneca Falls Lake carried actors cast as the early heroes of the woman's suffrage struggle, who alighted to the Strains of Handel's *Largo* sung by Madame Van Der Ver. Amplifying her 1915 Susan B. Anthony pageant, MacKaye included Elizabeth Cady Stanton and Lucretia Mott as characters, in addition to Anthony. In her history of women's long struggle to win equal rights, MacKaye provided a *pièce de résistance* that caused the audience to gasp. An electric sign that flashed "Declaration of Principles," a reference to the 1848 Manifesto, illuminated the evening sky.

The show was a hit, and two months later in September, the Colorado

Springs suffragists recreated it in an impressive natural setting, the Garden of the Gods near Colorado Springs. Here, appropriately, the pageant was expanded with a scene of women pioneers on the Overland Trail.[76] The following summer, fortified this time with a new scene including women of ancient Egypt, the Holy Land, Greece, and Rome, the pageant, now entitled *Forward into Light,* had its final presentation at the National Woman's Party annual conference in Westport-on-Lake Champlain in New York State. There it served as a tribute to the recently deceased suffrage heroine, Inez Milholland.[77]

The three Equal Rights pageants of 1923–24 were the swan song of pageants by Hazel MacKaye in particular, and by women's activist groups in general. They summarized an exciting era of experimentation in using amateur theatre for political ends. All-women's pageants had served the women's movement well, strengthening the skills of actors and all the other contributors, building a feeling of pride in women's achievements and abilities in participants and audiences alike, creating joyous spectacles to encourage women to strive for a fuller place in society, burying sanctions against women on the stage and women in public life, and advocating women's rights.

By the mid-1920s, however, the form was exhausted. So were the players and patrons. Although there is not yet a consensus as to the cause, scholars tend to agree that the vibrant women's movement of the turn of the century had begun to dissipate, not grow, with the women's suffrage victory in 1920. As women battled unsuccessfully for child labor laws, federal aid for maternity care, a cabinet post for education, and disarmament, their enthusiasm for pageantry seemed to decline.

At this time critics emerged to attack pageantry in biting terms. Pageant lyricist Herman Hagedorn noted:

> Most pageants are spectacles, some of them involved and tedious, some of them childish and tedious, and some of them only tedious, which have bored millions of honest citizens who did not have the courage to confess how bored they were.[78]

New technological entertainments—the radio, the Victrola, the movies, and the automobile—rivaled theater in their appeal to the average American. Many of those who had been involved in pageantry were drawn to the flourishing Little Theatre Movement of the 1920s. That movement gave rise to community theater, which produced formal plays, classics as well as experimental programs, for more limited audiences than the pageants had enjoyed. Amateur little theaters created a healthy variety of theatrical experiences for children as well as adults throughout the 1920s, and should in many ways be regarded as a positive evolution of pageantry. No other era in American history, however, sustained such a broad effort to produce successfully such an ambitious form of amateur theater as the pageant. Organized womanhood was a prime contributor to that phenomenon at the same time that she shaped pageantry to serve her changing needs.

SIX

The Little Theater Movement

The massive effort required to produce pageants was simply too taxing to be sustained, and the little theater movement emerged as the more durable successor to pageantry. While the production of plays by amateurs was smaller, easier, and cheaper to support, this brand of dramatic entertainment for neighborhood consumption could accomplish the same recreative, moral, and cooperative goals as pageantry. Between the years 1915 and 1930 multitudes of pageant supporters, as well as newcomers aboard the theatrical bandwagon, created and maintained a strong little theater movement in which amateur thespians cooperated for social as well as artistic purposes. While men were certainly present in this heyday of community drama, women's role can be said to be the key to its flourishing. Women's volunteer efforts made a substantial impact on the 1,000 little theaters that thrived in the 1920s, providing 32,500 productions per year and using 335,000 amateur actors for the pleasure of twelve and a half million spectators annually.[1]

Although the rage for amateur dramatics grew throughout the nation during this era, theater histories tend only to recognize the success of the Provincetown Players, moving from Cape Cod to New York City in 1915 to launch Eugene O'Neill's career as a playwright. In our reverence for this contribution to American commercial theater, we have forgotten that the Provincetown Players was not a unique phenomenon, but was representative of a larger movement. The enthusiasm to make plays in the 1910s and 1920s seemed to touch every social group. Young working people in Manhattan spent their two-week vacations at Catskill Mountain resorts, striving to replicate Broadway hits.[2] Immigrants in settlement houses, workers in labor colleges, children on playgrounds, students from primary grades to university-level, all joined amateur bands of thespians. Sinclair Lewis performed in *The Beau of Bath* in St. Paul, then satirized the experience in his novel *Main Street*. Louis Howe directed plays in Washington D.C., in off-hours from his responsibilities to Franklin Roosevelt. Poets Edna St. Vincent Millay and Amy Lowell played, as did Greenwich Village radicals John Reed and Louise Bryant. When Louise

Olivereau was sentenced to the federal prison at Leavenworth for urging draft resistance during World War I, her friend Minne Parkhurst entertained her with letters about the Seattle Workers' Playhouse.

What was the relationship between the older pageantry movement and the newer fashion for little theater? In both, women volunteers rallied to bring creative experiences to members of their communities. The amateur dramatic movement, however, was more efficient, refined, and durable than pageantry, thanks to the more manageable size of the company and support staff and to the lessened load of preparation for each play. Instead of requiring vast numbers in each town to abandon normal living patterns for months at a time, compact little theater companies could undertake a series of productions as simple as a series of one-act plays to accomplish similar goals.

Little theater and pageantry supporters shared a great number of goals and techniques. Both welcomed, at least in theory, widespread participation in the production and viewing of the plays; that is, they eschewed exclusivity. Both attempted to tailor the productions to the needs of the players and audiences. For instance, little theater companies devised plays for all-women casts when no male volunteers appeared, and located plays for children when the needs of the schools seemed paramount. Both the pageantry and little theater movements capitalized on the allure of story line, combined with color, costume, music, poetry, dance, and dramatic conflict, to absorb the players and audiences. Both also hoped to challenge the shallowness of commercial offerings by creating more ambitious alternatives and consciously developing material that was both wholesome and provocative, particularly to challenge the youth in their audiences. Both bemoaned the audience passivity that modern commercial entertainments invited, and sought to involve as many participants as possible in the creation of their productions—although the numbers in little theater were always small in comparison with the lavish cast sizes in community pageants. Both required generosity from volunteers, running on inadequate budgets as they did, and both movements utilized the womanpower of leisured middle-class women, who were organized through associations to deliver the labor required for success. Both pageantry and little theater enabled participants to enjoy the sense of cooperation and creativity involved in play making as well as the acclaim of the community that viewed and supported the effort.

However, genuine differences also existed between the little theater and pageantry movements. Little theaters were smaller and less demanding, and therefore likely to lure more sustained effort and ensure continuity. Instead of producing one show and disbanding forever, as pageant makers did, little theater companies could learn from their mistakes and grow more refined in their skills over time. In general, little theater casts could fit indoors, allowing audiences to better hear, see, and understand the productions. Talent was more even, insofar as involvement was limited to committed supporters rather than inviting every town organization to lend its entire membership to the company.

While little theaters reached more people in the course of their runs, they tended to be less effective than pageantry in reaching out to the general populace. The actors and support staff could become clubby, using the same individuals over and over again. For example, Black members of the community would be invited to play only the stereotypical roles of servants. Likewise, the audiences were only as broad as outreach programs created; playmakers "served" the culturally needy, rather than inviting them to contribute their talents to the production. The subject matter of the plays chosen also limited the audiences, insofar as the favored Shakespeare and Broadway comedies did not enlist the same wide community interest that town histories did. Nevertheless, little theaters pushed pageantry from the limelight in the 1920s and enjoyed the fervent support of women volunteers, most notably through the work of the Drama League of America.

From the start, women were the mainstay of the movement in every capacity from audience member to player, donor to seamstress, director to founder. They were conspicuous as playgoers, filling, one foundation study estimated, seventy percent of the theaters.[3] "Our matinee audiences are composed almost entirely of women," noted a contemporary observer,

> and our evening audiences are composed of women also, and the men that they have brought with them. Every contemporary playwright knows that it is by the suffrages of women that his work must stand or fall; in fact, the theatre is today the one great public institution in which "votes for women" is the rule, and men are overwhelmingly outvoted. Any movement to improve the theatre-going public, any movement to uplift the audience, must therefore be directed toward the women of America; and it is logical and fitting that the campaign of education and the campaign of organization should be conducted by women and by women's clubs.[4]

Women also ran playhouses throughout the nation, building fine reputations for their little theater companies. Many distinguished names emerged: Jessie Bonstelle at the Detroit Civic Theatre; Laura Sherry at the Wisconsin Players in Milwaukee; Laura Dainty Pelham at Hull House; the Lewisohn Sisters, Irene and Alice, in New York's Neighborhood Settlement House; Hallie Flanagan at Vassar College; and Cora Mel Patten with children's theater. Frequently, women in codirectorships with their spouses were overlooked when their husbands were credited, but Ellen Van Volkenberg deserves considerable credit, with Maurice Browne, for establishing the Chicago Little Theatre in 1912. Susan Glaspell worked alongside George Cram "Jig" Cook at the Provincetown Players; Florence James with Burton James in Seattle, and Rowena Jelliffe with Russell Jelliffe in Cleveland's Karamu Theatre. The list of women who made a stamp on little theater in the second and third decades of this century, as founders, directors, and also donors, is long and impressive.[5]

In their organizations particularly, women embraced little theater. Some clubs or departments in clubs saw members content to study plays and attend local amateur productions en masse. Often, however, clubwomen formed amateur companies of their own for the occasional or regular performance of plays. They frequently went on to found groups of community players or to support existing little theaters. In his classic *History of American Theatre* Glenn Hughes, drama professor at the University of Washington during the Progressive era, credited clubwomen as "important supporters."[6] Harold A. Ehrensperger, editor of the *Little Theatre Monthly,* was more generous:

> The renewed interest in the drama, the extraordinary activity in women's clubs and study groups organized over the entire country created a demand which the commercial theatre could not meet. Women with leisure had set in motion a gigantic undertaking in club work.[7]

Why were so many women attracted to amateur theatre activities at this time? As in the case of pageantry, they related these activities to democratic values to which they subscribed. Much like the other advocates of community uplift whom we have met in earlier chapters on visual arts, music, and pageantry, Mary Russell spoke for many women of her era when she argued that a healthy public theater in America not only built democracy but also reflected its strength. She said drama allowed the "development of initiative, invention or originality" in preparation for "cooperative government"; that is, it developed an appreciation of the necessity for rules, rather than blind obedience to authority. She spoke of drama "as an effective means of teaching the social principles and ethical truths necessary for harmony and progress in society,"[8] while itself demonstrating the rewards for such behaviors. Other progressives of the day echoed her sentiments about amateur theater:

> It is the most widely appealing and influential of all forms of story-telling and or amusements; its democracy inheres in these facts. Hence, anything done to make it clean, artistically attractive, mentally and emotionally stimulating in the best sense, is directly a service to the public.[9]

In an attack on the passivity invited by the popular culture of the day, advocates asserted that little theater appealed because it furnished the opportunity for active participation in creative endeavors, in welcome contrast to the "ever increasing inertia in the creation of our coming generation."[10]

In a plea to include rural populations in the quest for artistic expression, another little theater supporter declared, "There are literally millions of people in country communities to-day whose abilities along various lines have been hidden, simply because they have never had an opportunity to give expression to their talents, due to the narrow-minded attitude of society toward those who till the soil."[11]

Finally, devotees linked the new rage for little theater with the growing emphasis on developing good citizenship. Percy MacKaye, for example, spoke of "a conscious awakening of a people to self-government in the activities of its leisure,"[12] and captured the mood of considerable numbers of progressive reformers of his day. He embellished his theme:

> To this end, organization of the arts of the theatre, participation by the people in these arts (not of merchants in art), elimination of private profit by endowment

and public support, dedication in service to the whole community; these are chief among its essentials, and these imply a new and nobler scope for the art of the theatre itself. . . . a new expression of democracy.[13]

Such emphasis on the capacities of theater to enhance the democratic tradition in America had an impact on the types of plays performed in little theaters. That is, although participants recognized the origins of their movement in Europe, specifically in the experimental art theater tradition from Berlin, Moscow, and Dublin, they tended to downplay the international connection and favor works most accessible to American audiences. According to a survey of 3,619 plays reported in *Drama Magazine*'s Billboard listings from October 1925 through May 1929, by far the most popular form of play offered by little theater was comedy, accounting for 54 percent of all amateur productions.[14] Next followed drama (21 percent), farce (7 percent), tragedy (6 percent), fantasy (5 percent), melodrama (2 percent), and miscellaneous (5 percent).

While one quarter of all little theater plays produced in the 1920s were written by amateurs, and those mostly women, a survey of the period indicated that the little theaters generally offered rather predictable fare to its audiences.[15] That is, the works of George Bernard Shaw, in particular *Candida*, were performed more than those of anyone else. The plays of A. A. Milne were second in popularity, with *Mr. Pim Passes By* favored among his writings. William Shakespeare ranked third, with *Twelfth Night* his most-performed play. Next in popularity were James M. Barrie (especially *Dear Brutus*), Eugene O'Neill *(Anna Christie)*, and Henrik Ibsen *(A Doll's House)*.

Unlike the clubwomen who aspired to bring an understanding and appreciation of the arts to the general public, little theater supporters met little resistance. The rage to make and see plays was widely embraced by a broad population. However, the efforts of the theater women were obscured, then and now, by the women's willingness to contribute their energies to a product, that is a play, that was not plainly identified as a women's effort. (In this, they resembled the women who shaped town history pageants.) The little theater supporters were no less willing than other clubwomen to devise numerous mechanisms to educate themselves about the theater, to hone skills they could apply to theatrical productions, and to organize their communities to take advantage of this knowledge and skill. Yet their national organization, the Drama League of America, and frequently their local efforts, as we shall observe in the Pasadena branch, invited a small but visible male participation, which rather effectively obscured women's critical role in American play making and created the public perception that women's role was minor. This story reflects a pattern observable in the other areas of clubwomen's activity—their setting of specific and reasonable goals, determination to acquire substantial background for their projects, and zeal and creativity in bringing these tasks to completion. However, it also documents a commitment to the arts that excluded a concern to win recognition for women's substantial role in delivering theater to America's communities.

The Drama League of America, 1910–1930

The Drama League of America, a largely women's group that quickly became one of the most influential theater organizations of the 1910s and 1920s, was an outgrowth of a woman's club. Its object, to make social change through uplifting drama, was stated plainly in the league's charter of 1910:

> to stimulate an interest in the best drama and to awaken the public to the importance of the theatre as a social force and to its great educational value if maintained on the high level of art and morals. To harmonize and unify forces already existing for making this movement nation-wide. To co-ordinate the work of all associations and individuals interested in educating the public to appreciate and demand the best drama.[16]

These goals held enormous appeal, particularly among other women's organizations, which immediately accorded the Drama League the publicity and support to ensure it would flourish. Sixty-three existing drama societies, with a membership of ten thousand, united at the founding of the Drama League of America in 1910. Within a year and a half, the League had attracted twenty thousand members in thirty-five states. By 1913, eighty thousand members had joined; by 1914, ninety thousand; and by 1915, membership peaked at one hundred thousand.[17]

Alice Cushing Donaldson Riley (1867–1955) was instrumental in founding and sustaining the Drama League of America. She is representative of the energy and talent that were tapped by the organization. Born in Illinois and raised in Iowa, she studied music in Germany and married an attorney, Harrison Barnett Riley, when she was twenty-two years old. He climbed the corporate ladder at Chicago Title and Trust Company, finally serving as its president and chairman of the board from 1907 to 1928. They had a son and a daughter. While raising the family, she wrote and published children's plays and verses.[18] She also became enormously active in a wide range of voluntary associations, found time to assemble bibliographies on the drama for other theater enthusiasts, and ran Chicago's Municipal Pier Children's Theatre. She and her husband retired to Pasadena, California in 1924, where she wrote plays, forged alliances with the Pasadena Drama League and Pasadena Playhouse, and not surprisingly once again joined numerous organizations.[19]

The Drama League had its beginnings in 1901, when Alice C. D. Riley invited a few friends to sew and read plays at her Evanston home, where she could also keep an eye on her two children. The Riley Circle turned out to satisfy its participants handily, and its members met every Thursday for twenty years, long after the children had grown. The regular meeting permitted the women to familiarize themselves with an astonishing number and range of plays while in the company of good friends.

Riley's immersion in American amateur theatrical life was a direct outgrowth of the drama-reading Riley Circle she had founded, and the club would serve others similarly. Reflecting a pattern of ambition developed in many women's groups, the Riley Circle's members sponsored a drama lecture course only six years after the club began. Their profits of $154 encouraged them to incorporate their association, rename it the Drama Club of Evanston, and take on more and more dramatic challenges.[20] The club members began not only reading and discussing plays, but also performing occasionally for each other and even for small audiences, like YWCA members. In addition, they alerted each other to professional touring productions in nearby Chicago, so that their theater-loving friends would be sure to enjoy the best fare available.

Considering their enthusiasm for the theater, it is not surprising that the women of Evanston's Drama Club came to criticize the mediocre quality of commercial productions traveling through America under the auspices of the consolidating drama syndicates. The low standards evident in popular burlesque and vaudeville shows also troubled them. They sought a higher level of drama for themselves and the rest of the population, and began to organize to improve drama standards by building a market for more intellectually challenging and morally uplifting entertainment.

First, the members visited other women's clubs throughout the region, persuading them to study drama, both classics and contemporary works, as their group did. Next, in a move that would have broad repercussions for American theater history, they called together sixty representatives, from clubs with membership totalling ten thousand, to a conference in Chicago in April 1910. Assembled there were delegates from the range of women's clubs that would support the work of the budding theater organization, including the Evanston Woman's Club, the Catholic Women's League, and college clubs and civic societies from Louisville, Kentucky, and Milwaukee.[21] At this initial meeting, the women formed the Drama League of America to unite like-minded theater enthusiasts in small women's clubs into a national pressure group for better theater for all American audiences.

The leader of the new organization, who would retain key influence for two decades, was a woman of means. Marjorie Ayres Best (1874–1942) was born on Cape Cod, but spent most of her first twenty-five years in New York City. There she enjoyed a privileged education, by governess and private school, including lessons in voice and elocution. She attended the theater avidly. At the age of fifteen, she entered Smith College, where she became active in extracurricular dramatics. In 1896, she married Albert Starr Best, who founded Best Department Stores, specializing in children's clothing. They raised two sons and two daughters in Evanston, Illinois, but Marjorie also found plenty of time to steer the amateur theater movement, not only through the Drama League but also through her church and in wartime programs. Even after her stroke in 1933, neighborly thespians read plays to her each week until she died in 1942.[22]

For all her reliance on women's groups to fuel the enthusiasm for amateur theater that was growing in this country, Best continually sought male involvement in the Drama League, whose goals, she insisted, had relevance for both sexes. If women's beliefs were to have wide impact and transform all of society, she felt men must embrace them. Although Best would retain a key role in the Drama League of America, she hastily relinquished the presidency to men,[23] boasting early in its history:

> In its short time, the movement has even outlived the "ignominy" of being a woman's movement—it was started by the women's clubs of Chicago—and now has men as president in nearly half of the established centers; there are more men than women on its National Board of Directors, men representing all parts of the country and all types of interest.[24]

A decade later, she continued effectively to place men in prominent positions throughout the organization:

> The League rejoices in a board composed of a very loyal group of noted experts, mostly distinguished for service along drama lines. The officers are all men and there are only four women among its numbers, showing that it is no longer a "woman's movement" but a devoted group giving its best effort to the solution of recreational problems of the times.[25]

With Best's blessing, the editor of the league's journal was also a man, high school teacher Theodore B. Hinckley, and at the annual conventions the dais was dominated by male speakers, largely educators, publishers, philanthropists, and writers who were included to provide status, expertise and financial security. At the fifteenth annual convention in Cincinnati, for example, only two of the twenty-eight speakers were women. Likewise, male actors, donors, and dramatists were always welcome to take leadership positions in Best's Drama League. On the 1926 board of directors, seventeen men and five women served; in 1929, twenty-one men and three women. At first glance, then, the Drama League appears to have embodied Best's dream of demonstrating male enthusiasm for the goals framed by the female founders of the league. In reality, however, the men were largely figureheads in the organization, lending the luster of their reputations but little else. Their contributions never matched the considerable efforts of the female rank and file. Worst of all, by robbing the women of the control and visibility they deserved for their substantial volunteerism, the consistently male leadership would hasten the day when clubwomen's disenchantment with the league would put it out of business.

The rapid growth and success of the Drama League was due to the organizer's ingenuity at tapping the knowledge and enthusiasm of women's groups. Five hundred Chautauquas and teacher's institutes publicized the league. A strong alliance was begun with the General Federation of Women's Clubs in 1910, when the Cincinnati Biennial Conference gave Mrs. Best a forum to explain her new group and its goals to a huge delegation. The Federation supported Best immediately, urging its department clubs to establish theater sections that could join the league. Many did so. The warm relationship never abated. We will trace the GFWC's organizational impact on the Drama League and observe their cooperation on a number of issues. Finally, we will note the ways in which federated clubs filled the ranks of the Drama League.

The initial work of the Drama League revolved around members' dissatisfaction with the shallow and even immoral commercial theatrical offerings of the day. These women were "alive to the danger inherent in the powerful influence of the drama over the public, if that influence is not ennobling, uplifting."[26] The new membership was attracted by the hope of correcting "the dismal state of theatre now corrupting or at least failing to stimulate Americans" and to meet with "worthy plays the present tendency to tawdriness and uncleanliness on the boards."[27]

Cognizant of the dangers to civil liberties inherent in outright censorship of bad plays, the Drama League simply organized the "ticket-buying audience—for good, clean, well-written drama, well produced."[28] In boosting reputable productions rather than censoring disapproved ones, they took their cue from the feminists who had established the Consumer's League in 1910. Even the name of the Drama League reflects their emulation of the Consumer's League activist methods. The Consumer's League was an association of women who sought to discourage manufacturers and merchants who engaged in unfair labor practices against women and other employees, and to reward those who initiated fair working conditions, by issuing a White List of fair-minded businessmen. No censorious black list was ever employed. After their inspection of the commercial establishments, the Consumer's League publicized, as widely as possible, a recommended number of good companies with which consumers could trade in good conscience.

The Drama League quickly established committees along similar lines in many cities, whose members would view each play when it opened. "Bulletins" were published and distributed, listing the plays considered appropriate and satisfying for discerning audiences. A single page in length, the bulletins provided a plot summary and critique of the playwriting, acting, and staging for each production they endorsed. The Chicago branch of the Drama League, for instance, sent its Playgoing Committee of five women and three men to all forty-five non-musical plays that were performed in Chicago in 1914. (They had insufficient numbers of volunteers to examine the musicals as well.) From this total, the committee approved eighteen plays,[29] and placed copies of the "white list" of recommended productions in settlement houses, women's clubs, and the Chicago Art Institute. Not surprisingly, established classics were approved—works by Euripides, Shakespeare, Racine, and Molière. Modern plays of worth by Ibsen, George Bernard Shaw, Chekhov, and J. M. Barrie, and light productions like Percy MacKaye's *Anti-Matrimony* also won approval by the Chicago branch. New plays by women playwrights such as Rachel Crothers were also endorsed. Plays that dealt with the daring subjects of divorce and sex appeared on the approved list, as did Philip Moeller's *Madame Sand*, about the love affairs of the French novelist. The Drama League was not stuffy.

The New York branch was more critical. Its members saw fifty plays in the last five months of 1917, and found less than ten to have merit. They had praise for *Peter Ibbetson, Boomerang, A Kiss for Cinderella, Turn to the Right, Thirteenth Chair, Lady of the Camellias* with Ethel Barrymore, *Once Upon a Time, Karen,* and *Madame Sand,* but rejected such plays as *The Very Idea* which had been bulletined in Chicago.[30] The committee also declined to endorse *Polly with a Past, Leave It to Jane, Eve's Daughter, What's Your Husband Doing?,* and *The Naughty Wife.* The previous year, the New York chapter had effectively publicized the efforts of Ridgeley Torrence, an African-American playwright, author of *The Rider of Dreams, Simon the Cyrenian,* and *Granny Maumee,* the latter a tragedy about three Southern Black women dealing with lynching:

> A delightful evening is in store for those who visit the Garden Theatre and find three one-act plays by Mr. Ridgeley Torrence, each of which presents a different phase of negro character, and is at the same time universally human. Viewed as a whole it is the best bill of one-act plays recently presented. Its unity in variety, its fundamental poetic truth, and its beauty of presentation make it a performance not to be passed by.[31]

The idea behind the strategy was to encourage the production of high quality drama by promoting the best plays and thereby boosting their ticket sales. Full houses and fat profits for theater managers influenced impresarios to reject bad productions for good. The "theater party," or the booking of an entire bank of seats by a woman's club early enough in a play's run to extend it, demonstrated to theater backers that an aware clientele guaranteed good box office. The Drama League boasted that it saved a good many plays—like Galsworthy's *Skin Game*—from withering, and brought financial success with its stamp of approval.[32] In a survey of the impact of the Chicago bulletins, it was determined that the 687 members bought 17,182 tickets for fifteen plays, or forty percent of the houses. In Philadelphia, the league claimed even greater successes, namely that sixty percent of ticket sales were due to League influence.

Despite the Drama League's insistence on the impact of their bulletins, the plan exhibited many drawbacks. Each city's branch of the league held autonomy in decision making. A play championed in New York might be conspicuously absent on the Boston rolls. Therefore, a lack of uniformity undermined the strength of the lists. The white list criteria were not articulated, and there were diverse grounds on which a play might be judged good or bad. Moreover, there were small towns that were so seldom visited by traveling productions that only one or two of the lauded shows might ever appear there. Still smaller villages never saw decent theater at all, and the league was in no immediate position to correct this deficiency. Finally, and most disadvantageous of all, many profit seekers regarded the approval of the Drama League as the kiss of death:

> We think it is fair to say that most managers dread a Drama League endorsement. It hurts business instead of helping it . . . the general public is apt to get the

impression that there is something tedious and pretentious to be avoided at all cost.[33]

Many other producers, however, embraced the concept wholeheartedly. The "blessed" Chicago managers, for example, reprinted bulletins at their own expense to fill their houses.[34]

However it was regarded, the bulletin project came to play second fiddle to the other greatly expanded activities of the league after 1915. By that time, numbers of schoolteachers and clubwomen had become interested in amateur theater. In response, the league's focus shifted away from the role of watchdog of the commercial theater, toward the new responsibility of encouraging and guiding community amateur dramatic troupes—or, as they came to be known, little theaters. From 1915 until its demise in 1930, the Drama League of America served primarily as a catalyst in the countrywide explosion of enthusiasm for community amateur theater.

The organization now escalated its efforts to educate amateur theater enthusiasts about ways to improve their own dramatic efforts. Emulating the Women's Christian Temperance Union, the General Federation of Women's Clubs, and the National American Woman Suffrage Association, the league borrowed many techniques that had proven effective in women's organizational efforts. Annual conventions, contests, newsletters, and summer institutes were among the systems the Drama League borrowed, with good results, to tend and feed the new national interest in the potential of amateur theater.

An annual conference was held almost unfailingly from 1910 to 1931, and was open to any dues-paying member of the Drama League. Amateur theater enthusiasts were invited to these conferences at a different American city each spring for instruction and exchange of information.[35] This practice encouraged those already involved in theater to share their expertise, and informed and inspired potential organizers of local drama clubs (called centers or sometimes circles), as well as players. Some important exchanges between delegates took place informally, over convention dinners, receptions, and teas, often sponsored by a local woman's club.

The attraction of the sociability was as great as that of the theater information to be gained at Drama League conventions. At the Philadelphia convention in 1914, the Philomusian Club held a party for conferees at the luxurious New Century Club. Pasadena hospitality was extended at the 1924 convention, through tea parties and receptions at the estates of affluent members. At the Cincinnati meeting, it was the Cincinnati Woman's Club that hosted a gala. Trips to artistic sites in the region also provided an opportunity for camaraderie. Women-supported institutions, like the Rookwood Pottery in Cincinnati and the Chicago Art Institute, offered tours to Drama League delegates, whose arts interests encompassed a full range of creative enterprises in addition to the theater.

Naturally, however, local amateur theater productions were of key interest to the conventioneers; almost half a dozen plays, of all stripes, might be showcased in a single weekend. In Philadelphia, Plays and Players performed the fifteenth-century play *Maître Patelin*. The Vassar Players came to Chicago in 1921 with *Aria del Capo* by Edna St. Vincent Millay. Members also attended Percy MacKaye's *Pilgrim Pageant*. Mary E. Hamlin's *The Rock,* a religious play that won the Drama League's playwriting prize, was executed by the Pilgrim Players at the First Congregational Church of Evanston for the attentive and appreciative convention delegates in 1921. Local groups were featured, as well as troupes that traveled to the conventions for the special purpose of performing prize-winning productions. The rich theatrical fare served to further educate and inspire delegates about the calling that had brought them to the convention.

Not surprisingly, the conventions offered a formal slate of speeches on subjects related to theater, by acclaimed experts in the field. The mostly female audiences took in the special expertise of the mostly male speakers at lectures and workshops. Not professional actors, but educators, officers of the Drama League, drama critics, and little theater directors spoke on technique and theory. For example, George Pierce Baker, a Harvard professor, spoke to the group on his experiences in teaching drama. George Junkin gave an account of his success with rural productions, while Alexander Dean and Gordon Davis provided advice for financing little theaters, and Daniel Quirk, Jr. described his directorship of the players in Ypsilanti, Michigan. To be sure, some women were also represented at the dais. Hazel MacKaye, fresh from her victory with woman suffrage pageantry, spoke on the "Use of Pageantry" in 1914. Constance D'Arcy Mackay and Cora Mel Patten regularly addressed questions about children's theater, and Alice C. D. Riley reported on her playwriting.

Local talent, often considerable, was shared at the meetings for the benefit of the delegates. When the 1927 conference was held in Tacoma, Washington, the nearby city of Seattle provided an array of its amateur drama movers and shakers. Even though they generally did not get along with one another, five talented figures pooled their knowledge for the conventioneers in Tacoma: Glenn Hughes, drama professor at the University of Washington; Maurice Browne and Ellen Van Volkenberg, drama teachers at Cornish School, and widely respected for founding the first little theater in America; and Florence and Burton James, who had left Cornish School and the University of Washington to form a Seattle Repertory Playhouse, which would become the WPA Washington State Theatre during the Great Depression.

The meetings also included reports on the growth of Drama League circles. Delegates gave joyful accounts of new centers springing up in cities large and small—not only in the United States, but in Canada and England as well. While few centers could emulate the work of the unusually active New York City Center, which annually honored renowned celebrities like Eugene O'Neill and Eva Le Gallienne, it gave all centers confidence that Drama League ideals commanded respect among the worthies. Moreover, when delegates from one center identified their problems in putting on a particular play or coping with a common difficulty, representatives from other cities could deliver solutions. The conferences served to spread workable ideas generously and efficiently.

The Drama League also used the conventions to publicize its newest programs. A Lecture Bureau was established, modeled on those of older women's organizations. Convention delegates learned that the bureau would send experts with sparkling lectures or grand reputations to women's groups yearning for qualified speakers. The league began another bureau to solve costuming questions. Susan Taft, daughter of sculptor and drama enthusiast Lorado Taft, ran this service, even sewing samples and sending patterns for puzzled volunteers in the wardrobe departments of little theaters.

Thus, the Drama League provided services and education beyond the sessions at the annual conventions. When novices within the organization expressed interest in a brief course in dramatic production, the Summer Institute was founded in Chicago in 1920. For ten days in August the leading Chicago experts in drama, who were also Drama League officers, presented an intensive series of classes from 9:00 a.m. to 5:00 p.m. each day, with attendance at evening performances in the city. High school drama, religious drama, folk dancing, stagecraft, costuming, community recreation, pageantry, batik, and junior Bible were among the subjects treated by a broad range of instructors. The program was successful, a big money maker for the organization, and grew each summer. It filled three weeks by 1925, encompassing little theater management, dancing, voice, puppetry, makeup, and storytelling. It was probably the most ambitious crash course in theater available at the time.[36]

Obviously, this form of study was accessible only to a few. For wider instruction, the Drama League employed other, more traditional means. From the start, it kept members informed through the *Drama Quarterly* (later entitled *Drama Monthly* or *Drama Magazine*).[37] This publication reprinted officer reports and guest speeches for those who did not attend the conventions, listed successful productions of the many little theater groups around the country, and offered study guides, book lists, and monologues. These services were expensive. Like those of most voluntary organizations, the Drama League's periodical experienced continual financial difficulties. Despite the stable editorship of Theodore Ballou Hinckley, it never achieved financial security.

A steady stream of queries to Drama League headquarters soon pinpointed the need for a publishing program beyond its regular periodical. In response, the leadership solicited bibliographies on various subjects, such as "Plays for Children" and "Plays for Amateurs."[38] Study guides were published on Shakespearean tragedies and comedies, commedia dell'arte, pageantry, and modern English, Scandinavian, or Spanish plays. Each guide included an annotated bibliography, notably rich in women's contributions. The league made alliances with publishers such as George H. Doran Company, which published the Junior Play Series in which Alice Riley's *Ten Minutes by the Clock* was included. In 1914, Doubleday, Page and Company began publication of an inexpensive series of plays, American and foreign. Paperbacks were fifty cents, hardbacks seventy-five, priced to reach broad audiences. In New York City, the Drama League opened a bookstore in the theater district, near Broadway at Times Square, for walk-in traffic.

Many of the plays published were prize-winning efforts by amateur playwrights, most of them women. Contests seemed to excite women to try a hand at writing for the stage as nothing else did. The Drama League of America held competitions for one-act plays, children's plays, and Bible plays. Local Drama League centers, like the Pasadena Drama League, held their own competitions. One hundred and forty plays were entered into one Patriotic Play Competition during wartime, in February 1918. The contests sometimes identified and encouraged talent that would be developed further through Drama League channels. Hallie Flanagan (who became the director of the New Deal-funded Federal Theatre Project in 1935) won a competition prize from the Des Moines Little Theatre Contest for her play, *The Curtain*. She saw it subsequently published in the Drama League's magazine.[39] Sometimes the rewards were even greater than simply honor and publicity. In cooperation with Longmans Green Publishing Company, the prize-winning plays of 1928 were published, giving royalties and fame to Allison Gaw and Ethelean Tyson Gaw, who won the biblical prize with *Pharaoh's Daughter*. Samuel French, a well-respected publisher of plays, published an entry contributed by a member of the Drama League's Shreveport Center.

Not only did Drama League borrow methods of disseminating information and enthusiasm from other women's clubs, but they also shared many concerns, among them children, patriotism during World War I, and education. Such overlapping concerns enabled the league to grow steadily, in tandem with the broader women's club movement.

A range of issues dealing with child welfare engaged Drama League members no less than other clubwomen, although solutions tended to be related to drama. The league opposed child labor on the stage as well as in the factory. It attempted to solve the problem of rural children's boredom and isolation through the stimulation of rural theater, especially in North Dakota, Iowa, and North Carolina, where clubwomen were already addressing themselves to the problems of rural life.

Drama League conventions and publications expended considerable effort on promoting children's theater. Much touted was the Chicago Drama League's summer project, which began in 1917 and continued throughout the 1920s as the Children's Civic Theatre at the Municipal Pier. Securing money from the city council, members initiated theater workshops for children in the Pier Auditorium. To stimulate the imagination of children from ethnic backgrounds, they provided free classes in storytelling, pantomime, interpretive dance, and choral singing. Finally, participants put on plays for other children, costumes courtesy of the mothers. Sponsors of the Children's Civic Theatre claimed to unveil local talent and teach democracy at the same time.[40] This effort inspired similar projects by Drama League centers throughout the country, enhanced by alliances with playground associations, government recreation departments, and educators.

During World War I the Drama League was ignited by patriotic fervor no less than other women's organizations of its day. Inspired by an outburst of

Americanism, the league moved its national headquarters from Chicago to Washington D.C. for the duration of the war. The publications of the organization praised local efforts toward patriotism, such as the San Diego branch's sponsorship of Liberty Plays for forty thousand servicemen, and the activities of the circle in Buffalo, where the members sold six hundred dollars' worth of Liberty Bonds in theaters. The St. Louis convention of 1917 was all war talk, calling for a native drama instead of plays by foreigners, and recommending theater for the building of a national spirit.[41]

The Drama Leaguers, like other clubwomen of the era, made a priority of educating the general public about their topic. Every winter, the league sponsored a Drama Week which was implemented in other women's clubs. Members and their supporters circulated appropriate editorials, club papers, speeches, and sermons to the community. Many periodicals published lists of ideas for activities to make groups aware of the theater during the winter, such as club costume parties, play readings, games of matching playwrights with the titles of their plays, group attendance at a play, or putting on a play. Since mid-February was an occasion for club celebrations of Washington's and Lincoln's birthdays, productions with patriotic impact were the most widely enacted.

The Drama League and other clubs worked together during the celebration of the Shakespeare Tercentenary of 1916, and the Pilgrim Tercentenary of 1920. The bibliographies and scripts for community celebrations supplied by the Drama League for the General Federation of Women's Clubs is a useful illustration of the services the league was proud to offer to stimulate increased theater activity.

While the GFWC was firmly a secular organization, the Drama League attached itself to religious institutions for mutual benefit, although the focus was on instruction rather than beliefs. League officers realized the potential for growth through churches. Some clergymen had expressed opposition to the burgeoning popularity of amateur dramatics; the American Federation of Catholic Societies, for example, published a "Manifesto of 1915" against "immoral and demoralizing plays."[42] After World War I, Drama Leaguers began to argue that the Oberammergau pageant, performed since 1633, effectively advanced the cause of Christianity. They also reminded clerics that medieval morality plays had been a mainstay of the church in centuries past.

Churchgoers came to accept the use of drama for religious education because it appealed to young members that they hoped to win and keep. They were perturbed that fifteen million children received no religious instruction and that thirty-five million Americans over the age of ten lived without church affiliation. If drama was alluring to young people, then the church would use it to bolster their congregations.[43] Marjorie Best had achieved practical results when she formed the Pilgrim Players and Junior Pilgrim Players at her Evanston church in 1916.[44] Especially at Easter and Christmas, religious drama took hold, keeping youth interested in the church by teaching its precepts in a dramatic form. In the 1920s Dr. S. Parkes Cadman, last president of the

Drama League, wrote a regular column on religious drama for the league's publication. By 1930, the league held its conference in tandem with the Religious Drama Association, and for a time merged with it.

How effectively did women's civic and study clubs support the Drama League? Was there true reciprocity in the arrangement? Most emphatically, yes. The general population of women's club members supported league goals by sponsoring drama contests, and providing publicity, showcases, and monetary prizes that generated wide interest in amateur playwriting and acting. The Chicago Woman's Club, for example, awarded a fifty dollar prize for the group with the best voices and action. The New York State Federation of Women's Clubs, the California Federation of Women's Clubs, the Iowa Federation of Women's Clubs, and the Texas Federation of Women's Clubs all sponsored playwriting contests. The New Jersey Federation of Women's Clubs held an annual five-day little theater tournament in the 1920s to which affiliated clubs sent troupes of players to compete.[45]

The Drama League also cooperated with women's groups eager to produce a play for community causes. For instance, the Tacoma, Washington Drama League worked with the local Daughters of the American Revolution on a play to help the YWCA raise money. The Pittsburgh Drama League worked with the First Unitarian Church Woman's Alliance for similar purposes.

It had become clear to women's groups that the theater could serve the needs of any women's group. The Woman's Peace Party, for example, sought out the Chicago Little Theatre when World War I broke out in Europe. They paid five thousand dollars to sponsor a tour of Euripides' *Trojan Women*, regarded by members as the world's greatest peace play. In fifteen weeks, forty-two performances in thirty-one cities reached thirty-three thousand viewers, including audiences at San Francisco's International Exposition. However, the play folded in Spokane when the company ran out of money.[46]

For all its service to the goals of women's clubs and those of the larger Progressive reform community, the strength of the Drama League, like that of most of the organizations examined in these pages, waned considerably toward the end of the 1920s. After responding to the needs of literally millions of theater enthusiasts, the league dissolved in 1931.

Explanations for the organization's demise can be found in both internal and external conditions. Within the organization, the problems concerned leadership and finance. The decision makers of the Drama League emerged and remained firmly entrenched in the Midwest, based most emphatically in Chicago under the supervision of Marjorie Best and her circle. The failure to distribute power to other regions of the country, notably New York—then the unchallenged center of professional theatrical life—weakened the willingness of other regions to participate. In fact, the New York chapter of the Drama League, unable to wrest its fair share of influence from the Chicago group, remained separate from the national organization for most of their histories.

It is likely that Best's proclivity for selecting male presidents for her organization, almost exclusively from the Midwest, also discouraged wider support. Talented officers throughout the United States, women as well as men, could have delivered broader involvement. The individuals who did reach the top, while certainly capable and celebrated in the field, held such extensive commitments to other projects and institutions that they were clearly incapable of devoting much attention to the specific needs of the Drama League. Most were figureheads. This was perhaps as Best intended it; however, the lack of new blood in league directorship served the organization badly.

The league's relatively narrow base inevitably made fund-raising difficult, particularly when members developed aspirations of serving rural and school populations, as well as the community drama enthusiasts. Efforts to build an endowment to pay for those services failed continually. In 1922, the leadership launched a campaign to raise $25,000 for the purpose of hiring additional staff workers. Millionaire arts philanthropist Otto Kahn, who had been courted as a potential benefactor for years, contributed only $250 to the fund. In 1925, the Drama League applied for two major grants, from the Carnegie Foundation and from the Laura Spelman Rockefeller Memorial Foundation. It was disappointed in both endeavors. In December of 1927, it launched still a third unsuccessful fund-raising campaign. A theatrical tour of Europe earned some much-needed income in 1928, but the tour lost money the following year. The lean budget, coupled with the loss of key volunteers—as in the 1929 death of Theodore Hinckley, who had served as the league's magazine editor for sixteen years—hampered the organization in planning for its future.

1929 saw an ambitious plan to resurrect the organization by merging with the Church and Drama Association of New York City, an organization that enjoyed backing by the Rockefeller Foundation and appeared to be on firm financial footing. For all the financial sense it made, this alliance outraged a significant part of the Drama League membership. Six important Drama League centers withdrew from the organization in protest over the organizational modification. Boston, Charleston, Chicago, Los Angeles, Pasadena, and Worcester were large chapters; the league rocked with their withdrawal. Only eleven centers, with 5,305 members, now remained. The merger, which had proved to be so disastrous, was undone.

Despite this retraction, the blow dealt by the attempted merger proved fatal. At the May 1931 league conference in New York City a mere three hundred members appeared. Noting the scanty treasury of $34, this handful voted to dissolve the organization. They closed down the headquarters, fired the staff, suspended all publication plans, and maintained only a mailing address, from which volunteers would continue to function. While National Drama Week continued to be celebrated by many institutions, only one remnant of the organization hung on. That remnant was in New York City, where ties to professional theater remained strong, and where members still meet for an annual dinner at which theater personalities are honored.

For all the trials specific to the Drama League's operation, however, other forces need to be considered for an understanding of the demise of the organization and of the little theater movement, which sank alongside it. In part, the fashion for amateur dramatics simply abated as society moved on to other infatuations—such as the more and more splendid moving picture shows—

and coped with such major tragedies as the Great Depression. However, even those with more than a passing interest in the little theater eventually faced the limits and frustrations of the movement. One writer, for example, observed the seemingly irreconcilable tension between the little theater's wish to challenge mass culture and its hunger for mass support. Helen Deutsch admitted that her peers in the little theater movement "expect little theatres to be experimental."[47] Most audiences simply wanted plays to be fun.

Disenchantment was also expressed by the women volunteers who had delivered so many services and received so little glory. "The little theatre is sick!" complained commentator Harold Ehrensperger as early as 1927, attributing the ailment to the displacement of women by professional directors entering the little theater.[48] To be sure, some of these professionals were women; and large numbers of women students would be the beneficiaries of the burgeoning university drama programs that emerged from this wave of excitement. But the texture had changed. The Drama League, which had built its empire on the labor of women volunteers, failed to retain their loyalty. The catalyst for people's play making moved to another arena within the community, away from the playhouses and into the schools.

If the Drama League disintegrated, amateur dramatics did not. The vitality of little theater has hung on in more than a few towns and cities, and professional and semiprofessional community theaters today can trace their origins to this early twentieth century hope for strengthening the nation on the stage.

The Drama League at the Pasadena Playhouse, 1916–1928

Those who were lucky enough to obtain tickets to a performance of the brand new Pasadena Community Playhouse during the month of May 1925 must have been dazzled indeed by all that they saw. The $400,000 Spanish-style stucco theater was ornamented with tile roof, lush greenery, a broad patio, and a baroque-style fountain. The courtyard would have been abuzz with proud citizens as well as "snowbirds" who were visiting Southern California for its mild winter. Hollywood moguls, creative neighbors like writers Upton Sinclair or Pulitzer Prize winner Zoë Akins, glittering tourists—perhaps an oil baron or Maria Montessori—were likely to have been present along with Pasadena socialites, students, or working people. Musicians dressed in costume played tunes appropriate to the era of the play, setting the tone for the production. Young women wearing full skirts and Spanish shawls welcomed ticketholders with programs. Once inside the 820-seat theater, an impressive production with elaborate scenery, costumes, and props, all rendered by amateur volunteers from the community, awaited the audience. After the applause subsided for the company of local amateur thespians' presentation of Victor Mapes's new play *The Amethyst,* the audience could hurry to the Green Room to drink hot cocoa while meeting their neighbor/actors and the director.

For all its glamour, however, the experience of the ticketholder would have paled in comparison to that of a Pasadena Drama League member on the occasion of the opening season of the new facility. Her satisfaction arose not from the glamour of the setting, the aura of the play, or the surprising amount of talent in her town, but from her realization that it was her efforts that had established this healthy community theater. Not only did she have a hand in every aspect of production, but she had also created ties that linked the production to every corner of her city. The Drama Leaguer would be attending this play surrounded by many of the six hundred members of the Pasadena Drama League. The actors she applauded would be her friends and other Pasadena citizens who had auditioned and won parts, from starring roles to spear-carrying cameos in mob scenes. She herself might have donated props, sewn costumes, or painted scenery for either this play or the one that would follow in two weeks' time. Perhaps she had invited her Garden Club to donate the greenery onstage or the flowers in the lobby. It is likely she would have viewed this splendid theater with self-congratulation, recalling all the fund-raising she had accomplished for it, perhaps by chaperoning public dances all summer long.

She would have been responsible for winning the acceptance of Miss Hoit, the town librarian, whom she had coaxed into endorsing an exhibition of miniature stage sets in the downtown library foyer; and Mr. Vroman, with whom she had arranged for his bookstore window to contain a display of copies of the play. She might observe many other Pasadena residents who also had a stake in the production's popularity: the schoolteachers expressing their delight that their students could view a play they were reading in English class; community boosters from the Chamber of Commerce and Kiwanis noting the presence of vacationers who, properly entertained, were likely to return again next year to spend money at Pasadena businesses; the Red Cross officers, who had reserved the balcony, delighted to be raising relief funds from the resale of the tickets.

As for herself, the Drama League member had gained as much as she had given to the theatrical enterprise. She had probably read the play for the last club meeting, where expert speakers had addressed its technical or philosophical aspects. She might even have tried her hand at writing a spoof on it for the amusement of her peers. She must have been pleased to have initiated this community feast for eye and ear, to have created this cohesion in her town, to have provided wholesome entertainment in a society all too accustomed to chasing hollow pleasures. She would devour the laudatory review in the next day's *Pasadena Star-News* with genuine interest, for she felt herself to be as much a player in this drama as any actor on the stage.

The little theater experience in Pasadena was not typical of American community drama history. However, it deserves attention here as a case study of a local branch of the Drama League of America because it reflects the success that clubwomen could achieve under optimal conditions. The relationship between the community's playhouse and the Pasadena Drama League demonstrates that women could accomplish a great deal to build an institution as well-supported, vigorous, and esteemed as the Pasadena Community Playhouse.

The Pasadena women's enthusiasm for little theater sprang from a series of women's organizations devoted to the drama. Since 1888, the Shakespeare Club had devoted a considerable portion of its program to the study, discussion, and performance of the Bard's plays, holding a Shakespeare birthday party every April and inviting theater experts to speak at their meetings. In 1917, the membership endorsed the creation of a department devoted to modern drama, which showcased several experts as lecturers each year.[49] Meanwhile, the College Women's Club of Pasadena developed a drama section more plainly infatuated with the magic of movie making. The department offered monthly trips—including a tour of the Max Factor makeup factory in nearby Hollywood and another of the Calkin's Studio, which made stage scenery.[50] The Tuesday Morning Drama Class, formed in 1912 under the leadership of Mrs. J. B. Durand, thrived for over forty years, its members meeting regularly for the sole purpose of reading and discussing new plays.[51] Such activity nurtured a nucleus of well-read and enthusiastic patrons of the drama, women who would provide Pasadena's theatrical experiments with appreciative audiences and informed supporters.

The two most important events in Pasadena's theater history occurred in 1916. First, the Pasadena women separated from Los Angeles' Drama League to form their own center of the Drama League of America, at the instigation of Alice C. D. Riley who was visiting from Evanston. Secondly, a troupe of professional actors, under the direction of Gilmor Brown, made a failed attempt to establish a stable repertory company in Pasadena and then fell upon a brilliant alternative, the establishment of a community theater. Both elements deserve consideration.

Like the other one hundred and fifteen Drama League centers of the era, the objects of the Pasadena Drama League were to encourage and support good drama, to discourage vicious or poor plays by attending good ones, to build up audiences for good drama through study courses, reading circles, and lectures, and to develop better plays for better audiences, better audiences for better plays.[52] In truth, these goals were rarely a priority. Instead, the organization used the drama as a cause around which to rally the community and facilitate a cooperative interaction that they viewed as an artistic expression of democracy. Members' insistence on ambitious theatrical fare was subsidiary to these civic ends.

At the start of Pasadena's Drama League, president Sibyl Eliza Jones attracted influential members of the community to give the group immediate social standing. No doubt she had learned the wisdom of such action through her participation in other Pasadena clubs: the Shakespeare Club, the Tuesday Morning Drama Class, and the Woman's University Club. As an amateur playwright, with a B.A. from the University of California at Berkeley and an M.A. in comparative literature, she had a love and knowledge of theater, but her social status was equally valuable to the league.[53] One woman invited to serve as vice-president was Virginia Pease Hunt, active in her community through the Women's Civic League and the World War I Camp Committee. Hunt carried some social importance from her husband, Myron, who was the architect of most of the grand structures in the city: the Henry E. Huntington Library, the California Institute of Technology, the Rose Bowl, and resort hotels and lavish residences. Similarly, Elma Stuart, who served as the league's second vice-president, was the wife of Holloway Stuart, considered to be the premier banker of the city.[54]

A handful of men were also involved in the founding of Pasadena's Drama League. One of these was Dr. Robert Freeman, pastor of the Presbyterian Church for thirty years, "as much an integral part of Pasadena as the City Hall,"[55] and a figure who bestowed moral sanction on an enterprise often associated with immorality. Another was attorney James Morin, senior partner in the law firm of Morin, Newell, Brown, and Hamell, and organizer of the First Federal Savings and Loan Association of California.

It is important to note that Pasadena's Drama League was absolved, by its proximity to the Los Angeles League, from the obligation to bulletin the plays evaluated by the latter group.[56] Therefore, Pasadena members were freer to attend to community outreach. They put their initial efforts into raising the impressive sum of seven hundred dollars for prize money, which they offered in a playwriting contest. The winner, Mrs. Walton Wood of South Pasadena, also won a staging of her play *Scapegoat,* and became an active member in the league. The league would continue to hold contests throughout its history, although the prize money dropped to three hundred dollars for a one-act play. These competitions drew great numbers of entries (165 entries in 1922; 329 in 1926; 240 in 1927) from amateur playwrights, particularly women, throughout the nation.

Although the Pasadena Drama League charged only one dollar for dues at the start, the organization did not immediately attract great numbers of citizens. By 1920, there were sixty members. When Miss Eleanor Bissell assumed the presidency for five years, however, she sought a larger local following to construct a suitable playhouse for the town. Although the annual dues rose to two dollars, the membership grew. 1923 saw 357 on the membership rolls; in 1924 there were 500 members, and in 1925, 600 members. Most of these were Pasadena women, although the group also appealed to some men, like Desaix Myers and Louis Winchester Jones, both Caltech professors, and to snowbirds, so captivated by the Drama League's wintertime programs that they were willing to provide this modicum of formal support.

Most Drama League members were white, Protestant, married people with one to three grown children. Pasadena's unusual demographic patterns were reflected in the league's active membership, which included a strong percentage of monied, blue-blooded senior citizens and widows, enjoying status and carrying a sense of social responsibility. These women tended to have a history of activity and influence in a number of associations, connections they would tap to solicit increasing support for the Drama League's projects.[57] Many of the women active in the league as officers, board members, committee heads, or steady workers on committees and projects were wives of prominent professional men in Pasadena.

Greta Irvin Blanchard Millikan, President of the Drama League from 1927 to 1928, was the wife of Robert A. Millikan, director of the California Institute of Technology who won the Nobel Prize for Physics in 1923. Typical of Drama Leaguers, she volunteered her energies generously to many other worthwhile voluntary organizations—the Red Cross, the Community Chest, the Visiting Nurse Dispensary, the Southern California Symphony Association, the Brahms Club, Pasadena's Woman's Club, the Neighborhood Church, the Women's Civic League, the Women's Committee of the Pasadena Philharmonic Society, World War I relief efforts, and the Alliance Française. Despite these wide-ranging interests, her correspondence attests to her fervor for the amateur theater in Pasadena. She raised $125,000 in two weeks for the new theater building, tried a hand at playwriting, and also managed to perform and sing in many productions.[58]

Some of the active women Drama League members were unmarried and enjoyed lives of leisure due to inherited wealth. Like Millikan, they were not single-minded in their devotion to theater. Eleanor Bissell, heiress to the Bissell carpet sweeper fortune, was a member of the Smith College Alumnae Association (she was class of '97), the Valley Hunt Club, the Universalist Church, the Republican Party, Colonial Dames of America, the Huntington Library and the California Institute of Technology, among other organizations.[59] Her housemate of forty years, Miss Flora Harper, divided her time between the Drama League, the Daughters of the American Revolution, the Garden Club, and the First Universalist Church.[60]

Some of the active members, however, had to work to support themselves. Grace Nicholson sold Native American artifacts and Asian antiques so successfully that she would bequeath a Pacific Asia Museum to Pasadena. The teachers in the club included Mrs. Harriet L. Green, who edited the Drama League's *Bulletin,* the Southern-born Fairfax Proudfit Walkup, a history instructor at a private girls' academy. Among the writers were playwright Marjorie Penney and poet and playwright Hildegarde Flanner.

Two nationally-known clubwomen also migrated to Pasadena and became active in the Pasadena Drama League. Alice Riley, founder of the Evanston club that initiated the national association, wintered in Pasadena in the 1910s and finally retired there. She was among the most talented of Drama Leaguers and her presence, advice, and connections enabled the league to maintain its leading role in little theater circles. Minnesota-born clubwoman Alice Ames Winter also retired to Pasadena in the mid-1920s. Her claim to fame was her presidency of the General Federation of Women's Clubs from 1920 to 1924 and her monthly column on women's clubs in the *Ladies' Home Journal,* but her long record of club life well acquainted her with the organizational circles in which her Pasadena colleagues traveled.[61]

Like every Drama League center in the nation, Pasadena's organization tried to provide an opportunity for theater-lovers to meet like-minded people. For the most casual student there was the large annual business meeting and election, held around the first of June, which included a performance by members of a one-act play, or a lecture by a well-known theatrical personage. For more avid enrollees, speeches were offered by the nation's leading drama experts, attracted to the community by Pasadena's climate or cultural life. Between 1925 and 1930 for example, Maurice Browne, often called the father of the little theater movement, travelled from Seattle to offer members a talk on "The Value of Community Theatre to the Public"; his ex-wife, Ellen Van Volkenberg, cofounder of the Chicago Little Theatre, spoke about *What Every Woman Knows,* a play the Pasadena League presented; Dhan G. Mukerji spoke on "Tagore and the Hindu Drama"; Mrs. William C. De Mille came from Los Angeles to present her thoughts on "The Value of Motion Pictures to the Drama League"; and Zoe Kincaid (Mrs. John Pendlington), a local playwright, offered a lecture on "Kabuki: What Asiatic Theatre Holds for the West."

The most devoted members of the Drama League registered for regular courses, generally held from October through June. For six dollars, one could attend fifteen play readings, held every other Monday evening in a private corner of the public library. Open only to members, each class involved the reading by members of a new play, such as Zona Gale's *Neighbors,* or a familiar play about to be performed in town. Sometimes a visiting playwright would read her work. Alice Riley, for instance, read her own *Radio, Taxi,* and *Their Anniversary* for the audience.

For those thirty members fluent in the French language, local teacher Elizabeth Segalle read fifteen new plays each year, fresh from the Paris stage. Members of the Alliance Française were invited as well. *Jeanne d'Arc* (translated from George Bernard Shaw's *St. Joan*) and *L'Âme en Peine* by Jean-Jacques Bernard were among the choices Segalle presented and directed the discussion on.

Still another regular course offered by the Drama League throughout the 1920s was the Playwriting Class, meeting twice a month under the tutelage of University of Southern California English professor Laurabelle S. Dietrich.[62] Many of the students' efforts, destined to be submitted to local, regional, and national playwriting competitions, were inspired not only by the Drama League of America and its centers, but also by publishing company competitions. Mrs. A. A. Maxfield, secretary of the class in Pasadena, won a Longmans Green contest for *Ruth,* a Biblical play, and saw it performed by high school students in Omaha. Anna Nissen's *Thirty,* Clare Kummer's *Good Gracious Annabell,* and Margaret Penney's *Elusive Cynthia* are only a few of the members' plays produced by the Pasadena Playhouse.

A poetry class also met regularly under the auspices of the Pasadena Drama League, directed by Hildegard Flanner. A young woman of twenty-one, who had just won the University of California poetry prize, she began to publish her own work while lecturing to the Drama League members on Emily Dickinson, Carl Sandburg, and "Hardy and Robinson as Landmarks of this Poetical Generation."

Not content to listen and write, several members of the Pasadena Drama League also put on plays of their own. Their membership performed many of the plays that were submitted for contests, especially if their authors were local. Their most successful productions were shared with the community. For example, a trio of one-act plays were performed at a meeting of the College Woman's Club of Pasadena. The Drama League also delivered drama workshop leaders to the YWCA, Whittier College, and the California Federation of Women's Clubs convention.

At the same time that the Pasadena Drama League was taking shape, a troupe of professional actors, calling themselves the Crown Stock Company while they toured California's communities, identified Pasadena as an appropriate resting place in 1916. Gilmor Brown, the company's manager, director, and leading man, hoped to install his newly-christened "Savoy Players" at the Savoy Theatre (formerly burlesque house) on North Fair Oaks Avenue. Josephine Dillon, married to Clark Gable, was one of the leading ladies of the company. The players had a difficult time covering costs in Pasadena, even though they offered ten shows each week. Brown noticed that his production of a Drama League play, *White Bird* by Marjorie Driscoll, attracted the first full house he commanded in the city, for Drama League members filled the Savoy to capacity for the November 1916 production. After that, he was eager to cultivate an alliance with the League, envisioning a symbiotic relationship which would be fruitful for both organizations. Now he padded his crowd scenes with Drama League members. He permitted the club to perform three brief "curtain raisers" before each Tuesday evening performance, in hopes of attracting the amateur players' friends and relatives into his professional theatre.

In an effort to broaden his Pasadena following, Brown tried a variety of ingenious methods to elicit new interest among potential theater-goers. He brought *Oedipus Rex* to the high school under the sponsorship of the PTA. He held monthly receptions for ticketholders. He sent brief scenes to the luxury hotels to pique the interest of vacationers.

Within a few years, the Playhouse won accolades beyond those accorded to other city entertainments. "Although the Community Playhouse is an activity of, for and by the people of Pasadena, nothing here contributes more uniquely to the entertainment of the Crown City's large tourist population," one publication declared.[63]

Continuing his efforts to capture the public's attention and respect, Brown ordered that scenery be shifted before viewers, makeup applied onstage, and amateur night invitations be extended to budding thespians. A pie eating contest welcomed children; and on one occasion, Brown reversed men and women actors in female and male roles.[64] None of this, unfortunately, yielded the financial stability his company required. In May 1917, Brown admitted defeat. After presenting an ambitious slate of thirty-six full-length plays, seventeen one-acts, and ten special programs in the space of a year, he dissolved his professional company.

Pasadena's theater enthusiasts, with whom Brown had developed a rapport, were eager to use his talents in another capacity. The Drama League called a community meeting which brought out two or three hundred drama lovers to discuss ways of securing a resident theater company in Pasadena. A committee of twelve persons devised a plan whereby Gilmor Brown would be paid a salary to direct amateur actors, to be called the Pasadena Community Players. To institutionalize the plan, they formed a Pasadena Community Playhouse Association (PCPA),

> a non-profit association legally incorporated to foster educational recreation for adults and children. Its purpose is not to make actors, but to afford individual opportunity for self-expression in the Allied Arts of the Theatre. The players, all volunteers, are amateurs in the best sense of the word, as they play for the love of it rather than as a business. Democracy being the Association's ideal, it welcomes all who desire to participate in or to encourage the communal endeavors for which it stands.[65]

The members of the PCPA board of directors, like the Drama League, consisted of a Pasadena who's who. Leading educators, scientists, clergymen, businessmen, clubwomen, and even the wealthy socialist, Kate Crane Gartz, were invited. Sibyl Eliza Jones, as president of the Pasadena Drama League, served on the board, as would succeeding directors of the league. Astronomer George Ellery Hale; Max Farrand, director of the Huntington Library; noted craftsman Ernest Batchelder; H. H. Doty, vice-president and treasurer of the First Trust and Savings Bank; all lent their influence to the cause.

Generally, when the story of Pasadena's amateur playhouse is told, the leadership of founder and director Gilmor Brown (1886–1960) is accorded all credit from its origin in 1917 until his retirement in 1958. There is little or no acknowledgement of the work of the voluntary associations featured in this chapter. There is no denying the man's talent and effort were extraordinary. Under Gilmor Brown's leadership, the Pasadena Community Playhouse enjoyed one of the finest and most enduring reputations in the amateur theater world. But his real genius lay in his talent for utilizing the efforts of volunteers, particularly the women volunteers, who enabled the playhouse to flourish.

As soon as it was formed, the Pasadena Community Playhouse Association invited citizens to contribute to the creation and maintenance of an amateur company of actors. Thousands of people came forward with two dollars and thereby earned the title "Associate Members." Drama League members were especially responsive to the call for support. Drama League President Eleanor Bissell poured some of her family fortune into the playhouse. Such acts of generosity occasioned a debate in 1925 over whether to merge the Pasadena Community Playhouse Association with the Drama League:

> In the interests of 'good theatre' the Community Playhouse group and the Drama League are trying team work this winter. Though both are impelled by the same motive force toward the same objective point, their approach is not identical and it would weaken the situation to attempt a merger. Without loss of individuality on either side they are working together for their common end at the Playhouse on El Molino.[66]

The Pasadena Community Players presented their first program in November 1917, drawing on the Drama Leaguers for much of the casting, as would be true for the next decade. Some of the original Savoy Players played in this production as well, for love rather than money. Held at the women's swank Shakespeare Club, the Community Players' production consisted of a bill of four one-act plays, including Zona Gale's *Neighbors*. The first actress onstage was a young Santa Barbara woman, Martha Graham, who introduced *Song of Lady Lotus Eyes* with a Chinese dance. Her career would later blossom, as would that of Agnes De Mille and batteries of other fledgling performers who debuted on the stage of the Pasadena Community Playhouse.

The playhouse hit many snags before it became a little theater of renown. At first, the general public failed to understand that they were welcome, because of the initial presentation at a private club of Pasadena's elite women. This misunderstanding led to meager audiences for the early productions and necessitated a move from the Shakespeare Club back to the shabby and inadequate Savoy Theatre. The Shakespeare Club members were glad to see the actors go, for the players had disrupted club routine. But its members continued to support the little theater with audiences and actors, and assisted generously in the effort to build a lavish replacement for the inadequate Savoy. An eight-year fund-raising effort ensued, culminating in the building of one of the finest playhouses of the day.[67] The influenza epidemic of 1918 posed another, more immediate threat to the stability of the budding amateur company. For a time, the actors and audiences attempted to carry on wearing white gauze masks; but finally the theater, like all public facilities, was closed down for the duration of the contagion.

World War I diverted attention from artistic endeavors to patriotic efforts, and for a time this seemed to jeopardize the theatre's success. Oddly enough, the demands of the emergency strengthened the ties to schools, clubs, and other community institutions that Gilmor Brown had initiated in 1916. This proved to be the key to success. The re-emergence of the theater's sense of responsibility to the community provided the focus the little theater needed to survive, indeed to flourish, and to steer the city's cultural life. The members of the playhouse network—the Drama League members, as well as those in the Pasadena Community Playhouse Association—who were providing actors, money, and audiences, were impressed by the theater's ability to serve their community interests. They could have abandoned the little theater in order to roll bandages in their clubs, raise money at their charity balls, donate hours to the Red Cross, and sell Liberty Bonds to their neighbors. Instead, they discovered that they could use the theater to supplement their war efforts. Thus, the playhouse initiated a series of patriotic events—free tickets to military men for certain performances, skits presented at nearby soldiers' homes. Five thousand citizens responded to the playhouse call for a community sing in wartime.[68] Such programs endeared the amateur thespians to Pasadena's residents.

Playhouse personnel, both paid and volunteer, never forgot this lesson. With every innovation—the one-thousand player *Peace of Victory* pageant in 1919,[69] the elaborate Rose Parade float with thirty-two maidens in Greek attire,[70] the Easter ceremony on the lawn of the Huntington Hotel, the May

Festival[71]—the Pasadena Community Playhouse Association strengthened its image of commitment to provide public ritual in a colorful but serious fashion and to attract and serve the public. In fact, these goals quickly superseded the original Drama League impulse to improve taste among audiences. The public praised this democratic direction warmly. On the society page of the *Pasadena Post,* one reporter likened the burgeoning community spirit at the playhouse to wartime patriotism. Recalling the days when women of leisure put their efforts into war-related efforts, Anne Goodwin Nissen wrote,

> Now a task almost as great as making the world safe for democracy ... is keeping the world safe for the democracy of ideals and expression ... the embryo of this splendid opportunity is the Community Theatre.... It is in a position to be a sort of artistic Liberty Loan for Pasadena society.[72]

Announcements inviting participants from all strata of Pasadena society bolstered an image of non-exclusivity: "Needle experts asked to help players out: Girls—young, middle-aged and along in years—who want to help the costume committee of the Pasadena Community Players, are requested to come to the Playhouse tomorrow afternoon, armed with needles, scissors, and thimbles."[73] Such openness was commended throughout the press. The *Star-News,* for example, endorsed the effort to touch every citizen in Pasadena with theatrical events:

> There is a cozy atmosphere about the local playhouse. Those who take part in its activities are like a large family. They know each other and are interested in the efforts of one another. It is far from being a 'closed corporation.' The membership lists are always open and everyone who would like to join is heartily invited.[74]

The playhouse sought to involve many of its neighbors, especially through community institutions like schools, churches, and clubs that might otherwise not have joined in play making. However, while the efforts of playhouse supporters to reach widely for volunteers were vigorous, ingenious, and admirable, they fell short of touching all segments of society. For example, the democratic thrust was limited in its inclusion of minorities in Pasadena. Only one black actor, Napoleon Simpson, routinely participated in roles that called for "Negroes." He was acceptable because "he was seen to know his place,"[75] reported one rueful white volunteer actor of unenlightened times. Even so, some players refused to share a dressing room with him. Pasadena's African-American population was three percent. Its Mexican-American population was ten percent, yet there were no plays dealing with the minority experience.

On the other hand, the attitudes toward race expressed by the Playhouse were somewhat progressive, given the era's general distinterest in racial problems. Occasional theater programming in Pasadena attempted to include non-Anglo culture, albeit modestly. The little theater addressed Native American issues by producing *Red Bird,* by William Ellery Leonard, a play set in faraway Wisconsin. The production was presented with considerable fanfare. Between the acts, Boy Scouts demonstrated their skills in woodcraft; Sioux performed ceremonials around a campfire; and Hopi dances choreographed by Katherine Edson were staged for the public. However limited the playhouse programming may have been, it was generous in the context of a largely unconcerned society. Those who were distressed at the plight of the Native American population appreciated even the modest concern the playhouse provided. *Red Bird,* for example, brought out the membership of the American Indian Defense Association en masse.[76]

Some social barriers were broken at the playhouse. Socialite Frances Boniface played alongside "social inferiors," like the superintendent of the Edna-Alter Mexican-American Settlement House. Rural people were portrayed without the customary condescension often accorded them. Deeply decent farm women and men appear in, for example, *The Neighbors* and *Trifles,* mainstays on the little theater stage. Feminists fared best at the playhouse, for the volunteers, in Pasadena as nationally, admired the strong women in Ibsen's *Hedda Gabler* and the complex female characters in works by American playwrights Rachel Crothers, Susan Glaspell, and Zona Gale. The playhouse performed their works to full houses.

In choice of plays, the worth of their content did not weigh more heavily than their mass appeal. Following national trends, the Pasadena Community Playhouse offered a variety of plays, more intent on attracting all tastes than molding public preferences to a high plane. Thus, Shakespeare, Molière, Congreve, and Goldsmith shared center stage with naive works to which parents could bring their children: *Mrs. Wiggs of the Cabbage Patch, Rebecca of Sunny Brook Farm, Little Women,* and at Christmastime, *Cricket on the Hearth.* As was true of most amateur theaters, the playhouse did not attempt musicals, for the expense and complexity of adding musicians and singers were prohibitive. Instead, they provided Saturday morning fairy tales for preschoolers; Broadway hits like Noel Coward's urbane *Hay Fever* for the sophisticates on holiday; and neighborhood "reviews" or "follies" containing skits by neighbors of uneven abilities. To balance these productions, the playhouse publicity staff made much of its intellectual forays. Most notably, the world premier of Eugene O'Neill's *Lazarus Laughed,* too expensive to attempt on Broadway, was staged in Pasadena thanks to endless volunteer hours spent making 350 costumes and 350 masks.[77]

A survey entitled "Playhouse Productions Meet Variety of Tastes," compiled after a decade of Pasadena activity, shows a balance between serious and lighter fare. The PCP productions which had drawn "the largest and most enthusiastic audiences" were solid. At the top of the list was the work of Shakespeare (especially *The Merry Wives of Windsor*), followed by Ibsen *(Peer Gynt, Hedda Gabler, Wild Duck,* and *An Enemy of the People),* and G. B. Shaw. Yet the spoof on amateur thespians by George Kelly, *The Torchbearers,* and a revue by Pasadena talents, *Head Acres,* also won wide support.[78]

The little theater that got off to a rocky start in 1917 rallied quickly to perform a staggering number of classics and new plays at the creaky Savoy

Theatre. From its beginning until the fire department condemned the facility in 1925, the volunteers swarmed around the playhouse in sufficient numbers to produce 163 plays at a rate of two per month. This pace was surpassed after May 1925, when a luxurious modern Spanish-style theater was erected on El Molino Avenue. While estimates of the number of contributors to the new theater vary widely, from 3,000 to 8,000, it is clear that the volunteers supported the playhouse mightily at this time, by donating generously and urging their friends to do so, in order to purchase the property, build the $400,000 theater, and staff it.

By 1921, the payroll had increased beyond Gilmor Brown's salary to $1,000 per month for a stage manager, a business manager, an assistant business manager, a music director, and Sibyl Jones, who directed a children's theater until her accounts were audited for irregularities. In 1925, when the PCPA secured twelve hundred donations to build the new theater, it could also afford a monthly payroll of $3,280 each month. At that time, Brown had four associate directors, seventeen staff members under business manager Charles Prickett, and a crew of five.[79]

The physical expansion permitted the playhouse to serve as a community center, providing headquarters for a number of women's groups. Not only the Drama League, but also the Junior Tuesday Musicale and the Women's Choral Club were among the many clubs meeting there.[80] Public speeches of interest to women were offered. Margaret Sanger, for example, spoke about birth control, and Halide Edib lectured on Turkish feminism.[81]

A windfall from Fannie E. Morrison, Pittsburgh steel widow, paid the $200,000 balance on the mortgage, and added a school in 1928 that sent multitudes of young actors to the Hollywood film industry.[82] In the mid-1930s, when the rest of the world was paralyzed by the Great Depression, Morrison added a six-story building containing sixty-six rooms for classes and meetings, three fifty-seat theaters for experimental and amateur productions, shops, storage areas for props, scenery and ten thousand costumes, a cafe, and a kitchen. The physical space was well used. Celebrating its twenty-fifth birthday in 1941, the Playhouse calculated that it had produced 1,348 plays by twelve hundred actors, to multitudes of viewers.[83]

In significant ways, the Drama League was a crucial support group to the Pasadena Community Playhouse, vital for establishing and maintaining its good health and reputation. League members joined the PCPA board and its committees. The league played a significant role in the unending fund-raising—for the new playhouse, its interior and furnishings, and student scholarships. In addition to the league's collective and individual financial contributions to the playhouse, its members invented special money-making projects. Among the most popular of these was one that renewed the outreach to the community, even as it raised the ire of Methodists, Quakers, and First Adventists.[84] This somewhat controversial project was a series of community dances, initiated in the summer of 1920. The organization charged ten cents at first, a quarter by the mid-1920s, and provided a hundred Drama League chaperones who supervised eleven to sixteen dances on the tennis courts of the city's parks each summer. These dances attracted as many as twenty thousand young people each summer.[85]

The Drama League members used their networks of influence in other clubs and in the schools to feed the playhouse with support in the form of audiences and financial contributions. In so doing, they simultaneously addressed the goal of delivering theater to new audiences. Members pressed the other organizations to which they belonged to donate sums to the playhouse. The Women's Civic League, the College Woman's Club, the Shakespeare Club, and the Pasadena Business and Professional Women's Club all complied. Drama League members appointed some of their own to serve as liaisons with women's clubs to sell tickets for each production. Representatives to the Shakespeare Club, the Browning Club, the Tuesday Morning Drama Club, the Red Cross, the Navy League, and the Federated Parent-Teachers' Association were among the bridge-builders.[86] Members also coaxed their other clubs to create theater parties, reselling banks of seats to members at inflated prices to win profits for their own causes. The Occidental College Woman's Club, for example, raised money for its scholarship fund in this way. The Shakespeare Club attended the Shakespearean productions in full force, the Junior Hadassah came en masse for *Dybbuk,* a play about Hasidic Jews. When a convention of librarians, teachers, commercial secretaries, or clubwomen came to the area, their evening's entertainment was provided by the playhouse. For certain functions, Junior League debutantes were invited to usher.

Efforts such as these enabled the Pasadena Playhouse to have one of the biggest budgets in American amateur theater. In 1927–28, its budget reached $123,400. With box office sales amounting to $112,000 and $10,000 from memberships, the playhouse could spend a thousand dollars for cast hospitality and $240 for the workers' tea, and still emerge with a profit of $8,896.[87]

While some little theaters operated on a shoestring (the Provincetown Players, for example, spent a maximum of three dollars per set), the Pasadena Community Playhouse found seventeen thousand dollars for *Lazarus Laughed.* Admittedly, this was its most expensive production; but its average costs were still high in relation to many other amateur theaters. Figures from 1927–29 place Pasadena among the most ambitious and successful of the little theaters in the country.

Drama Leaguers, as mothers, teachers and lovers of literature, forged com-

THEATRE	BUDGET	EMPLOYEES	PRODUCTIONS PER YEAR	PERFORMANCES PER YEAR	ADMISSIONS PER YEAR
Ypsilanti, Mi.	$1,900	0	5	25	5,000
Memphis	12,000	3	6	42	10,000
Dallas	35,000	7	12	89	34,500
Pasadena	146,000	40	28	322	132,986
Detroit Civic	220,000	51	35	400–500	200,000
Cincinnati	275,000	61	35–40	360	250,000[88]

fortable alliances with the schools of Pasadena and used their ties to broaden support for the community theater. Players who were performing the Shakespearean tragedies that high school students studied in their classrooms were urged to bring scenes to the school auditorium, or to provide special student matinees. The Drama Leaguers publicized competitions, like the Oral Arts Association of Southern California contest, awarding prizes to pupils who delivered twenty-five lines of the Bard's canon from memory. Under Drama League auspices, actors also performed plays of special interest to beginning theater-goers; *The Little Princess,* for instance, was performed for those in primary grades. An entire learning unit was developed around the show in which teachers read to classes the book on which the play was based, and assigned pupils a book review. The league awarded free tickets to the playhouse to the authors of the finest school essays. In addition, league members sent costumes for display at the South Pasadena High School and the Westridge School, to tantalize and educate schoolchildren.

Education of the broader public followed naturally from Pasadena members' efforts with schoolchildren and adolescents, and from women's customary posture as bearers of useful, moral, and artistic endeavors. Thus the annual February Drama Week occasioned efforts by the Pasadena League, as it did among Drama League centers all over the country, to pique the curiosity of the general population about amateur dramatics. Considering how effective the Pasadena women were all year long, it seems superfluous for them to have stepped up their energies for the month of February. Nevertheless, in 1926 the members induced the four clergymen from some of their own congregations to announce the events of Drama Week from the pulpit. Representatives from the league gave speeches to local organizations and high schools, and succeeded in securing a page for publicity in the *Pasadena Star-News*. All connections of the members were tapped to alert Pasadena's citizens to recognize Drama Week.

The group excelled in other educational efforts on behalf of the theater as well, notably the sponsorship of summer training institutes, conferences, and a Service Bureau to advise other community theaters in the region. In many ways, these programs replicated those maintained by the Drama League National headquarters in Chicago. Conducted thousands of miles away, however, Pasadena's instructional outreach served constituencies far removed from the Midwestern sphere of influence and did not usurp responsibilities staked out by the national leadership. In fact, national publications of the Drama League of America regularly publicized the Pasadena programs, commended the efforts of the membership, and generally encouraged other branches to admire and emulate the energy and inventiveness put forth by the Pasadena women.

In the summer of 1920, the Drama League of Pasadena provided its first four-week summer institute, similar to the one offered by the experts at national headquarters in Chicago. For twenty-five dollars, thirty-four registrants could select two courses from a list including costume design, practical stage design and lighting, stage action and speech, dramatic dancing, playmaking, stage direction, and makeup. Instruction was offered by Drama League members or local experts teaching at Los Angeles colleges and universities. The effort drew enthusiastic young people, alerting the playhouse to the market for a regular acting school. The program also managed to yield a much-needed profit of $191. The first class brought enrollee Lenore Shanewise to Gilmor Brown's attention, and he invited her to become his associate director, a post she held for several years until other theatrical work lured her to Hollywood. The summer school boasted forty-six students in 1921, and continued to draw amateur enthusiasts in 1922 and 1923. The following summer, due to concerted efforts to get the new playhouse built, it was disbanded. The school resumed in 1929 as an extension of the regular year-round school program, a program that prided itself on launching many professional careers in the theater.

The Pasadena Drama League shared members' knowledge of the theater in other formats as well. Again in the footsteps of the national association in Chicago, it offered a Service Bureau that served as a clearinghouse of plays, technical information, and emergency aid for costume or scenery problems. Harriet Green, as director of the bureau, was authorized to correspond with troubled directors or clubwomen and attempt to satisfy their inquiries. Thus, western area community playhouses did not have to reach as far as the Drama League headquarters in Chicago for assistance.

As the Drama League in Pasadena won a wider renown for its enthusiasm and expertise, it logically fell to its membership to host a number of little theater conventions. The largest of these, the annual conference of the Drama League of America, was held in 1924. This occasion was also the fiftieth anniversary of the city of Pasadena, the occasion of the groundbreaking of the new playhouse, and the date of the General Federation of Women's Clubs' huge biennial meeting in Los Angeles. The city preened, the Pasadena League broke ground with fanfare for their new headquarters—the playhouse—and the conference swelled with clubwomen in town for the other meetings. As was customary at such conferences, a great number of experts spoke, formally and informally, about the mechanics of playmaking. The wealthiest Drama League members had occasion to open their homes and lawns for grand tea parties and receptions.

Smaller conferences also took place at the behest of Pasadena's Drama League. Eighty delegates attended a Regional Conference for Little Theatre in June 1927, basking in the glory of the new playhouse facilities. In March 1929, still another western states little theater convention was planned and hosted by the Drama League.

While the generosity of the outreach programs became legendary, the members of the Pasadena Drama League also used hospitality to serve themselves and the playhouse in a number of significant ways. Social amenities took the form of providing coffee into the wee hours for their neighbors in rehearsal. Clubwomen made hot chocolate for the members of the audiences who came backstage to the Green Room after the performances to congratulate the cast. On the third Friday of every month, they hosted a new workers' tea, enabling newcomers to feel comfortable immediately, and the league also gave a regular party for the costume workers. Members held cast parties at the Valley Hunt

Club or in their spacious homes. Most glamorous was the opportunity to fete visiting personalities such as the Stratford-upon-Avon Players, who brought Shakespearean productions from Britain. When pageant makers Thomas Wood Stevens and Percy MacKaye came to town, they were hosted by the club. For playwrights Alice Riley, Lulu Vollmer, and Ellen Van Volkenberg, and Harvard drama teacher George Pierce Baker, the club offered splendid receptions. The playhouse could flatter its visitors and workers in style, enhance the sociability of the common creative effort, and engage the hosts in a useful but enjoyable task, all diminishing further the distance between stage and community.

On the face of it, the Drama League contribution to Pasadena's ambitious little theater might appear to be quite traditional in nature. Reaching out to school children and their own neighbors and friends in other associations seemed to reinforce traditional proscriptions against women's involvement in wider circles. Entertaining playhouse visitors and workers could be seen as a mere extension of domestic routine. Certainly members' sewing of costumes and pouring of tea evokes unremarkable images of women's behavior.

This view of the Drama League endeavor, however, is to overlook its novel aspects. The women created a safe environment for personal development at the Drama League and the Pasadena Playhouse. Here was a semi-public setting where women could indulge their own intellectual, creative, and social needs. For themselves, they read widely of plays and related literature. They discussed the works, prepared roles, and wrote plays. Satisfying their social needs, they planned and executed productions, often measuring success not in terms of artistic excellence, but in terms of a camaraderie achieved. The Drama League approach made women so comfortable in their theater that they dominated most of its working committees. In 1920, for example: Casting Committee (three women out of five members); Costume (all fourteen); Courtesy (five out of six); Decoration (three women); Educational (four out of five); Entertainment (one woman and one man); Hospitality (eight women and their spouses); House (three women); Library (four women); Manuscript (three women, three men); Publicity (five out of eight); Social Services (eight women and two of their husbands). In only a few committees did the women fail to dominate in numbers: Production (twelve women out of twenty-three); Music (four women out of fifteen); Ways and Means (three women out of fourteen).[89]

The Drama League championed great numbers of plays by women in their own productions and at the playhouse, among them works by Anna Cora Mowatt, Louisa May Alcott, Harriet Beecher Stowe, and contemporaries like Rachel Crothers, Constance D'Arcy MacKaye, Zona Gale, and Susan Glaspell. No doubt members' steady appreciation of women's work encouraged the Playhouse in its presentation of over fifty woman-authored plays on its main stage and countless others in its smaller forums before the advent of the Great Depression.[90]

It was useful to both the hosts and the guests when the Drama League women met and feted such playwrights as Lulu Vollmer, Ellen Van Volkenberg, and Alice Riley, studying their works, examining the women characters, and praising the authors. Naturally, the heroines whom the Drama Leaguers met vicariously in the drama varied considerably. For every wise and humane Marmee from *Little Women,* Mrs. Wiggs from "Cabbage Patch," Kentucky, or farm woman from Susan Glaspell's *Trifles,* there were the cruel slave mistresses in *Uncle Tom's Cabin,* the empty-headed ingenues, and the malicious female villains. By the same token, the members sought and found strong women characters such as Hedda Gabler in plays by male authors, as well as inept if well-meaning and amateur actresses in George Kelly's popular *Torchbearers* or pouty fortune hunters in Noel Coward's *Hay Fever.* Regardless of the stage roles Drama Leaguers admired or rejected, however, they had built for themselves a woman's place where they might read, think, talk, plan, and develop among themselves.

These tasks, in a public setting rather than a cloistered one at home, gave women a new landscape for their ingenuity, intelligence, organizational ability, administrative talents, and managerial skills. Most importantly, amateur theater provided a broad focus for their work. Women's capacity to develop an ideal, envision concrete goals and strategies, marshall resources, and carry plans through using their influence and hard work, speaks to their range of abilities, but also to the strength of their commitment to the theater and their local audiences. They cemented their community, winning the approval of government, church, educational institutions, service clubs, and businesses because of their ability to synthesize the recreational, social, educational, moral, and material needs of Pasadenans and their visitors. Their contribution ultimately lies in their assimilation of community requirements and their distribution of theatrical services to meet those needs. Their allegiance was to their townspeople first, not to the stage, but the stage served them well.

For all their success, the establishment of a school for the drama at the Pasadena Community Playhouse in 1928 proved to be a watershed for the Pasadena Drama League. The clubwomen were pushed out by its presence, never again to shape the community theater as they had in the past. Suddenly, students could do the jobs clubwomen had once done. The students paid tuition, and the school became profitable even when the productions were not. A stronger emphasis on the importance of professionalization contributed to a diminution of volunteer activity. In a world where the experts lent their knowledge to ambitious students, Drama Leaguers felt peripheral to the real business of the playhouse. Admittedly, Gilmor Brown, an ingenious marshall of volunteer energy, did not acquiesce to the forces undermining clubwomen's efforts. When asked to eliminate the volunteers in order to produce more excellent productions, he declined to do so. The *Playhouse News* reported, "Referring to the difference of opinion as to whether the Playhouse should be an art theatre or a community theatre, Mr. Brown said that the fusion of the two types would make the Playhouse one of greater usefulness and distinction."[91] Still, the women saw the writing on the wall and fell away. Where once they had filled opening night audiences, considering it a privilege to support the first performance, they now had to be coaxed to attend. In 1928 the *Playhouse News* reported:

> A few years ago it was the acknowledged duty of a good Drama Leaguer to be faithful in attending the opening night of each new production.... In a recent address... Gilmor Brown, recognizing many old-time supporters in the audience, spoke of his sense of loss in the dropping away of the Drama League First Night audience and pleaded for its restoration. He felt that the Playhouse should have a representative Pasadena audience for the opening night of every new play with a renewal and strengthening of the old feeling of friendly interest and cooperation.[92]

The old feeling was never restored, and the Great Depression only escalated the distance between Drama Leaguers and their playhouse. The women's ability to make financial contributions to the enterprise was severely diminished. Referring to the 1930s, Associate Director Ralph Freud spoke of the "gradual weakening of the creative fiber of the organization ... financial too" which resulted from the absence of the volunteers.[93] The Pasadena Community Playhouse name was changed in 1937 to Pasadena Playhouse. The removal of the word "community" was long overdue. The allegiance of women declined with the prominence of the school, not to be restored. The theater and the school closed in 1969. However, the grand facility still stands, enjoying a recent renaissance fueled by commercial investments, a magnificent monument to the unheralded women who built it for themselves and for their city.

SEVEN

The Clubhouse as Arts Center

Among the earliest projects undertaken by American clubwomen were their efforts to create physical spaces for the betterment and enrichment of women's lives. Clubwomen saw this work as a natural and necessary dimension of their Municipal Housekeeping. Creating spaces in which to serve women's needs was a step toward alleviating the social problems they were trying to solve. Thus, they built homes for unwed mothers, maintained orphanages, and established training centers for delinquent girls, "well baby" clinics, day care centers, women's hospitals and children's hospitals, rest stations for farm women, and residences for one-room school teachers called "teacherages." Women's clubs created campus meeting places for women students; residences for working girls and women, and for women students of the arts; facilities for women engaged in commercial and professional pursuits; libraries; summer camps; and industrial homes. The structures clubwomen built for welfare purposes are far too numerous to describe here in detail. Suffice it to say, the list is long and the range wide.

While clubwomen early on embraced a tradition of creating structures for altruistic purposes, it was not until the decade after World War I that they focused on erecting their own ambitious clubhouses, to facilitate the pursuit of their civic and artistic projects. The extensive purchase of war bonds by clubwomen made possible this costly venture into the field of clubhouse building. It was an endeavor that met with extraordinary, even brilliant, success. But the strains occasioned by building and maintaining clubhouses served to divide and deplete the women's club movement that had flourished for decades. Ultimately, the financial responsibilities of their new and grandly decorated structures diverted the attention of clubwomen from social reform, undermining their public voice. Coupled with other challenges of the 1920s, clubhouse building led to the clubs' decline—and with it, the close of the heyday of the women's amateur arts movement. Yet the building boom brought the members back full circle to their original intention of helping themselves.

More than any other segment of women's clubs, it was the clubwomen devoted to the arts who were most conspicuously served by the blossoming of the clubhouses. In the new clubhouses were to be found the most luxurious art centers of the day. The most tangible of clubwomen's arts achievements, many of these buildings still stand today, evidence of the significance of the arts for the organized womanhood of the twentieth century. At about the same time that Virginia Woolf formulated her theories on the importance to women of "A Room of One's Own," American clubwomen were acting on them.

Clubhouse building flourished among multitudes of women's voluntary associations during the decade after World War I. The sizeable urban, civic, and study clubs in the General Federation of Women's Clubs set the trend, completing, by conservative estimate, twelve hundred clubhouses by the end of the era.[1] As early as 1920, the General Federation of Women's Clubs surveyed its member clubs and found one thousand clubhouses were reported even though eighteen states did not reply.[2] In addition, the local branches of the Daughters of the American Revolution, the Daughters of the State Pioneers, and the Junior League, populated by debutantes from America's most affluent families, were quick to build. As a result, the country became peppered with graceful homes-away-from-home for American clubwomen.

The clubhouse building fever that overtook Progressive Era women was fed by the arts-loving members seeking superior facilities for their ambitious club programs for arts study and enjoyment. They yearned for command over large and well-equipped theaters, with modern lighting, up-to-date film projection equipment, comfortable seating, well-appointed rehearsal spaces and dressing rooms, and spacious reception areas, in order to sponsor musical and theatrical events by their own membership, by the amateurs and professionals in their communities, and by nationally-regarded arts celebrities who came to town. Readings by poets, performances by dance troupes, productions by drama leagues, orchestral and chamber concerts, song and instrumental recitals, and speeches and demonstrations by arts educators, critics, scholars, and patrons of the arts all necessitated regular access to one or more modern auditoria, large enough to hold all interested club members and their guests. Not insignificantly, smaller arts clubs, daunted by inadequate community facilities, would come to depend on the theaters erected by women's clubhouses for activities they could not offer in their more modest clubrooms.

Clubwomen also expected new clubhouses to contain libraries to house reference materials, picture books, fiction, song collections, sheet music, anthologies of plays, popular periodicals, programs of past arts events, and calendars of the city's current cultural fare. In addition, clubwomen sought attractive and secure gallery spaces to exhibit art objects. These needed to be well-lit, accessible to members and visitors at the club, and yet sufficiently safe to ensure that the loaned paintings, pottery, baskets, sculpture, textiles, and metalwork would not suffer damage. Clubwomen devoted to the arts, expecting to fete the artists who lent their luster to the club, insisted that new clubhouses contain modern kitchens, dining areas, and reception centers, so that they could provide refreshments in elegant spaces where artists and members could mingle. A wide variety of meeting rooms was vital as well—to plan future activities and to hold book discussions, dance classes, painting workshops, dramatic readings, and program rehearsals. In all of these spaces other goals of arts-supporting clubwomen would also be achieved: exchange of opinion about the arts events they had just enjoyed together, announcements of other arts activities throughout the city, a general nurturance of arts appreciation among the membership, and a cultivation of the women's club as arts oasis, a beacon for cultural excellence in the community. Such services, under one roof, tailored to the desires of members, came to be feasible to multitudes of women's clubs.

Without question, even clubwomen with no interest in the arts also had a decided interest in the erection of improved meeting places. Those committed to political reform, municipal improvement, charitable endeavors, business opportunities for their sex, and legal advancement likewise sought meeting places in which to plan their programs and strategies, libraries where they could research and study the issues, halls for noteworthy speakers, and pleasant reception areas in which to greet them. These women were very willing supporters of the new clubhouses. Still, it was the arts activities that demanded the most specialized facilities, and the arts advocates who had the most to gain from the 1920s rage for clubhouse building.

The Friday Morning Club

A clear illustration of the impact of the clubhouse on women's club arts programming can be seen in the Friday Morning Club of Los Angeles, the largest woman's club in America, from the year 1909, when it had 1,000 members, until 1920, when 1,834 women belonged to the organization.[3] The club was created in 1891 by Caroline Severance, who had earlier distinguished herself by founding one of the first women's clubs in the country, the New England Woman's Club of Boston, in 1868.

The Friday Morning Club soon discovered that rented rooms designed for other types of activities did not provide satisfactory spaces in which to plan gatherings and events, stage concerts, plays, or readings, hold receptions for visiting artists, exhibit works of art, or host luncheons with guest speakers. The club members who were primarily interested in politics or reform likewise craved more suitable facilities for their discussions and debates. Therefore, in 1897, with a membership of three hundred women, the club initiated a campaign to raise $4,500 to purchase land near downtown Los Angeles, at South Figueroa Street and Tenth Avenue. There they succeeded in erecting and furnishing an elegant two-story Spanish-style clubhouse, valued at $25,000, which served the arts and civic needs of the membership. On 12 January 1900 the group, which had grown to five hundred in size, celebrated the dawn of the twentieth century by commanding a new auditorium, reception area, meeting rooms, library, and exhibit spaces.

With their own building, the Friday Morning Club could plan an impressive slate of arts instruction and entertainment for themselves. Polish-born actress Helena Modjeska appeared at the clubhouse to speak about her career. California author Mary Hunter Austin spoke on the art of the American Indian. L. Frank Baum, author of the *Oz* books, lectured on "Folk Lore and Folk Tales." The women mustered the highest fee they had ever paid, $250, to bring Henry James to address the membership on "The Lessons of Balzac." The club's healthy departments of drama, music, art, and book review delivered to the general membership productions of George Bernard Shaw's *Pygmalion* and John Synge's *Playboy of the Western World,* a harpsichord recital, a discussion of Delsarte's dance movements, and a review of John Galsworthy's *Island Pharisee.*

By 1905 the clubwomen already felt the need for expanded space, yet the Building Committee members debated the logistics and finances of an improved clubhouse for another decade. Finally, in 1915, the 1,432 members settled on a remodeling of their original building. With a new auditorium, seating 650, the club could deliver larger crowds to famous artists who commanded high fees. Among these artists were Ruth St. Denis, who demonstrated her theories of modern dance, and authors William Butler Yeats, Max Eastman, Upton Sinclair, Rheta Child Dorr, Kate Douglas Wiggin, and Charlotte Perkins Gilman. Euripides' *Alkestis* was presented, as was August Strindberg's *The Stronger.* Marian MacDowell performed compositions by her late husband Edward at the piano, and the Tuskegee Jubilee Singers performed "Negro Spirituals." Princess Redfeather provided a presentation of "American Indian Music," and the members also heard a lecture on Richard Wagner's "Use of Pagan Myths" in his operas. In 1916, a pageant celebrating William Shakespeare's plays marked the 300th anniversary of the Bard's death.

Although more regular and broad arts programming became feasible as a result of mid-decade reconstruction, World War I drew unexpectedly large numbers to the Friday Morning Club, and the growing membership hungered for grander facilities to further improve the menu of club arts events. Unquestionably the membership required a newer, larger clubhouse for its meetings. The original property at 940 S. Figueroa Street, which had cost $4,500 in 1900, was now situated in the heart of downtown Los Angeles and worth $150,000. In terms of finances and the desirability of a central location, it made sense to the membership for the Friday Morning Club to remain at the same address and erect a larger structure. Dismantling the old building and selling it with its furnishings to the Catholic Women's Club, the Friday Morning Club broke ground in March 1923 for one of the most splendid clubhouses that would be built in the nation. One year later, the membership of 2,546 women unveiled their six-story, half-million-dollar showplace, a building that stands today and serves the club still.[4] The superior facilities assured an optimal setting for a membership determined to support a wide range of arts activities. The structure contained two auditoria, one seating 1,100, and another seating 550. A state-of-the-art kitchen serviced a dining area for 500, where authors and musicians steadily provided after-luncheon entertainment. An art gallery displayed regular exhibits for members' edification, where any faithful attendant of the club's gatherings could become familiar with an impressive number of the world's most renowned artists and their works.

Speeches were offered in the club auditoria or dining room by writers Hamlin Garland, Thornton Wilder, Sherwood Anderson, Floyd Dell, Bertrand Russell, Kathleen Norris, Carl Sandburg, Vachel Lindsay, Upton Sinclair, and Edna St. Vincent Millay; by actors Hedda Hopper and Edward Everett Horton; and by little theater director Gilmor Brown. Olga Steeb, concert pianist, performed in recital. The Women's Orchestra of Los Angeles played for the club. Five California women composers came to offer their own compositions. The Hallelujah Quartet sang "Negro Spirituals," the Russian String Quartet played the classics, and "Court Songs of France" were presented by singers in medieval costume.

Plays presented under the auspices of the drama department included *Surgery* by Anton Chekhov, *Lady Windemere's Fan* by Oscar Wilde, *The Great God Brown* by Eugene O'Neill, *Success* by A. A. Milne, *The Queen Was in the Parlor* by Noël Coward, *Weary Blues* by Langston Hughes, and *The Constant Wife* by W. Somerset Maugham. Eighteen members of the club entered the playwriting competition in 1925, and two winning works were performed. Scholarly experts delivered papers on "Creative Women from Sappho to Mme. de Staël"; "Women in Modern Drama"; "Emily Dickinson"; and "Bassoon History." Members reviewed Theodore Dreiser's new novel, *An American Tragedy*. Hundreds of feature films and childrens' films were previewed at the club and the members' endorsements were publicized throughout the city. The women celebrated Shakespeare's 362nd birthday in 1926, lobbied the Mayor to appoint a Municipal Arts Commission for the city of Los Angeles, and urged the new city library to exhibit works by California artists and sculptors.[5] In 1929, the club gallery offered an exhibition of work by women painters of the West.

The constant stream of arts programming in superior arts facilities served to attract to the Friday Morning Club more and more members with knowledge of and experience in the arts, which further enriched the cultural life of the members. The new recruits were more than willing to share their ideas, enthusiasm, and connections within the arts world, formally and informally, thus broadening the arts interests of other members. Anna De Mille, wife of playwright William C. and sister-in-law of film director Cecil B., was one of these new members. She made regular trips to New York to view theatrical fare on Broadway, and reported her observations to the club. She also sponsored her choreographer daughter, Agnes, in a dance recital at the clubhouse.[6]

Other members similarly lent their arts expertise when they joined the club; among them, composer and first vice-president of the Los Angeles Symphony Orchestra, Harriet William Russell Strong, and club president Margaret Collier Graham, who wrote philosophy and fiction for the *Atlantic Monthly* and *Century* and published *The Wizard's Daughter and Other Stories* (1895). The range of accomplishments by club members was extensive. Josephine Hilty Abramson, for example, composed children's songs, while poet Sarah Bixby Smith published *My Sagebrush Garden* and *Adobe Days*. Mrs. John W. Mitchell directed the Bridges Art Gallery in San Diego. Both Mrs. E. K. Foster and Mrs. Kreider were appointed by the Los Angeles city manager to serve on the Board of Motion Picture Censorship. Eleanor Toll organized the Glendale Symphony Association to aid the orchestra, and Carrie Parson Brant chaired the fund-raising breakfast for the Hollywood Bowl for eight seasons.

The clubhouse, then, served as an ideal spot for women's networking in support of the region's growing professional and amateur arts organizations. The opportunity for members' arts interests to thrive in such an atmosphere was unquestionable. Friday Morning Club members, like clubwomen throughout the nation, succeeded in their efforts to build unparalleled arts facilities for themselves. In doing so, they launched a new stage of arts activity, desired and achieved by clubwomen of the 1920s.

Clubwomen's political activities also benefitted from the new clubhouse facilities. Those members who cared more about W. E. B. DuBois's judicial efforts on behalf of the Black population than the performances of Black singers filled the Friday Morning Club's largest hall to hear his speech. The municipal reformers used the auditorium to interview mayoral candidates at election time. Similarly, disarmament, international relations, peace, and environmental committees also planned their strategies in club committee rooms. Civic activists raised money and announced special events alongside their arts-minded sisters in the most spectacular arts center in their city.

The Post–World War I Building Boom

A similar story developed in every corner of American clubdom, and we can still observe the luxurious facilities for ambitious cultural activities that thousands of clubs undertook. However, the demands of the new buildings, to plan, build, maintain, and pay for them, exposed the drawbacks of real estate investment and contributed to the decline of club life as an attraction for women.

It is important to note that well before World War I, a few women's reform and literary clubs had raised the money to build and furnish clubhouses of their own. Even before the turn of the century, there was evidence that clubwomen desired their own spaces for club activity. The Milwaukee Woman's Club claimed to have built the first clubhouse in 1890, while the Grand Rapids Ladies' Literary Club was second.[7] Increasingly, rising real estate values enabled clubwomen to sell donated or purchased properties at a great profit, with which they financed grander building plans. It was World War I, however, that catapulted the majority of women's organizations into financing their own structures. The patriotic impulse to participate in the war effort swelled club ranks. Huge numbers of traditional women, totally devoted to their homes and families, suddenly decided to taste club life. Within the clubs, all suffrage, educational, municipal, and arts projects had come to a virtual halt, so that members might devote their full attention to wartime relief. The homebody could serve her country in the club by rolling bandages, knitting socks for soldiers, absorbing advice on the proper canning of Victory Garden fruit for hospitals, and pledging to observe meatless or wheatless days when she cooked for her family. The many new members enjoyed their new acquaintanceship with large numbers of women, the solace of camaraderie in turbulent times, the opportunity to leave the home for novel activity, and the sense of accomplishing as a group member large jobs that could not be done alone. These experiences had long been appreciated by millions of early clubwomen, but until now had remained untried by other middle-class, married, and busy mothers.

Many of these new members had realized that their families and homes, generally smaller than those of their forebears and containing new labor-saving devices, required less commitment than home life had required of their mothers and grandmothers. One historian of housework, Ruth Schwartz Cowan, has termed this era "The Golden Years" for the middle-class housewife."[8] These women felt they were freer to devote some time to work other than domestic, and this attitude encouraged women's ongoing participation in clubs.

When the clubs attempted to shift back to their original agendas after the war, the new women stayed on and continued to bring along their friends and relatives. Even the widespread influenza epidemic, which necessitated the cancellation of all public meetings for the autumn of 1918, failed to moderate the steady flow of new members. As a result, previously small societies of women grew to a size that made spacious meeting places essential.

In addition, the war provided many women's clubs with a comfortable nest egg of savings. The groups had rallied handsomely to the call to purchase Liberty Bonds. In fact, one-third of all war bonds were bought by women, many of whom had never invested before.[9] It was not uncommon for clubs to have raised thousands of dollars to acquire several bonds for each of the four Liberty Loan drives. After the war, these bonds paid three-and-a-half percent interest, which the members were now free to spend on their organizations. Women's activities in raising large amounts of money for bonds, as well as for war-related causes such as ambulances, French orphans, and Christmas gifts for soldiers, provided them with the skills and experience to amass and spend large sums. The experiences of approaching potential donors, arranging rummage sales, and compiling cookbooks in wartime had demonstrated to clubwomen that building another treasury for a clubhouse would hardly tax their talents.

Thus, the war freed women to confront their dissatisfactions with meeting in each others' homes or renting public space from landlords. Certainly the disruption of using one's house for a meeting, overfilling it with club members, after scouring it thoroughly, borrowing chairs and dishes, baking refreshments for all, perhaps even buying new furnishings for the parlor or shrubs for the front lawn, was a responsibility no one enjoyed on a regular basis.

However, the clubs that graduated from members' homes to rented meeting places also suffered discomforts. Venues such as the Odd Fellows Hall, churches, the YWCA, the public library, the historical society, or the girls' academy (for meetings of alumnae associations) were not ideal meeting places.

As renters, the women had no control over the rising costs of their space or its cleanliness. Unless they maintained the room year-round, they could not determine which furnishings might be available to them at each gathering. For arts performance planners in particular, rented spaces could be deadly. A poorly-maintained piano, a too-small stage, indifferent acoustics, the absence of a curtain, houselights that did not dim, curtains that admitted light, an insufficient pitch in the hall which limited sight lines for viewers, all proved disturbing. The clubwomen were never free of the possibility of eviction—as when the Chicago YMCA revoked the lease of the Women's Christian Temperance Union, because the YMCA officers had decided not to rent to women anymore.[10] Club members found that space was not always available to them at their own convenience, for the owner could displace them for such occasions as his daughter's wedding reception. The safety of club supplies, minutes, the president's podium and gavel, or a favored and valuable silver tea service, would be uncertain in a building that was irregularly patrolled for theft, fire, or water damage. Yet public meeting rooms were sufficiently scarce that members could seldom voice their dissatisfactions and move on to other quarters.

Soon after the war, then, it made sense to clubwomen to apply their treasuries toward building their own clubhouses. Members felt sure that structures owned by their organizations would make several important statements to the community. As the President of the General Federation of Women's Clubs, Alice Ames Winter, pointed out to her two million members, "A building would serve as a visible symbol for strength."[11] It would also demonstrate the stability of the group. "The woman's club has come to stay. It gets itself a home as a manifestation of that permanence," said Winter, a steady champion of clubhouse building.[12] The buildings, it was argued, would provide expanded performance facilities for the community.

In addition, a building could show off women's newfound capability to deal with banks and to manage corporations without the assistance of men:

> The new conception of a clubwoman as a competent business woman who has learned to manage her affairs with an efficiency born of her contact with the business world and her swift assimilation of its methods, is rapidly impressing itself, the country over.[13]

The business sense that women marshalled to create and maintain their clubhouses was considerable. Despite general assumptions that they were incapable of managing money, services, or legal questions on such a large scale, they managed to give the lie to the myth of female financial irresponsibility. "The notion that women have little business sense has had a hold on the human race for a considerable time, and is still powerful," one clubwoman complained. Yet, she observed that clubwomen had managed the business of clubhouse operation successfully for years, investing millions of dollars, an activity that "involved such presumably masculine matters as bonds, balances and mortgages."[14] In short, the women were succeeding in still another male-dominated realm.

As for the women themselves, they could devise a comfortable setting to their own specifications in which to relax, build friendships, entertain with ease, and initiate and carry out artistic and political projects of importance. Thus, they kept a promise they had made to themselves in the 1890s—to use clubs to nurture their own membership. In the clubhouse, observers noted, a woman could be "a guest" with "shelter and living conditions that [were] comfortable and private—where a woman may have a 'room of her own' where she may exercise hospitality without the burden of preparation."[15] For the single career woman without a family, the building would additionally provide companionship unavailable to her at home.

In order to gain these advantages, women were willing to invest a great deal of themselves in clubhouse planning. For women who maintained households for their husbands and children, who created as warm a haven as possible, who supervised the details of daily life to smooth the path of family happiness, there was an evident need for a place of their own. Within the clubhouse walls, women might be sustained by the very same womanly nurturance they provided for everyone else. Had women felt completely fulfilled by their self-sacrifice for their loved ones, as convention had it, the clubhouse would not have been regarded as such a welcome hideaway from voracious domestic demands. As it was, the clubhouse became a setting for a separate existence, where a woman could be her own person and develop herself. She could entertain her friends there, without cleaning, cooking, or washing. She could peruse the literary magazines to which the organization subscribed or perform an art song for her friends. She could regularly enjoy exposure to new people and new ideas, relieving the isolation of the family. Even the initials on the dishes and towels were not those of her spouse; they were those of her very own club.

Simultaneously, members justified the clubhouse as providing offices, meeting rooms, archives, clearing houses, and lecture space that they needed for tackling the social problems of the day. Arts devotees could here launch their lobbying for war memorials, celebratory pageants, or National Music Week. This place—neither public nor private, but both—provided its members with a homelike environment, while at the same time it served the community through the membership's labors.

As soon as the war was over, clubwomen in every region of the country reoriented their priorities, making preparations to establish their own buildings. Within the decade, over 1,200 ambitious new edifices had emerged all over the nation. Over 172 of them cost between $50,000 and $3.5 million, serving a total of a half million women; another 626, more modestly priced, served another quarter million women.[16] Seattle saw the completion of the Woman's Century Club, the Women's University Club, the Sunset Club, and buildings for the Daughters of the American Revolution, the YWCA, and the Seattle Federation of Women's Clubs. In Atlanta and its immediate environs, the women built clubhouses for the Atlanta Woman's Club, the West End Club, the Grant Park Club, the Capitol Hill Club, the Decatur Club, the College Park Club, the local section of the National Council of Jewish Women, and two chapters of the Daughters of the American Revolution.[17] The New York State Society of the Society of Colonial Dames of America built an uptown replica of a pre–Revolutionary War mansion which had once stood at 34 Wall Street.[18]

Black women, unwelcome in most of the clubs of the General Federation of Women's Clubs, federated into the National Association of Colored Women, which reported 1,181 clubs with 20,155 members in 1933.[19] Among the clubhouses black women funded in the 1920s were the Mary Tolbert Club in Tampa, Florida, the Hallie Q. Brown Club in Palakta, Florida, the Indiana State Club House, and several structures in California.

California led the way, with more clubs, more club members, and more clubhouses (three hundred), than any other state.[20] Among California's new structures were four of the most splendid in the country. Three of these stood in Los Angeles: the Ebell Club (costing one million dollars), the Friday Morning Club (costing a half million), and the Women's Athletic Club (at a cost of over a million). San Francisco's Woman's Club cost two million dollars.[21] Very quickly, envious clubs strived to set regional, if not national, standards of extravagance. The Atlanta Woman's Club, for example, sold its old facility, purchased from the Christian Scientists for $12,000 in 1908, for $35,000 in 1920. Members then moved into the splendid 1898 Wimbish House on Peachtree Street, for which they paid $47,000. Two years later, however, they found it too small, and put another $110,000 into the addition of a club theater.[22]

Not to be surpassed by mere member clubs, the national associations to which these groups belonged scrambled to erect institutional headquarters. Lest member societies create such lavish dwellings that they appeared to surpass the strength and importance of the muscle-flexing, expanding administrative offices, the national leadership sought to ensure that national headquarters, too, resided in impressive dwellings. Only the Women's Christian Temperance Union had succeeded in acquiring a headquarters building before the 1920s. In 1892 its member clubs paid for a twelve-story WCTU office building in Chicago at a price of $1.2 million, with much hard feeling over the great expense.[23]

By the 1920s, however, no group wanted to be without a national headquarters of size and elegance, to host meetings, publish a newsletter and other pertinent guides and publications, entertain dignitaries, house the growing number of administrative offices, and, occasionally, provide private apartments for the executive officer. For the most part, club leaders selected structures in Washington, DC because of the proximity to legislators for lobbying purposes. The General Federation of Women's Clubs paid $70,000 for an 1873 mansion, at 1734 N Street NW, opening their headquarters in 1922.[24] In 1927 the National Society of Colonial Dames of America acquired the 1751 Dumbarton House of Georgetown. Similarly, the National Society, United States Daughters of 1812 purchased a D.C. building in 1928, on Rhode Island Avenue N.W.

By 1917 the Daughters of the American Revolution had paid off the Memorial Continental Hall it had erected in 1905 with an auditorium and a museum of furnished rooms decorated from donations. Immediately after this they began raising $385,000 for an adjacent administration building, which opened in 1923 at 1776 D Street in Washington. Next, the organization began building its Constitutional Hall, with one of the largest auditoriums in the nation's capital.[25] On the opposite end of the political spectrum the National Woman's Party was unwilling to divert its energy from the Equal Rights Amendment for a building campaign. However, the wealthy Alva Vanderbilt Belmont bought the handsome Sewall-Belmont Mansion, a short distance from the Capitol building, and presented it to the party for its headquarters. The National Association of Colored Women dedicated its headquarters on 12th and O Street NW in 1928.[26] The American Association of University Women, formed in 1921 as a result of the merger of the Association of Collegiate Alumnae with the Southern Association of College Women, bought a headquarters on Eye Street NW in 1921.[27]

New York City also saw its share of women's national headquarters. The YWCA built an imposing structure on Lexington Avenue, including lodgings for young working women more affordable than those at the Waldorf-Astoria, half a block away. The Junior League spent $1.25 million on new offices. In 1929, Panhellenic House provided accommodations for its sorority membership. In all, American women had never done so much building before, and would not do so again.

In theory, the typical woman's club required just a simple room, large enough to seat all its active members, plus facilities to boil water for tea after the business meetings or lectures. Most clubs had endured little more than this in rented spaces. Now, however, members began to demand much more. The obligatory setting came to consist of splendid facilities for the pursuit of the arts, for socializing, and for meeting and planning. Most clubhouses held at least one auditorium, seating from two hundred to twelve hundred people.[28] The typical auditorium also included a balcony, orchestra pit, motion picture equipment, dressing rooms, footlights, storage for scenery, box office, coatrooms, lobby, and bathrooms with spacious anterooms. In addition, clubhouses included classrooms of several sizes, board rooms and offices, a large reception hall for teas or balls, a modern commercial sized kitchen, an art gallery, and a comfortable parlor and library with fireplace and shelves for donated books and magazines and newspaper subscriptions.

Not all clubs could afford to meet the aforementioned standard, but many surpassed them, providing athletic facilities (swimming pool, gymnasium, massage room, sauna or Turkish bath, showers, lockers), a soundproof music room with a grand piano, an elevator for elderly members, a solarium, or private interior gardens. The San Antonio Junior League gave the five stables on its property over to the use of artists for studios. Some club members demanded bedrooms to accommodate downtown shoppers in need of naps, career women without a home, or mobile clubwomen visiting from another town.[29] The Women's Athletic Club in Los Angeles, for example, rented one hundred and fifty hotel rooms. Frequently, dining rooms or cafeterias were constructed either for members only or for the general public. Apartments for hired managers were common, the concept of a paid woman superintendent catching on so quickly that 125 of them attended a 1928 convention in Detroit.[30] Occasionally, clubs even built tennis courts or a dog room for the care of one's pets. A beauty parlor and exercise rooms were features at the New York Junior League and the Providence Plantations Club in Rhode Island. Only parking lots seem to have remained unconsidered, since most dwellings either stood downtown or in fashionable districts of the city, accessible by public transportation, or were located within the neighborhoods of the membership.

Rather than keeping their buildings all to themselves, some clubwomen made a decision to share their facilities with other groups of women. Altruism was evident in the uses to which some club buildings were put. The New York Junior League installed a baby shelter with a separate entrance in its building, where twelve pink and twelve blue cribs held babies for low-income mothers who were temporarily unable to keep them at home.[31] Other clubs housed women's exchanges, whose profits went to the housebound women who made the objects that were sold, or sponsored rummage shops, whose profits went to charity. The Rockford, Illinois, Woman's Club, encouraged by the success of its rummage shop, aspired to create a gymnasium for children.[32] In other instances, the clubwomen charged a rental fee to outsiders who used their building. Even so, the scarcity of public meeting places for women meant that their policy appeared magnanimous. As we shall see, however, this form of generosity sometimes brought more trouble than it was worth.

When clubwomen had built structures solely to meet a social need, such as an orphanage, their goals were generally realistic, and their plans were ruled by the size of their purse. When they built for themselves, however, they attempted to realize their collective dreams. When they realized their desires to provide modern club women with the spaces they had long been denied, the sky was the limit. Clubwomen strived to make their clubrooms as elegant as possible, by selecting property in fashionable locations, building as large and ornate club residences as they could possibly imagine managing, and decorating them in as luxurious a manner as feasible.

It is likely that many club members devoured *The House in Good Taste* (1913), in which interior decorator Elsie De Wolfe described her 1905 designs for Stanford White's Colony Club for New York City society women. The decor was so widely praised for its elegance that De Wolfe went on to earn a fortune decorating the private homes of Colony clubwomen, including the Vanderbilts, the Whitneys, the Morgans, the Harrimans, and other industrialists.[33] Clubwomen had access to De Wolfe's methods through wide press coverage of the Colony Club decor and through her book, which carefully provided a blueprint of her efforts. The decorator described the roof garden, with its white lattice covering the walls and supporting a profusion of growing vines, blossoming flowers, and singing birds. It was comfortable even on the bleakest winter days, she insisted, thanks to two huge stoves of green majolica which she ordered from Germany. Ceiling lights, hidden in huge branches of pale green grapes, illuminated furniture in grape-patterned chintz and green and white striped linen.[34]

De Wolfe's Trellis Room was no less extravagant, boasting a fountain on the brim of which was posed a youthful figure upheld by two dolphins and surrounded by formal pedestals, curved urns, boxed trees, statues, marble benches, and a red tile floor. The 22' × 60' basement pool, sunken below a marble floor, was surrounded by white columns, marble benches, and walls panelled with mirrors, permitting endless reflections of columns and shimmering lights which hung from bunches of green-white artificial grapes. "Surely the old Romans knew no pleasanter place than this city-enclosed pool," asserted the designer.[35] Clubwomen devoured these descriptions, widely publicized at the time with generous photographs of the palatial settings.[36] While no clubs had the resources to outdo De Wolfe's Colony Club decor, all had the imagination to aspire to match it.

Thus, many a clubhouse tried to outdo the others in devising fabulous settings, decorating one room in Colonial American style, another in Pompeian, another in Egyptian, another in Oriental. Dutch colonial was popular in New York, while in New England, Early American was the rage; in the Southwest, Spanish decor predominated, in keeping with the growing regional loyalties of the era. The Boston Junior League opted for the avant-garde, selecting a modern art deco setting with severe, angular, salmon pink and silver-colored decor in the reception area of its new building at Zero Marlboro Street. The two-story ballroom was done in pale apricot and Venetian blue. The members of the Los Angeles Ebell on Wilshire Boulevard installed frescoes in their clubhouse atrium,[37] French Provincial furniture in the bedrooms, and heavy wrought-iron gates in the medieval grand parlor. It is not surprising that Hollywood movie studios now rent the clubhouse to film in its period sets.

The building of opulent clubhouses all over the nation made glittering arts functions rather commonplace. In Grand Rapids, Michigan, the 1925 remodeling of the St. Cecilia Music Society Building occasioned a gala concert by Lauritz Melchoir, the renowned Wagnerian *Heldentenor,* just arrived from Europe to make his Metropolitan Opera debut. Boasting a stained-glass window of St. Cecilia at the organ, designed by American artist Frederick S. Church and executed by the Tiffany studios, the new hall has continued to facilitate decades of rich musical performances by prominent artists. Similarly, in 1924 the New York Junior League clubhouse could offer a show of seventy-five works by contemporary artists, including Georgia O'Keeffe, Stuart Davies, and Charles Demuth. When the Los Angeles Ebell dedicated its million-dollar clubhouse in 1927, its members enjoyed a steady diet of exposure to the fine arts, including a folksong recital, a poetry contest, a wood block demonstration, the dedication of a memorial fountain commemorating 250 World War I casualties who were relatives of Ebell women, and the depiction of *Four Sibyls* by Maxine Albro in the clubhouse garden's patio frescoes. Whenever and wherever a regional, state, or national women's club conference was held, local clubhouses provided impressive settings for concerts, art shows, and dramatic interludes.

It was only after considerable discussion that groups of women were able to decide whether to build a clubhouse, where it should be located, what services it should provide, how much money it should cost, how the money should be raised, and who should be hired as architect, banker, lawyer, decorator, and manager. Some clubs weathered this process better than others. In Clark's Summit, Pennsylvania, every single member of the town's women's club dutifully visited the available properties in town before the group voted on its purchase. In many clubs, the entire group embarked upon a series of lectures on interior decoration, so all might be competent to make judgments about the decor. These collective decision-making procedures seemed to tax the sisterhood among the members. Thus, President Brady of the Pomona, California, Ebell Club spoke of the effort with weariness:

> You are familiar with the effort to secure a lot for a club home. The effort has been filled with joy and trouble, calm and storm, assertion and denial; hopes and fears, plans made and plans revoked, but I rejoice to say all has passed off without dissension, and when the papers are finally adjusted, I trust we will all be satisfied, even if everything is not just as we would have it. We must remember that with 125 different minds, the final decision will be a composite and stand for everyone. I trust the club will grow in usefulness when we are in a club home. Environment counts for much.[38]

At the 1927 dedication of the Los Angeles Ebell Club, it was member cooperation that clubwomen praised:

> Let us dedicate this building to friendship, one of the most prized human possessions; dedicate it to the most satisfying form of friendship, not that which comes from mere social acquaintance, but that which comes from thinking, planning, and working together.[39]

Money Troubles and Fund-Raising Efforts

How did the women manage to pay for the land, building, and decor of these clubhouses? Some did not. The St. Paul Junior League gave up in its fund-raising efforts. The Woman's Club of Harvard in Massachusetts became discouraged and moved its thousand dollars to its student loan fund. In 1930 the National Association of Women Painters and Sculptors, in New York City, sold the house its members had purchased five years earlier, finding it prohibitively expensive, costing more than they had anticipated and certainly more than they had budgeted for.[40] But many other women's groups persevered in spite of financial difficulties. These difficulties, ironically underlining the financial dependence of supposedly prosperous women, were overcome only by a careful calculation of expenses and of the club's ability to pay them. This careful attention to financial detail for even the most ostentatious of projects demonstrated members' financial responsibility, and at the same time allowed women to build edifices that provided facilities well beyond the bare minimum of their needs.

A few fortunate clubs received donations of property and therefore needed only to furnish their dwellings. Mrs. Watson bought a building for the Fine Arts Club in North Dakota. The Des Moines Woman's Club was able to secure a ninety-nine year lease to "rent" the Hoyt Sherman Farm for a dollar a year. One member of the Cleveland Art Club donated a country cottage as a club studio. When Elizabeth P. Taylor joined the Little Rock Junior League, her parents presented the association with a home.[41]

Few clubs were so fortunate as to receive a gift of a house, however. Those clubs that had property to sell at a profit did so to improve their dwelling spaces. For example, Pomona Ebell sold its original clubhouse lot to the Congregational Church and moved its building to a new location, one of a size that permitted a generous addition. We have already observed the successes of the Los Angeles Friday Morning Club and the Atlanta Woman's Club in this kind of activity.

Many clubs debated whether to build a new clubhouse or to refurbish a standing structure. The preservation of an historical building was often the favored solution, especially among patriotic organizations of women, who emphasized history as part of their program. The National Society of Colonial Dames of America, for example, remodeled the 1751 Dumbarton House in Georgetown, District of Columbia. Branches of the organization, known as state societies, followed suit. They moved into Wilmington's First Presbyterian Church, New York City's Abigail Adams Smith House at 421 East 61st Street, and Savannah's Andrew Low House. In Virginia, members occupied the Wilton Mansion, ten miles outside of Richmond.[42]

The Daughters of the American Revolution were responsible for restoring numerous historic buildings. Atlanta's Daughters of the American Revolution bought an 1895 replica of the Longfellow home, known as the Craigie House of Cambridge, Massachusetts, which had been erected as the Massachusetts State Building at the Atlanta Cotton States and International Exposition.[43] The New Jersey branches restored several colonial estates: Fleming Castle, the Thomas Revel House, and George Washington's headquarters in Plainfield and in Rocky Hill. The Schuyler-Hamilton House became chapter houses for the Flemington, Burlington, Plainfield, Princeton, and Morristown women.[44] A contemporary survey of DAR chapters nationwide revealed seventy-five historical structures of great diversity occupied by member clubs, from the Burnham Tavern in Machias, Maine, to the Exchange Building and Custom House in Charleston, South Carolina; the El Cuartelejo Indian Pueblo in Scott City, Kansas; suffragist May Wright Sewall's private school in Indianapolis; Stephen Douglas's birthplace in Rutland County, Vermont; Fort Pitt Blockhouse in Pittsburgh; Jones Point Lighthouse in Alexandria, Virginia; and a log cabin in Fairbury, Nebraska.[45]

Even women's groups not specifically devoted to patriotic causes found historical preservation a sound idea. The Santa Clara Woman's Club managed to restore an 1818 adobe building, while the Poughkeepsie Junior League purchased the eighteenth-century Glebe House. The Indiana Federation of Women's Clubs raised ten thousand dollars to purchase Fauntleroy House in

New Harmony, reputed to be the birthplace of the club movement in that women held discussions there as early as 1859.[46] The Des Moines Woman's Club inhabited the Hoyt-Sherman farm, owned by the brother of William Tecumseh Sherman.[47] The Woman's Club of Jackson, California, received a gift of the Constitution Saloon, enabling them to devote their savings to its refurbishment.[48] The Tacoma Woman's Club moved into a residence built by pioneers of the Pacific Northwest.[49] The Junior League of Philadelphia restored "Sweetbrier," a 1797 house in Fairmount Park, for its headquarters.

Whether the goals were grand, like the two-million-dollar San Francisco Woman's Club, or more modest, like the Memphis Nineteenth Century Club, whose two thousand members spent $12,500 on its facility,[50] most clubs sold shares to members to help pay for the building. In 1919, the Friday Morning Club of Los Angeles urged its 2,130 members to contribute ten dollars each to the Foundation Fund, justifying this practice as more fitting than soliciting gifts from outsiders:

> We have asked for money from our own members because that is the only dignified and independent thing to do. We are willing to accept gifts from anyone, but we do not intend to ask help of outsiders, for we must control and operate this building ourselves. We did not wish to organize a stock company because our experience in financing the present clubhouse showed the great disadvantage of such a plan.[51]

Club spokeswomen need not have been so apologetic. Some members, at least, were eager to help: "I would rather go hungry all the rest of my life than not have my part in the new clubhouse," said one. "For twenty-nine years the Club has filled so large a place in my life, and it is still my dearest interest outside my own family."[52]

Naturally, the clubs cashed in their Liberty Bonds as soon as they matured. They also revived many of the fundraising techniques they had developed in wartime. The Atlanta Woman's Club netted $6,000 by selling a cookbook. The Pasadena Shakespeare Club, saving for a new auditorium that would cost $127,187 and a remodeling that required $29,000, collected $5,000 when four thousand people attended its Spanish Fiesta at the Benjamin Hahn Rancho in October 1925. Its members also sold postcards that portrayed their clubhouse, and invited the public to attend, for a fee, their violin recitals, their lectures on Shakespeare, their Yellowstone Park travelogues with stereopticon lantern slides, and a four-day exhibit of the Sistine Madonna in needlework. They raised another $1,000 when they sponsored Helen Keller's first West Coast lecture.[53] The Friday Morning Club of Los Angeles made $3,000 when donated cooked foods were resold to members, and their Forest Fete earned another $11,000. The bake sales, raffles, card parties, dances, amateur theatricals, and rummage sales were plentiful. Clubwomen also skimped on their annual yearbooks, making a single volume do for two years.[54]

Still clubwomen ran short of money and turned to the banks for mortgages. One assumes that ex–Friday Morning Club president Margaret Sartori had no difficulty in getting a ten-year $300,000 loan at five and a half percent interest from the Security Trust and Savings Bank. Her husband was its president. The Pasadena Shakespeare Club members had no such connections. They paid six and a half percent interest on their million-dollar mortgage, paying five thousand dollars per year until it was paid off in 1944.

Clubhouse building, then, was not without its drawbacks. The incurrence of large debts insured that bake sales and raffles would remain on the scene for a long time, continuing to divert members from the clubs' more basic goals and interests. The new entrepreneurship also undercut the sisterhood that had formerly flourished. For example, heavy expenses tended to ensure a tougher dues policy. In most cases, admission fees and/or yearly dues were doubled.

Los Angeles Ebell had to do more than simply double its dues to collect $200,000 for the purchase of one-and-a-third acres on Wilshire Boulevard at Lucerne Avenue in 1925. The luxurious clubhouse, with 68 rooms, 185 windows and 54 French doors, cost $985,000. The furnishings cost another $150,000. The mortgage of $750,000 plus $350,000 in interest was not paid off until 1948. In its attempt to pay these costs, the club raised its dues from $25 to $50 in 1926, while the new-member fee rose from $50 to $100 and the cost of life membership rose from $300 to $500. The club collected new member fees immediately, "to relieve embarrassing situations" for those who were slow to meet their financial obligations. Club budget officers initiated strict policies regarding tardy dues payers, observing that "out of a total of 121 members fifty were delinquent in their dues, twenty of whom were listed as "Hopeless."[55] The new rules required that those who resigned but returned later had to pay again the initiation fee required of newcomers. In 1920–21, officers rescinded an old rule that had permitted ten-year members, or those over the age of seventy, to attend club gatherings without paying dues. Finally, the club increased its fee to temporary members, such as visitors who were vacationing for the winter with Southern California relatives who held memberships.[56] Despite all these measures, the Ebell barely escaped the outcome that befell the Atlanta Woman's Clubs, for which "financial difficulties became so severe that personal loans were taken out in the club's behalf by several of its members."[57]

In addition to a closer watch on the treasury, clubs now urged members to make donations of cash, fine furnishings, and other objects. Anniversary Day was an annual occasion that celebrated the dedication of the building, and formalized the ritual of presenting the clubhouse with gifts—a painting, a silver pitcher, or at least a library book. Many a 1920s clubhouse was furnished through the steady largesse of its members.

Clubs worked at winning more members as a way of acquiring more needed funds. For example, the Woman's Club of Hollywood, built in 1913 by 250 members, grew to 1,400 women in 1922.[58]

However, the influx of new members had a significant impact on the quality of club life and unalterably changed the character of clubwomen's interactions. The membership drives brought in new members with different interests, as well as younger women with whom older women found it hard to share experiences. Earlier membership drives by exclusive clubs had not had so drastic an effect. The new growth altered not only the numbers, but also the type of membership perceptibly. While wives of the professional and business elite in a community never invited factory workers' wives to join, they did coax their mildly interested neighbors and daughters-in-law to apply, where once an invitation had been reserved for those who appreciated that it was a precious thing to come by. Some clubs also initiated new policies whereby the wives of clergymen or foreign consuls could join for half price. This tactic padded the membership lists with "nice" women and filled voracious club coffers with their dues, but it also filled the ranks with women selected for a husband's status more than for the newcomers' commitment to club work.

Most clubs decided to feed their treasuries by inviting Junior Auxiliaries to form. Teenagers and young brides could belong at a discount and use the clubhouse to develop activities of their own. It was hoped that they would grow accustomed to club life and linger, as full dues payers, in later life. The members of this age group tended to be interested in social programming, which relieved the tedium of burdensome housekeeping and child-raising tasks. They required clubs to provide entertainments of a type that had never been prevalent before—fashion shows, Halloween costume balls, and bridge parties. While it was the young new members that carried out the organizational effort to execute these festivities, the new programs that met their needs changed the tone of club life. Few senior citizens wished to discuss diaper rash. They had long ago met such obligations; their purpose in joining clubs had been to move on to different concerns. The sudden presence of great numbers of young women made older members less comfortable than they had been when they dominated the clubs. By the same token, the younger women were aware of and uncomfortable with the seniors about them. Schisms arose, created by differences in age and lifestyle.

The new relative ease of club admissions also resulted in a membership less committed to club life and club work, less willing to participate on commitees, less likely to attend events and support special projects. The dedication on which club leadership had relied was eroded by the very efforts to grow more powerful through numbers.

On a national level, the headquarters of women's voluntary organizations attempted the same strategies to bolster their membership lists and national treasuries. Seeing rural women as an untapped source of membership, the General Federation of Women's Clubs scrambled to persuade farm women to form clubs and to join the federation. Many urban women, the mainstay of club life, were reluctant to embrace programs designed for agricultural, unsophisticated, and less affluent women. Consequently, the urban membership became estranged from club life. The costs of building the membership, then, were high, undermining the unity and the appeal of elitism that had given strength to club life over generations.

Still, the need for funds to pay for physical expansion was not satisfied. Clubs expected that important revenue would come from the rental of their reception rooms. While we have already observed that they gave some space away for good causes, clubwomen became comfortable with charging other organizations for the use of clubhouse facilities. The commercial vulgarity of renting was tempered by the notion that in charging worthy causes for space the clubs were still performing a community service, particularly in localities with a dearth of meeting places. Members expected to make a steady income from the rental of their clubrooms to the Rotary Club, drama societies, and other women's groups such as the local women's press club, the Daughters of the British Empire, or the Ladies' Catholic Benevolent Society. Thus, clubhouses housed numerous lectures, Sunday school services, graduation exercises, Girl Scout meetings, card parties, luncheons, dances, dinners, local orchestral performances, meetings, traveling art exhibitions, and college extension courses. To members in need of space for family birthday parties, wedding receptions, and anniversary dinners, the clubhouse generally was let at a twenty-five percent discount.[59]

Earning money through rentals was not without its difficulties. Clubs sometimes grew concerned over the propriety of events held on their premises, as when the Friday Morning Club objected to the embarrassing new plays produced by a drama group. When the thespians threatened to leave after a rate increase was quoted, the clubwomen decided to renew the contract at the old rate, keeping their reservations about the good taste of the plays to themselves.[60] In contrast, the Ladies' Literary Club of Salt Lake City so carefully limited the types of events it sponsored that in 1926 the treasurer managed to extend the club's nonprofit, tax-free status to the groups that rented its space.[61] Other clubs occasionally decided to grant free use of their rooms to such worthy groups as the Scouts or the Red Cross, abandoning the intent to earn cash through their rentals.

Another method by which clubs aspired to pay their own way and make a profit was to provide food service. Teas, once a staple in club life, were now accompanied by luncheons. Sometimes clubs opened their food service to the public, as did the Women's Educational and Industrial Union in Boston, and the Woman's City Club in Cleveland; but generally clubs served food only to members. The new kitchens had acquired modern conveniences such as refrigerators, dishwashers, steam tables, bread slicers, scales, can openers, toasters, and fans.[62] Club members attempted to create efficient arrangements of workspace, not only by using the latest equipment, but by inventing sensible patterns of traffic for workers and diners. Making the dishwasher convenient to waiters, placing the coffee close to the guests so that it would arrive at the table hot, and devising a theft-proof storage system, were techniques that clubwomen learned by trial and error. But members' aim of providing modern, efficient, and attractive service with good low-priced food usually proved a failure under an inexperienced management. The dining facilities in clubhouses seldom made a profit, despite Herculean efforts.

Numerous considerations were involved in creating an attractive atmosphere for the dining rooms. The Chicago Woman's City Club, despite its impressive view of the river, was not exempted from the necessity of supplying good ventilation to clear the air of cooking odors. They also needed to provide bright lighting, clean windows, polished silver, cheery decor, quality china, linens, and glassware, small tables for intimate chats, and larger ones for business banquets. Members wanted a homey atmosphere in their dining rooms, and managed this by decorating with members' pottery or artwork. But the institutional feeling was hard to eradicate altogether in a dining room like that of the Woman's City Club of Detroit, which served fifteen hundred women each day.

Furthermore, it was not immediately obvious what clubwomen liked to eat. This, too, had to be determined by experimentation. In general, it seemed that the basic meal should be light. Steaks and chops were less popular than dainty salads, diet bread, muffins, fresh fruits, and light custards. The Grand Rapids Woman's City Club nevertheless admitted that women's restraint did not extend to the banishment of gooey desserts, which were unfailingly popular as well.[63]

In an effort to reduce their financial miseries, some clubs replaced waitress service with a buffet or a cafeteria. Clubwomen met this innovation and economy measure with resistance; but it survived when it succeeded in saving the patrons money. By the late 1920s it was possible to observe: "A few years ago it would have been ridiculous for anyone to assume that women of social standing and dignity would consent to carry their own trays of food at luncheon, but that is exactly what the members do."[64] In the face of escalating expenses at the Chicago Woman's City Club, half the dining room was allotted to more expensive waitress service for the old-fashioned patron. The others could pay seventy-five cents for a lunch offering three choices of meat plus a vegetable, salad, dessert, roll, butter, and coffee. A la carte, members could dine out on a shoestring by selecting one or two inexpensive dishes from the following menu: omelet (35 cents), meat (40 cents), salad (25 cents), a meat substitute like macaroni and cheese (25 cents), fresh green vegetable (15 cents), and dessert (15 cents). Fourteen workers, including a cook, cashier, dishwasher, and busboy managed to serve lunch to 180 and dinner to 20 patrons daily.[65]

Many clubs never managed to solve all these culinary tangles. New York's Woman's City Club gave up its food service, unable to compete with restaurants in the vicinity. The Woman's City Club in Rochester found itself with a deficit of four thousand dollars.[66] Meals turned out to be a service to the membership rather than the hoped-for profit-maker to pay for the fancy new clubhouse.

Maintaining the clubhouses also turned out to be more difficult than clubwomen had anticipated. After the first flush of enthusiasm died, the clubwomen still had to cope with the problems of depreciation. The gorgeous buildings were not perfectly constructed. The Friday Morning Club, having won an award from the Southern California Branch of the American Institute of Architects for the beauty of its clubhouse, discovered some expensive problems during the third year of operation. Seepage during a storm caused damage requiring a contractor to adjust the basement walls. The expenditures and the committee work required for the allocation of funds taxed many committee members, women who might have been attending to matters of greater significance.

The expenses of maintaining the building, of course, were greater and more complicated than those of any home. Regular payments had to be made to the bank, the telephone company, the water company, the electric company, the hauler of ashes, the gardener, the manager, and to suppliers of goods and services. Clubwomen made mistakes for which they paid dearly, for example, when they furnished with pretty items rather than practical ones. Heavy traffic in a hallway soon ruined poor carpets. Women found they could not live with bold patterns in curtains. Laundering caused drapes to fade, shrink, or lose their glossy finish.[67]

Keeping the clubhouses clean was an expensive proposition as well. The membership of the Bryn Mawr Club in New York City was not content to hire six full-time and six part-time cleaning staff. Once a month, another woman scoured from roof to cellar, shaking drapes down, washing woodwork, waxing and polishing the hardwood floors. Twice a week, the club silver had to be polished. The Town Hall Club, too, hired a contractor to wash its clubhouse windows weekly.[68]

Orderly operation required exacting supervision. Clubs kept inventories of supplies and noted which products were most and least effective.[69] Pomona Ebell acquired a safety deposit box at the bank to insure the safekeeping of its legal documents. Its minutes recorded attention to new awnings, bad radiators, bulbs for the stage torches, a gardener to trim the edge of the lawn and rose bushes, sidewalk repair ($6.25), a new cement walk ($129.75), the purchase of a carpet sweeper ($4), a new toilet tank ($23), furniture insurance ($3), a new broom ($1.75), piano mover ($2.50), hardwood expenses, wiring materials ($1.85), grass carrier for the lawn mower, heating for the stage and dressing rooms ($432.25), new French doors, floor polish ($.85), toilet paper ($75), a window shade ($1), oil for the floor ($1.30), a light for the telephone room, gas installed in the fireplace, a plumber ($4.50), city taxes ($50.49), having the hall rug sized, painting and tinting the clubhouse ($185), cleaning the rugs, putting away the window drapes and curtains, and finding a carpenter to fix the window box. No wonder the stockholders voted to "send a note of thanks and affection to Mr. Sheets for tuning and fixing the piano gratis."[70]

Members made a sincere effort to secure good service at modest prices. In order to retain their control and demonstrate their managerial and financial abilities, they worked long hours in committees to run their clubhouses as smoothly as they could. Clubs that did not hire managers to run their buildings on a daily basis devised shifts for volunteer members.[71]

Another way in which clubwomen preserved order was to hire a woman superintendent to perform as many services as could be delegated. Typically, she was a mature unmarried woman who lived on the premises or kept regular hours there. Her presence, presumably, would discourage thieves and vandals. She could keep an eye out for leaks, storm damage, running toilets, and could admit repairmen when necessary. She could receive deliveries of food, flowers, mail, and packages; supervise the cleaning staff; take telephone messages, or direct inquiries to the appropriate officers; and air out the facilities before group functions. The solution of hiring a superintendent was not a universal custom, but it was a common one.

Likewise, clubwomen trusted professional decorators and architects of their own sex to conduct the artistic affairs of clubhouse development. Once Elsie De Wolfe plucked the task of interior decoration from men's hands, clubs turned to their own members or to professional women decorators. Confident that the female sex possessed special abilities, Anne Harriman Sands Rutherford Vanderbilt, who had married the wealthy William Kissam Vanderbilt in 1903, took charge of furnishing the American Woman's Association Building.[72] Similarly, Elsie Cobb Wilson assisted the members of the New York Junior League in decorating their building.[73] The Republican Women of Philadelphia relished the Violet Oakley murals on the walls of their Hannah Penn House. The Alameda County Woman's Athletic Club in California hired Helen Wills to design the ideal tennis courts for them, while Native Daughters of the Golden West in San Francisco hired Margaret Herrick to paint frescoes and stencils in their clubhouse. The Monday Club in San Luis Obispo commissioned Doris Day to paint, stencil, and decorate their clubhouse.[74]

Clubwomen generally sought out an architect of local importance to design their precious buildings, sometimes a woman architect. Julia Morgan, who created a great many western women's clubhouses, is the most renowned of the women's clubhouse architects.[75] Of all her California clubhouses, her Berkeley Woman's City Club is probably the most admired. Clubwomen's commitment to women architects was sufficient to win Morgan commissions to design their charitable institutions as well, and she designed many buildings, notably for the YWCA.[76]

Morgan did not monopolize clubhouse design. Mrs. Minerva P. Nichols designed the New Century Clubs in Wilmington and Philadelphia.[77] In both Worcester and Lynn, Massachusetts, Josephine Wright Chapman designed the Woman's Clubhouses.[78] Sophia Hayden designed the 1893 Woman's Building at the Chicago Fair; Elise Mercur designed the Woman's Building for the Atlanta Cotton States and International Exposition in 1895; Hazel Wood Waterman designed the Wednesday Club in San Diego;[79] and Gertrude Sawyer designed the Junior League Building in Washington D.C. Blanche Geary, the YWCA inspector of buildings, worked with William F. Thompson to design the YWCA building in Evansville, Indiana.[80] Marcia Mind designed the YWCA buildings in Jersey City, Buffalo and Bridgeport.[81]

Women were grateful for the club environment developed for the pleasure of the membership. A Muncie, Indiana, woman revealed that "a friend of mine belongs to several clubs and won't resign from any of them even though her husband has been laid off three months. She says she'll give up her home before her clubs."[82] Such loyalty did not surprise the shapers of club life. In 1877, when the club movement was in its infancy, the secretary of the Rhode Island Woman's Club had fantasized about the ideal club:

> The ideal club has a house and home of its own; has heavy deposits in many banks; perhaps controls railroads and steamboat lines, and so has a powerful

voice on Change. In its beautiful palace, on the finest street of the ideal city, its members can at any hour drop in to chat with friends, and ladies fatigued with shopping always find the daintiest lunch at their call. Their artist-members have their studios, and sounds of exquisite music steal faintly through lofty halls from the distant music-rooms. In the stately library book-worms delve, and in the elegant lecture room Hypatia holds forth daily. Refinement and strength, richness and delicacy, are combined in every appointment, and accurately photograph the mental characteristics of this club.[83]

Although Ms. Eddy did not live to see it, her dream of club life came close to complete realization in the typical women's clubs of the 1920s.

Clubhouses were established throughout the nation through the vision, energy, talent, and efficiency of modern women willing to undertake financial, managerial, and bureaucratic responsibilities of a type and magnitude previously unheard of. They demonstrated, in a new arena, the capabilities of the new American female.

Conclusion

While the immediate satisfactions of clubhouse building were many, the problems arising from them were greater. Most obviously, the increased numbers of women recruited to support the new structures altered the character and the quality of club life, to the dissatisfaction of many members. By 1925, women's clubs were swollen in size, having continued to capitalize on the willingness of new groups of women to enter their once-exclusive ranks. Although the General Federation of Women's Clubs' membership figures are not to be trusted for this period—their claim of two million members is certainly an inflated figure; the real figure was probably closer to one million—individual club rosters indicate that department club memberships tended to peak in 1926–27. In the late 1920s, however, club memberships began to fall off steadily, crumbling the foundation beneath and the energy behind Progressive reform and the women's rights struggle.

Why did club life cease to be an important vehicle for women in the late 1920s? Scholars have looked at clubwomen's declining organizational enthusiasm and clout, and attempted to explain it via external forces. Some have related the erosion of club life to the Great Depression of the 1930s, which forced Americans to concentrate on economic survival, thereby reducing public activism to a luxury many had to dispense with. Others have suggested that the impact of Freud's theories, especially those revealing women's sexual drives, made heterosexual women self-conscious about working with each other, for fear of the label of lesbianism. Still others have identified as crucial the Red Scare of the era, particularly the Spider Web chart of the War Department and the attacks made by the Daughters of the American Revolution against the socialist and pacifist aspects of club programs. It has also been observed that this era offered women the vote and broader opportunities in the professions, providing new outlets for their talents. Young clubwomen are also blamed for underestimating the pleasure and importance of cooperating with other women now that they could mix more freely with the opposite sex, and for ignoring civic responsibility and yielding to their interest in adornment and recreation.[84]

We need, however, to look as well at certain internal forces in the clubs that may have undermined vitality and weakened women's interest in working through these organizations. The enthusiasm for building women's clubhouses did considerable damage to the club movement. The creation of these elaborate structures symbolized the new clubwoman's intention of adorning herself, or at least her surroundings, at the expense of serving others, as women had in stage two of the development of the club movement; neither did the new clubwomen invent ways to involve the community in their programs of service, as they had in stage three. In a way, clubhouse building was a crowning achievement of the Woman Movement, the expression of woman's desire to please herself before she pleased her loved ones. It recalls the earliest stages of club life, when women sought to gain a place of their own in which to attain their best selves. However, the earliest clubwomen were determined to cultivate their individual capabilities, while the clubwomen of the 1920s were bent on a showier enterprise, ornamentation that ultimately stagnated. Clubhouse building was the most self-directed, some would say selfish, undertaking of clubwomen in the Progressive Era, and it became a focal point for major stresses within club life. Before long, this expensive phenomenon cost clubs the trust, admiration, and cooperation that members had built with each other.

Clubhouses were easily the grandest spaces that women had ever erected and surely put clubwomen on the map both literally and figuratively. The structures were impressive architectural statements to their communities that club members had established organizations which were a real presence to be reckoned with. The problem was paying for it all. Raising money to sustain these grand houses became the overriding concern of club leaders in the 1920s. The mechanics of running and financing houses demanded a great deal of clubwomen's time, energy, and financial resources, and diverted them from other issues they might have addressed, new programs they might have invented, and new goals they might have set for their membership and for society in general.

The tactic of increasing membership so as to meet financial needs was a solution that backfired. Older and long-time members responded to the anonymity that came with size by forming small cliques. They felt displaced and displeased by the young mothers with their frivolous demands for parties and frolics during their rare afternoons out of the house and away from small children. The seniors, accustomed to devoting long hours to lobbying for a law or to organizing a community sing, were disappointed that the newer members did not have the time to devote to larger projects. These new members, who had not been required to wait for the privilege of admission to the club, took meetings rather casually. They came late; they did not volunteer to participate fully; they failed to attend with any reliability; and worse still, they did not always remember to pay their dues. And certainly, in a club the size of three thousand, to whom would it matter if they did not exert great effort for club programs? Neither would it have been especially interesting to attend a reception full of strangers. Furthermore, the women who did organize gatherings did not feel appreciated. Strangers seemed to take for granted that some hard worker would produce a program, party, or reception. Both the hesitant newcomers and the diligent old-timers, then, felt peripheral to the organization. And still the dues went up.

The tug of war is reflected at national conventions as well as local club meetings. Home economics figured prominently in the 1920s, to serve the rural women and the newlyweds, but was considered a poor substitute for social activism by those who had settled their domestic questions decades before and had gravitated to clubs because they yearned for challenging new work.

The most devoted clubwomen, observing the reluctance of many members to contribute effort, time, or money to club life, sought to repair the problem. Officers made a notable attempt to implement business methods as a means of curing club ills. Unfortunately, this and kindred approaches had a dehumanizing effect. The bureaucratization of club life—the distribution of surveys, issuance of reports, calls for increased funding for national headquarters—distanced members further from the warmth they had once associated with clubs.

Clubwomen around the nation were offered two-week Club Institutes that promised to instruct them in the implementation of standardized methods and programs. A rigorous series of sessions was designed to turn volunteers quickly and efficiently into practical, trained leaders. Apparently the old-fashioned custom of apprenticeship in a committee chaired by a senior, experienced clubwoman was viewed as a slow, cumbersome, and therefore unsuitable route to securing skilled volunteers to carry on club work in the 1920s. The innovation failed to heal the wounds modern club life had sustained. Members fell away. Older members, who could remember the pleasures of volunteering alongside good friends, died off. Newer members, who had never experienced the same intimate club atmosphere, did not push their sisters to solve internal club problems they did not understand. They did not invent new goals for their clubs to achieve. The members who remained were those who were content to follow the well-worn paths cut by their forebears.

It would be misleading to suggest that the crises of the 1920s killed women's club life, for women's clubs continue to attract members today throughout the United States. Small art, music, literary, and little theater societies still meet, entertain, and instruct their members. Department clubs still support healthy art, music, drama, and book review departments. Women's clubhouses continue to hold great varieties of cultural events for their members and the wider community. However women's clubs, which had explored and experimented with new and successful methods for change, by the late 1920s had ceased to lead their membership toward untested and challenging expressions of influence.

As long as neighborhood issues were perceived by society as synonymous with national issues, club life stood for daring and progress. Once clubwomen's goals were met, however—the community theaters established, the music and painting classes offered in the schools, the cultural and other civic programs in place—most members were unable to move beyond the rationale of nurturing community needs as a basis for their activities. This impasse explains the decline not only of the initiatives of women's arts clubs but also of the larger women's club movement. By the last half of the 1920s women in the arts clubs, like those in the civic clubs, had accomplished a great deal, because their families' needs were the nation's needs. But although an impressive number of problems had been ameliorated by Progressive reforms, problems on a global scale began to surpass those of a developing American nation. These problems included world peace, international relations, disarmament, and racism; and only a few clubwomen were able to make the leap to tackle these issues that lay beyond the neighborhood.

Two kinds of women dominated clubs between 1890 and 1930, although braver types also participated. The original, late nineteenth-century members would go to any lengths to serve their communities unselfishly. For these women, however, global concerns were generally beyond realization. Their unsuccessful campaigns in the 1920s—for a permanent Sheppard-Towner Act for federal aid for maternal and infant health care, for a Department of Education, and for a child labor law—had taught them that their impact on the federal level was slight, the barriers obstinate. On the other hand, the New Woman, "selfish" by the standards of her seniors, felt strongly about her entitlement to a space of her own. Burdened by her duties as the caretaker of luxurious clubhouses, she too failed to assume a role of influence much beyond her immediate surroundings. Thus, while the turn-of-the-century woman could not move beyond her town even in her activism, her daughter did not want to. For only a brief time in history, generally labeled the Progressive Era, the activities of the woman burdened with the lady's interest in her immediate loved ones coincided with the nation's cultural needs, as well as with the aspirations of women's rights activists, and produced impressive change. In the long run, however, these changes were finite and the momentum was spent.

NOTES

Introduction

1. Louis B. Wright, *Culture on the Moving Frontier* (New York: Harper and Brothers, 1955), 234.
2. Henry Nash Smith, *Virgin Land: The American West as Symbol and Myth* (New York: Random House, 1950), 304.
3. John William Ward, *Andrew Jackson: Symbol for an Age* (New York: Oxford University Press, 1969), 43.
4. Ibid., 30.
5. Arthur M. Schlesinger, Jr., *The Age of Jackson* (Boston: Little, Brown, 1953), 38.
6. Neil Harris, *The Artist in American Society: The Formative Years, 1790–1860* (New York: George Braziller, 1966), 117.
7. Morton White and Lucia White, "The American Intellectual versus the American City," in *American Urban History: An Interpretive Reader with Commentaries,* ed. Alexander B. Callow, Jr. (New York: Oxford University Press, 1969), 354–55.
8. As quoted in Richard Hofstadter, *Anti-Intellectualism in American Life* (New York: Knopf, 1963), 299.
9. Ruth Elson, "American Schoolbooks and 'Culture' in the Nineteenth Century," *Mississippi Valley Historical Review* 46 (December 1959): 414.
10. Susan L. Allen, "Progressive Spirit: Oklahoma and Indian Territory Federation of Women's Clubs," *Chronicles of Oklahoma* 66 (Spring 1988): 4–21; Mrs. N. F. Mossell, *The Work of the Afro-American Woman* (New York: Reprint. Schomburg Library of Nineteenth-Century Black Women Writers, Oxford University Press, 1990); Darlene Clark Hine, ed., *Black Women in United States History from Colonial Times to the Present,* 16 vols. (Brooklyn: Carlson Publishing, 1990); Beverly W. Jones, "Mary Church Terrell and the National Association of Colored Women, 1896–1901," *Journal of Negro History* 47 (Spring 1982): 20–33; Lynda F. Dickson, "Toward a Broader Angle of Vision in Uncovering Women's History: Black Women's Clubs Revisited," *Frontiers* 9 (1987): 62–68; Ralph Watkins, "A Reappraisal of the Role of Voluntary Associations in the Afro-American Community," *Afro-Americans in New York Life and History* 14 (July 1990): 51–60; Darlene Clark Hine, *When the Truth Is Told: A History of Black Women's Culture and Community in Indiana, 1875–1950* (Indianapolis: National Council of Negro Women, 1981); Anne Firor Scott, "Most Invisible of All: Black Women's Voluntary Associations," *Journal of Southern History* 56 (February 1990): 3–22; Stephanie J. Shaw, "Black Club Women and the Creation of the National Association of Colored Women," *Journal of Women's History* 3 (Fall 1991): 10–25; Cynthia Neverdon-Morton, *Afro-American Women of the South and the Advancement of the Race, 1895–1925* (Knoxville: University of Tennessee Press, 1989); Lillian Williams, "'And Still I Rise': Black Women and Reform, Buffalo, New York 1900–1940," *Afro-Americans in New York Life and History* 14 (July 1990); Earline Rae Ferguson, "The Women's Improvement Club of Indianapolis: Black Women Pioneers in Tuberculosis Work, 1903–1933," *Indiana Magazine of History* 84 (September 1988): 237–61; Kathleen C. Berkeley, "'Colored Ladies also Contributed': Black

Women Activists from Benevolence to Social Welfare, 1866–1896," in *The Web of Southern Social Relations: Women, Family and Education,* ed. Walter J. Fraser, Jr. (Athens: University of Georgia Press, 1985), 181–203; Tulia Kay Brown Hamilton, "The National Association for Colored Women, 1896–1920," (Ph.D. diss., Emory University, 1978).

11. Daniel Scott Smith, "Family Limitation, Sexual Control and Domestic Feminism in Victorian America," in *Clio's Consciousness Raised,* ed. Mary Hartman and Lois W. Banner (New York: Harper and Row, 1974), 11–36, applies the term "Domestic Feminism" to women who gained autonomy by using the lady's traits to their advantage. I borrowed the phrase in my book on literary clubs, *The Clubwoman as Feminist: True Womanhood Redefined, 1868–1914* (New York: Holmes and Meier, 1980), and it has also been employed by Barbara Leslie Epstein, *The Politics of Domesticity: Women, Evangelism, and Temperance in Nineteenth-Century America* (Middletown, Conn.: Wesleyan University Press, 1981).

12. Myrna G. Eden, *Energy and Individuality in the Art of Anna Huntington, Sculptor and Amy Beach, Composer* (Metuchen: Scarecrow, 1987), 159–60.

13. Louis S. Lyons, ed., *Who's Who among the Women of California* (San Francisco: Security Publishing Company, 1922), 1.

14. John Anderson, "And What's Become of the Torchbearers?" *Theater Magazine* 51 (January 1930): 21–22; Eleanor Bissell, "Report of the Drama League of America, Fourteenth Convention," *Drama* 15 (December 1924): 64.

15. Mary I. Wood, *The History of the General Federation of Women's Clubs* (Norwood, Maine: Norwood Press, 1912), 312.

16. New York: Holmes and Meier, 1980.

17. *Highbrow/Lowbrow: The Emergence of Cultural Hierarchy in America* (Cambridge: Harvard University Press, 1988).

18. Roy Rosenzweig, *Eight Hours for What We Will: Workers and Leisure in an Industrial City, 1870–1920* (New York: Cambridge University Press, 1983); Kathy Peiss, *Cheap Amusements: Working Women and Leisure in Turn-of-the-Century New York* (Philadelphia: Temple University Press, 1986); John F. Kasson, *Amusing the Million: Coney Island at the Turn of the Century* (New York: Hill and Wang, 1978); Joanne J. Meyerowitz, *Women Adrift: Independent Wage Earners in Chicago, 1880–1930* (Chicago: University of Chicago Press, 1988); Mary P. Ryan, *Women in Public: Between Banners and Ballots, 1825–1880* (Baltimore: Johns Hopkins University Press, 1990).

19. Estelle Freedman, "Separatism as Strategy: Female Institution Building and American Feminism, 1870–1930," *Feminist Studies* 5 (Fall 1979): 512–29; Lynn D. Gordon, *Gender and Higher Education in the Progressive Era* (New Haven: Yale University Press, 1990); Ruth Bordin, *Women and Temperance* (Philadelphia: Temple University Press, 1981); Barbara Leslie Epstein, *The Politics of Domesticity* (Middletown, Conn.: Wesleyan University Press, 1981).

20. Robyn Muncy, *Creating a Female Dominion in American Reform, 1890–1935* (New York: Oxford University Press, 1991); Paula Baker, "Domestication of Politics: Women and American Political Society, 1780–1920," *American Historical Review* 89 (June 1984): 620–47; Paula Baker, *The Moral Frameworks of Public Life: Gender, Politics, and the State in Rural New York, 1890–1930* (New York: Oxford University Press, 1991); Anne Firor Scott, "After Suffrage: Southern Women in the Twenties," *Journal of Southern History* 30 (August 1964): 298–318; Nancy F. Cott, *The Grounding of Modern Feminism* (New Haven: Yale University Press, 1987).

21. Cott, *Grounding of Modern Feminism;* Scott, "After Suffrage"; Muncy, *Creating a Female Dominion;* J. Stanley Lemons, *The Woman Citizen: Social Feminism in the 1920's* (Urbana: University of Illinois Press, 1973).

22. Kathleen D. McCarthy, *Noblesse Oblige: Charity and Cultural Philanthropy in Chicago, 1849–1929* (Chicago: University of Chicago Press, 1982); Kathleen D.

McCarthy, *Women's Culture: American Philanthropy and Art, 1830–1930* (Chicago: University of Chicago Press, 1991).

1. The Arts in Nineteenth-Century American Women's Lives

1. Barbara Welter, "The Cult of True Womanhood, 1820–1860," *American Quarterly* 18 (Summer 1966): 151–74.

2. A compact source is Barbara Welter, *Dimity Convictions: The American Woman in the Nineteenth Century* (Athens, Oh.: Ohio University Press, 1976).

3. One notable exception is Judith Tick, whose excellent discussions of "The Tradition of Music as a Feminine Accomplishment," and "Accomplishment Becomes Middle Class," are both in *American Women Composers before 1870* (Ann Arbor: UMI Research Press, 1983).

4. My observations are based on a study of the women's periodicals and etiquette books collected by the Henry E. Huntington Library, San Marino, California. The periodicals are: *Lady's Companion*, (1839–43) *Godey's Lady's Book* (1830–88), *Lady's Almanac* (1854–78), *Ladies' Wreath* (1846–62), *Ladies' World* (1880–1918), *Ladies' Weekly Museum* (1788–1817, 1825–26), *Ladies' Souvenir* (1846–56), *Ladies' Repository* (1841), *Ladies' Magazine of Literature, Fashion and Fine Arts* (1844–46), *American Ladies Magazine* (1828–36), *Philadelphia Album and Ladies' Literary Port Folio* (1826–34), *Ladies' Companion* (1839–44), *Ladies' Garland* (1824–28, 1839), *Ladies' Literary Cabinet* (1819–22), *Young Ladies' Offering* (1848–57), *Young Ladies' Mentor* (1858), *Young Ladies' Oasis, Lady's World* (1842–48), *Lady's Pearl* (1840–43), *Arthur's Home Magazine* (1853–98), *Lady's Gift* (1850–51), *Ladies' Diadem* (1848–51), and *Lady's Friend* (1864–73). The published books are: Almira H. L. Phelps, *Female Student* (New York: Leavitt, Lord, 1839); Lydia Sigourney, *Letters to Young Ladies* (New York: Harper and Bros., 1837) and *Ladies' Companion and Letters to My Pupils* (New York: Robert Carter and Brothers, 1860); Catharine Beecher, *Treatise on Domestic Economy for the Use of Young Ladies at Home & at School* (Boston: Marsh, Capen, Lyon and Webb, 1841); *Young Lady's Own Book* (Philadelphia: Desilver, Thomas, 1836); *Young Lady's Mentor* (Philadelphia: H. C. Peck and Theodore Bliss, 1860); *Young Lady's Guide* (New York: American Tract Society, 1870); *Ladies' Keepsake* (New York: J. S. Taylor, 1852–54).

5. Other artists were J. I. Pease, A. L. Dick, P. F. Rothermel, and J. A. Dallas. Frank Luther Mott, *A History of American Magazines*, vol. 1 (1741–1850) (Cambridge: Harvard University Press, 1930) 592.

6. Florence Hartley, *Ladies' Book of Etiquette* (Boston: G. W. Cottrell, 1860), 185, 188, 179.

7. Mrs. I. M. E. Blandin, *A History of Higher Education of Women in the South Prior to 1860* (New York: Neale Publishing, 1909).

8. Tick, *American Woman Composers*, 42–45.

9. Thomas Woody, *A History of Women's Education in the United States*, vol. 1 (New York: Science Press, 1929), 351.

10. Arthur C. Cole, *A Hundred Years of Mount Holyoke College* (New Haven: Yale University Press, 1940), 57.

11. Anna C. Brackett, *Woman and the Higher Education* (New York: Harper and Brothers, 1893), 20; Alma Lutz, *Emma Willard, Daughter of Democracy* (Boston: Houghton Mifflin, 1929), 83.

12. "Troy Female Seminary," *American Ladies' Magazine* 8 (1835): 104.

13. Peter C. Marzio, *The Art Crusade: An Analysis of American Drawing Manuals, 1820–1860* (Washington, D.C.: Smithsonian Institution Press, 1976).

14. Maria Turner, *Young Ladies' Assistant in Drawing and Painting* (Cincinnati: Corey and Fairbank, 1833); Maria Turner, *Rudiments of Drawing and Shadowing Flowers in Pencil in Sixty-Four Lessons* (Boston: Munroe and Francis, 1827); Mrs. Anne Hill, *Drawing Book of Flowers and Fruit* (Philadelphia: E. C. Biddle, n.d.).

15. William Minifie, *Three Lectures on Drawing and Design* (Baltimore: William Minifie, 1852), 3.
16. Almira Hart Lincoln Phelps, *Female Student* (New York: Leavitt, Lord, 1836), 369, 365.
17. Mrs. S. T. Martyn, ed., "Books in the Family Circle; or, the Importance of a Taste for Reading," *Ladies' Wreath* 2 (1849): 5.
18. Charles Burton, quoted in "The Beauties of Music," *Ladies' Garland* 1 (1838): 6.
19. *Young Ladies' Assist*, vi.
20. Sigourney, *Letters to Young Ladies*, 114.
21. "Thoughts on Domestic Education" by a Mother (1829), quoted in Woody, *A History of Women's Education*, 51.
22. Sigourney, Letter Seven: "Manners and Accomplishments," in *Letters to Young Ladies*, 110.
23. "A Plan for Improving Female Education," in *Woman and Higher Education*, ed. Anna C. Brackett (New York: Harper and Brother's, 1893), 29.
24. "The Cultivation of the Mind," in *Young Lady's Mentor: A Guide to the Formation of Character in a Series of Letters to Her Unknown Friends,* by a Lady (Philadelphia: H. C. Peck and Theodore Bliss, 1858), 162.
25. "On Cultivation of Taste," *Ladies' Garland,* 1 (April 15, 1837): 12.
26. 19 (August 1843): 207. Similar attitudes regarding women's moral influence on others are expressed in *American Ladies' Magazine* 4 (1831): 256, and throughout *Ladies' Companion* 13–14 (1840–41).
27. A Pupil of Troy Female Seminary, "Incorporated Female Seminary," *American Ladies' Magazine* 8 (June 1835): 342.
28. "Poetry, Its Province and Influence on Society," *Ladies' Keepsake and Home Library* 4 (June 1854): 182.
29. Sigourney, Letter Seven: "Manners and Accomplishments," in *Letters to Young Ladies,* 111.
30. "The Beauties of Music," *Ladies' Garland* 1 (June 3, 1837): 62.
31. Florence Hartley, "Accomplishments," in *Ladies' Book of Etiquette and Manual of Politeness* (Boston: G. W. Cottrell, 1860), 178.
32. "Music," *Ladies' Diadem* 2 (1851): 286.
33. Jane Eyre, *Needles and Brushes and How to Use Them, a Manual for Fancy Work* (Chicago: Belford, Clark, 1887); Almon C. Varney, *Our Homes and Their Adornments* (Chicago: People's Publishing, 1885); Maria Turner, *The Young Ladies' Assistant in Drawing and Painting* (Cincinnati: Corey and Fairbank, 1833); Woody, *A History of Women's Education.*
34. Woody, table I, *A History of Women's Education,* 418.
35. Charles Butler, *American Lady* (Philadelphia: Hogan and Thompson, 1836) 96, 105; and "Conversations at the Fireside No. 2—Dancing," *American Ladies Magazine* 6 (1833): 539–45.
36. Butler, *American Lady,* 96–100.
37. Blandin, *History of Higher Education of Women in the South,* 47.
38. Butler, *American Lady,* 113.
39. Catharine Beecher, *Treatise on Domestic Economy* (Boston: Narsh, Cooper, Lyon and Webb, 1841), 256.
40. Henry Rogers, "Novel Reading from the Greyson Letters," *Young Lady's Guide* (1870): 157.
41. Mrs. H. O. Ward, *Sensible Etiquette of the Best Society* (Philadelphia: Porter and Coates, 1878), 405.
42. Hartley, *Ladies' Book of Etiquette,* 178; *Young Lady's Own Book* (1836): 103–105.
43. Rogers, "Novel Reading," 167.

44. *Hand-Book for Home Improvement: How to Talk* (New York: Fowler and Wells, 1867), 146.

45. Rev. Charles Burroughs, "Female Education," *American Ladies Magazine* 1 (1828): 26.

46. Butler, *American Lady,* 156–57.

47. *Young Lady's Own Book* (1836): 65–73.

48. Ann S. Stephens, "Women of Genius," *Ladies' Companion* 11 (1839): 89.

49. Phelps, *Female Student,* 370.

50. Sigourney, *Letters to Young Ladies,* 112; "Education of Women," By a Lady, in *Young Lady's Mentor* (Philadelphia: H. C. Peck and Theodore Bliss, 1860), 233.

51. George Hogarth, "Music as an Accomplishment," in *Lady's Companion,* ed. By a Lady (Philadelphia: H. C. Peck and Theodore Bliss, 1856), 19–25.

52. "Education of Women," by a Lady, in *Young Lady's Mentor,* 240.

53. Ibid., 237.

54. Ibid., 240.

55. Sarah J. Hale, "Village Schoolmistress," in *Sketches of American Character* (Philadelphia: Perkins and Purves, 1843), 106.

56. "Female Education in England," *American Ladies Magazine* 5 (May 1832): 230–32.

57. "Female Education," in *Young Lady's Own Book: A Manual of Intellectual Improvement and Moral Deportment* (Philadelphia: Desilver, Thomas, 1836), 61–62.

58. "On Female Education," *Ladies' Literary Cabinet* 1 (July 17, 1819): 76.

59. Helen Lefkowitz Horowitz, *Alma Mater: Design and Experience in the Women's Colleges from Their Nineteenth-Century Beginnings to the 1930s* (New York: Knopf, 1984), 11–12.

60. Shirley Phillips Ingebritsen, "Ednah Dow Littlehale Cheney," in *Notable American Women,* vol. 1, ed. Edward T. James, Janet Wilson James, and Paul S. Boyer (Cambridge: Harvard University Press, 1971), 325–27; Karen J. Blair, *The Clubwoman as Feminist: True Womanhood Redefined, 1868–1914* (New York: Holmes and Meier, 1980), 15–38.

61. Phyllis I. Peet, "The Emergence of American Women Printmakers in the Late Nineteenth Century" (Ph.D. diss, UCLA, 1987).

62. Emily Sartain, "The Pioneer in Industrial Art Education: Philadelphia School of Design for Women, An Address to the Art Club of Philadelphia, 1890," published as "Philadelphia School of Design for Women," *Woman's Progress* 2 (October 1893): 22–25; Joseph E. Holliday, "Sarah Anne Worthington King Peter," in *Notable American Women,* vol. 3, 54–56; and Lea J. Brinker, "The Charitable Impulse of Sarah Worthington King Peter," *Queen City Heritage* 42 (Winter 1982): 27–40.

63. Woody, *A History of Women's Education,* vol. 2, 78.

64. Tick, *American Women Composers,* 33, 52–53.

65. See William Lichten Wanger, "Clara Louise Kellogg," in *Notable American Women,* vol. 2, 319–21; Edwin Tribble, "Adelina Patti," in ibid., vol. 3:30–31; and Judith Tick, "Women in Music," in *New Grove Dictionary of American Music,* ed. H. Wiley Hitchcock and Stanley Sadie, vol. 4 (London: Macmillan, 1986), 551.

66. Elizabeth Fries Lummis Ellet, *Women Artists in All Ages and Countries* (New York: Harper and Brothers, 1859), Chapters 18–20.

67. *Notable American Women* (op cit.), and *Notable American Women: The Modern Period,* ed. Barbara Sicherman (Cambridge: Harvard University Press, 1980) are rich sources for the biographies of women in the arts.

68. Eliza Leslie, *The Behavior Book: A Manual for Ladies* (Philadelphia: Willis P. Hazard, 1854), 274–84, 256.

69. Ann S. Stephens, "Women of Genius," *Ladies' Companion* 11 (1839): 90.

70. "Female Literature of the Present Age," *Ladies' Garland* 1 (April 15, 1837): 12.

71. Sylvester Rosa Koehler compiled descriptions of these societies in *The United*

States Art Directory and Year Book (New York: Cassell, Pelter, Galpin, 1882; New York: Cassell, 1884).

72. Woody, *History of Women's Education;* Peet, "Emergence of American Women Printmakers;" Robert R. Preato, *The Genius of the Fair Muse; Paintings and Sculpture Celebrating American Women Artists, 1878–1945* (New York: Grand Central Art Galleries, 1987); Lois Marie Fink and Joshua C. Taylor, *Academy: The Academic Tradition in American Art* (Washington, D.C.: Smithsonian Institution, 1975).

73. Frederick P. Keppel, *The Arts in American Life* (New York: McGraw Hill, 1933), 41, cites Royal B. Farnum, educational director of the Rhode Island School of Design and surveyor of dozens of American art centers.

74. Ray Edwin Robinson, "A History of the Peabody Conservatory of Music" (Doctor of Music Education Degree, Indiana University, 1969), introduction; William S. B. Mathews, *A Hundred Years of Music in America* (Chicago: G. L. Howe, 1889).

75. The Paris Conservatory was founded in 1795; other conservatories were established in Vienna (1817), Brussels (1833), the Royal Academy of Music's London Conservatory (1822), Leipzig (1843), Cologne (1849), Moscow (1866), Berlin (1869), Royal College of Music (1882).

76. Amy Fay, *Music-Study in Germany* (New York: Macmillan, 1900); Helen L. Kaufmann, "Amy Fay," in *Notable American Women,* vol. 1, 602–603.

77. Fay, *Music-Study in Germany,* 28, 23–27, 117.

78. *Crisis* (Magazine of the National Association for the Advancement of Colored People), 5 (January 1913), 116; ibid. (December 1912), 67.

79. J. Huneker, *Overtones: A Book of Temperments* (New York: Charles Scribner's Sons, 1904), 91.

80. Otto Ebel, *Women Composers* (Brooklyn: F. H. Chandler, 1902), preface. Cited in Judith Tick, "Passed Away Is the Piano Girl," in *Women Making Music: The Western Art Tradition, 1150–1950,* ed. Jane Bowers and Judith Tick (Urbana: University of Illinois Press, 1984), 339.

81. Judith Tick, "Women in Music," *New Grove Dictionary of American Music,* vol. 4 (New York: Grove's Dictionaries of Music, 1986), 550.

82. Claire Richter Sherman, *Women as Interpreters of the Visual Arts, 1820–1979* (Westport, CT: Greenwood, 1981), 44.

83. Huneker, *Overtones,* 92.

84. Florence Converse, *Wellesley College, a Chronicle of the Years, 1875–1938* (Wellesley: Hathaway House Bookshop, 1939); Lida Rose McCabe, *The American Girl at College* (New York: Dodd, Mead, 1893); Horowitz, *Alma Mater.*

85. B. V. B. Dixon, *A Brief History of H. Sophie Newcomb Memorial College, 1887–1919: A Personal Reminiscence* (New Orleans: Hauser, 1928), 65.

86. Mary Ann Stankiewicz, "The Creative Sister: An Historical Look at Women, the Arts, and Higher Education," *Studies in Art Education* 24 (1982): 48–56.

87. Dena J. Epstein, "Amy Marcy Cheney Beach," in *Notable American Women,* vol. 1, 117–19.

88. Dorothy Gradfly, "Cecelia Beaux," in *Notable American Women,* vol. 1, 119–21.

89. Louis Auchincloss, "Edith Newbold James Wharton," vol. 3, 570–73, and Leon Edel, "Alice James," vol. 2, 267–68, in *Notable American Women,* vols. 2 and 3.

90. Others included contralto Anna Louise Cary; operatic singers Emma Abbot and Minnie Hauk; composers Amy Beach, Mabel Daniels, and Carrie Jacobs Bond; soprano Grace Hiltz; music teachers Sara Hershey Eddy, Clara E. Munger, and F. Jeannette Hall; writers Louisa May Alcott, Sarah Orne Jewett, Kate Douglas Wiggin, and Mary Wilkins Freeman; illustrator Mary Hallock Foote; and painters Mary Cassatt and Cecilia Beaux.

91. Also London-born harpist Josephine Chatterton; Viennese-born and American-raised singer Emma Juch; Madrid-born operatic singer Adelina Patti; singer Helena Modjeska from Poland; English actors Ellen Terry, Eleanora Duse, and Sarah Bern-

hardt; and London-born music teacher Clara M. Brinkerhoff. See also biographies in *Notable American Women;* Louis C. Elson, "American Women in Music," in *The History of American Music* (New York: Macmillan, 1925), 293–310; Mathews, *A Hundred Years of Music in America.*

92. Huneker, *Overtones,* 301.

93. D. S. M., "Women Artists," *Living Age* 220 (March 18, 1899): 730–32.

94. Edith Brower, "Is the Musical Idea Masculine?" *Atlantic Monthly* 73 (March 1894): 336.

95. George P. Upton, *Woman in Music: An Essay* (Boston: James R. Osgood, 1880).

96. Kate Chopin, *The Awakening* (New York: Capricorn, 1964), 165.

97. *Woman: A Vindication* (New York: Knopf, 1923), 302.

98. "Opening Doors," *Woman Citizen* 6 (November 19, 1921): 187–88.

99. John H. Mueller, *American Symphony Orchestra* (New York: Knopf, 1969), 309, cites Beecham, "The Position of Women," in *Vogue's First Reader* (Garden City: Halcyon House, 1944), 420.

100. See alumnae newsletters for Wellesley College, Radcliffe College, Smith College, Vassar College, and Mount Holyoke College.

2. Arts and Activism

1. Jane Cunningham Croly, *The History of the Woman's Club Movement in America* (New York: Henry G. Allen, 1898), 15–83; for an extended examination of the origins of women's clubs, see Karen J. Blair, *The Clubwoman as Feminist: True Womanhood Redefined, 1868–1914* (New York: Holmes and Meier, 1980).

2. Mary I. Wood, *The History of the General Federation of Women's Clubs* (Norwood, ME: Norwood Press, 1912), 76, reports that the federation alone, excluding all non-affiliated clubs, numbered 495 clubs and 21 state federations of 800 clubs, "giving a total individual membership in round numbers of one hundred thousand" for November 1896.

3. "Woman's Mission and Woman's Clubs," *Ladies Home Journal* 22 (1905), 3–4.

4. Frank Luther Mott, *A History of American Magazines,* vol. 4 (New York: D. Appleton, 1930), 147.

5. Deann Meecham, "Hagerstown Club and the Public Library" (Ph.D. diss., University of Maryland, 1991).

6. Ednah Dow Cheney, *Reminiscences* (Boston: Lee and Shepard, 1902), 155.

7. Julia Ward Howe to Ednah Dow Cheney, 26 January 1876, Julia Ward Howe Papers, File A, Schlesinger Library, Radcliffe College, Cambridge, Massachusetts.

8. Jane Cunningham Croly, *History of Sorosis: Its Origin and History* (New York: J. J. Little, 1886), 26.

9. Jane Cunningham Croly, *History of the Woman's Club Movement in America* (New York: Henry G. Allen, 1898), xi.

10. Ibid., 45.

11. Wood, *History of the General Federation of Women's Clubs,* 166, reports on the May, 1904 membership with painstaking precision: "At that time the General Federation included forty-five state federations with a membership of about three hundred thousand; four distinct federations with a membership of about forty-two clubs; six city federations with a membership of one hundred clubs; two national societies and nine hundred and seventy-one individual clubs with a membership of about ninety thousand active members."

12. (New York: Charlton Co., 1914), chapter 4.

13. Biographies in *Notable American Women,* vols. 1–3, ed. Edward T. James et al. (Cambridge: Harvard University Press, 1971); vol. 4 "The Modern Period," ed. Barbara Sicherman (Cambridge: Harvard University Press, 1980).

14. (Chicago: Forbes, 1913), 41–42.
15. "Editorial: Woman and Music," *Etude* 47 (November 1929): 793.
16. Massachusetts State Federation of Women's Clubs, *Federation Manual* (1921–22).
17. Mrs. H. P. Pierce, "Department of Fine Arts Report," Washington State Federation of Women's Clubs, *Bulletin* 10 (November 1925): 12.
18. "Editorial: Women and Music," 793.
19. Massachusetts State Federation of Women's Clubs, *Federation Manual* (1922–23): 28–29.
20. New York State Federation of Women's Clubs, *Yearbook* (1917): 48. See also quotations in yearbooks of Bellingham Woman's Music Club, Music Library Archives, Western Washington University.
21. Introduction to John Farrar, "The Club Program: A Contemporary Outline of Contemporary American Literature," *Ladies Home Journal* 39 (November 1922): 8.
22. Among the excellent new accounts of civic reform in clubs that treat arts activities only peripherally are Linda Vance, *May Mann Jennings: Florida's Genteel Activist* (Gainesville: University Presses of Florida, 1985); Gail Stanislaw, "Domestic Feminism in Wilmington: The New Century Club, 1889–1917," *Delaware History* 22 (Spring/Summer 1987): 158–85; J. Stanley Lemons, *Woman Citizen* (Chicago: University of Illinois Press, 1975); Nancy Cott, *The Grounding of Modern Feminism* (New Haven: Yale University Press, 1987); William L. O'Neill, *Everyone Was Brave* (Chicago: Quadrangle, 1969); Anne Firor Scott, *The Southern Lady* (Chicago: University of Chicago Press, 1970).
23. *American Art Annual* (1934): 147, 211.
24. Croly, *History of the Woman's Culture Club Movement*, 759, 599. Croly's work includes hundreds of examples of the department club phenomenon, including the Athene Club of Bangor, Maine (current events, science, economy, literature, art, music, education); Ray Palmer Club of Newark, New Jersey (literature, art, philanthropy, home, current events); and Nineteenth Century Club in Memphis, Tennessee (literature, art, education, music, philosophy, science, social economy, philanthropy).
25. See annual yearbooks of each arts organization.

3. "Hear America First"

1. Quoted in Mildred Adams, "Foster-Mothers of Music," *Woman Citizen* (January 1924): 7.
2. Bessie Ryan, "A Pageant of the National Federation of Music Clubs," NFMC 1940 Papers, Library of Congress, Music Division, Washington, DC.
3. The clubs that responded to Thomas's invitation by sending delegates are listed in *National Convention of Women's Amateur Musical Clubs* (Chicago: Stromberg, Allen, 1893).
4. She was the sister of Amy Fay, author of a widely read autobiography describing the life of a music student in nineteenth-century Germany.
5. *National Convention of Women's Amateur Musical Clubs*, 1893, 2.
6. Rose Fay Thomas, "Women's Amateur Musical Clubs," NFMC *Proceedings* (1901): 48.
7. Rose Fay Thomas, "Address of Welcome to the Clubs," *National Convention of Women's Amateur Musical Clubs*, 4.
8. Ibid., 5.
9. *National Convention of Women's Amateur Musical Clubs*, 9.
10. "Schubert Club History," Zylpha Morton Papers, 5, Minnesota Historical Society.
11. Ibid., 74.
12. "Rubenstein Club Report," *National Convention of Women's Amateur Music Clubs*, 62.

13. *National Convention of Women's Amateur Musical Clubs*, 96, 50, 39, 12, 8.
14. Ibid., 39.
15. Ibid., 7, 22, 86, 88.
16. NFMC 1927 Bluebook, 1, NFMC Papers, Library of Congress, Washington D.C.
17. Ibid., 7.
18. Ibid., 9.
19. *National Convention of Women's Amateur Musical Clubs*, 64.
20. Ibid., 19.
21. Among the women present were Florence Edith (Mrs. Theodore) Sutro, Mrs. Russell R. Dorr, Mrs. F. Marion Ralston, and Mrs. Chandler Starr. See Ruth Haller Ottaway, "Historical Highlights of the Federation, 1898–1935," NFMC *Proceedings* (1935): 221–22; Ruth Haller Ottaway, "Music Clubs, a Significant Factor in National Development," Music Teachers' National Association Proceedings (Oberlin: MTNA, 1931), 120.
22. Homer Ulrich, *Centennial History of Music Teachers' National Association* (Cincinnati: Music Teachers National Association, 1976).
23. Florence Sutro Papers, New York Historical Society, New York, New York.
24. Adopted at June 1925 biennial convention in Portland, Oregon.
25. Woman's Choral Society of New Haven, *Report*, 1937–39, New Haven Colony Historical Society, CT.
26. The committees were as follows: At State and County Fairs; Public School Music; College Museums; Philanthropic Museums; Correlation of Music and the Arts; Music in Industry; Music in the Home; Music Subsidization; National Music Week; Radio Music; Motion Picture Music; Choral Music; American Composers; Opera; Orchestra; Library Extension; Religious Education; International Music Relations; Chamber Music; Fellowships and Memorials for American Composers; American Folk Songs; Program Exchange; Church Music; Community Music; Festival and Pageantry; and Junior Work, which included Toy Orchestra and Rhythm and Harmonic Bands.
27. The First Biennial (1899) was held in St. Louis; the following Biennials were: 1901 in Cleveland, 1903 in Rochester, 1905 in Denver, 1907 in Memphis, 1909 in Grand Rapids, 1911 in Philadelphia, 1913 in Chicago, 1915 in Los Angeles, 1917 in Birmingham, 1919 in Peterboro, 1921 in Tri-Cities of Davenport, Iowa/Moline and Rock Island, Illinois, 1923 in Asheville, 1925 in Portland, 1927 in Chicago, 1929 in Boston, 1931 in San Francisco, 1933 in Minneapolis, and 1935 in Philadelphia.
28. For example, conference delegates heard Mme. Ernestine Schumann-Heink and the Pittsburgh Orchestra, conducted by Victor Herbert, at the second biennial convention in Cleveland in 1901; the Philadelphia Orchestra at the 1911 convention; Rafael Joseffy in recital in 1903; and the Boston Pops in 1929.
29. The twelve presidents were: Alice F. (Mrs. Edwin F.) Uhl of Grand Rapids (1898–1901); Helen C. (Mrs. Curtis) Webster, a founder of the Fortnightly Musical Club of Cleveland (1901–1903); Helen Storer (Mrs. Winifred B.) Collins, of the Tuesday Musical Club of Akron and the Fortnightly Club of Cleveland (1903–1905); Louise B. (Mrs. Russell Ripley) Dorr, nine-year president of the Schubert Club of St. Paul, and first vice-president of the Monday Music Club of Portland (she served only briefly in 1905 and resigned to organize the federation's Artists Bureau); Leila B. (Mrs. Julius E.) Kinney of Denver, who completed Dorr's term (1905–1907) and was elected in her own right (1911–1915); Mrs. Charles B. Kelsey, past president of the St. Cecilia Club of Grand Rapids (1907–11); Mrs. A. J. Ochsner of Chicago (1915–19); Gertrude F. Penfield (Mrs. Frank A.) Seiberling of the Tuesday Musical Club of Akron (1919–21), who declined to run for the traditional second term to direct the Finance and Legislative Department to raise an endowment for the organization; Lucille M. (Mrs. John F.) Lyons, president of the Harmony Club of Fort Worth for eighteen years (1921–25); Jessie Gregg (Mrs. Edgar Stillman) Kelley of Oxford, Ohio, where her renowned com-

poser husband taught at Western College (1925–29); and Ruth Haller (Mrs. Elmer James) Ottaway of Port Huron, Michigan (1929–33).

30. B. D. Ussher, "Federation More than Doubles Clubs During Mrs. Frankel's Incumbency," *Musical America* (July 21, 1923): 1, 9; see also clippings in scrapbook of Bessie Bartlett Frankel Papers, Special Collections, UCLA, Los Angeles.

31. National Federation of Music Clubs, *Official Bulletin* 1 (January 1922): 5, 8; (March 1929): 8.

32. The figures on the top ten clubs for April 10, 1927, can be found in *Music Club Magazine* 9 (October 1929): 30; Texas (221 clubs), Missouri (205), Ohio (236), Michigan (158), Indiana (105), Oklahoma (109), Tennessee (118), Virginia (135), Alabama (145), Pennsylvania (101).

33. Membership figures have been gleaned from NFMC publications and papers, Music Division, Library of Congress. 1899 (76 clubs); 1901 (124 clubs with 10,733 members); 1903 (106 clubs); 1905 (125 clubs); 1906 (145 clubs with ten thousand members); 1911 (200 clubs); 1917 (440 clubs); 1919 (557 clubs); 1923 (1903 clubs); 1925 (3,000 clubs with 130,411 members); 1927 (3,252 clubs); 1928 (3,863 clubs and 450,000 members); 1929 (4,470 clubs or 2,173 senior clubs and 2,306 junior clubs with 750,000 [*sic*]); 1930 (5,000 clubs including 2,000 junior clubs, with 400,000 members); 1935 (500,000 members); 1937 (4,300 clubs with 400,000 members); 1935 (500,000 members); 1937 (4,300 clubs with 400,000 members); 1948 (4,000 clubs).

34. Among the southern states in 1923, Alabama boasted 53 junior clubs, Georgia 43, Texas 51, Tennessee 49, and Missouri 81, while Virginia and West Virginia reported none at all. See Addye Yeargain (Mrs. William John) Hall, *History and Outlook of the Junior Department of the National Federation of Music Clubs* (New York: National Bureau for the Advancement of Music, 1923).

35. Ibid., 33.

36. General Federation of Women's Clubs, *Biennial Report* (1930): 35; Massachusetts Federation of Women's Clubs, *Federation Manual* (1922–23): 77; Washington State Federation of Women's Clubs, *Bulletin* 2 (November 1917): 42–44; Rhode Island Federation of Women's Clubs *Yearbook* (1915–16): 71; Minutes, Sorosis Papers, (May 1916) Smith College; Marie Meyer-Ten Broech, "How the Mother Can Make the Child's Music Study Irresistibly Interesting," *Etude* 46 (January 1928): 25, 63; Alice Ames Winter, "The Technic of Being a Clubwoman," *Ladies Home Journal* 41 (August 1924): 6.

37. See GFWC, *Bulletin* (August 1921): 16.

38. Other popular selections included *O Sole Mio,* an Italian folk song; Felix Mendelssohn's *Overture* to *A Midsummer Night's Dream;* Beethoven's *Fifth Symphony;* Franz Schubert's *Unfinished Symphony;* Dvorak's *Largo* from the *New World Symphony; Scheherazade* by Rimsky-Korsakov; and so-called Native American themes in Cadman's *From the Land of the Sky-Blue Water* and Edward MacDowell's *Love Song* from his *Indian Suite.* See National Federation of Music Clubs, *Junior Bulletin* (April 1928): 9.

39. Hall, *History and Outlook of the Junior Department,* 85.

40. *National Notes* 28 (July–August 1922): 2.

41. Hall, 29.

42. Ibid., 36.

43. National Federation of Music Clubs, *Junior Bulletin* (April 1928): 16.

44. Gail Stanislow, "Domestic Feminism in Wilmington: The New Century Club, 1899–1917," *Delaware History* 22 (Spring–Summer 1987): 170.

45. GFWC, *Proceedings* (1910): 82.

46. Mrs. Lawrence Maxwell, "Report of the Department of Music," GFWC, *Twelfth Biennial Proceedings* (1914): 194.

47. Delegates heard works by Mrs. H. A. A. Beach, Augusta Holmes, Amy Woodford Finden, Liza Lehmann, Clara Schumann, Cecile Chaminade, and Harriet Ware,

and attended a performance of the Women's Chorus of St. Paul. Mary I. Wood, *History of the General Federation of Women's Clubs,* 215.

48. The most popular of these was written in 1913 for the Victor Talking Machine Company. *What We Hear in Music, a Laboratory Course of Study in Music History and Appreciation, for Four Years of High School, Academy, College, Music Club or Home Study* (Camden, New Jersey: Educational Department, Victor Talking Machine Company, 1913) was issued thirteen times in eleven years, continuing its impact into the 1940s.

49. Lawson addressed such subjects as "The Religion of the American Indian," "Indian Childhood," "Nature," "Tribal Music," "Indian Love Songs," "Ghosts and Legends," which drew on examples from Pueblo, Navaho, Sioux, Kickapoo, Winnebago, Seminole, Apache, and Pawnee cultures.

50. GFWC, *Fourteenth Biennial Proceedings* (1918): 205. Later the list expanded to include American composers, American women composers, Berlioz, Christmas music, Civil War music, conservatories of music in the United States, the effect of immigration on American music, famous orchestral conductors, opera, history of the piano, and Negro music. *General Federation News* 1 (August 1921): 31.

51. National Federation of Music Clubs, *Official Bulletin* 3 (September 1923): 18.

52. Massachusetts State Federation of Women's Clubs, Scrapbook, May 17, 1908 clipping of *Providence Sunday Journal.*

53. Mildred White Wells, *Unity in Diversity: The History of the General Federation of Women's Clubs* (Washington, D.C.: General Federation of Women's Clubs, 1953), 179; Merlin H. Aylesworth, "The Influence of National Radio Broadcasting," GFWC, *Nineteenth Biennial Proceedings* (1928): 382; Frank A. Arnold, "America's Great Musical Opportunity," GFWC Council *Proceedings* (1927): 71–75.

54. GFWC *Bulletin* 1 (August 1921): 16.

55. Ibid., 16; Susan Baldwin Walker, "Report of the American Music Committee," National Federation of Music Clubs, *Biennial Proceedings* (1915): 37–41; National Federation of Music Clubs, *Official Bulletin* 3 (September 1923): 15; Mrs. T. S. Robinson, "American Composers," GFWC, *Biennial Proceedings* (1927): 140.

56. John Warren, "Women who are Making a Musical America," *Delineator* 76 (September 1910): 201.

57. Glenn Dillard Gunn, "The American Musician and His Opportunity," National Federation of Music Clubs, *Biennial Proceedings* (1913): 33.

58. Susan Baldwin Walker, "Report of the American Music Committee," National Federation of Music Clubs, *Biennial Proceedings* (1915): 37–41.

59. Catherine Parsons Smith and Cynthia S. Richardson, *Mary Carr Moore* (Ann Arbor: UMI Press, 1987).

60. James G. MacDermid, Edward MacDowell, Hans Barth, E. S. Barnes, Andrew C. Haigh, Paul Tiegens, James H. Rogers, Frederic Vanderpool, Harvey Gaul, and Louis Baker Philips were those whose work was heard at the New York State Federation of Music Clubs' series of three "American Composers and Artists" concerts in 1923.

61. Also musicians Mary Turner Salter, Harriet Ware, Margaret Ruthven Lang, Mabel Daniels, Helen Hood, Edith Noyes Porter, Fannie Bloomfield Zeisler, Laura S. Collins, Carrie Jacobs Bond, Marguerite Melville, Julia Rive-King, Mary Knight Wood, Fanny Knowlton, Natalie Curtis, Fay Foster, Harriet P. Sawyer, Mrs. L. E. Orth, Mrs. Jessie L. Gaynor, Mrs. Eleanor Freer, Patty Stair, and Mrs. Clara Korn. (Chittenden Turner, "Music and the Women's Crusade," *Arts and Decoration,* 19 (Sept. 1923), 29, 70–71, 73.)

62. *Crisis* 5 (February 1913): 168.

63. Wells, *Unity in Diversity,* 181; Mrs. Maxwell, "Report of Music Department," GFWC, *Twelfth Biennial Proceedings* (1914): 198; National Federation of Music Clubs, *Official Bulletin* 3 (September 1923): 15.

64. Gladys Livingston Graff, "The Most Outstanding American Woman—Mrs.

Edward MacDowell, Zeta, Wins Achievement Award," *The Lyre* 28 (March 1925): 349.

65. Abbie Farwell Brown, *The Boyhood of Edward MacDowell* (New York: Frederick A. Stokes, 1924), ix; Harriette Moore Brower, *Story-Lives of Master Musicians* (New York: Frederick A. Stokes, 1922), 348.

66. "A Brief History of the MacDowell Colony," MacDowell Colony Archives, Peterborough, New Hampshire.

67. See "Edward MacDowell Fund," 10 May 1907, Box 7, Miscellany File, Marian MacDowell Papers, Library of Congress Manuscript Division.

68. The annual reports of the MacDowell Colony invariably reveal the generosity of women's groups, listing them as donors of dormitories, private studios, a swimming pool, forest acreage, cash, and furnishings. Annual Reports, 1911–35, Box 72, MacDowell Colony Papers, Library of Congress Manuscript Division.

69. From 1907 to 1926, the breakdown is: awards to writers: male 52, female 78; awards to painters and sculptors: male 15, female 16; awards to interpretive artists: male 0, female 19; awards to composers: male 29, female 14, for a total of 96 males and 121 females. However, an additional list of twenty-one names, all women, appears in "Early Colony residents, omitted from printed list," in Parker Fillmore's records and office card files in Box 72, MacDowell Colony Papers, Library of Congress Manuscript Division, which suggests that 142 women were sponsored. The colony invited the most promising women talents of the day to enjoy its facilities. Composer Amy Beach and writers Elinor Wylie, Sara Teasdale, and Constance Rourke were among those who worked at the colony. Others included composers Mabel W. Daniels and Camilee W. Zechwer; painters and sculptors Lillian Link, Helen Farnsworth Mears, Gertrude Monophan, Lilla Cabot Perry, Elizabeth Sparhawk-Jones, Ida McClelland Stout; playwrights Dorothy Haward, Elizabeth McFadden, Josephine Preston Peabody; poets and prose writers Grace Hazard Condling, Louise Driscoll, Eloise Robinson, Leonora Speyer, Eunice Tietzens, Aline de Villale, Anne Shannon Monroe, and Margaret Widdemer.

70. MacDowell Folder, Clara Bradley Burdette Papers, Huntington Library, San Marino, California.

71. "Quality of Woman's Greatness," *Woman Citizen* 9 (March 9, 1925): 16–17.

72. GFWC, *Biennial Proceedings* (1926): 264.

73. Glenn Dillard Gunn, "The American Musician and His Opportunity," NFMC, *Biennial Proceedings* (1913): 34.

74. NFMC, *Third Biennial Proceedings* (1903).

75. *Crisis* 11 (December 1915): 60.

76. M. Marguerite Davenport, *Azalia: The Life of Madame E. Azalia Hackley* (Boston: Chapman and Grimes, 1947), 146–48.

77. F. L. C. B., "Show Beauty of Negro Folk Songs in Unique Concert in St. Paul," *Musical America* 28 (August 3, 1918): 10.

78. For example, the NFMC *Magazine* listed the Boston Woman's Symphony Orchestra, conducted by Ethel Leginska, among American women's ensembles recently hired for important engagements. "American Music Department," NFMC, *Magazine* 8 (October 1928): 15.

79. Friday Morning Club, *Yearbook* (1926–27).

80. "Federation of Music Clubs Plan Prepared by Mrs. Cecil Frankel of Hollywood Give Fine Program," undated clipping, Bessie Bartlett Frankel Scrapbook, UCLA Special Collections, Los Angeles; GFWC, *Biennial Proceedings* (1902): 39.

81. NFMC, *Official Bulletin* (June 1927): 14.

82. Arthur Elson and Everett E. Truette, *Woman's Work in Music* (Boston: L.C. Page, 1931), 245.

83. "Woman's Symphony Is Now Largest in Country," *Los Angeles Evening Express* (April 17, 1923); John C. Freund, "Why Should We Not Have Symphony Orchestras Composed of Women?" *Musical America* (August 23, 1913): 3; Judith Tick,

"Passed Away Is the Piano Girl: Changes in American Musical Life, 1780–1900," in *Women Making Music*, ed. Jane Bowers and Judith Tick (Urbana: University of Illinois Press, 1986), 329; Christine Ammer, *Unsung: A History of Women in American Music* (Westport, CT: Greenwood, 1980), 39, lists several all-women's chamber ensembles as well.

84. Wells, *Unity in Diversity*, 179.

85. Mrs. Alfred Burrit Andrews, *Guido Ferranti*; Eleanor Everest Freer, *Legend of the Piper*; Celeste Heckscher, *The Rose of Destiny*; and Emma R. Steiner, *Light Operas*, were listed in Mrs. Archibald Freer, "American Opera," NFMC, *Official Bulletin* 2 (May 1923): 12.

86. Chittenden Turner, "Music and the Women's Crusade," *Arts and Decoration* 19 (Sept. 1923): 29, 70–73.

87. "American Opera in Chicago," NFMC, *Magazine* 9 (Nov. 1929): 13; "Success of American Opera Company in Closing Season," NFMC, *Official Bulletin* 7 (May 1928): 9.

88. "Greetings from the Baroness Von Klenner of the American Opera Club," GFWC, *Sixteenth Biennial Proceedings* (1922): 117.

89. Nina Marchetti Archanbal, "Frances Densmore: Pioneer in the Study of American Indian Music," in *Women of Minnesota: Selected Biographical Essays*, ed. Barbara Stuhler and Gretchen Kreuter (St. Paul: Minnesota Historical Society Press, 1977), 96–97, identifies a December 1895 lecture before the Schubert Club of St. Paul as Densmore's debut. Joan Mark, *A Stranger in Her Native Land: Alice Fletcher and the American Indians* (Lincoln: University of Nebraska Press, 1989) discusses Fletcher's activity in Sorosis, a New York City club, in the 1870s. See Karen J. Blair, *The Clubwoman as Feminist: True Womanhood Redefined, 1868–1914* (New York: Holmes and Meier, 1980), 47, on her role in the Association for the Advancement of Women.

90. NFMC, *Proceedings* (1921).

91. See, for example, "The Meaning of Community Music," *General Federation Magazine*, 17 (March 1918), 29, 32.

92. Anne Shaw Faulkner (Mrs. Marx) Oberndorfer, "Music for Every Home: A Substitute for Jazz," *Fruit, Garden and Home* (March 1924): 9.

93. "Preserving the Negro Spiritual," *Musician* 34 (June 1929): 13.

94. NFMC, *Official Bulletin* 3 (September 1923): 3.

95. GFWC, *Proceedings* (1924): 447–49.

96. NFMC, *Eleventh Biennial Proceedings* (1919): 48.

97. Mrs. Harold Vincent Milligan, "Folk Music of America," GFWC, *Proceedings* (1924): 420–23; Marx Oberndorfer and Anne Oberndorfer, *A Century of Progress in American Song* (Chicago: Hall and McCreary, 1933).

98. Nicholas John Cords, "Music in Social Settlement and Community Music Schools, 1893–1939: A Democratic-Esthetic Approach to Music Culture" (Ph.D. diss., University of Minnesota, 1970), 287; additional quotations on settlements are collected in Robert F. Egan, *Music and the Arts in the Community: The Community Music School in America* (Metuchen, NJ: Scarecrow Press, 1989).

99. Clarence A. Grimes, *They Who Speak in Music: The History of the Neighborhood Music School* (New Haven: Neighborhood Music School, 1957), 18.

100. *Music in Thirty-Eight Settlements in New York City* (New York: Welfare Council of NYC, 1930), 11.

101. Mrs. A. P. Pierce, "Department of Fine Arts," Washington State Federation of Women's Clubs, *Bulletin* 10 (October 1925): 12.

102. "Survey of Music Instruction in Settlement Houses of New York," *Musician* 34 (July 1929): 7–8.

103. Deborah B. Thomas, "Mary Louise Curtis Bok Zimbalist," in *Notable American Women: The Modern Period*, ed. Barbara Sicherman and Carol Hurd Green (Cambridge: Belknap Press, 1980), 757–59.

104. Clarence A. Grimes, Papers of the Neighborhood Music School, New Haven Colony Historical Society, New Haven, CT.
105. Schubert Club History, Schubert Club Papers, Minnesota Historical Society.
106. "Music Settlement Department," NFMC, *Official Bulletin* 8 (March 1929): 8.
107. Mrs. W. B. Nickels, "Music Settlements," NFMC, *Official Bulletin* 2 (April 1923): 14.
108. In 1921 alone, its volunteers provided 1,037 piano lessons, 309 violin lessons, and 18 voice lessons in six settlement houses. GFWC, *News* 3 (September–October 1922): 5; GFWC, *Sixteenth Biennial Proceedings* (1922): 343.
109. Janet D. Schenck, *Adventures in Music: A Reminiscence, Manhattan School of Music, 1918–1960* (New York: Manhattan School of Music, 1961), 11.
110. Adella Prentiss Hughes, *Music Is My Life* (Cleveland: World Publishing Company, 1947), 154–55.
111. NFMC, *Official Bulletin* 8 (March 1929): 8.
112. "What Ebell Women Are Doing," *Ebell Magazine* (May 1930): 31.
113. Karen J. Blair, "The Seattle Ladies Musical Club, 1890–1930," in *Experiences in a Promised Land: Essays in Pacific Northwest History*, ed. G. Thomas Edwards and Carlos A. Schwantes (Seattle: University of Washington Press, 1986), 133.
114. Massachusetts State Federation of Women's Clubs, *Federation Manual* (1919–1920): 22.
115. Mildred White Wells, "Public Affairs," in *Unity in Diversity* (Washington, DC: General Federation of Women's Clubs, 1953), 198–209.
116. The NFMC met in the spring of 1917 when the war had just begun and peacetime programs had already been planned.
117. "A Brief History of the Schubert Club, 1882–1962," 18, Zylpha Morton Papers, Minnesota Historical Society.
118. Wells, *Unity in Diversity*, 179.
119. "Department of Music," GFWC, *Fourteenth Biennial Proceedings* (1918): 204.
120. Hughes, *Music Is My Life*, 229; Rhode Island State Federation of Women's Clubs, *Yearbook* (1918) reported on Buffalo.
121. Hughes, 196–97.
122. Ida B. McLagan, "Music," Washington State Federation of Women's Clubs, *Bulletin* (November 1917).
123. "The Future American Orchestra: Some Drastic Truths and High but Justifiable Hopes," in *Who's Who in Music and Dance in Southern California*, ed. Bruno D. Ussher (Hollywood: Bureau of Musical Research, 1933), 42–44; "Music Necessary, Say Proponents," *Portland Oregonian*, 12 June 1925, 1.
124. Minutes, October 1918, New England Conservatory Club, Special Collections, University of Oregon, Eugene, Oregon.
125. "Music Report," Rhode Island State Federation of Women's Clubs, *Yearbook* (1918–19): 34; Hughes, *Music Is My Life*, 232–39.
126. Woodrow Wilson to Florida Federation of Women's Clubs, November 21 1917, May Mann Jennings Papers, Box 11. Cited in Linda D. Vance, *May Mann Jennings: Florida's Genteel Activist* (Gainesville: University Presses of Florida, 1985), 98.
127. Eleanor De Cisneros, "Are American Artists Being Denied a Square Deal in Their Own Country?" *Etude*, 40 (Oct. 1922): 665–66.
128. "Carillon as Women's Peace Memorial Proposed by Arts Club," GFWC, *News* 1 (October 1920): 1. However, the Daughters of the American Revolution succeeded in financing a carillon at Valley Forge.
129. Mrs. William D. Steele, "Department of Music," GFWC, *Magazine* 17 (November 1918): 27.
130. Frank Damrosch, "Music Education and Music Culture," GFWC, *Biennial Proceedings* (1916): 306–315.

131. "Report of Music Department," GFWC, *Biennial Proceedings* (1916): 294.

132. "Ten Thousand Join in Community Singing," *San Francisco Examiner*, 9 September 1918.

133. John Orlando Northcutt, *Magic Valley: The Story of the Hollywood Bowl* (Los Angeles: Osherenke Pub. Co., 1967), 42; Grace G. Koopal, *The Miracle of Music: The History of the Hollywood Bowl* (Hollywood: The Hollywood Bowl, 1972), 26–27; "Liberty Loan," B. B. Frankel Scrapbook, 59, UCLA Special Collections.

134. Dr. J. L. Erb, "Musical Awakening of Today," GFWC, *14th Biennial Proceedings* (1918): 211.

135. Other favorite songs of the period included: *1620* by Edward MacDowell, *Victory* by Mrs. H. A. A. Beach, *Home Road, Americans Are Coming* by Fay Foster, *Ten Thousand by Ten Thousand* by Carrie Jacobs Bond. All these songs were sung at the NFMC Peterborough Biennial of 1919.

136. Erb, "Musical Awakening of Today"; "Music Committee Report," GFWC, *Fourteenth Biennial Proceedings* (1918): 208; Kenneth S. Clark, "The Making of a Singing Army," GFWC, *Fourteenth Biennial Proceedings* (1918): 218; Addie W. Hunton and Kathryn M. Johnson, "The Salvation of Music Overseas," in *Two Colored Women with the American Expeditionary Forces* (Brooklyn: Brooklyn Eagle Press, 1920), 217–25.

137. C. M. Tremaine, *New York's First Music Week* (New York: National Bureau for the Advancement of Music, 1920), 18.

138. GFWC, *14th Biennial Proceedings* (1918): 213.

139. *American Art Annual* 20 (1923): 13.

140. *American Art Annual* 17 (1920): 27.

141. C. M. Tremaine, *History of National Music Week* (New York: National Bureau for the Advancement of Music, 1925), 27.

142. Ibid., 17–19.

143. Tremaine, *History of Music Week*, 78, 198, lists over twenty active Arkansas clubs.

144. Tremaine, ibid. credits 85 women's clubs across the nation with significant support.

145. Ibid., 43.

146. Ibid., 35.

147. The Carnegie Foundation awarded five thousand dollars to New York's celebration in 1925. "Notes," *American Magazine of Art* 16 (July 1925): 382.

148. C. Turner, "Music and the Women's Crusade," *Arts and Decoration* (1923): 71.

149. Tremaine, *History of Music Week*, 11.

150. Idem, "Music Week Possibilities," NFMC, *Nineteenth Biennial Proceedings*: (1935): 82–84.

151. Tremaine, *New York's First Music Week*, 69–73.

152. Tremaine, *History of Music Week*, 8.

153. Ibid., 74, 75.

154. NFMC, *Official Bulletin* 7 (October 1927): 6.

155. Otto H. Kahn, in Tremaine, *History of Music Week*, 9.

156. Tremaine, ibid., 9–16.

157. Ibid., 16.

158. Ibid., 10.

159. Tremaine, *New York's First Music Week*, 20.

160. Ibid., 20.

161. Anne Oberndorfer, "Music as a Power in the Community," GFWC, *Sixteenth Biennial Proceedings* (1922): 393.

162. Walter Damrosch, *My Musical Life* (New York: Scribner's, 1926), 323.

163. "The Feminine Nuisance in American Literature," *Yale Review* 10 (July 1921): 722.

164. Earl Barnes, *Woman in Modern Society* (New York: B. W. Huebsch, 1912), 82.
165. GFWC, *Twentieth Biennial Report* (1930): 363.
166. Curtis Institute of Music enrollment figures, 1924–1931, G. Spofford Papers, Box 13, Sophia Smith Collection, Smith College, Northampton, Massachusetts.
167. Massachusetts State Federation of Women's Clubs, *Federation Manual* (1921–22).

4. Women's Societies for the Visual Arts

1. Rose Berry, "Report of the Art Division," GFWC, *Biennial Proceedings* (1926): 233.
2. Ibid.
3. Annie Prescott, "History of Auburn Art Club, 1880–1920," Papers of Auburn Art Club, 1920, Auburn, ME, Public Library; Lucy Pope Taylor, Harriette Barney, and Mary Salinda Foster, comps. "The First Fifty Years, Mankato Art History Club, 1896–1946," Papers of Mankato Art History Club, Blue Earth County Historical Society, Mankato, MN; Papers of Hartford Art Club, Stowe-Day Foundation, Hartford, CT; Laurene Alliott, "Ruskin Art Club History, 1888–1948," Ruskin Art Club Papers, Southwest Museum, Los Angeles; Suzanne M. Pate, "The History of the Spokane Art League," (Senior Honors Thesis, Eastern Washington University, 1985); Stella Rausch, *History of the Women's Art Club of Cleveland: Our First Twenty Years, 1912–1932* (Cleveland: Central Publishing House, 1933); Massachusetts State Federation of Women's Clubs, *Federation Manual* (1914–15): 43; *American Art Annual* 8 (1910–11): 177; 5 (1906–1907): 199; 4 (1903–1904): 205; 14 (1917): 215; 9 (1911): 117; 14 (1914): 231–32; 8 (1910–11): 128.
4. See *National Notes;* Mary Salmon, "The Study Club Movement," *Catholic World* 124 (February 1927): 679–81.
5. "Professional Art Schools in the United States," *American Art Annual* 8 (1910–11): 41.
6. *American Art Annual* 11 (1914): 17.
7. See annual convention reports, AFA Papers, Smithsonian Institution, Washington, DC.
8. AFA, *Conference Proceedings* (1917): 2, AFA Papers, Smithsonian Institution, Washington, DC.
9. Leonard K. Eaton, "Florence Nightingale Levy," in *Notable American Women,* vol. 2, ed. Edward T. James, Janet Wilson James, and Paul Boyer (Cambridge: Harvard University Press, 1971), 395–97.
10. *Art and Progress* 1 (April 1910): 154–58.
11. See, for example, vol. 12 of *Magazine of Art* on E. Christine Lumsdon (Nov. 1921), 384–85; vol. 13 on Ethel L. Coe (September 1922), 308–12; Grace Ravlin (May 1922); vol. 14 on Lilla Cabot Perry, Ruth St. Denis, Grace Mott Johnson, Florence K. Upton; vol. 15 on Susan H. Bradley, Else Hasselriis, and Nellie Verne Walker; vol. 16 on Jessie Wilcox Smith, Katherine McEwen, Harriet Frishmuth, Mary Butler, Clara E. Sipprell, Eleanor Norcross, Cora Holden, Anne Taylor Brown, Lydia Longacre, Elsie Dodge Pattee, Laura Coombs Hills, Helen Winslow Durkee, Maria J. Strean; and vol. 17 on Myra Albert Wiggins, Alice R. Guger Smith, Susan M. L. Wales, Florence Este, Violet Oakley, Lilla Cabot Perry, Lilian Westcott Hall, Nan Sheets, Mary Cassatt, and Caroline Armington.
12. *American Art Annual* 18 (1921): back cover verso.
13. In 1909, the AFA assembled three exhibitions and found nine societies, both member chapters and non-affiliated groups, willing to exhibit these works in clubs, schools, museums, libraries, and art associations. By 1914, the AFA located 23 exhibits to tour in 114 places. These were seen by 300,000 individuals. By 1914, 45 exhibits went to 168 locations. In 1922, 56 exhibits toured 257 locations. In 1929, 46 exhibits

toured 300 locations. In the first twenty years of the traveling exhibition program, 675 shows went to 3,369 communities. *American Art Annual* 26 (1929).

14. Talks supplied by the AFA included the following topics: American painting; American sculpture; civic art; American mural paintings; Whistler's etchings; tapestries; and furniture. Any member chapter that had already paid its ten dollars in dues could obtain a speech and fifty slides for the modest sum of three dollars.

15. Jane Cunningham Croly documents thirteen early art clubs in *The History of the Woman's Club Movement* (New York: Henry G. Allen, 1898).

16. GFWC, *Biennial Proceedings* (1898): 42.

17. GFWC, *Biennial Proceedings* (1896): 81.

18. Mary Quick Burnet, *Art and Artists of Indiana* (New York: Century, 1921), 275. See also Ella Bond Johnston, "An Art Association for the People," *Outlook* 85 (27 April 1907): 943–51; Thomas A. Mott, "Schools as Art Centers," *National Educational Association Proceedings and Addresses* (1913): 586–89; Ella Bond Johnston, "The High School as the Art Centre of the Community," in *The Modern High School*, ed. Charles Hughes Johnston (New York: Scribner's, 1914): 692–706; "Mrs. M. F. Johnston, Art Leader, Is Dead," *Richmond Palladium-Item*, 25 April 1951; *Art in Richmond, 1898–1978* (Richmond: Art Association, 1978); Papers of Ella Bond Johnston, Richmond Art Museum, Richmond, Indiana.

19. "American Sculpture at the Palace of the Legion of Honor," *University of California Chronicle* (October 1929); *Dream City* (San Francisco: W. N. Brunt, 1915); "John Singer Sargent," *Art and Archaeology* 18 (1924): 81–112; *What Do You Know about American Art?* (New York: Scribner's, 1928).

20. "Art Department," GFWC, *Magazine* (April 1914): 9–10.

21. Mrs. Rose V. S. Berry, "Appreciation of Art Is a Social Necessity," *General Federation Clubwoman* 1 (December 1920): 1.

22. Among the artists featured were Brenda Putnam, Edith Baretto Parsons (with *Laughing Fountain*), Bessie Potter Vonnoh, Grace Mott Johnson, Laura Gardin Fraser, Anna Vaughn Hyatt Huntington *(Diana)*, Harriett Payne Bingham *(Bird Bath)*, and Harriett Fishmuth. See Rose V. S. Berry, "The Spirit of Art," GFWC, *Eighteenth Biennial Proceedings* (1926): 270–73.

23. Twenty-four women painters are cited in *Scribner's Magazine* 83 (June 1928): 792 g,h, and 76.

24. "Report of the Art Department," *General Federation Magazine* 17 (October 1918): 6.

25. Mrs. Walter S. Little, "Art for the Home's Sake," GFWC, *Fifteenth Biennial Proceedings* (1920): 109.

26. GFWC, *Biennial Proceedings* (1900): 89; *American Art Annual* 6 (1907–1908): 199; "Report of Art Committee," GFWC, *Biennial Proceedings* (1902): 36.

27. "Modern Development in Indian Art," GFWC, *Twentieth Biennial Proceedings* (1930): 110.

28. Joan Siegfried, "American Women in Art Pottery," *Nineteenth Century* 9 (Spring 1984): 12–18; and Andrea Callen, *Angel in the Studio: Women and the Arts and Crafts Movement, 1870–1940* (London: Architectural Press, 1979), 87, list numerous American potteries directed or established by women.

29. "Prize Winners," *General Federation Magazine* 13 (July 1914): 15–16.

30. *American Art Annual* 6 (1907–1908): 163.

31. "Art Department," *General Federation Magazine* 12 (April 1914): 9–10.

32. "Report of the Committee on Art," GFWC, *Fifth Biennial Proceedings* (1900): 37–39.

33. Burnet, *Art and Artists of Indiana*.

34. Catherine Kaiser, "Those One Hundred Friends," *Carnegie Magazine* (September/October 1984): 22–24; "List of Purchases for 1917–1981 for the One Hundred Friends of Pittsburgh Art Collection of Paintings for the Pittsburgh Public Schools."

35. Mary Gibson, *A Record of Twenty-Five Years of the California Federation of*

Women's Clubs, 1900–1925 (n.p.: California Federation of Women's Clubs, 1927), 212.

36. "The Greatest Service to Art," *American Magazine of Art* 15 (August 1924): 436.

37. Miss L. Pearl Saunders, "Aims of the Art Department, Tennessee Federation of Women's Clubs," in *Women's Work in Tennessee* (Memphis: Jones-Briggs, 1916), 228–31.

38. Charles L. Hutchinson, "The Democracy of Art," *American Magazine of Art* 7 (August 1916): 397.

39. "Art for the Schoolroom," *American Magazine of Art* 16 (March 1925): 142–44.

40. The official list suggested: George Inness, *The Home of the Heron;* Madonnas by Botticelli and by Raphael; Vermeer's *Music Lesson;* Rembrandt's *Holy Family;* Reynolds's *Age of Innocence;* Van Dyck's *William II of Nassau;* Hals's *Laughing Cavalier;* and Velasquez's *Infanta Margareete Theresa.* In sculpture: *Nike Fastening Her Sandal,* panels of horsemen from the frieze of the Parthenon, della Robbia's boys playing drums or trumpets and singing, and Donatello's cherubs dancing.

41. The list of objects placed by the Chicago society appears in Kimberly Dawn Finley, "Cultural Monitors: Clubwomen and Public Art Instruction in Chicago, 1890–1920," (Ph.D. diss., Ohio State University, 1989), 271.

42. "An Exhibition in a Kansas High School," *American Magazine of Art* 9 (January 1918): 111–13.

43. Adelaide S. Hall, "Practical Art among Club-Women," *Chautauquan* 31 (Sept. 1900): 621–24.

44. Other examples include Percy F. Albee's *Youth Instructed* and *Youth Endowed* in Bridgham School, Providence, Rhode Island; Armin O. Hansen's *Audubon Birds;* Edith Brown's frieze of twelve tiles at the Forsyth Dental Infirmary for Children, Fenway, Boston; and Frances Grimes's relief for Washington Irving High School in New York. See Rose Henderson, "Mural Paintings in Public Schools," *American Magazine of Art* 17 (May 1926): 241–44; Antonio Cirino, "Interior Decoration in a Grammar School," *American Magazine of Art* 17 (October 1926): 534–38; *Art and Progress* 6 (June 1915): 273, 288; Adeline Adams, "A Relief by Frances Grimes," *Art and Progress* 6 (May 1915): 215–17.

45. GFWC, *Biennial Proceedings* (1908): 207.

46. Effie Seachrest, "The Smoky Hill Valley Art Center," *American Magazine of Art* 12 (January 1921): 14–16.

47. *American Art Annual* 13 (1916): 154.

48. Finley, "Cultural Monitors," 48.

49. Forty-four pictures and casts for Public School 135 came from Mrs. J. J. White; one hundred items for P.S. 8 from Mrs. Robert DeForest, wife of the AFA president and Metropolitan Musuem of Art president; and 58 items for P.S. 105 from Mrs. V. Sorchan and Mrs. Edward Wharton. See *American Art Annual* 1 (1898): 42–43.

50. Ellsworth H. Plumer and Everett E. Robie, "Correlating Elementary Subjects with Art," *School Arts Magazine* 30 (June 1931): 665–68.

51. "Other Federation Activities," *American Magazine of Art* 16 (March 1925): 144–48.

52. "The Cleveland Convention," *American Magazine of Art* 16 (July 1925), 348–73.

53. Mary Powell, "Art in the Public Library," *American Magazine of Art* 13 (May 1922): 161–65.

54. Mrs. Everett W. Pattison, "Art and the Women's Clubs," *Federation Bulletin* 7 (March 1910): 189–91.

55. *American Art Annual* 8 (1910–1911): 166–67.

56. Ibid., 349.

57. Pattison, "Art and the Women's Clubs;" *American Art Annual* 11 (1914): 117;

Massachusetts State Federation of Women's Clubs, *Federation Manual* (1926–27): 92; *American Art Annual* 10 (1913): 155; "Painting to be Given as Prize; Golden Hours," *Jersey Observer* 28 March 1927; Scrapbook 1914–1934, Helen Maria Turner Papers, New York Historical Society, New York City; Lolita L. W. Flockhart to Helen Turner, 15 May 1928, Helen Maria Turner Papers, New York Historical Society; Metal Plaque from Woman's Art Club of New York to Helen M. Turner, 1910; Eleanor C. Winslow to Helen Turner, 24 February; Box 21, unidentified note to Helen Turner re Paducah Woman's Club. My thanks to Phyllis Peet for the material on Helen Maria Turner.

58. *American Art Annual* 26 (1929): 18; *American Art Annual* 24 (1927): 17; *American Art Annual* 25 (1928): 18; *American Art Annual* 28 (1931): 18; Vernon Loggins, "Elisabet Ney," in *Notable American Women*, vol. 2, 623–25; Bride Neill Taylor, *Elisabet Ney, Sculptor* (Austin: Thomas F. Taylor, 1938), 75–78.

59. Louisine Havemeyer, "Memories of a Militant: The Suffrage Torch," *Scribner's Magazine* 71 (May 1922): 528–39; Frances Weitzenhoffer, *The Havemeyers: Impressionism Comes to America* (New York: Harry Abrams, 1986).

60. Edith Mayo, "Adelaide Johnson," in *Notable American Women: The Modern Period*, 380–81.

61. GFWC, *Biennial Proceedings* (1918): 159.

62. Mildred White Wells, *Unity in Diversity: The History of the General Federation of Women's Clubs* (Washington, DC: General Federation of Women's Clubs, 1957), 178.

63. "Art Exhibits Ready for Club Circuit," GFWC, *News* 3 (September–October 1922): 7.

64. Wells, *Unity in Diversity*, 178.

65. "Shop Window Displays—the People's Picture Galleries," *American Magazine of Art* 12 (April 1921): 115–17; Massachusetts State Federation of Women's Clubs, *Federation Manual* (1929–30): 106.

66. Martha K. Schauer, "The Community and Art, Art Week in Dayton," *American Magazine of Art* 18 (April 1927): 252–54. For a fuller discussion of the activities of Art Week, see Margaret Montgomery, "Art Week: Philadelphia Innovation," *International Studio* 75 (July 1922): 352–55; "Art Week in Philadelphia," *American Magazine of Art* 13 (June 1922): 200–201.

67. "Art at the County Fairs," *Literary Digest* 55 (29 September 1917): 26–27; *American Art Annual* 14 (1917): 80; Suzanne M. Pate, "Spokane Art League, 1892–1913" (B.A. Honors Paper, Washington State University, 1986); Mina Humphrey Varnum, "Permanent Art Building for the Michigan State Fair," *American Magazine of Art* 8 (Jan. 1917): 106–107; Massachusetts State Federation of Women's Clubs, *Federation Manual* (1922–23): 22.

68. "At State Fairs," *American Magazine of Art* 13 (November 1922): 485–86.

69. Muriel Caswall, "The Children's Art Center," *American Magazine of Art* 9 (August 1918): 408–12.

70. Ernest Poole, "Art and Democracy: How the Chicago Art Institute Reaches the People," *Outlook* 85 (23 March 1907): 640–42, 665–74; Evans Woollen, "The Art Museum and the Public Schools," *Art and Progress* 2 (December 1910): 42–45; Henry W. Kent, "Art Museums and Schools," *Educational Review* 40 (June 1910): 78–81; Blake-More Godwin, "What the Small Museum Can Do," *American Magazine of Art* 18 (October 1927): 527–33; Harold Ward, "A Museum Makes Friends with Today," *American Magazine of Art* 17 (July 1926): 338–45; Florence N. Levy, "The Service of the Museum of Art to the Community," *American Magazine of Art* 15 (November 1924): 581–87; Anna Curtis Chandler, "School Children and the Art Museum," *American Magazine of Art* 15 (October 1924): 508–13; Thomas Whitney Surette, "Music in the Art Museum," *American Magazine of Art* 9 (August 1918): 418–20; Margaret Sawtelle Smith, "Children, Art Museums and Stories," *American Magazine of Art* 9 (June 1918): 328–34; Katharine Gibson, "An Experiment in Measuring Results of Fifth Grade Class Visits to an Art Museum," *School and Society* 21

(30 May 1925): 658–62; Minnie Cage, "Popularizing Art," *Art and Progress* 2 (September 1911): 333–35; "Methods of Using Art Museums," *American Magazine of Art* 12 (1915): 15–30.

71. Rose V. S. Berry, "Report of the Art Division," GFWC, *Nineteenth Biennial Proceedings* (1928): 176.

72. "Beautifying New York Discussed by Municipal Art Society, a City Planning Commission," *New York Times*, 13 April 1913, sec. 5, 14:1; C. Howard Walker, "Municipal Art," GFWC, *Ninth Biennial Proceedings* (1908): 128–30.

73. Elma Graves, "Municipal Art," *American Journal of Sociology* 6 (March 1901): 681.

74. Mrs. Joseph B. Dibrell, "Civic Commission Report," GFWC, *Biennial Proceedings* (1908): 125.

75. "Public Art in American Cities," *Municipal Affairs* 2 (March 1898): 1–13.

76. "Art Committee," GFWC, *Biennial Proceedings* (1908): 122.

77. C. H. Caffin, "Municipal Art," *Harper's Monthly Magazine* 100 (April 1900): 661.

78. "Art Commissions Confer," *American City* 8 (June 1913): 669–70; "City Beautifiers Hear Gaynor on Art," *New York Times*, 14 May 1913, 5.

79. "The Federation," *Art and Progress* 1 (November 1909): 19.

80. Mrs. Everett W. Pattison, "Municipal and State Art Commissions," *Federation Bulletin* 6 (May 1909): 211–13.

81. Richard B. Watrous, "Civic Art and Country Life," *American Academy of Political and Social Science Annals* 40 (March 1912): 193.

82. Caffin, "Municipal Art," 661.

83. Mrs. E. W. Pattison, "Art and the Women's Clubs," *Federation Bulletin* 7 (May 1909): 38–40; GFWC, *Eighth Biennial Proceedings* (1906): 106; Staff of the Minnesota Historical Society, "Brief History of the Minnesota State Art Society," and "Report of the Minnesota State Art Society, 1903–04," both in Minnesota Historical Society, St. Paul, MN, c. 1949; Mrs. Phelps Wyman, "State Art Society of Minnesota," *American City* 7 (August 1912): 142–43.

84. "What Ebell Women Are Doing," *Ebell Magazine* (May 1930): 31.

85. U.S. Commission of Fine Arts Papers, Box 6, National Archives; and American Federation of Arts Annuals.

86. Mrs. Everett W. Pattison, "Report of the Art Committee," GFWC, *Tenth Biennial Proceedings* (1910): 77.

87. George B. Ford, "Art Commissions and City Planning," *American City* 10 (February 1914): 118.

88. Martha Candler, "What a Village Art Commission Might Do," *American City* 36 (June 1927): 810–11.

89. W. W. Taylor, "Cincinnati Municipal Art," *American City* 2 (January 1910): 16–18.

90. Elma Graves, "Municipal Art," *American Journal of Sociology* 6 (March 1901): 678.

91. Lucy Fitch Perkins, "What Municipal Art Should Be," *Chautauquan* 36 (February 1903): 517.

92. George Wharton James, "Municipal Art in Western Cities: Eugene, Oregon," *Arena* 41 (August 1909): 515–24; George Wharton James, "Municipal Art in American Cities: Springfield, Massachusetts," *Arena* 37 (January 1907): 16–30; Charles Mulford Robinson, *Modern Civic Art or the City Made Beautiful* (New York: Putnam's, 1903).

93. Wells, *Unity in Diversity*, 195; Mrs. Harry L. Harcum, *The History of the Maryland Federation of Women's Clubs, 1899–1941* (Fredericksburg: J. W. Stowell, 1941), 93; Washington State Federation of Women's Clubs, *Bulletin* 5 (December 1920); "Save a Tree—Plea of State Federation of Women's Clubs for Purchase of Park," *Spokane Woman*, 18 November 1926, in Esther Maltby Scrapbook #1, University of

Washington Manuscript Collection; Papers of Shakespeare Club, 23 January 1925 clipping; Wells, *Unity in Diversity,* 447; Ann Marie Evans, *Women's Rural Organizations and Their Activities* (Washington, DC: Government Printing Office, 1918), 8.

94. Leila Mechlin of AFA and Mrs. Owen Wister of GFWC attended. See "The Baltimore Convention of the American Civic Association," *American City* 7 (December 1912): 583–85; Harlean James, "Civic Work of Women's Clubs: Baltimore Flower Market," *American City* 8 (April 1913): 390–92; "Progressive Club Work," *American City* 5 (October 1911): 232.

95. Among these were the Garden Club of America, the American Federation of Arts, the National Academy of Design, the National Association of Women Painters and Sculptors, several state federations of women's clubs, Sorosis in New York City, the Long Island Federation of Women's Clubs, and the Federated Garden Clubs of Long Island. See "Billboard File," Papers of U.S. Commission of Fine Arts, National Archives, Washington, DC.

96. Wells, *Unity in Diversity,* 196–97.

97. Among the companies that succumbed to the pressure to cooperate, in an effort to promote better public relations, were B. F. Goodrich, Pillsbury Flour Mills, Champion Spark Plug, Fleischmann, Gulf Refining, Standard Oil of California, New York and New Jersey, and International Harvester. See "Billboard File," Papers of U.S. Commission of Fine Arts, National Archives, Washington, DC.

98. "Those Country Billboards," *American Magazine of Art* 17 (March 1926): 146–48.

99. Mrs. W. L. Lawton, "Committee on Bill Board Restrictions," GFWC, *Biennial Proceedings* (1927): 142–43.

100. Ibid.

101. Mrs. Arthur J. Crockett, serving as the Massachusetts State Federation of Women's Clubs representative on the Billboard Law Defense Committee, is quoted in "Sign Tax Planned by Pennsylvania," *Washington Star,* 3 February 1931.

102. "A Buyers' Strike against Billboards," *New York Times,* 17 November 1929, Sec. 4, 4:6.

103. Lena M. McCauley, "Mid-West Art in Wartime," *American Art Annual* 15 (1918): 25–27; "Art and the Great War," *Magazine of Art* 11 (December 1919): 64–65; Dudley Crafts Watson, "Art during the War," GFWC, *Fourteenth Biennial Proceedings* (1918): 167–75; "Museum War Service," *American Magazine of Art* 10 (November 1918): 27; Duncan Phillips, "Art and the War," *American Magazine of Art* 9 (June 1918): 303–309; Dudley Crafts Watson, "Art during the War," *General Federation Magazine* 17 (October 1918): 7–9; Mrs. Cyrus W. Perkins, "Report of the Art Department," *General Federation Magazine* 17 (October 1918): 6–7.

104. "War Picture Exhibitions," *American Magazine of Art* 10 (December 1918): 71–72.

105. *American Magazine of Art* 10 (March 1919): 190.

106. "Art Committee Report," Massachusetts State Federation of Women's Clubs, *Federation Manual* (1917–1918): 45.

107. Watson, "Art during the War," GFWC, *Biennial Proceedings* (1918): 174.

108. "Art during the War," *American Art Annual* 15 (1918): 19–34.

109. "War Memorials," *American Magazine of Art* 10 (February 1919): 144–45; J. Monroe Hewlett, "War Memorials," *American Magazine of Art* 17 (October 1926): 512–14.

110. "War Memorials," *General Federation Magazine* 19 (January 1920): 18–19.

111. Andrew Wright Crawford's remarks were quoted in "Pennsylvania," *General Federation Magazine* 19 (January 1920): 23; see also Charles Moore, "Memorials of the Great War," *American Magazine of Art* 10 (May 1919): 233–47.

112. "War Memorials," *American Magazine of Art* 10 (February 1919): 137–38.

113. "War Memorials," *American Magazine of Art* 10 (May 1919): 270–72.

114. "Memorials for the Small Community," *American Magazine of Art* 10 (September 1919): 430–43.

115. Elihu Root, "The Memorial Spirit and the Future of America," *American Magazine of Art* 10 (September 1919): 407–409; Morris Gray, "War Memorials: Utility or Spirituality?" *American Magazine of Art* 10 (September 1919): 410–13.

116. "War Memorials," *American Magazine of Art* 13 (February 1919): 144–45.

117. Alice Ames Winter, "We and the Land God Gave Us," *Ladies' Home Journal* 41 (July 1924): 109; Mildred Marshall Scouller, *The Women Who Man Our Clubs* (Philadelphia: John C. Winston, 1934); Washington State Federation of Women's Clubs, *Bulletin* 10 (December 1925): 23.

5. Pageantry and the Women's Rights Movement, 1905–1925

1. David Glassberg, *American Historical Pageantry: The Uses of Tradition in the Early Twentieth Century* (Chapel Hill: University of North Carolina Press, 1990); Naima Prevots, *American Pageantry: A Movement for Art and Democracy* (Ann Arbor: UMI Research Press, 1990).

2. Ralph Davol, *Handbook of American Pageantry* (Taunton, MA: Ralph Davol, 1915), 1.

3. Historians who have noted working-class use of parades, festivals, and spectacles include: Mary P. Ryan, *Women in Public: Between Banners and Ballots, 1825–1880* (Baltimore: Johns Hopkins University Press, 1990); Roy Rosenzweig, *Eight Hours for What We Will: Workers and Leisure in an Industrial City, 1870–1920* (New York: Cambridge University Press, 1983); Maxine Seller, ed., *Ethnic Theatre in the United States* (Westport, CT: Greenwood Press, 1983); Sean Wilents, *Chants Democratic: New York City and the Rise of the American Working Class, 1788–1850* (New York: Oxford University Press, 1984), 87–89; Charles G. Steffen, *Mechanics of Baltimore: Workers and Politics in the Age of Revolution, 1763–1850* (Urbana: University of Illinois Press, 1984), 164; Michael A. Gordon, "Labor Boycott in New York City, 1880–1886," in *American Working-Class Culture*, ed. Milton Cantor (Westport, CT: Greenwood Press, 1979), 311; Jean Ann Scarpaci, "Immigrants in the New South: Italians in Louisiana's Sugar Parishes, 1880–1910," in *American Working-Class Culture*, 393; Francis G. Couvares, "Triumph of Commerce: Class Culture and Mass Culture in Pittsburgh," in *Working Class America*, ed. Michael M. Frisch and David Walkowitz (Urbana: University of Illinois Press, 1983), 132–33; Susan G. Davis, *Parades and Power: Street Theatre in Nineteenth-Century Philadelphia* (Philadelphia: Temple University Press, 1985); Lisa Tickner, *The Spectacle of Women: Imagery of the Suffrage Campaign 1907–14* (Chicago: University of Chicago Press, 1988).

4. Brief mention is made of pageantry in Max Kaplan, *Leisure in America* (New York: John Wiley, 1960), 144; Reynold Edgar Carlson et al., *Recreation in American Life* (Belmont, CA: Wadsworth, 1972), 434. Histories of leisure and recreation that overlook this popular pastime altogether: Frederick Lewis Allen, *Only Yesterday: An Informal History of the 1920's* (New York: Harper and Row, 1931); Russell Nye, *The Unembarrassed Muse: The Popular Arts in America* (New York: Dial Press, 1970); Foster Rhea Dulles, *A History of Recreation* (New York: Appleton-Century-Crofts, 1965).

5. Kenneth MacGowan, *Footlights across America: Towards a National Theatre* (New York: Harcourt, Brace, 1929), deals with pageantry; Howard Taubman, *The Making of the American Theatre* (New York: Coward-McCann, 1965); Oliver M. Sayler, *Our American Theatre* (New York: Brentano's, 1923); Glenn Hughes, *A History of the American Theatre, 1700–1950* (New York: Samuel French, 1951) deals solely with the pageants of Percy MacKaye. There is no mention of American pageantry in Elmer Rice, *The Living Theatre* (New York: Harper and Brothers, 1959); Barnard Hewitt, *Theatre USA, 1668–1957* (New York: McGraw Hill, 1959); Garff B. Wilson, *Three Hundred Years of American Drama and Theatre* (Englewood Cliffs, NJ: Pren-

tice-Hall, 1973); or Oscar G. Brockett, *History of the Theatre* (Boston: Allyn and Bacon, 1968).

6. Mary Porter Beegle, "Fundamentals of Successful Pageantry," American Pageant Association, *Bulletin* (15 September 1914); Davol, *Handbook of American Pageantry*, 104; Frederick George Walsh, "Outdoor Commemorative Drama in the U.S., 1900–1950" (Ph.D. diss., Western Reserve University, 1952), 165.

7. Martin Sidney Tackel, "Women and American Pageantry: 1908 to 1918" (Ph.D. diss., City University of New York, 1982), 27.

8. Mary Meek Atkeson, *Woman on the Farm* (New York: Century, 1924), 270.

9. Percy MacKaye, *Civic Theatre* (New York: Mitchell Kennerly, 1912), 42.

10. Davol, *Handbook of American Pageantry*, 67.

11. Constance D'Arcy MacKay, *Patriotic Drama* (New York: Holt, 1918), 63.

12. Davol, *Handbook of American Pageantry*, 62.

13. Box 1-12, Hazel MacKaye Papers, Dartmouth College Archives, Hanover, New Hampshire.

14. Percy MacKaye, *Civic Theatre*, 37.

15. MacKay, *Patriotic Drama*, 62.

16. Sheldon Cheney, "New Movement in the Theatre," *Forum* 52 (November 1914): 756; *Playground* 4 (February 1911): 8–9, 372–74.

17. In 1909, for example, Hadley, Massachusetts, celebrated its 250th anniversary. Other examples of anniversary celebrations in New England include those at Springfield, MA in 1908; Gloucester, MA, Duxbury, MA, and Worcester, MA in 1909; Ipswich, MA, Deerfield, MA, Peterborough, NH, and Charleston, ME in 1910.

18. New England towns celebrating town pageants after 1910 include Portsmouth, NH (300th); North Adams, MA; Brattleboro, VT (150th); Bennington, VT (150th); Warwick, MA; Pittsfield, MA; Warren, RI; Portland, ME (in 1913); Concord, NH; Medway, MA; Saugus, MA; Taunton, MA; Thetford, VT; Machias Valley (in 1913); Rockport, MA; Casco Bay, ME; Milton, MA; Arlington, MA (in 1913); Lake Minnetonka in Excelsior, ME; Marblehead, MA; Revere, MA; Manchester, NH; and Newton, MA.

19. Between 1910 and 1920: Schenectady, NY (250th); St. Louis, MO (150th); Winesburg, OH (100th); Piqua, OH; North Chillicothe, IL; Southold, Long Island, NY; Saluda, NC; Ravinia Park, IL; Fairmont, MN; Greenwich Village, New York City; Lake George, NY; Honolulu, HI; New Harmony, IN; West Chester, PA; Astoria, OR; Louisville, KY; Richmond, IN; St. Thomas, ND; Yankton, SD; Montevallo, AL; East Des Moines, IA; Oshkosh, WI; Reno, NV.

20. Mary Master Needham, *Folk Festivals: Their Growth and How to Give Them* (New York: B. W. Heubsch, 1912), 6.

21. Davol, *Handbook of American Pageantry*, 1.

22. Mary Porter Beegle and Jack Randall Crawford, *Community Drama and Pageantry* (New Haven: Yale University Press, 1916), 32.

23. Davol, *Handbook of American Pageantry*, 62.

24. Mrs. Mary McIntosh Hervey, "A Saner and Safer Fourth of July," GFWC, *Tenth Biennial Report* (1910): 201–12.

25. Margaret MacLaren Eager, American Pageantry Association, *Bulletin* (1 September 1915): 1.

26. Mary Ritter Beard, *Woman's Work in Municipalities* (New York: D. Appleton, 1916); Mrs. Milton Perry Smith, "A Peace Pageant," *American City* 13 (October 1915): 334–37; *American Art Annual* 19 (1922): 18–19; 25 (1928): 24; 24 (1927): 24.

27. Tackel, "Women and American Pageantry," and Walsh, "Outdoor Commemorative Drama" catalog the productions of these women pageant-masters.

28. Lotta Clark and Mary Cutler collaborated on *Torchbearers* in Minneapolis; Sue Lombard Horsley and Alice M. Tenneson on *Visions Fulfilled: A Symbolical Pageant of the Valleys of the Yakima*, Yakima, WA (1917); Miss McKenney and Miss Markley on *History of Education in Georgia* at Agnes Scott College, Decatur, GA;

Amelia Johnson and Louise Brooks on *The Girls of Yesterday and Today,* the YWCA Jubilee Pageant in Asilomar, CA; Cora Mel Patten and Elma C. Ehlich on the *Peace Pageant for Children and Young People;* Irene U. Telford and Lillian Keith on *Wheaton College Pageant* in Norton, MA; and Frances Dean and Genorie Solomon on *Normal School Pageant* in Salem, MA.

29. Beegle and Crawford, *Community Drama and Pageantry;* Esther Willard Bates, *Pageants and Pageantry* (Boston: Ginn, 1912); idem, *The Art of Producing Pageants* (Boston: W. H. Baker, 1925); Needham, *Folk Festivals;* Louise Burleigh, *Community Theatre in Theory and Practice* (Boston: Little, 1917); Constance D'Arcy MacKay, *Patriotic Drama in Your Town* (New York: Holt, 1918); idem, *Patriotic Plays and Pageants for Young People* (New York: Holt, 1912); Mary Russell, *How to Produce Plays and Pageants* (New York: George H. Doran, 1923); Linwood Taft, *Technique of Pageantry* (New York: A.S. Barnes, 1921).

30. For example, Alice C. D. Riley wrote *The Lover's Garden* with brief excerpts from *Midsummer Night's Dream, The Tempest, Winter's Tale, Romeo and Juliet, Hamlet, Twelfth Night,* and *As You Like It* and published it in *The Drama* for all to use. It was also published in Chicago: Clayton F. Summy, 1927.

31. Constance D'Arcy MacKay, "Pilgrims," *Woman's Home Companion* (April 1920): 24–25, 81.

32. Ethel Rockwell, "Children of Old Carolina: An Historical Pageant of North Carolina for Children," *University of North Carolina Extension Bulletin* 4 (1 April 1925).

33. Mary Porter Beegle, "Fundamentals of Successful Pageantry," *Bulletin* 7 (15 Sept. 1914); Virginia Tanner, "Dances of American Pageantry," *Bulletin* 64 (1 Nov. 1919); Mary Porter Beegle, "Pageant Dancing," *Bulletin* 34 (1 June 1916); Violet Oakley, "Spirit of the Pageant," *Bulletin* 39 (1 Sept. 1916); Lotta Clark, "Development of American Pageantry," *Bulletin* 9 (1 Nov. 1914).

34. Lotta Clark founded the American Pageantry Association in 1913. While men dominated the presidency and women held only the secretaryship regularly, Virginia Tanner became a vice-president at the 1921 annual meeting in Boston, and three of the six directors nominated at that meeting were Mary Cutter, Elizabeth Grumball, and Joy Higgins. See *Bulletin* 68 (1 June 1921).

35. Eleanor Randall Stuart, "Newer Aspects of Pageantry," *New England Magazine* 48 (January 1913): 540–41.

36. Constance D'Arcy MacKay, *Plays of the Pioneers: A Book of Historical Pageant-Plays* (New York: Hayes & Bros., 1915).

37. Walsh, "Outdoor Commemorative Drama," 71–73.

38. See "Acknowledgements," in Virginia Tanner, *Pageant of Portsmouth* (Concord, NH: Rumford, 1923), 94–95; *Seattle Post-Intelligencer,* 15 July 1922, 1.

39. "'Hey Nonny-Nonny' Age at Bryn Mawr," *College News Supplement, Fifty Years of Bryn Mawr College* (1935): 13–14; Evangeline W. Andrews, "With Good Queen Bess at Bryn Mawr," *Puritan* 8 (Sept. 1900): 641–55; "May Day at Bryn Mawr," *Outlook Magazine* 107 (23 May 1914): 147, "Elizabethan May-Day Festivals of Bryn Mawr College, *Bulletin* 26 (1 October 1915): 1.

40. "'Hey Nonny-Nonny' Age at Bryn Mawr."

41. Mary Patricia O'Donnell and Lelia Marion Finan, *Greek Games: An Organization for Festivals* (New York: A. S. Barnes, 1932), 105; Helen Eskine, ed., *To the Gods of Hellas; Lyrics of the Greek Games at Barnard College* (New York: Columbia University Press, 1930); Beegle and Crawford, *Community Drama and Pageantry* has good photographs of the Barnard Games.

42. O'Donnell and Finan, *Greek Games,* 105.

43. Jane Cunningham Croly, *The History of the Woman's Club Movement in America* (New York: Henry G. Allen, 1895) lists thirty-four clubs, but her list barely scratches the surface. Multitudes of Shakespeare clubs were founded in the twentieth

century, after Croly's survey was published. Also, large clubs of diverse interests have frequently formed Shakespeare Departments for a portion of their membership.

44. Pomona Shakespeare Club Papers, Pomona Public Library, Pomona, CA.

45. Isabelle J. Meaker, "Thirtieth Anniversary of the Drama Club, Oct. 13, 1937," Evanston Historical Society, 111.

46. One source that Shakespeare pageant-makers drew on was Percival Chubb et al., *Shakespeare Tercentenary: Suggestions for School and College Celebrations"* (New York: Drama League of America, 1916), which was distributed by the GFWC. It was based on Percival Chubb, "The Shakespeare Tercentenary," *Drama* (Aug. 1915): 531–36.

47. Ethel M. Smith, "Pageantry and the Drama League," *Theatre* 18 (Nov. 1913): 171; idem, "Independence Day Pageant at Washington," *Drama* (Feb. 1914).

48. YWCA Papers, National YWCA Headquarters, New York, New York.

49. *Good Will, the Magician*, Hazel MacKaye Papers. An annotated bibliography of children's peace plays of the era can be found in Elizabeth Miller Lobingier, *Educating for Peace* (Boston: Pilgrim Press, 1930). She includes sixteen plays.

50. *Woman of the Nations: A Pageant for Peace* or *War and Women's Awakening*, Hazel MacKaye Papers; "Pageant Develops New World Democracy," *Albany Argus*, 26 January 1919.

51. In 1916, the National Child Labor Committee presented *Sunshine and Shadow: A Child Labor Pageant* at the City College of New York stadium. In twelve episodes, pantomime and tableaux illustrated abuses against child workers. The program toured the country for two years, attempting to convince spectators of the need for an amendment outlawing child labor. The People's Institute on the Lower East Side in New York City collected children of seventeen nationalities in 1914 to illustrate the *History of New York*. At the Iowa State Fair, dancing potatoes and beans illustrated the importance of a balanced diet. Playground supervisors captivated their charges by contrasting the exuberance of Sunshine, Fresh Air, and Good Food with the somber roles of Disease, Germs, and Bad Teeth. See Mildred Marshall Scouller, *Women Who Man Our Clubs* (Philadelphia: John C. Winston, 1934); Maria Halsey Stryker, "Health Plays, Health Pageants and Health Fairies," *Child Welfare Magazine* 16 (July 1922): 290.

52. See Stella L. Christian, *The History of the Texas Federation of Women's Clubs* (Houston: Texas Federation of Women's Clubs, 1919), 386; Louise Driscoll, "A Pageant of Women," *Drama* 15 (May–June 1924): 263–65, on the New York State Federation of Women's Clubs' Albany pageant in 1923; Minutes of Pomona Woman's Club, (23 Jan. 1922), Pomona Woman's Club Papers, Pomona Public Library, Pomona, CA on their *Voices of the Ages* pageant.

53. Clara Bradley Burdette Papers, Huntington Library, San Marino, California; California Federation of Women's Clubs Papers, University of California at Santa Cruz, California.

54. *Fiftieth Anniversary of the Opening of Vassar College, October 10 to 13, 1915: A Record* (Poughkeepsie: Vassar College, 1916).

55. Ibid., 223.

56. Davol, *Handbook of American Pageantry*, 27.

57. Hazel MacKaye's unpublished memoirs, "Pioneering in Pageantry," are located in the Hazel MacKaye Papers, MacKaye Family Papers, Dartmouth College, Hanover, New Hampshire. Additional biographical detail is available in Lillian Leslie Tower, "Joy of Amateur Theatricals," *Boston Globe* 21 January 1912; Everett E. Truette, "Pageant of Darkness and Light," *Congregationalist and Christian World* (6 May 1911): 607–609; Durward Howes, ed., *American Woman: The Official Who's Who among the Women of the Nation* (Los Angeles: Richard Blank, 1935), 338; "Hazel MacKaye," in *Cyclopedia of American Women*, Box 8-12, Hazel MacKaye Papers; Obituaries: in *Driftwind, a Magazine of Poetry* (October 1944); *New York*

Times 14 August 1944; *New York Herald Tribune* 12 August 1944; *Fitchburg* (MA) *Sentinel* 26 August 1944.

58. Percy MacKaye, *Epoch: The Life of Steele MacKaye* (New York: Boni and Liveright, 1927), 19; Ted Shawn, *Every Little Movement; A Book about Francois Delsarte* (New York: Dance Horizons, 1954); Edwin Osgood Grover, ed., *Annals of an Era: Percy MacKaye and the MacKaye Family, 1826–1932* (Washington, DC: Pioneer Press, 1932).

59. A few details are contained in "Percy MacKaye," in *National Cyclopedia of American Biography*, vol. 14 (New York: James T. White, 1917), 159.

60. Ibid.; Grover, *Annals of an Era*.

61. The National Woman's Party commissioned *Pageant of Susan B. Anthony* or *A Dream of Freedom* in 1915; *Drama Ritual* for the unveiling of the suffrage statue at the Capitol Building in 1921; *Equal Rights Pageant* at Seneca Falls, Garden of the Gods in Colorado, and Westport, NY in 1923 and 1924; *Forward into Light: Inez Milholland Memorial Masque*, in 1924; the Congressional Union commissioned *Suffrage Allegory* in 1913; the Woman's Peace Party commissioned *War and Women's Awakening;* the National Council for the Prevention of War commissioned *Good Will, the Magician;* the YWCA commissioned the *Jubilee Pageant;* the Drama League of America commissioned *"Uncle Sam's Birthday Pageant"* in 1913; Vassar College commissioned *Pageant of Athena;* the Winchester Woman's Club commissioned *Pandora's Box* in 1911. Other causes of interest to women that called on Hazel's writing, organizing or lecturing talents include missionary work, education, the National Federation of Music Clubs, the New York City Men's Equal Suffrage League, the Second Pan-American Scientific Congress, and labor colleges. MacKaye assisted Radcliffe College's Idler Club, the Chelsea Woman's Club, and the Girls' Sewing Guild to prepare plays. She also wrote three lectures on women which she presented at many women's clubs: "Women and the Stage in the Eighteenth Century," "Theatre and Actresses," and "Seven Women Dramatists."

62. Hazel MacKaye, "Confessions of a Convert," *Equal Rights* 1 (19 May 1923): 109–10.

63. For accounts of British models on which Paul drew, see Cicely Hamilton, "Triumphant Women," in *Edy: Recollections of Edith Craig*, ed. Eleanor Adlard (London: Muller, 1949), 38–45; and Elizabeth Robins, *Way Stations* (New York: Dodd, Mead, 1913), 262–69.

64. Joe Mitchell Chapple, "Inauguration of President Wilson," *National Magazine* (April 1913): 17; "Ten Thousand Women March Down Avenue in Fight for Ballot," *Washington Times,* 3 March 1913; "Allegory 'On the Steps' Part of Suffragette Show in Washington," 5 February 1913 clipping in Hazel MacKaye Papers; "Mrs. Taft Will See Procession," *Woman's Journal* 1 March 1913; Hazel MacKaye Memoirs in Hazel Mackaye Papers; Percy MacKaye, "Art and the Woman's Movement," *Forum* 49 (June 1913): 680–85.

65. "Five Thousand Women March for Suffrage Cause," *New York Times,* 4 March 1913; Program for Procession, Hazel MacKaye Papers.

66. *Washington Herald,* 4 March 1913; *New York Times,* 4 March 1913. See also *Washington Times,* 3 March 1913.

67. "Parade Struggles to Victory Despite Scenes," *Woman's Journal,* 1 March 1913 and 8 March 1913.

68. Ibid., 8 March 1913; "Inaugural Crowd of 250,000 Nearly Swamps Great Woman Suffrage Parade," *Philadelphia North American,* 4 March 1914; "Woman's Beauty," *Washington Times,* 4 March 1913; *Washington Post,* 4 March 1913; "Women in Big Pageant, Unprotected, Battle through Avenue Mobs," *Washington Herald,* 4 March 1913; Hazel MacKaye Memoirs in Hazel MacKaye Papers. Some histories of women emphasize the mobs and riots at the expense of the pageant: Eleanor Flexner, *Century of Struggle: The Woman's Rights Movement in the United States* (New York: Atheneum, 1959), 264; William L. O'Neill, *Everyone Was Brave: A History of Femi-*

nism in America (Chicago: Quadrangle Books, 1969), 129; Linda K. Kerber and Jane De Hart-Mathews, eds., *Women's America: Refocusing the Past* (New York: Oxford, 1987), 301; Doris Stevens, *Jailed for Freedom* (New York: Boni and Liveright, 1920), 21; Inez Haynes Irwin, *Angels and Amazons: A Hundred Years of American Women* (Garden City, NY: Doubleday, Doran, 1933), 102; Harriot Stanton Blatch and Alma Lutz, *Challenging Years* (New York: Putnam's, 1940), 196.

69. Hazel MacKaye, quoted in Cynthia Patterson and Bari J. Watkins, "Rites and Rights," in *Women in American Theatre*, ed. Helen Krich Chinoy and Linda Walsh Jenkins (New York: Crown, 1981), 32.

70. "Plays and Pageants in Connection with Woman Suffrage: A Talk by Hazel MacKaye Delivered at the School for Suffrage in Washington, D.C.," 12 December 1913, Hazel MacKaye Papers, Box 1–18.

71. "Six Periods of American Life: A Woman Suffrage Pageant," 1914, in Hazel MacKaye Papers; *New York Times* 18 April 1914; "Pageant Credit to Men's League," *New York Telegraph,* 18 April 1914.

72. *Susan B. Anthony: A Chronicle Pageant,* 1915, Hazel MacKaye Papers; "Antis Refuse Honor Box at Anthony Suffrage Pageant," *Washington Herald,* 14 December 1915; "As Seen by Washington Women," *Washington Herald,* 9 December 1915.

73. Hazel MacKaye to Mrs. Norman de R. Whitehouse, 16 October 1916, Box 1-20 of Hazel MacKaye Papers.

74. MacKaye, "Pioneering in Pageantry," op. cit., 57.

75. "Women Open Fight for Real Equality in New Amendment," *New York Herald* 22 July 1923; "News from Seneca Falls and Rochester," *Equal Rights,* 14 July 1923, 173, 182; "Plans for Seneca Falls and Rochester," *Equal Rights,* 23 June 1923, 130; *New York Herald,* 22 July 1923, 1.

76. *Denver Express,* 23 August 1923; *Colorado Springs Evening Telegraph,* 19 September 1923; *Colorado Springs Sunday Gazette and Telegraph,* 23 September 1923; *Christian Science Monitor,* 24 September 1923; *East St. Louis Journal,* 14 September 1923; *Denver Post,* 23 August 1923; Hazel MacKaye, "Pioneering in Pageantry;" *Colorado Springs Gazette,* 11 September 1923; "Colorado Pageant," *Equal Rights* (1 September 1923): 229; "Memorial Ceremonial Pageant in the Garden of the Gods," *Equal Rights* 237–38, Box 8-12, Hazel MacKaye Papers; "Plans for Colorado's Memorial Pageant," *Equal Rights* (14 September 1923) 243, 247; "Colorado Pageant Inspires Multitudes," *Equal Rights* (6 October 1923), 269.

77. *Equal Rights* 11 (16 August 1924): 211.

78. Herman Hagedorn, "The Pageant at Plymouth," *Outlook* 128 (31 August 1921): 697.

6. The Little Theater Movement

1. Clarence Arthur Perry, *Work of the Little Theatres* (New York: Russell Sage Foundation, 1933), 26, counted 1,020 companies described in *Drama Magazine* from 1925 to 1931. Jack Poggi, *Theatre in America: The Impact of Economic Focus, 1870–1967* (Ithaca: Cornell University Press, 1966), 107, calculated 1,000 companies formed before 1929. Kenneth MacGowan also estimated 1,000 in *Footlights across America* (New York: Harcourt, Brace, 1929), 12.

2. Moss Hart, *Act One* (New York: New American Library, 1959).

3. Glenn Hughes, *History of American Theatre 1708–1950* (New York: Samuel French, 1951), 367.

4. Clayton Hamilton, "Organizing an Audience," *Bookman* 34 (October 1911): 163.

5. Albert McCleery and Carl Glick, *Curtains Going Up* (New York: Pitman, 1939), and MacGowan, *Footlights across America,* identify sixty-three active women.

6. Hughes, *History of American Theatre,* 367.

7. Harold A. Ehrensperger, "Women and the Little Theatre," *Drama* 18 (October 1927): 19–26.
8. *Drama as a Social Factor in Social Education* (New York: George H. Doran, 1924), 31, 47–48.
9. Richard Burton, "Drama League of America," *Nation* 99 (3 December 1914): 668–69.
10. Alexander Dean, *Little Theatre Organization* (New York: D. Appleton, 1926).
11. Alfred G. Arvold, *Little Country Theatre* (New York: Macmillan, 1923), 19.
12. Oliver M. Saylor, *Our American Theatre* (New York: Brentano's, 1923), 234.
13. Percy MacKaye, *Civic Theatre in Relation to the Redemption of Leisure* (New York: Mitchell Kennerly, 1912), 58.
14. Perry, *Work of the Little Theatres*, 56–57.
15. Ibid., 52.
16. Clippings File, Drama League, Lincoln Center Branch of the New York Public Library, New York, New York.
17. As the Drama League declined in size, it ceased to print its membership figures. Instead the league disguised its size by tabulating numerical records like these, for 1925: 115 circles, 350 clubs, 100 colleges, and 100 libraries in the current membership rolls.
18. Alice C. D. Riley's huge bibliography must be assembled from the Riley Scrapbooks, Evanston Historical Society, Evanston, Illinois; the Riley File, Newberry Library, Chicago; and "The Incredible Years" by Riley, an unpublished autobiography owned by her great-granddaughter Alison Blake Ramsey of Portland, Oregon. Among her most important works are the following. With composer Jessie L. Gaynor, Riley wrote children's songs. Her lyrics can be found in *Lilts and Lyrics for the School Room* (Chicago: C. F. Summy, 1907); *Songs of the Child World*, 3 vols. (Cincinnati: J. Church, 1897–1915); *Playtime Songs* (Chicago: C. F. Summy, 1898), which included their most popular song, "Slumber Boat." Many of these songs were sold individually as well. With her daughter Dorothy, Riley wrote fifty songs, collected in *Tunes and Runes* (Chicago: C. F. Summy, 1925). Riley also collaborated on operettas for children. With Gaynor, she wrote *The House that Jack Built* (Chicago: C. F. Summy, 1900); *The Toy Shop* (Chicago: C. F. Summy, 1922); *The Magic Wheel* (Cincinnati: J. Church, 1916); and *Welcome Spring!* (Chicago: C. F. Summy, 1909). With William Otto Miessner, she wrote *Dryad's Kisses* (Milwaukee: Miessner Institute of Music, no date); and with Frederick Fleming Beale she wrote *Fatima* (Boston: C. C. Birchard and Company, no date). Without collaborators, Riley wrote non-musical plays for children to perform. These include *Ten Minutes by the Clock, The Poet's Well, Tom Piper and the Pig,* and *The Blue Prince,* collected in *The Book of Plays for Young People* (New York: George H. Doran, 1923); *The Pool of the Wilful Princess, The Prize Zinnias, The Patchwork People, The King's Great Toe,* and *The Hole in the Wall* (Philadelphia: John C. Winston, no dates); *The Bubble Peddler, The Golden Touch, The Willow Tree,* and *The Ugly Duckling,* collected in *Let's Pretend* (Boston: Walter L. Baker, 1934). For adults she wrote several one-act plays. In *The Mandarin Coat and Five Other Plays for Little Theatres* (New York: Brentano, 1925) can be found *The Mandarin Coat, The Sponge, Their Anniversary, Radio, The Black Suitcase,* and *Skim-Milk.* Plays published by Samuel French in New York include *Taxi* (1927), *Uplifting Sadie* (1932), *The Weathervane Elopes* (1927), and a full-length play, *Little New Moon* (1929). *Rival Peachtrees* can be found in *Seven to Seventeen,* ed. Alexander Dean (New York: Samuel French, 1931). Riley wrote at least two pageants, *The Brotherhood of Man, a Pageant for International Peace* (New York: A. S. Barnes, 1924), and *The Lover's Garden, a Flower Masque arranged from Shakespeare for the Tercentenary* (Chicago: C. F. Summy, 1916). For the Drama League of America, Riley produced bibliographies for students of the theater, including "French Drama Chronologically Studied," *Drama Monthly* 1 (#4, 1916), 198–205, and "Study Course Outline on One-Act Plays," *Drama Monthly* 2 (February 1918), 617–29; 2 (March 1918), 639–46; 3

(April 1918), 8–13. Riley also wrote *Skimming Spain, in Five Weeks, by Motor* (Los Angeles: Saturday Night Publishing, 1931) and *The Elements of English Verse* (Chicago: C. F. Summy, 1905).

19. William L. Blair, *Pasadena Community Book* (Pasadena: A. H. Cawston, 1947), 504–505, identifies Riley's interest in such Chicago clubs as the Garden Club, MacDowell Club, Northwestern University Writer's Guild, Chicago Art Institute, Midland Authors, and Omega Epsilon, the latter a physical education sorority at the Comstock School of Oratory in Evanston. In Pasadena, she belonged to the Pasadena Art Institute, Southern California Women's Press Club, Pasadena Tuesday Morning Drama Class, Pasadena Town Club, and California Writer's Guild.

20. Isabelle J. Meaker, "Thirtieth Anniversary of the Drama Club, October 13, 1937," Evanston Historical Society, Evanston, Illinois.

21. Proceedings, First Annual Convention of the Drama League of America, Thursday, 26 January 1911.

22. Genevieve Wheeler Simpson, "Mrs. A. Starr Best," *Our Congregational Heritage* (1976), 188–90, First Congregational Church of Evanston Papers, Evanston Historical Society, Evanston, Illinois. See also obituaries of her husband in *Chicago Tribune*, 18 June 1950 and *Chicago Sun Times*, 19 June 1950.

23. The men who presided over the Drama League after the terms of Mrs. A. Starr Best (1910–12, 1913–14) and Mrs. Charles Besly (1912–13) were: Dr. Richard Burton (1914–15); Percival Chubb (1915–17); J. Howard Reber (1917–18); Professor Philip Sherman (1918–19); Percival Chubb (1919–20); John H. Stahl (1920–22); Francis Nielson (1922–25); Daniel L. Quirk, Jr. (1925–27); Levi J. Burgess (1927–30); Rev. S. Parkes Cadman (1929–30); and Walter Prichard Eaton, elected in 1931 but never taking office.

24. Mrs. A. Starr Best, "Drama League of America, 1914," *Drama* (February 1914): 136.

25. "Report of the Fourteenth Convention," *Drama* 15 (December 1924): 67.

26. Mrs. A. Starr Best, "Drama League of America," GFWC *Report Tenth Biennial Proceedings* (1910): 286–88.

27. Frank Chocteau Brown, "Drama League," *Theatre* 23 (March 1914): 13.

28. Best, "Drama League of America, 1914," 138.

29. "Drama League Convention, 1914," *Drama* (August 1914): 497.

30. *Drama Monthly* 2 (February 1918): 606.

31. Ibid.

32. J. Vandervoort Sloan, "But T'was a Noble Victory," *Drama* 12 (December 1921): 90.

33. *Drama* 14 (November 1923): 70.

34. Correspondence.

35. The cities where annual conventions were held included: Chicago (22–25 April 1912); New York (11–13 April 1913); Philadelphia (23–25 April 1914); Detroit (21–24 April 1915); New York City (26–29 April 1916); Pittsburgh (25–28 April 1917); Washington, DC (April 1918); Chicago (28–30 April 1921); Evanston (22–24 April 1922); Iowa City (19–21 April 1923); Pasadena (27 May–2 June 1924); Cincinnati (28–30 May 1925); New York (6–8 May 1926); Tacoma (1927); Kansas City, Missouri (19–23 April 1928); 1929—no convention held; dissolution in New York City (1931).

36. "Drama League Activities," *Drama* 11 (October 1920): 28–29; *Drama* 15 (May 1925): 184–85.

37. *Drama Quarterly* was published from February 1911 to May 1919; *Drama Monthly* from October 1919 to May 1930; *Drama Magazine* from February through June 1931.

38. Bibliographies on "Plays for Children" were compiled by Kate Oglesby in 1920 and Cora Mel Patten in 1923; Winifred Ward compiled "Plays for Amateurs" in 1922; see also "Selective List of Essays and Books About the Drama and the Theatre," (Chicago: Drama League of America, 1912).

39. Hallie F. Flanagan, *The Curtain, Drama* 13 (February 1923): 167–69.
40. "Children's Civic Theatre of Chicago," *Drama* 17 (October 1926): 12, 30–31; "A Civic Community Playground," *Theatre Magazine* 28 (December 1919).
41. Christopher Wenn Craig, "The Drama League of America; It's Conception, History, and Contribution to the American Theater, 1909–1931," (M.A. thesis, UCLA, 1965), 75, 58.
42. Thomas H. Dickinson, *Insurgent Theatre* (New York: B. W. Huebsch, 1917), 45.
43. Mary M. Russell, *Drama as a Factor in Social Education* (New York: George H. Doran, 1924), 86.
44. Mrs. A. Starr Best, "A Decade of Experience in Religious Drama," *Drama* (November 1929): 49.
45. Perry, *Work of the Little Theatres*, 185.
46. Maurice Browne, *Too Late to Lament: An Autobiography* (Bloomington, Indiana: Indiana University Press, 1956), 178–79.
47. Helen Deutsch, "The Social Contribution of Amateur Groups," *Drama* 21 (March 1931): 22.
48. Ehrensperger, "Women and the Little Theatre," 26.
49. Shakespeare Club Papers, Shakespeare Club, Pasadena, California.
50. College Woman's Club of Pasadena Papers, Pasadena Historical Society, Pasadena, California.
51. Jessie Ford Wilvas to Eleanor Bissell, 5 November 1953, Eleanor Bissell Papers, Pasadena Historical Society, Pasadena, California.
52. Constitution, Drama League of Pasadena.
53. "Miss Sibyl E. Jones Has Made Drama Main Study," *Pasadena Star-News* 9 October 1919; "Funeral of State College Instructor Set Tomorrow," *San Diego Union*, n.d., Biofile, San Diego Historical Society.
54. Blair, *Pasadena*, 544–45.
55. Ibid., 469–70.
56. Mrs. A. Starr Best, "Echoes," *Drama* 12 (June–August 1922): 322.
57. Biographical material is compiled from membership lists in Pasadena Drama League *Bulletin; Thurston's Pasadena City Directory* (Los Angeles: Los Angeles Directory Co., 1915–51); and Blair, *Pasadena*.
58. Greta Millikan Papers, California Institute of Technology, Pasadena, California.
59. Blair, *Pasadena*, 310–11.
60. Obituary, 1949, Eleanor Bissell Papers.
61. Winter held a B.A. and M.A. from Wellesley College, and wrote two novels, a history of women, and many publications pertinent to club life. In Minneapolis she served on the Child Labor Committee, the Visiting Nurse Association, the Playground Committee, the Public Safety Committee, and the wartime Minnesota Women's Council of Defense. President Harding appointed her to the Arms Limitation Advisory Committee, and she directed the Motion Pictures Procedures Committee in the late 1920s.
62. Alice Baskin, drama critic of the *Pasadena Star-News,* filled in when Dietrich toured Europe on sabbatical. Drama League member Miss Margaret Penney, occasional playwright, sometimes offered the course as well.
63. "Citizen Drama a Success," *Pasadena California Life* 18 (17 December 1921): 21–22.
64. Gail Leo Shoup, Jr., "Pasadena Community Playhouse: Its Origins and History from 1917 to 1942" (Ph.D. diss., UCLA, 1968), 71.
65. Alexander Dean, *Little Theatre Organization and Management* (New York: D. Appleton, 1926), 84–85.
66. "Pasadena Playhouse News," *Drama League Bulletin* (1 October 1925), 10.
67. Ibid.

68. Monroe Lathrop, "Topics in Stageland," *Los Angeles Express,* 13 November 1918.
69. Clipping, Pasadena Community Playhouse Scrapbook One, 25, 26 September 1919.
70. PCP Scrapbook One, 52, 9 December 1919.
71. "Mrs. Hoyt Lauded by Community Players," *Evening Post,* 21 May 1920; "Community Players," *California Life,* 1 May 1920, 21–22.
72. *Pasadena Post,* 10 October 1919.
73. *Star-News* 30 March 1920.
74. "Is Up-To-Date If Ten Years Old," *Star-News,* 24 September 1919.
75. Catherine Turney, interview with Karen Blair, August 1985.
76. Palmer Scrapbook.
77. F. M. Hersey, "Lazarus Laughed," *Drama* 18 (May 1928): 244.
78. Isabel S. Johnson, "Playhouse Productions Meet Variety of Tastes," *PCP News,* 15 November 1927.
79. Shoup, "Pasadena Community Playhouse," 79.
80. The College Women's Club, the Broadoaks Alumnae Association, the Martha Meservel Dancing Class, the Alliance Française, the Pasadena Historical Society, the California Chapter of Mt. Vernon Seminary, and the Cauldron Club also held meetings there.
81. John Langdon-Davies, author of *A Short History of Women* (New York: Viking, 1927), spoke on "Has Marriage a Future?," and Contessa Maria Loschi, Italian feminist and delegate to the International Congress of Women, spoke on "Pirandello."
82. For a list of the celebrities who studied at the school, see Diane Alexander, *Playhouse* (Los Angeles: Dorlese-MacLeish, 1984), 1.
83. "Twenty-Fifth Anniversary Celebration of the Pasadena Playhouse," 1941, Pasadena Playhouse Papers.
84. 12 October 1920 clipping, Bissell Scrapbook.
85. "PCP News," Drama League *Bulletin* (2 October 1928), 10; Mrs. A. Starr Best, "News from Centers," *Drama* 12 (December 1921): 94–95.
86. "Players Club Big Success," *Los Angeles Express,* 16 October 1919.
87. MacGowan, *Footlights across America,* 238–40.
88. Ibid., 233–34.
89. Program, *Bounty Pulls the Strings,* 1 and 2 June 1920, back cover.
90. MacGowan, *Footlights across America,* 334–43, calculated that there were fifty-four women playwrights on the main stage, as follows: 1917 (2); 1918 (3); 1919 (6); 1920 (5); 1921 (3); 1922 (9); 1923 (6); 1924 (5); 1925 (4); 1926 (2); 1927 and 1928 undetermined; 1929 (4) and 7 in workshop production.
91. PCP *News,* 1–21 July 1928.
92. "Drama League Bulletin," PCP *News,* 10 January 1928.
93. "A Career in Professional and University Theatre," 1969 interview with Ralph Freud, p. 112 in Pasadena Playhouse Oral History Project, University of California at Los Angeles.

7. The Clubhouse as Arts Center

1. No reliable compilation of women's clubhouses is known to exist. This figure comes from Sophonsiba P. Breckinridge, *Women in the Twentieth Century: A Study of Their Political, Social, and Economic Activities* (New York: McGraw-Hill, 1933), 82; *General Federation Magazine* 19 (June 1920).
2. See "Own Your Own Home," *General Federation Magazine* 19 (June 1920): 15–40; Ida Clyde Clarke, *Women of Today, 1928* (New York: Woman's Press, 1928), 334 estimated that 2,500 women's clubhouses were owned or rented.
3. See *Yearbooks* of the Friday Morning Club, Huntington Library, San Marino, California.

4. The club, unable to maintain the structure, sold it in 1977 to the Seven Arts Society with the stipulation that the club be permitted to lease the fifth floor for its activities. The building has since been threatened by the wrecker's ball for urban renewal but has survived as of this writing.

5. *Club Women,* the magazine of the California Federation of Women's Clubs, (July 1925): 8–10.

6. Agnes DeMille, interview with Karen J. Blair, autumn 1982.

7. Jane Cunningham Croly, *The History of the Woman's Club Movement in America* (New York: Henry G. Allen, 1898) includes dozens of examples of clubhouses built in the late nineteenth century.

8. Ruth Schwartz Cowan, *More Work for Mother: The Ironies of Household Technology from the Open Hearth to the Microwave* (New York: Basic Books, 1983), 154–60.

9. Ida Clyde Clarke, *American Women and the World War* (New York: D. Appleton, 1918), 110.

10. Ruth Bordin, *Women and Temperance* (Philadelphia: Temple University Press, 1982), 143.

11. "General Federation of Women's Clubs Permanent Home," Washington State Federation of Women's Clubs, *Bulletin* 5 (December 1921): 10.

12. "The Technic of Being a Club Woman," *Ladies Home Journal* 41 (August 1924): 6.

13. Ramona Herdman, "Clubhouse de Luxe," *Woman Citizen* 11 (April 1927): 25–27, 42.

14. "Women's Club Homes," *Woman Citizen* 7 (August 12, 1922): 8–9, 16–17.

15. Breckinridge, *Woman in the Twentieth Century,* 11.

16. This total figure is conservative, based solely on General Federation of Women's Clubs' figures, cited by the National Association of Colored Women, in Sallie W. Stewart, "The Clubhouse Movement," *National Notes* 31 (April 1929): 3–4.

17. Darlene Roth, "Feminine Marks on the Landscape: An Atlanta Inventory," in *American Material Culture: The Shape of Things around Us,* ed. Edith Mayo (Bowling Green, OH: Bowling Green State University Popular Press, 1984), 86.

18. For additional examples of clubhouses built by the end of the 1920s see "Woman's Club Homes," *Woman Citizen* 7 (12 August 1922); "Club Financing by the Extravagant Sex," *Woman Citizen* 7 (26 August 1922); "The Romance of the Atlanta Woman's Club," *Woman Citizen* 7 (7 October 1922); "The Women Did It— Again, Another New Clubhouse," *Woman Citizen* 7 (5 May 1923); "Leagueana," *Junior League Magazine* 16 (January 1930): 76–79.

19. Mrs. J. E. Johnson, "Statistical Report," National Association of Colored Women, *Conference Proceedings* (1933). Her figures were based on 30 replies from 44 state inquiries she sent out. The total does not include the 199 junior or girls' clubs, which contained 3,465 members.

Black women in the California Federation of Colored Women's Clubs built, among others, the Art and Industrial Club, the Madam C. J. Walker Club in San Francisco, the San Francisco Booker T. Mother's Club, the Los Angeles Iroquois, Friday Morning, Civic and Social Club; Stockton's San Joaquin Club; and the Ladies' Monday Club, Sorosis Club, and N.U.G. Art Club shared one building in Sacramento. See A. W. Hinton, "The Club Movement in California," *Crisis* 5 (December 1912): 90–91.

20. For California examples, see "Clubs in California," *Woman Citizen* 7 (4 November 1922): 4; Mrs. John M. Cage, "L.A. District Has Real Club Home," *General Federation Magazine* 9 (May 1929): 12; Marian Seifert, "History of the Woman's Club of Jackson, California, 1980" (Jackson, CA: Woman's Club of Jackson, 1980).

21. Mildred Adams, "Friday Morning's New Home," *Woman Citizen* 7 (7 April 1923), 13–14; Jessica Calhoun Anderson, "Women's Athletic Club of Los Angeles," *California Southland* 7 (October 1925): 9–11; Mary Foster, "The Athletic Club Idea," *Woman Citizen* 10 (March 1926): 22, 39–40.

22. Darlene Roth, "Matronage: Atlanta" (Ph.D. diss., George Washington University, 1978), 336; "The Romance of the Atlanta Woman's Club," 9, 22.
23. Bordin, *Women and Temperance*, 143.
24. GFWC, *Biennial Proceedings* (1924): 264–65.
25. Dorothy Strayer, *The DAR: An Informal History* (Washington, DC: Public Affairs Press, 1958), 206–27.
26. Sallie W. Steward, "With the President: Clubhouse Movement," *National Notes* (April 1925): 3–4; Elizabeth Lindsay Davis, *Lifting as They Climb* (Washington, D.C.: National Association of Colored Women, 1933), 83–84.
27. Marion Talbot and Lois Kimball Mathews Rosenberry, *History of the American Association of University Women, 1881–1931* (Washington, DC: AAUW, 1931), 258–65.
28. Minneapolis Woman's Club seated 650, Rockford, Illinois, Woman's Club (850), Philomusian in Philadelphia (450), Pomona Ebell (700), Woman's Century Club in Seattle (500), Friday Morning Club in Los Angeles (1,118 in Playhouse Theater, 357 in Assembly Hall, 65 in Studio A, 20 in Studio C, and if need be, 500 in the Banquet Hall).
29. Jean Whitby, "Making the Clubhouse Pay, II," *Woman's Journal* 13 (November 1928): 38–40.
30. Eva Noble, "Financing the Clubhouse," *Woman's Journal* 13 (April 1928): 34.
31. Frances Drewry McMullen, "Junior League at Home," *Woman's Journal* 15 (January 1930): 47–48.
32. Jessie I. Spafford, "A Club that Mothers a City," *Woman Citizen* 12 (October 1927): 20, 32, 33.
33. Henry Hope Reed, "Elsie De Wolfe," in *Notable American Women*, vol. 1, ed. Edward T. James et al. (Cambridge: Harvard University Press, 1971), 469–71.
34. *The House in Good Taste* (New York: Century, 1913), 277.
35. Ibid., 235–36.
36. Lillie Hamilton French, "The New Colony Club," *Harpers Bazaar* 41 (June 1907): 554–59; Bertha Damaris Knobe, "The New York Women's Colony Club," *Harper's Bazaar* 40 (April 1906): 340–46; Olivia Howard Dunbar, "The Newest Woman's Club," *Putnam's* 2 (May 1907): 196–206; Anne O'Hagan, "The Colony Club," *Century* 81 (December 1910): 216–24; Elsie De Wolfe, "The Story of the Colony Club," *Delineator* 78 (November 1911): 370–71.
37. *Ebell Magazine* (October 1933): 7–8.
38. Scrapbook, Pomona Ebell Club, Pomona Public Library, Pomona, California.
39. Charter Day Reminiscences (Los Angeles: Wilshire Ebell, 1977).
40. Ronald Pisano, *One Hundred Years: The National Association of Women Artists* (New York: National Organization of Women Artists, 1989), 15.
41. Janet Gordon and Diana Reische, *Volunteer Powerhouse* (New York: Rutledge Press, 1982), 83.
42. Sally M. Ferguson et al., comps., *National Society of the Colonial Dames of America Museum Houses, 1982* (Washington, DC: the organization, 1982); *National Society of the Colonial Dames of America: Its Beginnings, Its Purpose and a Record of Its Work 1891–1913* (Washington, DC: the organization, 1913); Mrs. J. W. E. Moore, "Evansview and Other Museum Houses of the Colonial Dames of America," *Historic Preservation* 16 (September–October 1964): 166–71; Mrs. Joseph Rucker Lamar, "Bellevue: The Home of the National Society of Colonial Dames," *Maryland Historical Magazine* 24 (June 1929): 99–112.
43. Roth, "Matronage," 349.
44. Grace Louis Camdus (Mrs. Henry Carr) Ward, comp., *State History of the New Jersey DAR* (Sea Isle, NJ: Atlantic Printing and Publishing, 1929), 102, 69, 114, 235, 186.
45. See Mollie D. Somerville, *Historical and Memorial Buildings of the DAR* (Washington, DC: DAR, 1979).

46. "Indiana Women to Buy Famous Old Club Home," *General Federation News* 2 (December 1921): 5.
47. "The Women Did It Again," *Woman Citizen* 7 (5 May 1923): 13, 29.
48. Marian Seifert, "History of the Woman's Club of Jackson, California, 1980" (Jackson, CA: Woman's Club of Jackson, 1980).
49. "Good Business Heads in Women's Clubs," *Woman Citizen* 7 (21 October 1922): 11.
50. "Club Financing by the Extravagant Sex," *Woman Citizen* 7 (26 August 1922): 8.
51. Friday Morning Club, *Yearbook* (1919–1920).
52. Ibid.
53. Minutes, Pasadena Shakespeare Club.
54. Ibid.; "Club Financing by the Extravagant Sex," 7–8, 16–17.
55. "History," Ebell, *Yearbook* (1927–28).
56. Frederica de Laguna, "Recent Amendments," *Ebell Magazine* 1 (January 1928): 5.
57. Roth, "Matronage," 106.
58. "Clubs in California," *Woman Citizen* 7 (4 November 1922): 4.
59. Pomona Ebell, in 1925 and 1926, offered the public rates such as these: entire clubhouse for an afternoon ($40) or an evening ($45); large auditorium for an afternoon ($20) or an evening ($25); small auditorium for an afternoon ($12.50) or an evening ($15); one parlor ($2.50) or two ($5); the kitchen for dinner ($7.50) or tea and punch ($5). In this way, club treasuries could accumulate considerable sums. See Pomona Ebell, *Yearbook* (1925–26). The Friday Morning Club of Los Angeles earned $4,084 from 250 rentals in 1920–21. The Pasadena Shakespeare Club earned $2,162 in that year, but earnings jumped to $5,995 in 1927–28 when its new auditorium opened.
60. Friday Morning Club, *Yearbook* (1926–27).
61. Katherine Barrette Parsons, *History of Fifty Years: Ladies' Literary Club of Salt Lake City, Utah, 1877–1927* (Salt Lake City: Arrow Press, 1927), 32.
62. Florence R. Clauss, "Refrigeration for Clubhouses," *Woman's Journal* (May 1928): 34–35; L. Ray Balderston, "Conveniences in the Kitchen," *Woman's Journal* 14 (December 1929): 38; Ferne E. Taylor, "Efficient Clubhouse Kitchen," *Woman's Journal* 14 (August 1929): 28–29; Elizabeth Ellam, "Club Laundry," *Woman Citizen* 12 (December 1927): 32–33; Cora S. Henry, "Club Restaurant," *Woman's Journal* 13 (January 1928): 34–35; "Club Kitchen," *Woman Citizen* 12 (November 1927): 30–31.
63. "What Clubwomen Eat," *Woman's Journal* 13 (March 1928): 34–35.
64. Mabel J. Carter, "A Clubhouse Cafeteria," *Woman's Journal* 13 (July 1928): 28–29.
65. Ibid.
66. Beatrice DeLima Meyers, "The Dining Room Shall Not Close," *Woman's Journal* 14 (April 1929): 38.
67. Jean Whitby, "Rugs and Carpets," *Woman's Journal* 14 (September 1919): 30; Ruth O'Brien, "Curtaining Home and Clubhouse," *Woman's Journal* 4 (November 1929): 36, 38; idem, "Clothing the Clubhouse," *Woman's Journal* 14 (June 1929): 36–38, 40.
68. Jean Whitby, "Keeping the Clubhouse Clean," *Woman's Journal* 13 (December 1928): 39–40.
69. Julia W. Bingham, "Beware's for Buyers," *Woman's Journal* 15 (January 1930): 36–38.
70. Pomona Ebell Minutes: 21 January 1918; 2 July 1917; 5 November 1917; 3 December 1917; 30 July 1920; 7 April 1919; 3 September 1919; 6 October 1924.
71. For example, the San Francisco Woman's Club. See "World News about Women," *Woman Citizen* 12 (November 1927): 28–29.
72. Florence Morton, "When Women Build for Women," *Woman's Journal* 14 (June 1929): 18–19, 44.

73. Frances Drewry McMullen, "The Junior League at Home," *Woman's Journal* 15 (January 1930), 15, 47–48.

74. Sara Boutelle, *Julia Morgan, Architect* (New York: Abbeville Press, 1988), 85.

75. These include the Berkeley Woman's City Club, the Monday Club House in San Luis Obispo, the Saratoga Foothill Woman's Club, the Sausalito Woman's Club, the Santa Maria Minerva Club, and the enlarged Woman's Century Club in San Francisco. Some sources suggest she also built the original turn-of-the-century Friday Morning Club in Los Angeles.

76. Julian C. Mesic, "Berkeley Woman's City Club," *Architect and Engineer* 105 (April 1931): 25–47; Boutelle, *Julia Morgan, Architect;* Elinor Richey, "Julia Morgan," in *Notable American Women, the Modern Period,* ed. Barbara Sicherman (Cambridge: Harvard University Press, 1980), 499–501.

77. Agnes Addison Gilchrist, "Minerva Parker Nichols," in *Notable American Women,* vol. 2, 629–30; Jane Cunningham Croly, *The History of the Woman's Club Movement in America* (New York: Henry G. Allen, 1898), 332–34 and 1021–1027.

78. *Ladies Home Journal* (October 1914): 3.

79. Harriet Rochlin, "A Distinguished Generation of Women Architects in California," *American Institute of Architects Journal* (August 1977): 38–42.

80. "New Association Building," *YWCA Association Monthly Magazine* (February 1926): 114.

81. Genevieve James Papers, Scrapbooks, Young Women's Christian Association, New York City.

82. Robert S. Lynd and Helen Merrill Lynd, *Middletown* (New York: Harcourt, Brace, Jovanovich, 1929), 63.

83. M. E. Eddy, First Annual Report of the Rhode Island Woman's Club (1877), 7.

84. Nancy F. Cott, *The Grounding of American Feminism* (New Haven: Yale University Press, 1987); J. Stanley Lemons, *The Woman Citizen: Social Feminism in the 1920s* (Urbana: University of Illinois Press, 1973); Carroll Smith-Rosenberg, *Disorderly Conduct: Visions of Gender in Victorian America* (New York: Oxford University Press, 1985); Estelle Freedman, "Separatism as Strategy: Female Institution Building and American Feminism, 1870–1930," *Feminist Studies* 5 (Fall 1979): 512–29.

SELECTED BIBLIOGRAPHY

While the citations in the endnotes offer many suggestions for readers, they do not enumerate all of the influential manuscript collections, unpublished materials, and primary and secondary sources that assisted me in creating this account. Here, I have identified the most significant bibliography on each topic in *The Torchbearers*.

Chapter 1: "The Arts in Nineteenth-Century American Women's Lives." My description of proscriptive literature on antebellum women's behavior relies on the extensive holdings of nineteenth-century periodicals and etiquette books for "ladies" at the Henry E. Huntington Library in San Marino, California. The periodicals include *American Ladies Magazine* (1828–34), *Arthur's Ladies' Magazine of Literature, Fashion and the Fine Arts* (1844–46), *Godey's Lady's Book* (1832–97), *Ladies' Companion* (1839–43), *Ladies' Diadem* (1848–51), *Ladies' Garland* (1824–28, 1837–39), *Ladies' Keepsake and Home* (1852–54), *Ladies' Literary Cabinet* (1819–25), *Ladies Museum* (1825–26), *Ladies' Musical Library* (1842), *Ladies' Wreath* (1846–62), *Ladies' Weekly Museum* (1788–1817), *Philadelphia Album and Ladies' Literary Portfolio* (1826–34), *Young Ladies' Fair* (1854–55), *Young Ladies' Offering* (1843–57), and *Young Lady's Guide* (1870). The etiquette books include *Young Lady's Mentor: A Guide to the Formation of Character in a Series of Letters to Her Unknown Friends. By a Lady* (Philadelphia: H. C. Peck and T. Bliss, 1858); *Young Lady's Own Book: A Manual of Intellectual Improvement and Moral Deportment* (Philadelphia: no publisher, 1836); Almira H. L. Phelps, *Female Student* (New York: Leavitt, Lord, 1839); Lydia Sigourney, *Letters to Young Ladies* (New York: Harper, 1837) and *Ladies' Companion and Letters to My Pupils* (New York: Robert Carter, 1860); Catharine Beecher, *Treatise on Domestic Economy for the Use of Young Ladies at Home and at School* (Boston: Marsh, Capen, Lyon and Webb, 1841); *Young Lady's Own Book* (Philadelphia: Desilver, Thomas, 1836); *Young Lady's Mentor* (Philadelphia: H. C. Peck and Theodore Bliss, 1860); *Young Lady's Guide* (New York: American Tract Society, 1870); *Ladies' Keepsake* (New York: J. S. Taylor, 1852–54).

The Winterthur Library at the Henry I. Dupont Winterthur Museum in Winterthur, Delaware, holds several instructional guides for young women of the period. Among these are Maria Turner, *Young Ladies' Assistant in Drawing and Painting* (Cincinnati: Corey and Fairbank, 1833); Maria Turner, *Rudiments of Drawing and Shadowing Flowers in Pencil in Sixty-Four Lessons* (Boston: Monroe and Francis, 1827); Mrs. Anne Hill, *Drawing Book of Flowers and Fruit* (Philadelphia: E. C. Biddle, n.d.); William Minifie, *Three Lectures on Drawing and Design* (Baltimore: William Minifie, 1852). On the subject of early education for women, Thomas Woody's *A History of Women's Education in the United States* (New York: Science Press, 1929) is a classic. On early art education, see Phyllis I. Peet, "The Emergence of American Women Printmakers in the Late Nineteenth Century," Ph.D. diss., University of California at Los Angeles, 1987. The author was extremely generous in sharing sources and details with me, on early women students and teachers. For the field of early music education, three authors stand out for their exemplary scholarship. They are Judith Tick, for

American Women Composers before 1870 (Ann Arbor: UMI Research Press, 1983) and "Passed Away Is the Piano Girl: Changes in American Musical Life, 1870–1900," in *Women Making Music,* ed. Jane Bowers and Judith Tick (Urbana: University of Illinois Press, 1986); Adrienne Fried Block and Carol Neuls-Bates, compilers and editors, *Women in American Music; A Bibliography of Music and Literature* (Westport, CT: Greenwood Press, 1979).

On the question of post–Civil War women as students of the arts, I turned to college catalogs at Vassar, Smith, Elmira, Wellesley, Radcliffe, and Mount Holyoke colleges. Amy Fay's autobiographical account, *Music-Study in Germany* (New York: Macmillan, 1900) is a classic. Lois Fink, in our conversations at the National Museum of American Art at the Smithsonian Institution in Washington, DC, and in her book, *American Art at the Nineteenth-Century Paris Salons* (New York: Cambridge University Press, 1990) provided many insights on painting studies abroad. The three-volume biographical encyclopedia *Notable American Women,* edited by Edward T. James, Janet Wilson James, and Paul S. Boyer (Cambridge, MA: Belknap Press of Harvard University Press, 1971), and its supplement, subtitled *The Modern Period,* edited by Barbara Sicherman (Cambridge: Belknap Press of Harvard University Press, 1980) provided numerous details about the lives of women artists in the American past.

Chapter 2: "Arts and Activism." The most valuable and under-utilized collection of women's club materials, from 1890 to the present, is held at the national headquarters of the General Federation of Women's Clubs in Washington, DC. The archive there contains conference proceedings, club periodicals, biographical files on officers, unpublished histories and reminiscences of club activities, newspaper clippings, and executive reports of the national organization and also of many local clubs and state and regional federations of clubs. Cynthia N. Swanson and Lisa C. Mangiafico's *Guide to the Archives of the General Federation of Women's Clubs* (Washington, DC: General Federation of Women's Clubs, 1992) has just been published.

Many state federation collections have proven immensely valuable to me as well. Among those I have visited are the Rhode Island Federation of Women's Clubs Papers at the Rhode Island Historical Society in Providence, Rhode Island; the New York State Federation of Women's Clubs Papers at Elmira College, Elmira, New York; the Washington State Federation of Women's Clubs Papers, currently at the University of Washington, Seattle; and the Massachusetts State Federation of Women's Club Papers at their headquarters in Quincy, Massachusetts. These collections contain newsletters, scrapbooks of clippings, correspondence, conference proceedings, bulletins, yearbooks, treasurer's reports, minutes, and periodicals, not only for the state federations but for many of their member clubs as well.

Local clubs have collected their minutes, yearbooks, treasurer's reports, news clippings, photographs, unpublished reminiscences, eulogies to deceased members, and even, occasionally, copies of papers delivered by the membership. Among the club records most useful to me were those of the Olympia Woman's Club in Olympia, Washington; the Friday Morning Club and Ebell of Los Angeles at the Henry E. Huntington Library; Sorosis of New York City at the Sophia Smith Collection, Smith College, Northampton, Massachusetts; the New England Woman's Club of Boston and fifty-four other New England clubs, at the Arthur and Elizabeth Schlesinger Library on the History of Women in America, Radcliffe College, Harvard University, Cambridge, Massachusetts; the Downey Women's Club in the Downey Historical Society, Downey, California; the Fortnightly Club at the Newberry Library, Chicago; the Worcester Women's Club at the Worcester Historical Society, Worcester, Massachusetts; the Pasadena Study Club and the Pasadena College Women's Club at the Pasadena Historical

Society, Pasadena, California; the Shakespeare Club of Pasadena; and the Pomona Shakespeare Club, Pomona Women's Club, and Pomona Ebell Club at the Pomona Public Library, Pomona, California.

The papers of several prominent clubwomen were helpful to me: the Esther Maltby Scrapbooks at the University of Washington, the Anna Pennybacker Papers at the University of Texas at Austin, and the Clara Bradley Burdette Papers and the Caroline Severance Papers at the Henry E. Huntington Library. Scholars who wish to locate additional manuscript collections of clubwomen and their organizations are advised to consult Andrea Hinding, *Women's History Sources* (New York: R. R. Bowker, 1979). Even though it is now out of date, it is still the most comprehensive listing of archival collections on women's voluntary activities.

Numerous periodicals from 1890 to 1930 published regular accounts of women's club activities. *The Ladies' Home Journal*, for instance, provided generous coverage from 1915 to 1930. In 1924, Alice Ames Winter, former president of the General Federation of Women's Clubs, joined the staff and contributed a monthly article on member projects. She was a columnist until 1929, when President Bettie M. Sippel began to offer articles about club progress during her administration, through 1932. Strong coverage of women's organizational development may be found in *California Club Woman*, 1900; *California Life* (later *Californian, Maryland-Huntington Life*, and *Pasadena California Life*), 1925–37; *California Southland*, 1919–30; *California Women's Bulletin*, 1912–16; *California Woman's Home and Club Journal*, 1909; *Clubwoman*, the Magazine of the California Federation of Women's Clubs, 1922–28; *Clubwoman*, 1909–19; *Connecticut Club Corner*, the Magazine of the Connecticut State Federation of Women's Clubs, 1928; *Connecticut Club Courier*, 1933; *Crisis*, the Journal of the National Association for the Advancement of Colored People, 1910–19; *Equal Rights*, 1923–30; *Federation Bulletin*, the Magazine of the Massachusetts State Federation of Women's Clubs, 1919–29; *The General Federation of Women's Clubs Magazine*, 1903–1920; *General Federation News*, 1920–30; *General Federation Clubwoman*, 1930; *Hartford Woman*, 1921–22; *Independent Woman*, 1922; *Junior League Magazine*, 1927–32; *Minnesota Clubwoman*, 1926–28; *National Notes*, the Official Magazine of the National Association of Colored Women, 1926–30; *North Dakota Club Bulletin*, 1922; *Oregon Woman's Magazine*, 1919; *Oregon Clubwoman* (later *The Oregon Federation News*), 1925–31; *Rhode Island Clubwoman*, 1926; Washington State Federation of Women's Clubs *Bulletin*, 1920–30; *Western Woman*, 1929–30; *Woman Patriot*, 1927–28; *Woman Voter*, 1911–16; *Woman's Home Companion*, 1925–28.

In addition, the University of North Carolina Extension in Chapel Hill, North Carolina, published a series of *Bulletins* for women's clubs during the 1920s. These were bibliographic guides for club study on a particular topic. For example, Cornelia Spencer Love prepared "Good Books of 1923–24: A Program for Women's Clubs," 3 (1 May 1924) and "Good Books of 1924–25," 3 (1 October 1925). Dougald MacMillan wrote "Recent Tendencies in the Theatre: A Program for Women's Clubs," 2 (1 April 1923); Russell Potter, "A Study of Shakespeare: A Program for Women's Clubs," 5 (1 January 1926); Ethel Theodora Rockwell, "A Study Course in American One-Act Plays: A Program for Women's Clubs," 4 (1 November 1924). In 1929, *Scribner's Magazine* offered a regular "Club Corner," and in June 1910, *The Chautauquan* published a special issue devoted to women's clubs.

Other collections of material for and about clubwomen include Alice Ames Winter, *The Business of Being a Clubwoman* (New York: Century, 1925); and Caroline French Benton, *Woman's Club Work and Programs, or First Aid to Club Women* (Boston:

Dana Estes, 1913) and *The Complete Club Book for Women* (Boston: L. C. Page, 1915). Simple lists of active clubs can be found in Helen M. Winslow, ed., *Annual Register of Women's Clubs*, vols. 1–31 (Shirley, MA: Helen M. Winslow, 1898–1930); Ida Clyde Clarke, *Women of Today* (Chicago: John C. Winston, 1923; New York: Women of Today Press, 1925–29); and Mrs. M. Burton Williamson, comp., *Ladies Clubs and Societies in Los Angeles in 1892* (Los Angeles: Historical Society of Southern California, 1892).

Dissertations that assisted me included B. A. Culp, "The History of the Gainesville XLI Club and Its Relation to the General Women's Club Movement" (M.A. thesis, North Texas State College, Denton, Texas, 1951); Gayle Gullett, "Feminism, Politics, and Voluntary Groups: Organized Womanhood in California, 1886–96" (Ph.D. diss., University of California at Riverside, 1983); Tulia Brown Hamilton, "The National Association of Colored Women, 1896–1920" (Ph.D. diss., Emory University, 1978); Lucile Evelyn LaGanke, "The National Society of the Daughters of the American Revolution: Its History, Policies, and Influence, 1890–1949" (Ph.D. diss., Western Reserve University, 1951); Dorothy Edwards Powers, "Chicago Woman's Club" (Ph.D. diss., University of Chicago, 1939); Ruth Reed, "Negro Women of Gainesville, Georgia" (M.A. thesis, University of Georgia, 1921); Barbara Spencer Spackman, "Women's City Club of Chicago: A Civic Pressure Group" (M.A. thesis, University of Chicago, 1930); Gillian Weiss, "As Woman and As Citizens: Clubwomen in Vancouver, 1910–1928" (Ph.D. diss., University of British Columbia, 1983).

My survey of 678 published sources on *The History of American Women's Voluntary Organizations, 1810–1960: A Guide to Sources* (Boston: G. K. Hall, 1989) provided substantial background for my interpretation of club records. The most outstanding titles are Jane Cunningham Croly, *The History of the Woman's Club Movement in America* (New York: Henry G. Allen, 1898); Mary I. Wood, *The History of the General Federation of Women's Clubs* (Norwood, ME: Norwood Press, 1912); Elizabeth Lindsay Davis, *Lifting as They Climb: The History of the National Association of Colored Women* (Washington, DC: National Association of Colored Women, 1933); Mildred White Wells, *Unity in Diversity: The History of the General Federation of Women's Clubs* (Washington, DC: General Federation of Women's Clubs, 1953). Mildred Marshall Scouller, *Women Who Man Our Clubs* (Philadelphia: John C. Winston, 1934) contains biographies of prominent clubwomen; Mary K. O. Eagle, *The Congress of Women: The World's Columbia Exposition, Chicago, USA, 1893* (Chicago: W. A. Reeve, 1895) contains 189 speeches delivered by clubwomen at the world's fair, on topics they had previously spoken about in their own clubs.

Numerous clubwomen published histories of their local societies. Among those works are Julia A. Sprague, *The History of the New England Woman's Club from 1868 to 1893* (Boston: Lee and Shepard, 1894); Katherine Barrette Parsons, *The History of the Fifty Years, Ladies' Literary Club, Salt Lake City, Utah, 1877–1927* (Salt Lake City: Arrow Press, 1927); Marguerite Dawson Winant, *A Century of Sorosis, 1868–1968* (Uniondale, NY: Salisbury Printers, 1968); Alice H. Williams, *Prologue: A History of the Birmingham Branch, American Association of University Women, 1907–68* (Birmingham: American Association of University Women, 1968); Henriette Greenebaum Frank and Amalie Jerome Hofer, comps., *Annals of the Chicago Woman's Club, 1876–1916* (Chicago: Chicago Woman's Club, 1916).

Histories of state federations include Mary S. Gibson, *A Record of Twenty-Five Years of the California Federation of Women's Clubs, 1900–1925* (Los Angeles: California Federation of Women's Clubs, 1927); Mrs. Frederick Hanger and Miss Clara B. Eno, *The History of the Arkansas Federation of Women's Clubs 1897–1934* (Lewisville, AR: Arkansas Federation of Women's Clubs, 1935); Ruth Kennerly Harcum et al., comps., *The History of the Maryland Federation of Women's Clubs, 1890–1941* (Federalsburg, MD: J. W. Stowell, 1941); Annie Laws, ed., *The History of the Ohio Federation of Women's Clubs for the First Thirty Years, 1894–1924* (Cincinnati: Ebbert and Richardson, 1924); Mildred Wells, *The History of the Alabama Federation of Women's Clubs 1917–1968* (Montgomery, AL: Paragon Press, 1968); Stella L. Christian, *The History of the Texas Federation of Women's Clubs* (Houston: Dealy-Adey-Elgin, 1919).

Many modern scholars have addressed themselves to the activities of women's organizations in history. See Paula Baker, "Domestication of Politics: Women and American Political Society, 1780–1920," *American Historical Review* 89 (June 1984): 620–47; Estelle Freedman, "Separatism as Strategy: Female Institution Building and American Feminism, 1870–1930," *Feminist Studies* 59 (Fall 1970): 512–29; Karen J. Blair, *The Clubwoman as Feminist: True Womanhood Redefined, 1868–1914* (New York: Holmes and Meier, 1980); Anne Firor Scott, *The Southern Lady: From Pedestal to Politics 1830–1930* (Chicago: University of Chicago Press, 1970), and *Natural Allies: Women's Associations in American History* (Urbana: University of Illinois Press, 1992): William L. O'Neill, *Everyone Was Brave: A History of Feminism in America* (Chicago: Quadrangle, 1969); Nancy F. Cott, *The Grounding of Modern Feminism* (New Haven: Yale University Press, 1987); J. Stanley Lemons, *The Woman Citizen: Social Feminism in the 1920's* (Urbana: University of Illinois Press, 1973); Cynthia Neverdon-Morton, *Afro-American Women of the South and the Advancement of the Race, 1895–1925* (Knoxville: University of Tennessee Press, 1989).

Chapter 3: "Hear America First." Materials on women's music clubs are accessible at the Library of Congress Music Division in Washington, DC, where the National Federation of Music Clubs publications and convention reports are available in full. Also available there are two accounts by Ruth Haller Ottaway: "Historical Highlights of the Federation, 1898–1935" *Proceedings* of the National Federation of Music Clubs (1935) and "Music Clubs, a Significant Factor in National Development," *Proceedings* of the Music Teachers National Association (1931); and the National Convention of Women's Amateur Music Clubs *Proceedings* from the 1893 Chicago Columbian Exposition. Marian MacDowell's Papers and the MacDowell Colony Papers are also held at the Library of Congress, in the Manuscript Division. The University of New Hampshire, Durham, New Hampshire, holds papers pertinent to the last years of MacDowell's life. Other useful collections of music materials: the Bessie Bartlett Frankel Papers at UCLA; Seattle Ladies Musical Club Papers, now at the Seattle Historical Society, Museum of History and Industry, Seattle, Washington; Bellingham Musical Club, Music Library of Western Washington University, Bellingham, Washington; the Wednesday Afternoon Music Club, Bridgeport, Connecticut at the Bridgeport Public Library, Bridgeport, Connecticut; Clef Club Papers, Forbes Library, Northampton, Massachusetts; Raleigh Music Club, State Library, Raleigh, North Carolina; New England Conservatory Club, University of Oregon, Eugene, Oregon; Tuesday Musicale Papers, Pasadena, California. The Grace Spofford Papers at the Sophia Smith Collection, Smith College, Northampton, Massachusetts, deal with women in conservatories; The Fadettes (Women's Orchestra of Boston) Papers are held by the Arthur and Elizabeth Schlesinger Library, Radcliffe College, Harvard University, Cambridge, Massachusetts. At the New York Historical Society in New York City, I used the Papers of Florence Edith (Mrs. Theodore) Sutro, concerning her efforts to win recognition for voicing the need for a music club federation in the early 1890s.

Unpublished music club histories include the Zylpha Morton Papers at the Minnesota Historical Society, St. Paul, which contain her unpublished "Brief History of the Schubert Club, 1882–1962." The Idaho Historical Society in Boise, Idaho, holds an unpublished "Idaho Federation of Music Clubs History, 1923–52"; Mrs. Arthur Leather and Mrs. Don Healy, "Music and Art Foundation, Seattle: Historical Sketch, 1923–27," is at the Seattle Music and Art Foundation; Mrs. Herbert Welker Coble, "History of the North Carolina Federation of Music Clubs, May 1961," in the Federation Papers and Mrs. B. W. Barnett, "Treble Clef Club of Charlotte, North Carolina: History," both at the North Carolina Department of Cultural Resources, State Library, Raleigh, North Carolina.

Periodicals useful to researchers include *Etude* (1901–34), *Musical America* (1898–1930); *Musical Courier* (1880–1930); *Musical Digest* (1920–30); *Musical Leader* (1895–1930); *Musical Monitor* (1914–24); National Federation of Music Clubs *Official Proceedings* (1898–1930), *Music Club Magazine* of National Federation of Music Clubs, *Official Bulletin* (1922–28), and *Music Clubs Magazine* (1928–30); General Federation of Women's Clubs *Magazine* (1903–20); *General Federation News* (1920–30); *General Federation Clubwoman* (1930) and Biennial Convention *Proceedings* (1890–1930); and Music Teachers National Association *Proceedings* (1928–31).

The published sources of note include Sir George Grove, ed., *Grove's Dictionary of Music and Musicians* (New York: W. W. Norton, 1938) and Stanley Sadie, ed., *New Grove Dictionary of Music and Musicians,* 20 vol. (London: Macmillan, 1980) and two memoirs; Adella Prentiss Hughes, *Music Is My Life* (Cleveland: World Publishing, 1947) and Walter Damrosch, *My Musical Life* (New York: Scribner's, 1926). See Agnes Martin, comp., *History of the Euterpe Club* (Greensboro, NC: Euterpe Club, 1939); Karen J. Blair, "The Seattle Ladies Musical Club, 1890–1930," in *Experiences in a Promised Land: Essays in Pacific Northwest History,* ed. G. Thomas Edwards and Carlos A. Schwantes (Seattle: University of Washington Press, 1986): 124–38; C. M. Tremaine, *The First Music Week* (New York: National Bureau for the Advancement of Music, 1920) and *The History of National Music Week* (New York: National Bureau for the Advancement of Music, 1925). A bibliography for music study is available in Paul John Weaver, "Great Composers 1600–1900: A Course of Study for Music Clubs," *University of North Carolina Extension Bulletin* 4 (1 May 1925).

Chapter 4: "Women's Societies for the Visual Arts." Art club material is plentiful at the library of the National Museum of American Art, Smithsonian Institution, Washington, D.C. I used the American Federation of Art's manuscripts, *American Art Annual* (v. 1–26, 1898–1929), and its magazine, entitled *Art and Progress* (1909–15), *American Magazine of Art* (1915–19), and *Magazine of Art* (1919–30). I also studied the Hartford Art Club Papers at the Stowe-Day Foundation, Hartford, Connecticut; the Ella Bond Johnston Papers at the Richmond Art Museum, Richmond, Indiana; the Ruskin Art Club Papers at the Southwest Museum Los Angeles; and U.S. Commission of Fine Arts Papers at the National Archives, Washington, DC.

Unpublished club accounts include the "History of the Minnesota State Art Society, 1903–04," at the Minnesota Historical Society, St. Paul; Laurena Alliott, "History of the Ruskin Club, 1888–1948" and Helen Williams Witmer, "History of the Ruskin Club, 1948–60" in the club papers, Southwest Museum, Los Angeles; Annie Prescott, "History of the Auburn Art Club, 1880–1920," in the Papers of the Auburn Art Club, Public Library, Auburn, Maine; and Lucy Pope Taylor, Harriette Barney, and Mary Salinda Foster, comps., "The First Fifty Years, Mankato Art History Club, 1896–1946," Papers of Mankato Art History Club, Blue Earth County Historical Society, Mankato, Minnesota. A valuable published work is Stella J. Rausch and Carrie B.

Robinson, *Our First Twenty Years, 1912–1932: The Women's Art Club of Cleveland* (Cleveland: Central Publishing House, 1933).

Also helpful was Suzanne M. Pate, "The History of the Spokane Art League" (Senior Honors Paper, Eastern Washington University, 1985). I am indebted to Kimberly Dawn Finley's "Cultural Monitors: Clubwomen and Public Art Instruction in Chicago, 1890–1920" (Ph.D. diss., Ohio State University, 1989), and to Elizabeth Roark, who supplied me with materials on the "Collection Presented to the Pittsburgh Schools by the One Hundred Friends of Pittsburgh Art," on exhibit 7–29 September 1985 at the University Art Gallery, University of Pittsburgh. Periodicals of importance, in addition to the aforementioned publications of the American Federation of Art, include *American City*, the General Federation of Women's Clubs *Magazine* and Biennial *Proceedings* (1890–1930), and Rose V. S. Berry's series of columns on art study for women's clubs in *Scribner's Magazine* 83 (1928).

Chapter 5: "Pageantry and the Women's Rights Movement, 1905–1925." The Papers of the American Pageantry Association are not collected at any single archive. Scholars of pageantry must patch together its history from collections of participants, its *Bullletin,* the programs and libretti of pageants, newspaper coverage, and women's club reports of specific pageants. Hazel MacKaye's story was assembled from her correspondence, photographs, and texts of pageants in the MacKaye Family Papers at Dartmouth College, Hanover, New Hampshire, and discussions with her nieces, Christy MacKaye Barnes and Arvia MacKaye Ege. The national headquarters of the Young Women's Christian Association, New York City, has archival materials relating to the many 1916 Jubilee Pageants that were celebrated by "Ys" all over the world. Two useful dissertations are Martin S. Tackel, "Women and American Pageantry: 1908–18" (Ph.D. diss; University of New York, 1982) and Frederick George Walsh, "Outdoor Commemorative Drama in the U.S., 1900–1950" (Ph.D. diss., Western Reserve University, 1952).

Periodicals worth combing include the American Federation of Arts' *American Art Annual* and magazine (*Art and Progress* from 1909 to 1915, *American Magazine of Art* from 1915 to 1919, and *Magazine of Art* after 1919), which made an effort to include not only painting news but information about other artistic endeavors as well. Likewise, the magazine of the Drama League of America discussed pageantry with some frequency, even though it stressed activities of little theaters. The March 1913 women's rights parade and pageant was widely reported by *Woman's Journal, New York Times, Washington Post, Philadelphia North American, Washington Times,* and *Washington Herald.*

Today's scholars are fortunate that David Glassberg has recently published a strong account of pageantry, *American Historical Pageantry: The Uses of Tradition in the Early Twentieth Century* (Chapel Hill: University of North Carolina Press, 1990). Its bibliography stands as the best survey of resources on the subject, and I recommend it wholeheartedly to researchers. Among the most useful overviews of pageantry are those of Percival Chubb, *Festivals and Plays in Schools and Elsewhere* (New York: Harper and Brothers, 1912); Percy MacKaye, *The New Citizenship: A Civic Ritual Devised for Places of Public Meeting in America* (New York: Macmillan, 1915), and Ralph Davol, *Handbook of American Pageantry* (Taunton, MA: Ralph Davol, 1915).

From the women's points of view, I recommend Mary Master Needham, *Folk Festivals: Their Growth and How to Give Them* (New York: B. W. Heubsch, 1912); Esther Willard Bates, *Pageants and Pageantry* (Boston: Ginn, 1912) and *The Art of Producing Pageants* (Boston: W. H. Baker, 1925); Mary Porter Beegle and Jack Randall Crawford, *Community Drama and Pageantry* (New Haven: Yale University Press, 1916);

Louise Burleigh, *Community Theatre in Theory and Practice* (Boston: Little, Brown, 1917); Constance D'Arcy Mackay, *Patriotic Drama in Your Town* (New York: Holt, 1918), *Plays of the Pioneers: A Book of Historical Pageant-Plays* (New York: Harper and Brothers, 1915) and *Patriotic Plays and Pageants for Young People* (New York: Holt, 1912); Mary Russell, *How to Produce Plays and Pageants* (New York: George H. Doran, 1923); and Elizabeth Burchenal, *May Day Celebration* (New York: Department of Child Hygiene, Russell Sage Foundation, 1910). Additional texts can be found in Ethel Theodora Rockwell, "Children of Old Carolina: An Historical Pageant of North Carolina for Children" *University of North Carolina Extension Bulletin* 4 (1 April 1925); Nina Lamkin, *The Passing of Kings: A Pageant* (Chicago: T. S. Denison, 1920); Alice C. D. Riley, *The Brotherhood of Man, a Pageant for International Peace* (New York: A. S. Barnes, 1924) and *The Lover's Garden, a Flower Masque Arranged from Shakespeare for the Tercentenary* (Chicago: C. F. Summy, 1916).

Contemporary scholars who have examined the uses of ritual include Naima Prevots, *American Pageantry: A Movement for Art and Democracy* (Ann Arbor: UMI Research Press, 1990); Roy Rosenzweig, *Eight Hours for What We Will: Workers and Leisure in an Industrial City, 1870–1920* (New York: Cambridge University Press, 1983); Mary Ryan, *Women in Public: Between Banners and Ballots, 1825–1880* (Baltimore: Johns Hopkins University Press, 1990); Sean Wilents, *Chants Democratic: New York City and the Rise of the American Working Class, 1788–1850* (New York: Oxford University Press, 1984); and Lisa Tickner, *The Spectacle of Women: Imagery of the Suffrage Campaign, 1907–14* (Chicago: University of Chicago Press, 1988).

In no field I have studied here are photographs as plentiful as they are for pageantry. Colleges, clubs, and guidebooks illustrated their accounts of pageants with images of the participants posed in dramatic settings.

Chapter 6: "The Little Theater Movement." The little theater story can be told with New York Drama League Papers at the Lincoln Center Branch of the New York Public Library, New York City, and at the Drama League headquarters in Manhattan. The Evanston Public Library in Illinois provided biographical material on Alice C. D. Riley and Ellen Best. Additional Riley papers, including her unpublished autobiography, "The Incredible Years," are held by her descendants, among them Alison Blake Ramsey of Portland, Oregon. The Otto Kahn Papers, William Seymour Theatre Collection, Princeton University, is helpful on the fund-raising efforts of the Drama League. The headquarters of the Parent-Teachers' Association in Chicago contains considerable material on children's theater. The Drama League's magazine, entitled *Drama Quarterly* (February 1911–May 1919), *Drama Monthly* (October 1919–May 1930), and *Drama Magazine* (February–June 1931) is informative. So is *Child Welfare Magazine* (1910–30), for its coverage of children's theater.

The Pasadena Community Playhouse account drew on the Pasadena Playhouse Papers, formerly held at the Pasadena Public Library. They have recently been given to the Henry E. Huntington Library, where they are being reorganized. The Greta Millikan Papers, at the California Institute of Technology in Pasadena, contain the diaries of a dedicated Playhouse volunteer. Eleanor Bissell's Papers, at the Pasadena Historical Society, illuminate the Pasadena Drama League's activities from the perspective of a board member. The Pasadena Playhouse Oral History Project, conducted at the University of California at Los Angeles, contains transcripts of interviews with several prominent playhouse personnel. The Pasadena Playhouse coverage for 1916 to 1930 was extensive in the *Pasadena Star-News*, the *Los Angeles Saturday Night*, the *California Southland*, the *California Life* (later *Californian, Maryland-Huntington Life*, and *Pasadena California Life*), and the *Bulletin* of the Pasadena Drama League.

Published works that provide a useful overview of the amateur theater movement include Clarence Arthur Perry, *The Work of the Little Theaters: The Groups They Include, the Plays They Produce, Their Tournaments, and the Handbooks They Use* (New York: Russell Sage Foundation, 1933); Kenneth MacGowan, *Footlights across America* (New York: Harcourt, Brace, 1929); Albert McCleery and Carl Glick, *Curtains Going Up* (New York: Pitman Publishing, 1939); Alexander Dean, *Little Theatre Organization and Management* (New York: D. Appleton, 1926); Percy MacKaye, *The Playhouse and the Play* (New York: Macmillan, 1909); A. G. Arvold, *Little Theatre County* (New York: Macmillan, 1922); Oliver M. Saylor, *Our American Theater* (New York: Brentano's, 1923). The University of North Carolina at Chapel Hill Extension *Bulletin* published three guides for drama clubs. These are Dougald MacMillan, "Recent Tendencies in the Theatre: A Program for Women's Clubs," 2 (1 April 1923); Russell Potter, "A Study of Shakespeare: A Program for Women's Clubs," 5 (1 January 1926), and Ethel Theodora Rockwell, "A Study Course in American One-Act Plays: A Program for Women's Clubs," 4 (1 November 1924).

Unpublished sources of value are Christopher Wenn Craig, "The Drama League of America; Its Conception, History and Contribution to the American Theatre" (M.A. thesis, University of California at Los Angeles, 1965); Barbara Mendoza, "Hallie Flanagan: Her Role in American Theatre, 1924–35" (Ph.D. diss., New York University, 1975); and the seven-hundred-page autobiography of Alice Gerstenberg, at the Chicago Historical Society.

Published resources on the history of the Pasadena Playhouse include Harriet L. Green, *Gilmor Brown: Portrait of a Man and an Idea* (Pasadena: Burns Printing, 1933); Gilmor Brown, *Too Late to Lament*; F. W. Hersey and Gilmor Brown, "Unusual Aspects of the Pasadena Community Theater," *Little Theater Monthly* 5 (November 1928): 499–500, also in *Drama* 19 (November 1928); Diane Alexander, *Playhouse* (Los Angeles: Dorlese-MacLeish, 1984); Catherine Turney, "Gilmor Brown: Founder of the Pasadena Playhouse," Program of the Pasadena Playhouse Hall of Fame (8 May 1982): 4–5, 10. An important unpublished source is Gail Leo Shoup, Jr., "Pasadena Community Playhouse: Its Origins and History from 1917 to 1942" (Ph.D. diss., University of California at Los Angeles, 1968).

For plays frequently performed by amateurs, see the plays of Alice C. D. Riley, Alice Gerstenberg, Cora Mel Patton, and the bibliography in Winifred Ward, *Theatre for Children* (New York: D. Appleton-Century, 1939).

Chapter 7: "The Clubhouse as Arts Center." When women's organizations devoted a great deal of time and money to build clubhouses, their manuscript collections generally reflect that effort. The papers of the Friday Morning Club and Wilshire Ebell Club, both of Los Angeles, formerly held by the clubs but now at the Henry Huntington Library, provide generous information on the topic. Likewise at the Arthur and Elizabeth Schlesinger Library of the History of Women, the papers of the Junior League of Boston and the Junior League of New York City are helpful. The latter collection has been returned to the officers of the club. The minutes and yearbooks of most clubs detail the uses of the club space and the treasurer's reports convey the expenses involved. The club records listed in chapter 2 provided the evidence for my analysis. The periodicals with strong coverage of clubhouse building and use include the *Woman's Journal,* especially 13–15 (1928–30); *Woman Citizen* (especially 1927); *Junior League Magazine* (especially 1930); and the General Federation of Women's Clubs *Magazine* (1915–30).

The writings of Dolores Hayden, for their consideration of women's use of space, have helped me shape this chapter. See *The Grand Domestic Revolution: A History* of *Feminist Designs for American Homes, Neighborhoods, and Cities* (Cambridge, MA: MIT Press, 1981). Published accounts of clubs, like Katherine Barrette Parsons, *History of Fifty Years, Ladies' Literary Club, Salt Lake City, Utah, 1877–1927* (Salt Lake City: Arrow Press, 1927), preserve details about clubhouse building. Unpublished accounts include Darlene Roth, "Matronage: Patterns in Women's Organizations, Atlanta, Georgia, 1890–1940" (Ph.D. diss., George Washington University, 1978).

INDEX

Abbey-Cheney Amateurs, San Francisco, 48
Abbot, Emma, 209n90
Abigail Adams Smith House, New York, 192
Abramson, Josephine Hilty, 182
African Americans, 9, 22, 56, 57, 58, 72, 75, 118, 112, 140, 145, 170, 183, 187, 214n50; spirituals, 4, 53, 60, 62, 63, 123, 181
Akins, Zoë, 160
Albee, Percy F., 221n44
Albro, Maxine, 190
Alcott, Louisa May, 21, 175, 209n90
Alexander, Mrs. John W., 83
Alliance Française, 164, 165, 234n80
Aloha Club, Tacoma, 87
Amateur Musical Club, Brooklyn, 47, 48
American Assn. of University Women, 29, 78, 188
American Civic Assn., 96, 101
American Federation of Arts, 29, 78–81, 85, 87, 89, 92, 101, 103, 221n49, 224n95; lecturers, 220n14; size, 80, 219n13
American Federation of Catholic Societies, 157
American Friends of Musicians in France, 66
American Indian Defense Assn., 170
American Indians. *See* Native Americans
American Institute of Architects, 79, 80, 197
American Opera Assn., 61
American Pageant Assn., 29, 126, 127, 227n34
American Society of Landscape Architecture, 79, 93
American Water Color Society, 79, 81
American Women's Assn., New York, 90, 199
Americanization, 62–63, 66, 69, 84
Ames, Winthrop, 136
Anderson, Sherwood, 182
Andrews, Mrs. Alfred Burrit, 216n85
Andrews, Evangeline W., 131
Anthony, Susan B., 6, 91, 140, 141, 229n61
Archaeological Institute of America, 79
Arche Club, Chicago, 86
Armington, Caroline, 219n11
Arms Limitation, 233n61
Art and History Club, St. Cloud, MN, 96
Art and Industrial Club, CA, 235n19
Art Associations, Leagues, or Societies, 96; Alabama, 97; Baltimore, 101; Charleston, IL, 89; Indianapolis, 33; Minnesota, 80; Nashville, 89; Newport, RI, 103; Richmond, IN, 89; Spokane, 92–93
Art Club, Fort Dodge, IA, 36
Art in Trades Club, New York, 80
Art Study Club, Natchez, 36
Art Week. *See* National Art Week
Arts and Crafts Club, Hartford, 36
Arundell Club, Baltimore, 82

Associated Craftsmen, 97
Association for the Advancement of Women, 216n89
Association of Collegiate Alumnae, 29, 188. *See also* Amer. Assn. of Univ. Women
Athena, 131, 134, 229n61
Athene Club, Bangor, 211n24
Atherton, Gertrude, 134
Audubon Society, 126
Austin, Mary Hunter, 181

Baermann, Carl, 26
Baker, George Pierce, 136, 154, 175
Barnes, E. S., 214n60
Barnum, P. T., 22
Barrie, James M., 147, 151
Barrymore, Ethel, 152
Barth, Hans, 214n60
Baskin, Alice, 233n62
Batchelder, Ernest, 167
Bates, Esther, 126
Bates, Katharine Lee, 58
Bauer, Harold, 44
Baum, L. Frank, 181
Beach, Amy Cheney (Mrs. H. A. A.), 26, 38, 58, 209n90, 213n47, 215n69, 218n135
Beaux, Cecilia, 26, 28, 79, 209n90
Beecham, Sir Thomas, 27
Beecher, Catharine, 17, 20
Beegle, Mary Porter, 124, 126
Belmont, Alva, 91, 188
Benét, Stephen Vincent, 59
Benoit Company, 102
Bernard, Jean-Jacques, 165
Bernhardt, Sarah, 209n91
Berry, Rose, 76, 83, 102
Berry, Virginia Stewart, 82–83
Besly, Mrs. Charles, 232n23
Best, Marjorie Ayres (Mrs. Albert Starr), 149–50, 157, 158, 159, 232n23
Better Homes Movement, 93
Billboard Law Defense Committee, of Massachusetts State Federation of Women's Clubs, 224n101
Billboards, 98, 99, 100, 101–102, 105
Bingham, Harriett Payne, 220n22
Bird Club, Meriden, NH, 137
Bissell, Eleanor, 163, 164
Black Americans. *See* African Americans
Blatch, Harriot Stanton, 91
Bok, Edward William, 31
Bond, Carrie Jacobs, 209n90, 214n61, 218n135
Bonheur, Rosa, 27
Boniface, Frances, 170

INDEX

Booker T. Mother's Club, 235n19
Bonstelle, Jessie, 145
Boston "Pops" Orchestra, 212n28
Bradley, Susan H., 219n11
Brahms Club, Pasadena, 164
Branscombe, Gena, 58
Brant, Carrie Parson, 183
Bridges Art Gallery, San Diego, 183
Brinkerhoff, Clara M., 210n91
Broadoaks Alumnae Assn., 234n80
Brooklyn Society of Etchers, 81
Brooks, Louise, 227n28
Brown, Anne Taylor, 219n11
Brown, Augusta, 22
Brown, Edith, 221n44
Brown, Gilmor, 162, 166, 167, 168, 171, 174, 176, 177, 182
Brown, Glenn, 79
Brown, Olympia, 6
Browne, Maurice, 145, 154, 165
Browning Club, Pasadena, 172
Bryn Mawr Club, New York, 198
Burgess, Levi J., 232n23
Burleigh, Cecila, 32
Burton, Henry, 47
Burton, Richard, 232n23
Business and Professional Women's Clubs. *See* National Federation of Business and Professional Women's Clubs
Busoni, Ferruccio, 24
Butler, Mary, 219n11

Cadman, Charles Wakefield, 62, 213n38
Cadman, Rev. S. Parkes, 157–58, 232n23
Camp Fire Girls, 52, 70
Capitol Hill Club, Atlanta, 186
Careno, Theresa, 26, 38
Carillon, 68, 104, 217n128
Carnegie Foundation, 159, 218n147
Carnegie Library, Lexington, KY, 89
Carter, Artee Mason, 39, 67
Cary, Anna Louise, 209n90
Cassatt, Mary, 28, 91, 209n90, 219n11
Castle Square Stock Company, Boston, 136
Cather, Willa, 59
Catholic Women's Club, Los Angeles, 181
Catholic Women's League, 149
Cauldron Club, Pasadena, 234n80
Cecilian Society, Duluth, 48
Chamber of Commerce, 74, 94, 96, 102, 161
Chaminade, Cecile, 38, 213n47
Chapman, Josephine Wright, 199
Chase, William Merritt, 82, 83
Chatterton, Josephine, 209n91
Chautauqua, 150
Cheney, Ednah Dow Littlehale, 21, 31, 32
Cheney, Seth, 21
Child, Lydia Maria, 22
Child Labor Committee, Minneapolis, 233n61
Children of the American Revolution, Thomas Welles Society, 132
Children's Educational Theatre, New York, 136
Children's Theatre, Chicago, 148, 156
Chopin, Kate, 27
Chromatic Club, Buffalo, 65
Chubb, Percival, 232n23

Church, Frederick S., 190
Church, institutional: Congregational, 192; First Adventist, 171; First Unitarian, 158; First Universalist, 164; Methodist, 171; Neighborhood Church, 164; Presbyterian, 163, 192; Quakers (Society of Friends), 171
—and the arts, 63, 69, 70, 71, 72, 73, 103, 118, 128, 130, 149, 154, 157, 173, 184 212n26
Church and Drama Assn., New York, 159
City Beautiful Movement, 100, 101
Civic and Social Club, Los Angeles, 235n19
Civil War, 214n50
Clark, Lotta, 7, 126, 226n28, 227n34
Cleavis, Helen, 83
Cleveland, Grover, 31
Cleveland Art Club, 192
Coe, Ethel L., 219n11
Cole, Mrs. Jirah D., 47
College Park Club, Atlanta, 186
College Women's Club, Pasadena, 162, 166, 172, 234n80
Colleges and universities, 71, 72, 79, 149, 173; Agnes Scott, 226n28; Barnard, 26, 41, 120, 131; Bryn Mawr, 25, 26, 41, 120, 131, 198; Calif. Institute of Technology, Pasadena, 163, 164; City College of New York, 228n51; Harvard, 154, 175; H. Sophie Newcomb Memorial, 26; Montana State, 127; Mount Holyoke, 25 (*see also* Schools: Mount Holyoke Female Seminary); Northwestern, 232n19; Occidental, 172; Radcliffe, 136, 229n61; Smith, 25, 149, 164; Syracuse, 26, 93; Univ. of Calif. at Berkeley, 162; UCLA, 165; Univ. of N. Dakota, 126; Univ. of S. Calif., 165; Univ. of Washington, 154; Vassar, 25, 134, 135, 145, 154, 229n61; Wellesley, 25, 233n61; Western, 212–13n29; Wheaton, 227n28; Whittier, 166; Yale, 64. *See also* Labor colleges; Normal schools; Schools
Collins, Helen Storer (Mrs. Winifred B.), 212n29
Collins, Laura S., 214n61
Colonial Dames. *See* National Society, Colonial Dames of America
Colony Club, New York, 189–90
Colored Jubilee Singers, 72. *See also* African Americans, spirituals
Community Chest, 164
Community Drama Assn., New York, 137
Community Sings, 37, 39, 40, 51, 57, 64, 68–70, 71, 168, 201. *See also* Liberty Sings
Competitions, 74, 97, 101, 173, 190, 197; art, 88, 89, 90, 129; essays, 72, 94; musical composition, 57, 58; musical memory contests, 53, 71; musical performance, 54; playwriting, 154, 156, 158, 163, 165, 182
Condling, Grace Hazard, 215n69
Congress of Women: International, 234n81. *See also* Council of Women
Congressional Union, 135, 141, 229n61. *See also* National Woman's Party
Conservation, 100–102, 105, 106, 134. *See also* Parks and forests
Consumer's League. *See* National Consumer's League
Contemporary Club, Newark, NJ, 90
Cook, George Cram "Jig," 145
Copland, Aaron, 59
Cosmopolitan Club, New York, 90

INDEX

Council of Women: International, 33; National, 33, 66, 70. See also Congress of Women
Coward, Noël, 170, 176, 182
Cowles, Ione (Mrs. Josiah E.), 66
Craft, 8, 16, 77, 79, 83, 84, 85, 92, 93, 106. See also Associated Craftsmen; Potteries/pottery
Croome, William, 13
Crothers, Rachel, 151, 170, 175
Crown Stock Company, CA, 166
Cult of True Womanhood, 12, 18, 20
Curtis, Natalie, 61, 214n6
Cushman, Charlotte, 22
Cutler, Mary, 226n28
Cutter, Mary, 227n34

Dalin, Virginia, 126
Damrosch, Walter, 73
Dana, C. E., 89
Dance, 12, 13, 14, 17, 56, 118, 120, 123, 124, 125, 126, 127, 128, 131, 133, 137, 138, 140, 155, 156, 171, 179, 196, 234n80
Daniels, Mabel, 209n90, 214n61, 215n69
Dassel, Hermionie, 22
Daughters of the American Revolution, 41, 90, 126, 132, 164, 179, 187–88, 217n128; specific chapters of, 125, 127, 158, 186, 187, 192. See also Children of the Amer. Revolution
Daughters of the British Empire, 196
Daughters of the Republic of Texas, 91
Daughters of the State Pioneers, 179
Davies, Stuart, 190
Davis, Gordon, 154
Day, Doris, 199
Dean, Alexander, 154
Dean, Frances, 227n28
Decatur Club, Atlanta, 186
De Ciseros, Eleanor, 68
Decker, Sarah Platt, 32–33, 35, 36, 56
DeForest, Robert, 79
DeForest, Mrs. Robert, 221n49
Dell, Floyd, 34, 182
Dello Joio, Norman, 59
Delsarte, François, 122, 128, 136, 181
De Mille, Agnes, 5, 168, 182
De Mille, Anna (Mrs. William C.), 5, 165, 182
De Mille, Cecil B., 41, 182
Demuth, Charles, 190
Densmore, Frances, 62–63, 216n89
de Pachmann, Vladimir, 71
Department of Fine Arts, 58
Department stores, 86, 92, 105
Deppe, Ludwig, 24
de Villale, Aline, 215n69
Dewey, Admiral George, 68
De Wolfe, Elsie, 189–90
Dickinson, Emily, 28, 165, 182
Dietrich, Laurabelle S., 165, 233n62
Dillon, Fannie, 58
Dillon, Josephine, 166
Domestic feminism, 7, 205n11
Donaldson, Mrs. Douglas, 83
Dorr, Louise B. (Mrs. Russell Ripley), 212n21, 212n29
Dorr, Rheta Child, 181
Doty, H. H., 167
Doubleday, Page and Company, Publishers, 155

Drama Circle, Evanston, 132
Drama Club, Evanston, 149
Drama League of America, 29, 137, 145, 147, 148–60, 173, 174, 179; bibliographies, 231n18; Boston, 152, 159; Buffalo, 157; Charleston, 159; Chicago, 151, 152, 153, 156, 159; Cincinnati, 153; Los Angeles, 159, 162, 163; New York, 151–52, 154, 158; and pageants, 125, 126, 127, 229n61; Pasadena, 147, 148, 153, 156, 159, 160–77; Philadelphia, 153; Pittsburgh, 158; St. Louis, 157; San Diego, 157; Shreveport, 156; Tacoma, 158; size, 39, 148, 231n17; Worcester, 159
Drama Week. See National Drama Week
Dreier, Dorothea, 34
Dreier, Katherine, 34
Dreiser, Theodore, 182
Drinker, Catharine Ann, 26
Driscoll, Louise, 215n69
Driscoll, Marjorie, 166
DuBois, W. E. B., 183
Duncan, Isadora, 122
Dunes Pageant Assn., 126
Duniway, Abigail Scott, 6
Durand, Mrs. J. B., 162
Durkee, Helen Winslow, 219n11
Duse, Eleanora, 209n91
Duthy, Jean, 54
Dyer, Susan Hart, 63

Eager, Margaret MacLaren, 126
Eastman, Max, 34, 181
Eaton, Walter Prichard, 232n23
Ebell Club: of Los Angeles (Wilshire), 39, 65, 97, 187, 190, 191, 194; of Pomona, 191, 192, 198, 236n28, 237n59
Eddy, Sara Hershey, 209n90
Edib, Halide, 171
Edna Alter Mexican-American Settlement House, 170
Edson, Katherine, 170
Ehlich, Elma C., 227n28
Ellet, Elizabeth, 18, 22
Elliot, George (Mary Ann Evans), 27
Elmore, Mrs. Frank, 97
Equal Rights Amendment, 137, 141, 188
Este, Florence, 219n11
Euterpe Club, Raleigh, NC, 37
Evans, Margaret J., 96
Expositions: Chicago (1893), 45, 46, 48, 199; Atlanta (1895), 192, 199; Paris (1900), 26; San Francisco (1915), 80, 83, 158

Farm Woman's Congress, 97
Farrand, Max, 167
Farwell, Arthur, 62
Faulkner, Anne. See Anne Faulkner Oberndorfer
Fay, Amy, 24, 34, 211n4
Fern, Fanny (Sara Willis Parton), 22
Filene's Department Store, Boston, 92
Finden, Amy Woodford, 213n47
Fine Arts League, Los Angeles, 81
Fishmuth, Harriett, 220n22
Flagg, Maurice Irwin, 97
Flanagan, Hallie, 145, 156
Flanner, Hildegarde, 164, 165
Fletcher, Alice, 38, 61, 62
Foote, Mary Hallock, 209n90

Fortnightly Musical Club, Cleveland, 65, 212n29
Foster, Mrs. E. K., 183
Foster, Fay, 214n61, 218n135
Foster, Stephen, 63
4-H Club, 52
Frankel, Bessie Bartlett (Mrs. Cecil), 51, 68
Fraser, Laura Gardin (Mrs. James Earle), 83, 220n22
Frazer, Mabel, 97
Freeman, Anna Mary, 22
Freeman, Mary Wilkins, 38, 209n90
Freeman, Rev. Robert, 163
Freer, Eleanor Everest, 214n61, 216n85
Friday Morning Club, Los Angeles: African-American membership, 235n19; largely Caucasian membership, 39, 193, 236n28, 237n59, 238n75; clubhouse, 180–83, 187, 192, 196, 197; and music, 61; and visual arts, 83
Frishmuth, Harriet, 219n11
Fuller, Margaret, 21

Gable, Clark, 166
Gabrilowitsch, Ossip, 71
Gale, Zona, 165, 168, 170, 175
Galsworthy, John, 152, 181
Garden Club of America, 100, 224n95; Chicago, 232n19; Long Island, 224n95; Pasadena, 164
Garland, Hamlin, 182
Garrison, Mabel, 66
Gartz, Kate Crane, 167
Gaul, Harvey, 214n60
Gaw, Allison, and Ethelean Tyson, 156
Gaynor, Jessie L., 214n61, 231n18
Geary, Blanche, 199
General Federation of Women's Clubs, 8, 29, 174, 187, 195; clubhouses, 179, 187, 235n16; music, 45, 49, 50, 53, 54–56, 58, 59–62, 70; officers, 4, 32, 35, 66, 97, 164, 185; pageants, 126, 127, 228n46; size, 32, 39, 82, 200–202, 210n2, 210n11; theater, 150, 153, 157; visual art, 76, 78, 80, 81–85, 87, 92, 100, 101; World War I, 66. *See also* State and Regional Federations of Women's Clubs
George H. Doran Publishing Company, 155
Gerstenberg, Alice, 38
Gibson, Mary, 86
Gilbert and Sullivan. *See* Operettas
Gilman, Charlotte Perkins, 6, 33, 181
Girl Scouts. *See* Scouts, Girl
Girls' Sewing Guild, 229n61
Glaspell, Susan, 170, 175, 176
Gottschalk, Louis, 13
Gottstein, Rose Morgenstern, 4, 5
Graham, Margaret Collier, 182
Graham, Martha, 168
Grange, 70
Grant, Ulysses S., 68
Grant, Zilpha, 13, 20
Grant Park Club, Atlanta, CA, 186
Green, Harriet L., 164, 174
Greenwich Settlement House, New York, 137
Grimes, Frances, 221n44
Grobe, Charles, 22
Grumball, Elizabeth, 227n34

Hackley, Azalia, 60
Hadassah, 172
Haigh, Andrew C., 214n60

Hale, George Ellery, 167
Hale, Sarah Josepha, 20
Hall, Adelaide S., 87
Hall, Anne, 22
Hall, F. Jeannette, 209n90
Hall, Lilian Westcott, 219n11
Hallelujah Quartet, 182
Hallie Q. Brown Club, Palakta, FL, 187
Hamilton, Mary A., 21
Hamlin, Mary E., 154
Hansen, Armin O., 221n44
Harding, Warren G., 233n61
Hare, Maud Cuney, 60
Harmony Club, Fort Worth, 212n29
Harper, Flora, 164
Harrison, Hazel L., 24
Hasselriis, Else, 219n11
Hauk, Minnie, 209n90
Havemeyer, Louisine, 91
Haward, Dorothy, 215n69
Hayden, Sophia, 199
Hearst, Phoebe, 80
Heckscher, Celeste, 216n85
Henrotin, Ellen M., 32
Henry E. Huntington Library, 163, 164
Heptorean Club, Somerville, MA, 82
Herbert, Victor, 212n28
Herrick, Margaret, 199
Herz, Henri, 13
Hewitt, John Hill, 22
Higgins, Joy, 227n34
Hildreth, Katherine, 35
Hill, Junius W., 26
Hill, Mabel Wood, 58
Hills, Laura Coombs, 219n11
Hillyer, Winthrop, 25
Hiltz, Grace, 209n90
Hinckley, Theodore Ballou, 150, 155
Historical Society, Pasadena, 234n80
Hohnstock, Adele, 13
Holden, Cora, 219n11
Hollywood Bowl, 39, 67, 69, 125, 183
Holmes, Augusta, 213n47
Hood, Helen, 214n61
Hoosier Salon, 86
Hopper, Hedda, 182
Horsley, Sue Lombard, 226n28
Horton, Edward Everett, 182
Hosmer, Harriet, 22
Housch, S. Henrietta, 81
Howard, Lucile, 90
Howe, Julia Ward, 32
Hughes, Adella Prentiss, 60
Hughes, Glenn, 146, 154
Hughes, Langston, 182
Hull, Mrs. C. L., 22
Hund, Alicia, 24
Hunt, Myron, 162–63
Hunt, Virginia Pease, 162
Huntington, Anna Vaughn Hyatt, 7, 38, 90, 94, 220n22
Huntington, Archer, 79
Hutchinson, Charles L., 79
Hutchinson, Mrs. Randall, 83

Idler Club, 229n61

INDEX

Immigrants, 4, 10, 37, 40, 45, 57, 62, 64, 65, 68, 73, 75, 77, 93, 128, 143, 214n50
Indiana Federation of Arts, 86
Indians. *See* Native Americans
Inness, George, 221n40
Iroquois Club, Los Angeles, 235n19
Iturbi, José, 27

Jackson, Andrew, 1–2
Jacobi, Frederick, 53
Jacobson, Oscar, 87
James, Alice, 26
James, Alice Archer, 7
James, Burton, 145, 154
James, Florence, 145, 154
James, Henry, 181
Jazz, 9, 53, 56, 62, 72
Jelliffe, Rowena, 145
Jelliffe, Russell, 145
Jewett, Sarah Orne, 209n90
Jewish War Relief Fund, 130
Joan of Arc, 134, 136, 165
Johnson, Adelaide, 91
Johnson, Amelia, 227n28
Johnson, C. Raymond, 87
Johnson, Grace Mott, 219n11, 220n22
Johnson, Rosamund, 58
Johnston, Ella Bond, 82
Jonas, Lucien, 103
Jones, Anna Maxwell, 102
Jones, Katharine Tift, 62
Jones, Sibyl Eliza, 162, 167, 171
Juch, Emma, 209n91
Junior Fortnightly Music Club, Indianapolis, 54
Junior League of America, 29, 52, 179, 188; Boston, 190; Little Rock, 192; New Haven, 65; New York, 65, 188, 190, 199; Pasadena, 172; Philadelphia, 193; Poughkeepsie, 192; St. Paul, 191; Washington, DC, 199
Junior Musical Club, Miami, 53
Junior Tuesday Musicale, Pasadena, 171
Junkin, George, 154ff

Kahn, Otto, 159
Keener, Anna, 87
Keith, Lillian, 227n28
Keller, Helen, 193
Kelley, Jessie Gregg (Mrs. Edgar Stillman), 212n29
Kellogg, Clara Louise, 22
Kelly, George, 7, 170, 176
Kelsey, Mrs. Charles B., 212n29
Kemble, Fanny, 22
Kincaid, Zoe (Mrs. John Pendlington), 165
Kinney, Leila B. (Mrs. Julius E.), 212n29
Kiwanis Club, 56, 161
Knowlton, Fanny, 214n61
Korn, Clara, 214n61
Krause, Martin, 24
Kreider, Mrs. (clubwoman), 183
Kullak, Franz, 24
Kummer, Clare, 165

Labor colleges, 143, 229n61; People's Institute, New York, 228n51
Ladd, Anne Coleman, 83
Ladies' Catholic Benevolent Society, 196

Ladies' Literary Club: Grand Rapids, 183; Salt Lake City, 196
Ladies' Monday Club, Sacramento, 235n19
Ladies Musical Club: Cincinnatti, 48; Seattle, 4, 37, 38, 48, 65
Ladies' Musical Club, Tacoma, 48
Lamkin, Nina, 126
Lander, Louise, 22
Lang, Margaret Ruthven, 214n61
Langdon, William Chauncy, 126
Langdon-Davies, John, 234n81
Laura Spelman Rockefeller Memorial Foundation, 159
Lawson, Roberta Campbell (Mrs. Eugene B.), 4, 55, 62
Lawton, Mrs. W. L., 102
Le Gallienne, Eva, 154
Legare, Mary Swinton, 22
Leginska, Ethel, 215n78
Lehmann, Liza, 213n47
Leonard, William Ellery, 169
Levy, Florence Nightingale, 80, 83
Lewis, Edmonia, 22
Lewisohn, Alice, 145
Lewisohn, Irene, 145
Liberty Bonds (or Loans), 42, 66, 68, 69, 103, 129, 132, 157, 168, 169, 178, 184, 193
Liberty Sings, 30, 63, 68, 104
Libraries, 31, 42, 63, 70, 71, 72, 86, 88, 89, 91, 101, 105, 138, 172, 178, 179, 180, 184, 194, 212n26, 219n13
Lind, Jenny, 22
Lindsay, Vachel, 182
Link, Lillian, 215n69
Liszt, Franz, 24
Little theaters, 145, 148, 230n1
Longacre, Lydia, 219n11
Longmans Green Publishing Company, 156, 165
Longworth, Maria, 85
Loschi, Contessa Maria, 234n81
Luddington, Sybil, 90
Lyon, Mary, 13, 20
Lyons, Lucille M. (Mrs. John F.), 212n29

McCarthy, Mary, 5
McCormick, Edith Rockefeller, 61
MacDermid, James G., 214n60
MacDowell, Edward, 5, 38, 59, 181, 213n38, 214n60, 218n135
MacDowell, Marian (Mrs. Edward), 5, 38, 58–59, 181
MacDowell Club of Chicago, 232n19
MacDowell Club of New York, 58
MacDowell Colony, 38, 44, 58, 60, 215n68
McEwen, Katherine, 219n11
McFadden, Elizabeth, 215n69
McFarland, Frances McElwee, 64
MacKay, Constance D'Arcy, 121, 126, 154, 175
MacKaye family: Harold Steele and Mary Keith Medbery (parents of Hazel and Percy), 135–36; Hazel, 10, 119, 121, 126, 130, 133, 135–42, 154; Percy, 120, 121, 126, 136, 139, 146, 151, 154
McKenney, Miss (pageant-maker), 226n28
McLaughlin, Mary Louise, 85
Madam C. J. Walker Club, San Francisco, 235n19
Maitland, Marguerite, 54

INDEX

Malby, Esther, 100
Mapes, Victor, 160
Marietta (OH) Woman's Assn., 120
Markley, Miss (pageant-maker), 226n28
Martha Meservel Dancing Class, 234n80
Mary B. Elling Prize, 90
Mary Tolbert Club, Tampa, 187
Mason, Maud, 83
Matinee Musicale Club, Lafayette, IN, 47
Maugham, W. Somerset, 182
Maxfield, Mrs. A. A., 165
Maxwell, Mrs. Lawrence, 54
Mears, Helen Farnsworth, 215n69
Mechlin, Leila, 80–81
Melchoir, Lauritz, 190
Mellon, Andrew, 79
Melville, Marguerite, 214n61
Mendelssohn, Fanny, 38
Men's Equal Suffrage League, New York, 139, 140, 229n61
Mercur, Elise, 199
Metropolitan Opera Company, New York, 66, 190
Mezquida, Anna Blake, 7
Midland Authors Club, 232n19
Milholland, Inez, 142, 229n61
Millay, Edna St. Vincent, 134, 143, 154, 182
Millikan, Greta Irvin Blanchard, 163–64
Millikan, Robert A., 164
Milne, A. A., 147, 182
Mind, Marcia, 199
Minerva Club, Santa Maria, CA, 238n75
Minnesota State Art Society, 80
Minorities, 40
Mitchell, Mrs. John W., 182–83
Modjeska, Helena, 181, 209n91
Moeller, Philip, 151
Monday Club, San Luis Obispo, CA, 199, 238n75
Monday Music Club, Portland, 212n29
Moneak, Elena, 61
Monophan, Gertrude, 215n69
Monroe, Anne Shannon, 215n69
Montessori, Maria, 160
Moore, Eva Perry (Mrs. Philip North), 55, 66
Moore, Mary Carr, 58
Morgan, Julia, 101, 199
Morin, James, 163
Morning Musical Club, Fort Wayne, IN, 48
Morning Musical Club, New York, 65
Morning Musicale, Greencastle, IN, 36
Morrison, Fannie E., 171
Motion pictures, 56, 70, 100, 142, 159, 165, 171, 179, 182, 183, 212n26
Motion Pictures Procedures Committee, 233n61
Mott, Lucretia, 91, 141
Mowatt, Anna Cora, 175
Muck, Karl, 67
Munger, Clara E., 209n90
Municipal (and state) arts commissions, 40, 85, 93, 94–100, 106; Alabama, 97; Cincinnati, 98, 102; Los Angeles, 97, 182; Minnesota, 80, 96, 97; Utah, 97
Municipal Housekeeping, 30, 33, 35, 40, 178
Murals, 88, 90, 220n14
Museums and Institutes of art, 10, 40, 77, 78, 79, 80, 82, 88, 93, 94, 99, 103, 105, 212n26, 219n13; Art I. of Chicago, 79, 80, 93, 126, 151, 153, 232n19

(*see also* Schools, Art Institute of Chicago); Art I. of Pasadena, 232n19; Baltimore M. of Art, 83; Cincinnati Art M., 89; Fogg M., 79; Heckscher M., 79; Henry Gallery, 79; Henry E. Huntington M., 79; Isabella Stewart Gardiner M., 79; Metropolitan M. of Art, 79, 93, 221n49; M. of Fine Arts, Boston, 79; National Gallery, 94; Pacific Asia M., 164; Utah Art I., 97
Music Club, Inglewood, CA, 72
Music Club, Monticello, AR, 71
Musical Club, Kansas City, 65
Music Week. *See* National Music Week
Mutual Welfare League, 56

National Academy of Design, New York, 21, 22, 24
National American Woman Suffrage Assn., 137, 140, 153; New York State Woman Suffrage Assn., 141
National Art Week, 92
National Assn. of Colored Women or (National Assn. of Colored Women's Clubs), 29; and art, 78; Calif. Federation, 235n19; clubhouses, 188, 235n16; competitions, 53; Indiana Federation, 187; size, 187, 235n19
National Assn. of Music Merchandisers, 70
National Assn. of Women Painters and Sculptors, 81, 83, 92, 191, 224n95
National Child Labor Committee, 228n51
National Committee for Restriction of Outdoor Advertising, 101–102
National Congress of Mothers, 70
National Conservatory of Music, 58
National Consumer's League, 151
National Council for the Prevention of War, 133, 229n61
National Council of Catholic Women, 78
National Council of Jewish Women, 70; Atlanta Branch, 186
National Dancing Masters Assn., 56
National Drama Week, 157, 159, 173
National Endowment for the Arts, 41, 106
National Federation of Business and Professional Women's Clubs: Pasadena Club, 172
National Federation of Music Clubs, 29, 45–54, 55, 56, 58, 59–62, 70, 71, 78; biennial convention, 66, 218n135; and children, 45, 52–54; magazine, 215n78; and pageants, 229n61; size, 32, 39, 52, 213n32, 213n33, 213n34; World War I, 66, 217n116. *See also* State Federations of Music Clubs
National League of Handicraft Societies, 79
National Music Teacher's Assn., 49
National Music Week, 45, 70–73, 186, 212n26; size, 218n143, 218n144
National Opera Club of America, 61
National Recreation and Playground Assn., 122
National Sculpture Society, 79
National Society, United States Daughters of 1812, 187
National Society of Colonial Dames of America, 126, 164, 192; New York State Society, 186
National Society of Mural Craftsmen, 79
National Society of Mural Painters, 79
National Society of the Daughters of the American Revolution. *See* Daughters of the Amer. Revolution
National Woman's Party, 91, 135, 137, 141, 142, 188, 229n61. *See also* Congressional Union
National Women's Trade Union League, 102

INDEX

Native Americans, 1, 2, 9, 55, 56, 57, 63, 75, 84, 118, 123, 125, 128, 129, 134, 139, 164, 169, 170, 181, 192, 213n38, 214n49; Chippewa, 22; Delaware, 4; Hopi, 55, 170; Onondaga, 93; Salish, 127; Sioux, 4, 169, 214n49; various other tribes by name, 214n49
Native Daughters of the Golden West, San Francisco, CA, 199
Navy League, Pasadena, CA, 172
New Century Club: Philadelphia, 153, 199; Wilmington, DE, 54, 199
New Deal, 41, 75, 156. *See also* WPA Federal Arts Projects
New England Conservatory Club, Portland, 67
New England School of Design for Women, Boston, 21
New Woman, 130, 131, 137
New York State Council on the Arts, 99
Ney, Elisabet, 91
Nicholas, Caroline, 61
Nichols, Minerva P., 199
Nicholson, Grace, 164
Nielson, Francis, 232n23
Nineteenth Century Club, Memphis, 193, 211n24
Nissen, Anna, 165
Nobel Prize, 164
Norcross, Eleanor, 219n11
Norfleet Trio, 54
Normal schools, 71; Boston, 23; Salem, CT, 21–22; Salem, MA, 227n28
Norris, Kathleen, 182
Northwestern Univ. Writer's Guild, 232n19
Nourse, Elizabeth, 38
N.U.G. Club, Sacramento, 235n19

Oakley, Violet, 83, 90, 199, 219n11
Oberndorfer, Anne Shaw Faulkner (Mrs. Marx E.), 55, 60, 62, 68
Ochsner, Mrs. A. J., 212n29
O'Keeffe, Georgia, 28, 190
Old masters, 76, 83, 84, 87, 88, 91, 100, 106
Olsen, Rena, 97
Omega Epsilon Sorority, 232n19
One Hundred Friends, Pittsburgh, 86
O'Neill, William, 143, 147, 154, 170, 182
Opera, 2, 55, 57, 61, 73, 212n26, 214n50. *See also* American Opera Assn.; National Opera Club of America
Opera in Our Language Federation, 61
Operettas, 26, 58, 71, 231n18
Oral Arts Assn., S. Calif., 173
Oratorio Society, Sunbury, PA, 72
Orchestras: Boston, 66, 67; Buffalo, 66; Chicago, 45; Cincinnati, 56, 68; Cleveland, 27, 60, 66; Glendale, 183; London, 27; Los Angeles, 39, 182; New York, 66, 67, 73; Philadelphia, 212n28; Pittsburgh, 212n28; Rochester, 27; San Francisco, 28; Seattle, 27, 38. *See also* Women's Orchestras
Orth, Mrs. L. E., 214n61
Ottaway, Ruth Haller (Mrs. Elmer James), 213n29

Pacifism, 33
Palmer, Mrs. J. Howard, 97
Panama Canal Zone, 90
Pan-American Scientific Congress, 229n61
Panhellenic House, 188

Parent-Teachers' Assn., 70, 166, 172
Parker, Louis N., 120
Parks and forests, 100, 220n22
Pasadena Community Playhouse, 148; Pasadena Community Playhouse Assn., 167, 168
Pasadena Drama League. *See* Drama League of America, Pasadena
Patriotism, 9, 10, 45, 50, 55, 57, 63, 65, 68, 69, 90, 100, 103, 104, 105, 106, 119, 121, 125, 130, 132, 156, 157, 183
Pattee, Elsie Dodge, 219n11
Patten, Cora Mel, 145, 154, 227n28
Patti, Adelina, 22, 209n91
Pattison, Alice M. Gould (Mrs. Everett W.), 80, 97
Paul, Alice, 41, 137, 140
Payne Tariff Bill, 94
Peabody, Josephine Preston, 215n69
Peace, 7, 64, 69, 103, 118, 119, 123, 126, 132, 133, 158, 183, 200, 203, 227n28, 228n49. *See also* Woman's Peace Party; National Council for the Prevention of War
Peale, Ann Leslie, 22
Peale, Mrs. Cornelius Dubois, 22
Peale, Mrs. Wilson, 22
Pelham, Laura Dainty, 145
Penney, Margaret, 164, 165, 233n62
Pennsylvania Academy of Design, 22
Pennsylvania Academy of Fine Arts, 21, 23
Pennybacker, Anna, 85
Perabo, Ernst, 26
Perkins, Mrs. Cyrus, 83, 104
Perry, Lilla Cabot, 215n69, 219n11
Peter, Sarah Worthington King, 21
Peterkin, Julia, 60
Phelps, Almira, 14, 19
Phelps, Elizabeth Stuart, 22
Philadelphia Music League, 69
Philadelphia School of Design for Women, 21
Philharmonic Society, Topeka, 47
Philips, Louis Baker, 214n60
Philomusian Club, Philadelphia, 153, 236n28
Pierce, Melusina Fay, 34
Pittman, Portia Washington, 24
Pittsburgh School of Design for Women, 23
Polk, Grace Porterfield, 53
Poole, Grace, 35
Poor, Henry V., 87
Popular culture, 53, 56, 62, 70, 75, 124, 125, 143, 144, 146, 148
Porter, Edith Noyes, 214n61
Potteries/pottery, 85, 92, 153, 179, 197
Powell, Maud, 26, 28, 38
Price, M. Elizabeth, 91
Prickett, Charles, 171
Professionals in the arts, 3, 4, 5, 6, 7, 9, 10, 25, 31, 34, 37, 38, 44, 45, 47, 48, 50, 55, 60, 70, 74, 77, 78, 79, 81, 88, 94, 98, 120, 124, 125, 179
Providence Plantations Club, 189
Provincetown Players, 143
Public Education Assn., New York, 88
Public School Art League, Houston, 88
Public School Art Society, Chicago, 87
Pulitzer Prize, 59, 160
Putnam, Brenda, 220n22

Quirk, Daniel L., Jr., 154, 232n23

256 INDEX

Quota Club, 56

Radio, 56, 70, 142, 212n26
Raemaekers, Louis, 103
Rallen, Mrs. Alvoni, 90
Rankin, Jeannette, 80
Ravlin, Grace, 219n11
Ray Palmer Club, Newark, 211n24
Reading Room Society, St. Cloud, MN, 96
Reber, J. Howard, 232n23
Recordings. *See* Victrola
Red Cross, 66, 99, 129, 133, 161, 164, 168, 172, 196
Redfeather, Princess, 181
Reed, John, 34
Religious Drama Assn., 158
Republican Party, 164
Republican Women's Club, Philadelphia, 90, 199
Reynolds, George, 221n40
Richardson, William H., 60
Richmond Art Assn., IN, 82
Riley, Alice Cushing Donaldson, 38, 148, 154, 164, 176; works of, 155, 162, 165, 175, 231n18
Riley, Harrison Barnett (husband of Alice C. D. Riley), 148
Riley Circle, Evanston, 148, 149
Rive-King, Julia, 26, 214n61
Robins, Margaret Dreier, 34
Robinson, Edward, 83
Robinson, Edwin Arlington, 59
Robinson, Eloise, 215n69
Robison, Mrs. E. J., 90
Rockefeller, Nelson, 99
Rockefeller Foundation, 159
Rockwell, Ethel, 126
Rogers, James H., 214n60
Roosevelt, Franklin, 71, 143
Roosevelt, Theodore, 90, 94
Root, Elihu, 79
Root, George, 13, 22
Rossi, Mrs. Herman, 83
Rotary Club, 56, 123, 126, 196
Rourke, Constance, 215n69
Rubenstein Club, Memphis, 47
Rural communities, 53, 69, 84, 88, 90, 100, 101, 121, 146, 154, 156, 170, 196. *See also* Farm Woman's Congress, 97
Ruskin Art Club, Los Angeles, 81, 97
Russell, Bertrand, 182
Russell Sage Foundation, 122
Russian String Quartet, 182

St. Cecilia Club, New York, 71
St. Cecilia Music Society, Grand Rapids, 190, 212n29
St. Denis, Ruth, 181, 219n11
Saint-Gaudens, Augustus, 79, 120, 136
St. Louis Musical Club, 55
St. Louis Symphony Society, 55
Salter, Mary Turner, 214n61
Samuel French Publishing Company, 156
San Joaquin Club, Stockton, 235n19
Sand, George, 61, 151
Sandburg, Carl, 165, 182
Sanders, L. Pearl, 83, 90
Sandzen, B., 87
Sanger, Margaret, 171
Sanitary Commission, 23

Sargent, John Singer, 83
Sartain, John, 13
Sartori, Margaret, 193
Saturday Morning Musical Club, Tuscon, 71
Sawyer, Gertrude, 199
Sawyer, Harriet P., 214n61
Scholarships, 44, 51, 54, 60, 65, 74, 88
Schools: Abbot's Institute for Young Ladies, 22; Academie Colorossi, 24; Academie Julian, Paris, 24; Andrew Jackson S., Chicago, 87; Art Institute of Chicago, 83, 88; Art Students' League, New York, 23, 28, 83; Bridgham S., Providence, 221n44; Cherry Valley Seminary, NY, 13; Chesapeake Female College, Hampton, VA, 22; Cleveland Music S. Settlement, 65; Cloonan S. Library, Stamford, CT, 88; Comstock S. of Oratory, Evanston, 232n19; Cooper Union, New York, 21; Corcoran S. of Arts, 80; Cornish S., Seattle, 154; Curtis S. of Music, 58, 74; Eastman S. of Music, 27, 58; Elizabeth Academy, Old Washington, MI, 17; Forsyth Dental Infirmary for Children, Fenway, Boston, 221n44; Girls' H.S., Montgomery, 87; Goodrich Public S., Chicago, 87; Greenwich Handicraft S., NY, 84; Hartford Female Seminary, 20; Ipswich Female Academy, 13, 20; John Herron Art Institute, Indianapolis, 33; Jones Public S., Chicago, 87; Juilliard S. of Music, New York, 58; McPherson H.S., KS, 87, 88; Minneapolis S. of Art, 88; Mississippi Industrial Institute and College for the Education of White Girls of the State of Mississippi, 24; Missouri S. for the Blind, 87; Moravian Female Seminary, Bethlehem, 13; Mount Holyoke Female Seminary, 13, 20, 28 (*see also* Colleges: Mount Holyoke College); Mount Vernon Seminary, 234n80; Music Settlement S., Los Angeles, 65; Nathaniel Hawthorne S., Indianapolis, 87; National Academy of Design, New York, 21, 24, 80, 93; Neighborhood Music S. Settlement, New Haven, 64; New England Conservatory, 24; New England S. of Design for Women, Boston, 21; New Haven Settlement Music S., 63; New York Public Schools (#8, #105, #135), 221n49; Paris Conservatory, 28; Philadelphia S. of Design for Women, 21, 85; Philadelphia Settlement Music S., 64; Pennsylvania Academy of Design, 22; Pennsylvania Academy of Fine Arts, 21, 28; Pittsburgh S. of Design for Women, 23; Polk Street S., Chicago, 87; Rhode Island S. of Design, 33; Richmond H.S., IN, 89; St. Louis S. of Design, 24; San Francisco S. of Design, 23–24; S. of Art and Applied Design, Nashville, 83; Settlement Music S., Seattle, 65; Shorewood Grade S., Milwaukee, 87; South Pasadena H.S., 173; Swope Music Settlement Music, Kansas City, 65; Tacoma H.S., 87; Troy Female Academy (Emma Willard S.), 13, 15, 20; Tuscaloosa H.S., 87; Tuskegee, 181; Union Music S., New York, 65; Washington Irving H.S., New York, 221n44; Wesleyan Female Seminary, Wilmington, 22; Western Reserve S. of Design for Women, 24; Westridge S., Pasadena, 173; Women's Art S., New York, 21. *See also* Colleges and Universities; Labor colleges; Normal schools
Schubert Club, St. Paul, 47, 64–65, 66, 212n29, 216n89
Schumann, Clara Wieck, 24, 38, 213n47
Schumann-Heink, Ernestine, 38, 212n28

Scott, Jeannette, 93
Scouts, 40, 52, 63, 118, 128, 196; Boy Scouts, 123, 169; Girl Scouts, 70, 123, 196
Scudder, Janet, 82, 90
Sculpture, 92, 95, 96, 98, 99, 103, 104, 220n14. *See also* War, memorials
Sedgwick, Catharine Maria, 17, 22
Segalle, Elizabeth, 165
Seiberling, Gertrude F. Penfield (Mrs. Frank A.), 212n29
Seneca Falls (NY) Women's Rights Convention, 141
Settlement Houses, 10, 39, 40, 41, 45, 51, 52, 57, 63–65, 68, 70, 74, 92, 118, 119, 128, 137, 143, 151, 216n98, 2l7n108. *See also* Schools
Seven Arts Society, Los Angeles, 235n4
Severance, Caroline Maria, 180
Sewall, May Wright, 6, 33–34, 192
Shakespeare Club or Society, 130, 136, 227n43; Pasadena, 100, 162, 168, 172, 193, 194, 237n59; Pomona, 132; Wellesley, 25
Shanewise, Lenore, 174
Shaw, Anne Howard, 66
Shaw, George Bernard, 147, 151, 165, 170, 181
Sheerer, Mary G., 26
Sheets, Nan, 219n11
Sherman, Philip, 232n23
Sherman Anti-Trust Law, 31
Sherry, Laura, 145
Sherwood, Mrs. Jean, 88
Sigourney, Lydia, 15, 16
Simpson, Napoleon, 169
Simpson, William, 138
Sinclair, Upton, 160, 181, 182
Sipprell, Clara E., 219n11
Slayden, John, 80
Sloman, Anne, 22
Sloman, Elizabeth, 22
Smith, Alice R. Guger, 219n11
Smith, Ella May (Dunning), 51, 65
Smith, Jessie Wilcox, 83, 219n11
Society for the Preservation of Spirituals, 62
Society of Arts and Crafts, Deerfield, MA, 85
Society of Decorative Art, New York, 85
Solomon, Genorie, 227n28
Song Birds Club, Philadelphia, 54
Sorchan, Mrs. V. (donor), 221n49
Sorosis: New York, 216n89, 224n95; Sacramento, 235n19; Wilmington, NC, 101, 127
Southern Assn. of College Women, 188. *See also* American Assn. of Univ. Women
Southern California Symphony Assn., 164
Sparhawk-Jones, Elizabeth, 215n69
Spencer, Lily M., 22
Spencer, Mary, 89
Speyer, Leonora, 60, 215n69
Stahl, John H., 232n23
Stair, Patty, 214n61
Standard Oil Co. of Calif., New York, and New Jersey, 102, 224n97
Stanton, Elizabeth Cady, 91, 140, 141
Starr, Mrs. Chandler, 212n21
State and county fairs, 77, 86, 92, 93, 105, 118, 212n26; Eastern (MA), 93; Iowa, 228n51; Mich., 93; Minn., 97; New York, 93; Tenn., 93; Texas, 41, 134; Oregon, 93. *See also* Expositions; Woman's Building

State Federations of Music Clubs: Calif., 51; New York State, 68, 214n60, 228n52; Wash. State, 51. *See also* National Federation of Music Clubs
State and Regional Federations of Women's Clubs, 224n95; Alabama, 87; Calif., 41, 80, 86, 101, 134, 158, 166; Conn., 80; Florida, 63; Illinois, 126; Indiana, 192; Iowa, 158; Kentucky, 80, 89; Long Island, 224n95; Maryland, 83; Mass., 35, 61, 66, 90, 224n101; Mich., 93; Minn., 82, 96; New Jersey, 90, 158; New York City, 84; New York State, 35, 158; Rhode Island, 67; Seattle, 186; Tenn., 83; Texas, 41, 158; Vermont, 84; Wash. State, 100. *See also* General Federation of Women's Clubs
Stebbins, Emma, 22
Steeb, Olga, 182
Steiner, Emma R., 216n85
Steiniger, Ms. (pianist), 24
Steinway and Sons, 70
Stevens, Neally, 26
Stevens, Nedda Hewitt, 62
Stevens, Thomas Wood, 126, 136, 175
Stocker, Mrs. Stella Prince, 48–49
Stokowski, Leopold, 56, 69
Stout, Ida McClelland, 215n69
Stowe, Harriet Beecher, 22, 175
Strean, Maria J., 219n11
Strindberg, August, 181
Strong, Harriet William Russell, 182
Stuart, Elma, 163
Suffrage. *See* Woman Suffrage
Sunset Club, Seattle, 186
Sutro, Forence Edith (Mrs. Theodore), 49, 212n21
Synge, John, 181

Taft, Lorado, 83, 86
Taft, Susan, 155
Tanner, Virginia, 126, 227n34
Tausig, Carl, 24
Taylor, Elizabeth P., 192
Tchaikovsky, Peter Ilich, 56
Teachers' Mutual Benefit Assn., Boston, 129
Teasdale, Sara, 215n69
Telford, Irene U., 227n28
Ten O'Clock Club, Indianapolis, 36
Tenneson, Alice M., 226n28
Terry, Ellen, 209n91
Theater troupes: Baltimore, 129; Chicago, 158; Evanston, 154, 157; Pasadena, 155, 168, 170–71; Philadelphia, 153–54; Provincetown, 143, 172; Stratford-upon-Avon, 175; Vassar, 154
Thomas, Rose Fay, 45, 46
Thomas, Theodore, 45, 70
Thompson, William F., 199
Thursday Musical Club, Minneapolis, 65
Tiegens, Paul, 214n60
Tietzens, Eunice, 215n69
Toll, Eleanor, 183
Torrence, Ridgeley, 151
Tourist Club, Minneapolis, 88
Town Club, Pasadena, 232n19
Town Hall Club, 198
Toy Orchestra, 54, 71, 212n26
Treble Clef Club, Los Angeles, 47
Treble Clef Club, Philadelphia, 48
Tsianina, Princess, musician, 62
Tucker, W. E., 13

258 INDEX

Tuesday Art and Travel Club, Chicago, 88
Tuesday Morning Drama Class, Pasadena, 162, 172, 232n19
Tuesday Musical Club, Akron, 212n29
Tuesday Musicale Club, Detroit, 48
Turner, Frederick Jackson, 1
Turner, Helen Maria, 90
Turner, Maria, 13
Tuskegee Jubilee Singers, 181
Twentieth Century Club, 31; Duluth, 89

Uhl, Alice F. (Mrs. Edwin F.), 212n29
Upton, Florence K., 219n11
U.S. Commission of Fine Arts, 80, 94, 99

Valentien, Anna, 91
Vanderbilt, Anne Harriman Sands Rutherford, 199
Vanderpool, Frederic, 214n60
Van Der Ver, Madame, 141
Van der Whelen, Adolf, 26
Van Volkenberg, Ellen, 145, 154, 165, 175
Victor Talking Machine Company, 70, 214n48
Victrola, 40, 53, 64, 66, 142
Visiting Nurse Assn., 164, 233n61
Vollmer, Lulu, 175
Vonnoh, Bessie Potter, 220n22

Wagner, Richard, 27, 56, 68, 181
Wales, Susan M. L., 219n11
Walker, Nellie Verne, 219n11
Walkup, Fairfax Proudfit, 164
War, 44, 45, 123, 124, 149, 200, 229n61; Amer. Revolution, 90, 123; anti-German feeling, 68; Civil War, 104, 129; memorials, 81, 83, 93, 98, 99, 100, 103–104, 106, 186; relief work, 11, 40, 66 (*see also* Women's Councils for National Defense); Spanish-Amer. War, 49, 68; World War I, 29, 37, 41–42, 44, 50, 57, 58, 63, 65–69, 71, 73, 77, 81, 89, 93, 99, 102–104, 118, 130, 132–33, 144, 156, 157, 158, 162, 164, 168, 178, 179, 181, 183, 190. *See also* Liberty Bonds; Liberty Sings
Warburg, Ms., pianist, 24
Ware, Harriet, 58, 213n47, 214n61
Washington, Booker T., 24
Waterman, Hazel Wood, 199
Webster, Helen C. (Mrs. Curtis), 212n29
Wednesday Club: Fort Worth, 89; St. Louis, 36; San Diego, 91, 199
West End Club, Atlanta, CA, 186
West Side Neighborhood House, St. Paul, 65
Weston, Margaret Pillsbury, 22
Wharton, Edith, 26
Wharton, Mrs. Edward, 221n49
Wheeler, Candace, 85
Whistler, James Abbott McNeill, 220n14
White, Mrs. J. J., 221n49
White, Stanford, 189
Whitney, Anne, 22
Whitney, Gertrude Vanderbilt, 90, 99
Widdemer, Margaret, 59, 215n69
Wiggin, Kate Douglas, 181, 209n90
Wiggins, Myra Albert, 219n11
Wilde, Oscar, 182
Wilder, Thornton, 59, 182
Willard, Emma, 13, 15, 20
Wills, Helen, 199

Wilson, Elsie Cobb, 199
Wilson, Woodrow, 57, 66, 68
Winter, Alice Ames, 35, 164, 185, 233n61
Woman Movement, 6, 7, 8, 29, 34, 201
Woman Suffrage, 3, 6, 10, 11, 34, 41, 57, 66, 91, 119, 130, 135, 154, 229n61; pageant, 137–42. *See also* National Amer. Woman Suffrage Assn.; National Woman's Party
Woman's Alliance, First Unitarian Church, Pittsburgh, 158
Woman's Assn., Marietta, OH, 120
Woman's Athletic Club, Alameda County, CA, 199
Woman's Building, New York State Fair, 93
Woman's Century Club, 31; San Francisco, 238n75; Seattle, 186, 236n28
Woman's City Club: Berkeley, 199, 238n75; Chicago, 196, 197; Cleveland, 196; Detroit, 197; Grand Rapids, 197; New York, 197; Rochester, 197
Woman's Club of: Amherst, 36; Arcata, CA, 72; Arlington, MA, 82, 125; Atlanta, 186, 187, 193, 194; Central Kentucky, 84; Chelsea, MA, 229n61; Cincinnati, 153; Clark's Summit, PA, 101; Des Moines, 89, 192, 193; Evanston, 149; Farmville, VA, 80; Harvard, 191; Hollywood, 68–69, 125, 194; Jackson, CA, 193; Lynn, MA, 199; Melrose, MA, 89; Milwaukee, 183; Minneapolis, 236n28; Natchez, 36; North Carolina, 80; Occidental College, Glendale, CA, 172; Paducah, KY, 90; Pasadena, 164; Pendleton, OR, 80; Raleigh, 129; Rhode Island, Providence, 199; Rockford, IL, 189, 236n28; San Francisco, 187, 193; Santa Clara, CA, 192; Saratoga (Foothill), CA, 238n75; Sausalito, 238n75; Sioux City, 126; Stoneham, MA, 60; Tacoma, 193; Winchester, 229n61; Worcester, 199
Woman's Department Club, Indianapolis, 36, 90
Woman's Exchange, 84
Woman's Peace Party, 133, 158, 229n61
Woman's University Club, Pasadena, 162
Women's Amateur Musical Club, 45, 48, 60
Women's Art Club: Cincinnati, 89; New York, 90
Women's Athletic Club, Los Angeles, 187, 188
Women's Choral Club, Pasadena, 171
Women's Chorus, St. Paul, 214n47
Women's Christian Temperance Union (WCTU), 7, 90, 101, 123, 153, 185, 187
Women's City Club, New York, 137
Women's Civic League, Pasadena, 162, 164, 172
Women's Civil League, Baltimore, 101
Women's Committee, Pasadena Philharmonic Society, 164
Women's Council, National Committee for Defense, 66; Florida, 63; Minnesota, 233n61
Women's Educational and Industrial Union, Boston, 23, 196
Women's Music Club, Columbus, 51, 65
Women's orchestras, 44, 48, 60–61, 136, 182, 215n78
Women's Outdoor Art League, 100
Women's Political Union, New York, 91
Women's Pottery Club, Cincinnati, 85
Women's Press Club, S. Calif., 232n19
Women's Rights Convention, Seneca Falls, 141
Women's Roosevelt Society, 90
Women's Trade Union League. *See* National Women's Trade Union League
Women's University Club, Seattle, 186

Wood, Mary I., 8
Wood, Mary Knight, 214n61
Wood, Mrs. Walton, 163
Woolfe, Virginia, 179
Worker's Playhouse, Seattle, 144
WPA (Works Progress Administration) Federal Arts Projects, 87, 106, 154
Writer's Guild, Calif., 232n19
Wylie, Elinor, 215n69

Yeats, William Butler, 181
Young Men's Christian Assn. (YMCA), 52, 66, 103, 123, 185
Young Men's Hebrew Assn., 52
Young Women's Christian Assn. (YWCA), 23, 41, 52, 70, 118, 123, 128, 129, 132, 134, 149, 158, 166, 184, 186, 188, 199, 227n28, 229n61
Young Women's Hebrew Assn., 52

Zechwer, Camilee W., 215n69
Zeisler, Fannie Bloomfield, 26, 214n61
Zimbalist, Mary Louise Curtis Bok, 64
Zoch Club, Minneapolis, 47
Zucca, Manna, 53

KAREN J. BLAIR is Professor of History at Central Washington University. She is the author of *The Clubwoman as Feminist: True Womanhood Redefined, 1868–1914* and *The History of American Women's Voluntary Organizations, 1810–1960: A Guide to Sources* and has edited *Women in Pacific Northwest History: An Anthology.*

NX 180 .F4 B63 1994
BLAIR, KAREN J.
THE TORCHBEARERS